D1811211

FOOD AND BEVERAGE PRODUCTION

FOOD AND BEVERAGE MANAGEMENT

(In 3 Volumes)

FOOD AND BEVERAGE PRODUCTION

(Volume-2)

Editor

Anupama Mukherjee

ISHA

ISHA BOOKS

DELHI-110033

Food and Beverage Production

ISBN: 81-8205-334-X (Set)
ISBN : 81-8205-336-6 (Vol. 2)

© Anupama Mukherjee

All rights reserved. No part of this book may be reproduced in any manner without written permission.

Published in 2006 in India by
Isha Books
D-43, Prithviraj Road,
Adarsh Nagar, Delhi-110033
e-mail : ishabooks@hotmail.com

Laser Typesetting at : Shiva Infosystem, Delhi
Printed at : Mehra Offset Press, Delhi

Preface

Food and beverage production is the process of transforming raw animal, vegetable, or marine materials into tasty, nutritious, and safe food products. The industry has its roots in ancient times, as humans have always needed to obtain food and store a portion for later use. Today a wide variety of methods are available to cook, maintain and enhance the appearance and taste of food. Modern food production methods also create products that are convenient for consumers, such as products that are ready to eat or require minimal preparation and cooking. Combining these methods with modern distribution networks makes seasonal crops available year-round in grocery stores all over the world.

This book explores the role of food production and the processes involved in it. It provides information on the objectives and methods of cooking, kitchen organisation, use of various equipment and tools in kitchen, procedures of making of tasty food items from vegetable and non-vegetable sources. It is hoped that the book will be highly informative to students, food industry professionals and all who are interested in food and beverage production.

Editor

Contents

1

Introduction to Cookery

Man, in his primitive state, lives upon roots and the fruits of the earth, until, by degrees, he is driven to seek for new means, by which his wants may be supplied and enlarged. He then becomes a hunter and a fisher. As his species increases, greater necessities come upon him, when he gradually abandons the roving life of the savage for the more stationary pursuits of the herdsman.

These beget still more settled habits, when he begins the practice of agriculture, forms ideas of the rights of property, and has his own, both defined and secured. The forest, the stream, and the sea are now no longer his only resources for food. He sows and he reaps, pastures and breeds cattle, lives on the cultivated produce of his fields, and revels in the luxuries of the dairy; raises flocks for clothing, and assumes, to all intents and purposes, the habits of permanent life and the comfortable condition of a farmer.

This is the fourth stage of social progress, up to which the useful or mechanical arts have been incidentally developing themselves, when trade and commerce begin. Through these various phases, only to live has been the great object of mankind; but, by-and-by, comforts are multiplied, and accumulating riches create new wants. The object, then, is not only to live, but to live economically, agreeably, tastefully, and well.

Accordingly, the art of cookery commences; and although the fruits of the earth, the fowls of the air, the beasts of the field, and the fish of the sea, are still the only food of mankind, yet these are so prepared, improved, and dressed by skill and ingenuity, that they are the means of immeasurably extending the boundaries of human enjoyments. Everything that is edible, and passes under the hands of the cook, is more or less changed, and assumes new forms.

Hence the influence of that functionary is immense upon the happiness of a household. In order that the duties of the Cook may be properly performed, and that he may be able to reproduce esteemed dishes with certainty, all terms of indecision should be banished from his art. Accordingly, what is known only to him, will, be made known to others.

In them all those indecisive terms expressed by a bit of this, some of that, a small piece of that, and a handful of the other, shall never be made use of, but all quantities be precisely and explicitly stated. With a desire, also, that all ignorance on this most essential part of the culinary art should disappear, and that a uniform system of weights and measures should be adopted, we give an account of the weights which answer to certain measures.

A Table-Spoonful is frequently mentioned in a recipe, in the prescriptions of medical men, and also in medical, chemical, and gastronomical works. By it is generally meant and understood a measure or bulk equal to that which would be produced by half an ounce of water. A Dessert-Spoonful is the half of a table-spoonful; that is to say, by it is meant a measure or bulk equal to a quarter of an ounce of water. A Tea-Spoonful is equal in quantity to a drachm of water.

A Drop is the name of a vague kind of measure, and is so called on account of the liquid being dropped from the mouth of a bottle. Its quantity, however, will vary, either from the consistency of the liquid or the size and shape of the mouth of the bottle. The College of Physicians determined the quantity of a drop to be one grain, 60 drops making one fluid drachm. Their drop, or sixtieth part of a fluid drachm, is called a minim.

Graduated glass measures can be obtained at any chemist's, and they save much trouble. One of these, containing a wine pint, is divided into 16 oz., and the oz, into 8 drachms of water; by which, any certain weight mentioned in a recipe can be accurately measured out. Home-made measures of this kind can readily be formed by weighing the water contained in any given measure, and marking on any tall glass the space it occupies.

This mark can easily be made with a file. It will be interesting to many readers to know the basis on which the French found their system of weights and measures, for it certainly possesses the grandeur of simplicity. The metre, which is the basis of the whole system of French weights and measures, is the exact measurement of one forty-millionth part of a meridian of the earth.

Art of Cookery

Excellence in the Art of Cookery, as in all other things, is only attainable by practice and experience. In proportion, therefore, to the opportunities which a cook has had of these, so will be his excellence in the art. It is in the large establishments of princes, noblemen, and very affluent families alone, that the man cook is found in this country.

He, also, superintends the kitchens of large hotels, clubs, and public institutions, where he, usually, makes out the bills of fare, which are generally submitted to the principal for approval. To be able to do this, therefore, it is absolutely necessary that he should be a judge of the season of every dish, as well as know perfectly the state of every article he undertakes to prepare. He must also be a judge of every article he buys; for no skill, however great it may be, will enable him to, make that good which is really bad. On him rests the responsibility of the cooking generally, whilst a speciality of his department, is to prepare the rich soups, stews, ragouts, and such dishes as enter into the more refined and complicated portions of his art, and such as are not usually understood by ordinary professors. He, therefore, holds a high position in a household, being inferior in rank, as already shown, only to the house steward, the valet, and the butler.

In the luxurious ages of Grecian antiquity, Sicilian cooks were the most esteemed, and received high rewards for their services. Among them, one called Trimalcio was such an adept in his art, that he could impart to common fish both the form and flavour of the most esteemed of the piscatory tribes. A chief cook in the palmy days of Roman voluptuousness had about £800 a year, and Antony rewarded the one that cooked the supper which pleased Cleopatra, with the present of a city. With the fall of the empire, the culinary art sank into less consideration. In the middle ages, cooks laboured to acquire a reputation for their sauces, which they composed of strange combinations, for the sake of novelty, as well as singularity.

Duties of Cook

The Kitchen and the Scullery Maids, are so intimately associated, that they can hardly be treated of separately. The cook, however, is at the head of the kitchen; and in proportion to her possession of the qualities of cleanliness, neatness, order, regularity, and celerity of action, so will her influence appear in the conduct of those who are under her; as it is upon her that the whole responsibility of the business of the kitchen rests, whilst the others must lend her, both a ready and a willing assistance, and be especially tidy in their appearance, and active, in their movements.

In the larger establishments of the middle ages, cooks, with the authority of feudal chiefs, gave their orders from a high chair in which they ensconced themselves, and commanded a view of all that was going on throughout their several domains. Each held a long wooden spoon, with which he tasted, without leaving his seat, the various comestibles that were cooking on the stoves, and which he frequently used as a rod of punishment on the backs of those whose idleness and gluttony too largely predominated over their diligence and temperance.

The Quality of early rising be of the first importance to the mistress, what must it be to the servant! Let it, therefore, be taken as a long-proved truism, that without it, in every domestic, the effect of all things else, so far as work is concerned, may, in a great measure, be neutralized. In a cook, this quality is most essential; for an hour lost in the morning, will keep her toiling, absolutely toiling, all day, to overtake that which might otherwise have been achieved with ease. In large establishments, six is a good hour to rise in the summer, and seven in the winter.

Her first duty, in large establishments and where it is requisite, should be to set her dough for the breakfast rolls, provided this has not been done on the previous night, and then to engage herself with those numerous little preliminary occupations which may not inappropriately be termed laying out her duties for the day. This will bring in the breakfast hour of eight, after which, directions must be given, and preparations made, for the different dinners of the household and family.

In those numerous households where a cook and housemaid are only kept, the general custom is, that the cook should have the charge of the dining-room. The hall, the lamps and the doorstep are also committed to her care, and any other work there may be on the outside of the house. In establishments of this kind, the cook will, after having lighted her kitchen fire, carefully brushed the range, and cleaned the hearth, proceed to prepare for breakfast. She will thoroughly rinse the kettle, and, filling it with fresh water, will put it on the fire to boil. She will then go to the breakfast-room, or parlour, and there make all things ready for the breakfast of the family. Her attention will next be directed to the hall, which she will sweep and wipe; the kitchen stairs, if there be any, will now be swept; and the hall mats, which have been removed and shaken, will be again put in their places.

The cleaning of the kitchen, pantry, passages, and kitchen stairs must always be over before breakfast, so that it may not interfere with the other business of the day. Everything should be ready, and the whole house should wear a comfortable aspect when the heads of the house and members of the family make their appearance. Nothing, it may be depended on, will so please the mistress of an establishment, as to notice that, although she has not been present to see that the work was done, attention to smaller matters has been carefully paid, with a view to giving her satisfaction and increasing her comfort.

By the time that the cook has performed the duties mentioned above, and well swept, brushed, and dusted her kitchen, the breakfast-bell will most likely summon her to the parlour, to "bring in" the breakfast. It is the cook's department, generally, in the smaller establishments, to wait at breakfast, as the housemaid, by this time, has gone up-stairs into the bedrooms, and has there applied herself to her various duties. The cook usually answers the bells and single knocks at the door in the early part of the morning, as the tradesmen, with whom it is her more special business to speak, call at these hours.

It is in her preparation of the dinner that the cook begins to feel the weight and responsibility of her situation, as she must take upon herself all the dressing and the serving of the principal dishes, which her skill and ingenuity have mostly prepared. Whilst these, however, are cooking, she must be busy with her pastry, soups, gravies, ragouts, &c. Stock, or what the French call consommé, being the basis of most made dishes, must be always at hand, in conjunction with her sweet herbs and spices for seasoning.

"A place for everything, and everything in its place," must be her rule, in order that time may not be wasted in looking for things when they are wanted, and in order that the whole apparatus of cooking may move with the regularity and precision of a well-adjusted machine – all must go on simultaneously. The vegetables and sauces must be ready with the dishes they are to accompany, and in order that they may be suitable, the smallest oversight must not be made in their preparation.

When the dinner-hour has arrived, it is the duty of the cook to dish-up such dishes as may, without injury, stand, for some time, covered on the hot plate or in the hot closet; but such as are of a more important or recherché kind, must be delayed until the order "to serve" is given from the drawing-room. Then comes haste; but there must be no hurry,– all must work with order. The cook takes charge of the fish, soups, and poultry; and the kitchen-maid of the vegetables, sauces, and gravies.

These she puts into their appropriate dishes, whilst the scullery-maid waits on and assists the cook. Everything must be timed so as to prevent its getting cold, whilst great care should be taken, that, between the first and second courses, no more time is allowed to elapse than is necessary, for fear that the company in the dining-room lose all relish for what has yet to come of the dinner. When the dinner has been served, the most important feature in the daily life of the cook is at an end. She must, however, now begin to look to the contents of her larder, taking care to keep everything sweet and clean, so that no disagreeable smells may arise from the gravies, milk, or meat that may be there. These are the principal duties of a cook in a first-rate establishment.

In smaller establishments, the housekeeper often conducts the higher department of cooking, and the cook, with the assistance of a scullery-maid, performs some of the subordinate duties of the kitchen-maid. When circumstances render it necessary, the cook engages to perform the whole of the work of the kitchen, and, in some places, a portion of the house-work also.

Whilst the cook is engaged with her morning duties, the kitchen-maid is also occupied with hers. Her first duty, after the fire is lighted, is to sweep and clean the kitchen, and the various offices belonging to it. This she does every morning, besides cleaning the stone steps at the entrance of the house, the halls, the passages, and the stairs which lead to the kitchen. Her general duties, besides these, are to wash and scour all these places twice a week, with the tables, shelves, and cupboards. She has also to dress the nursery and servants'-hall dinners, to prepare all fish, poultry, and vegetables, trim meat joints and cutlets, and do all such duties as may be considered to enter into the cook's department in a subordinate degree.

The duties of the scullery-maid are to assist the cook; to keep the scullery clean, and all the metallic as well as earthenware kitchen utensils. The position of scullery-maid is not, of course, one of high rank, nor is the payment for her services large. But if she be fortunate enough to have over her a good kitchen-maid and clever cook, she may very soon learn to perform various little duties connected with cooking operations, which may be of considerable service in fitting her for a more responsible place.

Now, it will be doubtless thought by the majority of our readers, that the fascinations connected with the position of the scullery-maid, are not so great as to induce many people to leave a comfortable home in order to work in a scullery. But we are acquainted with one instance in which the desire, on the part of a young girl, was so strong to become connected with the kitchen and cookery, that she absolutely left her parents, and engaged herself as a scullery-maid in a gentleman's house.

Here she showed herself so active and intelligent, that she very quickly rose to the rank of kitchen-maid; and from this, so great was her gastronomical genius, she became, in a short space of time, one of the best women-cooks in England. After this, we think, it must be allowed, that a cook, like a poet, nascitur, non fit.

Modern Cookery

Modern Cookery stands so greatly indebted to the gastronomic propensities of our French neighbours, that many of their terms are adopted and applied by English artists to the same as well as similar preparations of their own. A vocabulary of these is, therefore, indispensable in a work of this kind. Accordingly, the following will be found sufficiently complete for all ordinary purposes.

Aspic: A savoury jelly, used as an exterior moulding for cold game, poultry, fish, &c. This, being of a transparent nature, allows the bird which it covers to be seen through it. This may also be used for decorating or garnishing.

Assiette (plate): Assiettes are the small entrées and hors-d'oeuvres, the quantity of which does not exceed what a plate will hold. At dessert, fruits, cheese, chestnuts, biscuits, &c., if served upon a plate, are termed assiettes - Assiette volante is a dish which a servant hands round to the guests, but is not placed upon the table. Small cheese soufflés and different dishes, which ought to be served very hot, are frequently made assielles volantes.

Au-Bleu: Fish dressed in such a manner as to have a bluish appearance.

Bain-Marie: An open saucepan or kettle of nearly boiling water, in which a smaller vessel can be set for cooking and warming. This is very useful for keeping articles hot, without altering their quantity or quality. If you keep sauce, broth, or soup by the fireside, the soup reduces and becomes too strong, and the sauce thickens as well as reduces; but this is prevented by using the bain-marie, in which the water should be very hot, but not boiling.

Béchamel: French white sauce, now frequently used in English cookery.

Blanch: To whiten poultry, vegetables, fruit, &c., by plunging them into boiling water for a short time, and afterwards plunging them into cold water, there to remain until they are cold.

Blanquette: A sort of fricassee.

Bouilli: Beef or other meat boiled; but, generally speaking, boiled beef is understood by the term.

Bouillie: A French dish resembling hasty-pudding.

Bouillon: A thin broth or soup.

Braise: To stew meat with fat bacon until it is tender, it having previously been blanched.

Braisière: A saucepan having a lid with ledges, to put fire on the top.

Brider: To pass a packthread through poultry, game, &c., to keep together their members.

Caramel (burnt sugar): This is made with a piece of sugar, of the size of a nut, browned in the bottom of a saucepan; upon which a cupful of stock is gradually poured, stirring all the time a glass of broth, little by little. It may be used with the feather of a quill, to colour meats, such as the upper part of fricandeaux; and to impart colour to sauces. Caramel made with water instead of stock may be used to colour compôtes and other entremets.

Casserole: A crust of rice, which, after having been moulded into the form of a pie, is baked, and then filled with a fricassee of white meat or a purée of game.

Compote: A stew, as of fruit or pigeons.

Consommé: Rich stock, or gravy.

Croquette: Ball of fried rice or potatoes.

Croutons: Sippets of bread.

Daubière: An oval stewpan, in which daubes are cooked; daubes being meat or fowl stewed in sauce.

Désosser: To bone, or take out the bones from poultry, game, or fish. This is an operation requiring considerable experience.

Entrées: Small side or corner dishes, served with the first course.

Entremets: Small side or corner dishes, served with the second course.

Escalopes: Collops; small, round, thin pieces of tender meat, or of fish, beaten with the handle of a strong knife to make them tender.

Feuilletage: Puff-paste.

Flamber: To singe fowl or game, after they have been picked.

Foncer: To put in the bottom of a saucepan slices of ham, veal, or thin broad slices of bacon.

Galette: A broad thin cake.

Gâteau: A cake, correctly speaking; but used sometimes to denote a pudding and a kind of tart.

Glacer: To glaze, or spread upon hot meats, or larded fowl, a thick and rich sauce or gravy, called glaze. This is laid on with a feather or brush, and in confectionary the term means to ice fruits and pastry with sugar, which glistens on hardening.

Hors-D'oeuvres: Small dishes, or assiettes volantes of sardines, anchovies, and other relishes of this kind, served to the guests during the first course.

Lit: A bed or layer; articles in thin slices are placed in layers, other articles, or seasoning, being laid between them.

Maigre: Broth, soup, or gravy, made without meat.

Matelote: A rich fish-stew, which is generally composed of carp, eels, trout, or barbel. It is made with wine.

Mayonnaise: Cold sauce, or salad dressing.

Menu: The bill of fare.

Meringue: A kind of icing, made of whites of eggs and sugar, well beaten.

Miroton: Larger slices of meat than collops; such as slices of beef for a vinaigrette, or ragout or stew of onions.

Mouiller: To add water, broth, or other liquid, during the cooking.

Paner: To cover over with very fine crumbs of bread, meats, or any other articles to be cooked on the gridiron, in the oven, or frying-pan.

Piquer: To lard with strips of fat bacon, poultry, game, meat, &c. This should always be done according to the vein of the meat, so that in carving you slice the bacon across as well as the meat.

Poêlée: Stock used instead of water for boiling turkeys, sweetbreads, fowls, and vegetables, to render them less insipid. This is rather an expensive preparation.

Purée: Vegetables, or meat reduced to a very smooth pulp, which is afterwards mixed with enough liquid to make it of the consistency of very thick soup.

Ragout: Stew or hash.

Remoulade: Salad dressing.

Rissoles: Pastry, made of light puff-paste, and cut into various forms, and fried. They may be filled with fish, meat, or sweets.

Roux: Brown and white; French thickening.

Salmi: Ragout of game previously roasted.

Sauce Piquante: A sharp sauce, in which somewhat of a vinegar flavour predominates.

Sauter: To dress with sauce in a saucepan, repeatedly moving it about.

Tamis: Tammy, a sort of open cloth or sieve through which to strain broth and sauces, so as to rid them of small bones, froth, &c.

Tourte: Tart. Fruit pie.

Trousser: To truss a bird; to put together the body and tie the wings and thighs, in order to round it for roasting or boiling, each being tied then with packthread, to keep it in the required form.

Vol-Au-Vent: A rich crust of very fine puff-paste, which may be filled with various delicate ragouts or fricassees, of fish, flesh, or fowl. Fruit may also be inclosed in a vol-au-vent.

2

Kitchen Organisation

The kitchens of the Middle Ages, in England, are said to have been constructed after the fashion of those of the Romans. They were generally octagonal, with several fireplaces, but no chimneys; neither was there any wood admitted into the building. Some kitchens had funnels or vents below the eaves to let out the steam, which was sometimes considerable, as the Anglo-Saxons used their meat chiefly in a boiled state.

From this circumstance, some of their large kitchens had four ranges, comprising a boiling-place for small boiled meats, and a boiling-house for the great boiler. In private houses the culinary arrangements were no doubt different; a little kitchen with a chamber, even in a solarium, or upper floor.

A good kitchen, should be erected with a view to the following particulars.

- — Convenience of distribution in its parts, with largeness of dimension.
- — Excellence of light, height of ceiling, and good ventilation.
- — Easiness of access, without passing through the house.

— Sufficiently remote from the principal apartments of the house, that the members, visitors, or guests of the family, may not perceive the odour incident to cooking, or hear the noise of culinary operations.

— Plenty of fuel and water, which, with the scullery, pantry, and storeroom, should be so near it, as to offer the smallest possible trouble in reaching them.

The simplicity of the primitive ages has frequently been an object of poetical admiration, and it delights the imagination to picture men living upon such fruits as spring spontaneously from the earth, and desiring no other beverages to slake their thirst, but such as fountains and rivers supply.

Thus we are told, that the ancient inhabitants of Argos lived principally on pears; that the Arcadians revelled in acorns, and the Athenians in figs. This, of course, was in the golden age, before ploughing began, and when mankind enjoyed all kinds of plenty without having to earn their bread "by the sweat of their brow." This delightful period, however, could not last for ever, and the earth became barren, and continued unfruitful till Ceres came and taught the art of sowing, with several other useful inventions.

The first whom she taught to till the ground was Triptolemus, who communicated his instructions to his countrymen the Athenians. Thence the art was carried into Achaia, and thence into Arcadia. Barley was the first grain that was used, and the invention of bread-making is ascribed to Pan. The use of fire, as an instrument of cookery, must have been coeval with this invention of bread, which, being the most necessary of all kinds of food, was frequently used in a sense so comprehensive as to include both meat and drink. It was, by the Greeks, baked under the ashes.

In the primary ages it was deemed unlawful to eat flesh, and when mankind began to depart from their primitive habits, the flesh of swine was the first that was eaten. For several ages, it was pronounced unlawful to slaughter oxen, from an estimate of their great value in assisting men to cultivate the ground; nor was it usual to kill young animals, from a sentiment which considered it cruel to take away the life of those that had scarcely tasted the joys of existence.

At this period no cooks were kept, and we know from Homer that his ancient heroes prepared and dressed their victuals with their own hands. Ulysses, for example, we are told, like a modern charwoman, excelled at lighting a fire, whilst Achilles was an adept at turning a spit. Subsequently, heralds, employed in civil and military affairs, filled the office of cooks, and managed marriage feasts; but this, no doubt, was after mankind had advanced in the art of living, a step further than roasting, which, in all places, was the ancient manner of dressing meat.

The age of roasting we may consider as that in which the use of the metals would be introduced as adjuncts to the culinary art; and amongst these, iron, the most useful of them all, would necessarily take a prominent place. This metal is easily oxidized, but to bring it to a state of fusibility, it requires a most intense heat. Of all the metals, it is the widest diffused and most abundant; and few stones or mineral bodies are without an admixture of it. It possesses the valuable property of being welded by hammering; and hence its adaptation to the numerous purposes of civilized life.

Metallic grains of iron have been found in strawberries, and a twelfth of the weight of the wood of dried oak is said to consist of this metal. Blood owes its colour of redness to the quantity of iron it contains, and rain and snow are seldom perfectly free from it. In the arts it is employed in three states, – as cast iron, wrought iron, and steel. In each of these it largely enters into the domestic economy, and stoves, grates, and the general implements of cookery, are usually composed of it. In antiquity, its employment was, comparatively speaking, equally universal.

The excavations made at Pompeii have proved this. The accompanying cuts present us with specimens of stoves, both ancient and modern. One of kitchen stove found in the house of Pansa, at Pompeii, and would seem, in its perfect state, not to have been materially different from such as are in use at the present day. Another one was self-acting, simple open range in modern use, and may be had of two qualities, ranging, according to their dimensions, from £3. 10s. and £3. 18s. respectively, up to £4. 10s. and £7. 5s. They are completely fitted up with oven, boiler, sliding cheek, wrought-iron bars, revolving shelves, and brass tap.

Next kitchen stove is called the Improved Leamington Kitchener, and is said to surpass any other range in use, for easy cooking by one fire. It has a hot plate, which is well calculated for an ironing-stove, and on which as many vessels as will stand upon it, may be kept boiling, without being either soiled or injured. Besides, it has a perfectly ventilated and spacious wrought-iron roaster, with movable shelves, draw-out stand, double dripping-pan, and meat-stand.

The roaster can be converted into an oven by closing the valves, when bread and pastry can be baked in it in a superior manner. It also has a large iron boiler with brass tap and steam-pipe, round and square gridirons for chops and steaks, ash-pan, open fire for roasting, and a set of ornamental covings with plate-warmer attached. It took a first-class prize and medal in the Great Exhibition of 1851, and was also exhibited, with all the recent improvements, at the Dublin Exhibition in 1853.

Another kitchener, adapted for large families. It has on the one side, a large ventilated oven; and on the other, the fire and roaster. The hot plate is over all, and there is a back boiler, made of wrought iron, with brass tap and steam-pipe. In other respects it resembles Fig. 4, with which it possesses similar advantages of construction. Either maybe had at varying prices, according to size, from £5. 15s. up to £23. 10s.

From kitchen ranges to the implements used in cookery is but a step. With these, every kitchen should be well supplied, otherwise the cook must not be expected to "perform her office" in a satisfactory manner. Of the culinary utensils of the ancients, our knowledge is very limited; but as the art of living, in every civilized country, is pretty much the same, the instruments for cooking must, in a great degree, bear a striking resemblance to each other.

On referring to classical antiquities, we find mentioned, among household utensils, leather bags, baskets constructed of twigs, reeds, and rushes; boxes, basins, and bellows; bread-moulds, brooms, and brushes; caldrons, colanders, cisterns, and chafing-dishes; cheese-rasps, knives, and ovens of the Dutch kind; funnels and frying-pans; handmills, soup-ladles, milk-pails, and oil-jars; presses, scales, and sieves; spits of different sizes, but some of them large enough to roast an ox; spoons, fire-tongs, trays, trenchers, and drinking-vessels; with others for carrying food, preserving milk, and holding cheese. This enumeration, if it does nothing else, will, to some extent, indicate the state of the simpler kinds of mechanical arts among the ancients.

In so far as regards the shape and construction of many of the kitchen utensils enumerated above, they bore a great resemblance to our own. This will be seen by the accompanying cuts. In the manufacture of these utensils, bronze metal seems to have been much in favour with the ancients. It was chosen not only for their domestic vessels, but it was also much used for their public sculptures and medals. It is a compound, composed of from six to twelve parts of tin to one hundred of copper.

It gives its name to figures and all pieces of sculpture made of it. Brass was another favourite metal, which is composed of copper and zinc. It is more fusible than copper, and not so apt to tarnish. In a pure state it is not malleable, unless when hot, and after it has been melted twice it will not bear the hammer. To render it capable of being wrought, it requires 7 lb. of lead to be put to 1 cwt. of its own material.

The Corinthian brass of antiquity was a mixture of silver, gold, and copper. A fine kind of brass, supposed to be made by the cementation of copper plates with calamine, is, in Germany, hammered out into leaves, and is called Dutch metal in this country. It is employed in the same way as gold leaf. Brass is much used for watchworks, as well as for wire.

The braziers, ladles, stewpans, saucepans, gridirons, and colanders of antiquity might generally pass for those of the English manufacture of the present day, in so far as shape is concerned. In proof of this we have placed together the following similar articles of ancient and modern pattern, in order that the reader may, at a single view, see wherein any difference that is between them, consists.

Any display of taste in the adornment of such utensils, might seem to be useless; but when we remember how much more natural it is for us all to be careful of the beautiful and costly, than of the plain and cheap, it may even become a question in the economy of a kitchen, whether it would not, in the long run, be cheaper to have articles which displayed some tasteful ingenuity in their manufacture, than such as are so perfectly plain as to have no attractions whatever beyond their mere suitableness to the purposes for which they are made.

Some of the ancient utensils represented in the above cuts, are copied from those found amid the ruins of Herculaneum and Pompeii. These Roman cities were, in the first century, buried beneath the lava of an eruption of Vesuvius, and continued to be lost to the world till the beginning of the last century, when a peasant, in digging for a well, gradually discovered a small temple with some statues.

Little notice, however, was taken of this circumstance till 1736, when the king of Naples, desiring to erect a palace at Portici, caused extensive excavations to be made, when the city of Herculaneum was slowly unfolded to view. Pompeii was discovered about 1750, and being easier cleared from the lava in which it had so long been entombed, disclosed itself as it existed immediately before the catastrophe which overwhelmed it, nearly two thousand years ago.

It presented, to the modern world, the perfect picture of the form and structure of an ancient Roman city. The interior of its habitations, shops, baths, theatres, and temples, were all disclosed, with many of the implements used by the workmen in their various trades, and the materials on which they were employed, when the doomed city was covered with the lavian stream.

Amongst the most essential requirements of the kitchen are scales or weighing-machines for family use. These are found to have existed among the ancients, and must, at a very early age, have been both publicly and privately employed for the regulation of quantities. The modern English weights were adjusted by the 27th chapter of Magna Charta, or the great charter forced, by the barons, from King John at Runnymede, in Surrey. Therein it is declared that the weights, all over England, shall be the same, although for different commodities there were two different kinds, Troy and Avoirdupois.

The origin of both is taken from a grain of wheat gathered in the middle of an ear. The standard of measures was originally kept at Winchester, and by a law of King Edgar was ordained to be observed throughout the kingdom. An ancient pair of common scales, with two basins and a movable weight, which is made in the form of a head, covered with the pileus, because Mercury had the weights and measures under his superintendence.

It is engraved on a stone in the gallery of Florence. Modern weighing-machine, of great convenience, and generally in use in those establishments where a great deal of cooking is carried on. Accompanying the scales, or weighing-machines, there should be spice-boxes, and sugar and biscuit-canisters of either white or japanned tin. The covers of these should fit tightly, in order to exclude the air, and if necessary, be lettered in front, to distinguish them.

The white metal of which they are usually composed, loses its colour when exposed to the air, but undergoes no further change. It enters largely into the composition of culinary utensils, many of them being entirely composed of tinned sheet-iron; the inside of copper and iron vessels also, being usually what is called tinned. This art consists of covering any metal with a thin coating of tin; and it requires the metal to be covered, to be perfectly clean and free from rust, and also that the tin, itself, be purely metallic, and entirely cleared from all ashes or refuse.

Copper boilers, saucepans, and other kitchen utensils, are tinned after they are manufactured, by being first made hot and the tin rubbed on with resin. In this process, nothing ought to be used but pure grain-tin. Lead, however, is sometimes mixed with that metal, not only to make it lie more easily, but to adulterate it – a pernicious practice, which in every article connected with the cooking and preparation of food, cannot be too severely reprobated.–

As not only health but life may be said to depend on the cleanliness of culinary utensils, great attention must be paid to their condition generally, but more especially to that of the saucepans, stewpans, and boilers. Inside they should be kept perfectly clean, and where an open fire is used, the outside as clean as possible. With a Leamington range, saucepans, stewpans, &c., can be kept entirely free from smoke and soot on the outside, which is an immense saving of labour to the cook or scullery-maid.

Care should be taken that the lids fit tight and close, so that soups or gravies may not be suffered to waste by evaporation. They should be made to keep the steam in and the smoke out, and should always be bright on the upper rim, where they do not immediately come in contact with the fire. Soup-pots and kettles should be washed immediately after being used, and dried before the fire, and they should be kept in a dry place, in order that they may escape the deteriorating influence of rust, and, thereby, be destroyed.

Copper utensils should never be used in the kitchen unless tinned, and the utmost care should be taken, not to let the tin be rubbed off. If by chance this should occur, have it replaced before the vessel is again brought into use. Neither soup nor gravy should, at any time, be suffered to remain in them longer than is absolutely necessary, as any fat or acid that is in them, may affect the metal, so as to impregnate with poison what is intended to be eaten.

Stone and earthenware vessels should be provided for soups and gravies not intended for immediate use, and, also, plenty of common dishes for the larder, that the table-set may not be used for such purposes. It is the nature of vegetables soon to turn sour, when they are apt to corrode glazed red-ware, and even metals, and frequently, thereby, to become impregnated with poisonous particles. The vinegar also in pickles, by its acidity, does the same.

Consideration, therefore, should be given to these facts, and great care also taken that all sieves, jelly-bags, and tapes for collared articles, be well scalded and kept dry, or they will impart an unpleasant flavour when next used. To all these directions the cook should pay great attention, nor should they, by any means, be neglected by the mistress of the household, who ought to remember that cleanliness in the kitchen gives health and happiness to home, whilst economy will immeasurably assist in preserving them.

Without fuel, a kitchen might be pronounced to be of little use; therefore, to discover and invent materials for supplying us with the means of domestic heat and comfort, has exercised the ingenuity of man. Those now known have been divided into five classes; the first comprehending the fluid inflammable bodies; the second, peat or turf; the third, charcoal of wood; the fourth, pit-coal charred; and the fifth, wood or pit-coal in a crude state, with the capacity of yielding a copious and bright flame.

The first may be said seldom to be employed for the purposes of cookery; but peat, especially amongst rural populations, has, in all ages, been regarded as an excellent fuel. It is one of the most important productions of an alluvial soil, and belongs to the vegetable rather than the mineral kingdom. It may be described as composed of wet, spongy black earth, held together by decayed vegetables. Formerly it covered extensive tracts in England, but has greatly disappeared before the genius of agricultural improvement.

Charcoal is a kind of artificial coal, used principally where a strong and clear fire is desired. It is a black, brittle, insoluble, inodorous, tasteless substance, and, when newly-made, possesses the remarkable property of absorbing certain quantities of the different gases. Its dust, when used as a polishing powder, gives great brilliancy to metals. It consists of wood half-burned, and is manufactured by cutting pieces of timber into nearly the same size, then disposing them in heaps, and covering them with earth, so as to prevent communication with the air, except when necessary to make them burn.

When they have been sufficiently charred, the fire is extinguished by stopping the vents through which the air is admitted. Of coal there are various species; as, pit, culm, slate, cannel, Kilkenny, sulphurous, bovey, jet, &c. These have all their specific differences, and are employed for various purposes; but are all, more or less, used as fuel. The use of coal for burning purposes was not known to the Romans. In Britain it was discovered about fifty years before the birth of Christ, in Lancashire, not far from where Manchester now stands; but for ages after its discovery, so long as forests abounded, wood continued to be the fuel used for firing.

The first public notice of coal is in the reign of Henry III., who, in 1272, granted a charter to the town of Newcastle, permitting the inhabitants to dig for coal. It took some centuries more, however, to bring it into common use, as this did not take place till about the first quarter of the seventeenth century, in the time of Charles I. A few years after the Restoration, we find that about 200,000 chaldrons were consumed in London. Although several countries possess mines of coal, the quality of their mineral is, in general, greatly inferior to that of Great Britain, where it is found mostly in undulating districts abounding with valleys, and interspersed with plains of considerable extent. It lies usually between the strata of other substances, and rarely in an horizontal position, but with a dip or inclination to one side.

When fuel and food are procured, the next consideration is, how the latter may be best preserved, with a view to its being suitably dressed. More waste is often occasioned by the want of judgment, or of necessary care in this particular, than by any other cause. In the absence of proper places for keeping provisions, a hanging safe, suspended in an airy situation, is the best substitute. A well-ventilated larder, dry and shady, is better for meat and poultry, which require to be kept for some time; and the utmost skill in the culinary art will not compensate for the want of proper attention to this particular.

Though it is advisable that annual food should be hung up in the open air till its fibres have lost some degree of their toughness, yet, if it is kept till it loses its natural sweetness, its flavour has become deteriorated, and, as a wholesome comestible, it has lost many of its qualities conducive to health. As soon, therefore, as the slightest trace of putrescence is detected, it has reached its highest degree of tenderness, and should be dressed immediately.

During the sultry summer months, it is difficult to procure meat that is not either tough or tainted. It should, therefore, be well examined when it comes in, and if flies have touched it, the part must be cut off, and the remainder well washed. In very cold weather, meat and vegetables touched by the frost, should be brought into the kitchen early in the morning, and soaked in cold water. In loins of meat, the long pipe that runs by the bone should be taken out, as it is apt to taint; as also the kernels of beef.

Rumps and edgebones of beef, when bruised, should not be purchased. All these things ought to enter into the consideration of every household manager, and great care should be taken that nothing is thrown away, or suffered to be wasted in the kitchen, which might, by proper management, be turned to a good account. The shank-bones of mutton, so little esteemed in general, give richness to soups or gravies, if well soaked and brushed before they are added to the boiling.

They are also particularly nourishing for sick persons. Roast-beef bones, or shank-bones of ham, make excellent stock for pea-soup. When the whites of eggs are used for jelly, confectionary, or other purposes, a pudding or a custard should be made, that the yolks may be used. All things likely to be wanted should be in readiness: sugars of different sorts; currants washed, picked, and perfectly dry; spices pounded, and kept in very small bottles closely corked, or in canisters, as we have already directed.

Not more of these should be purchased at a time than are likely to be used in the course of a month. Much waste is always prevented by keeping every article in the place best suited to it. Vegetables keep best on a stone floor, if the air be excluded; meat, in a cold dry place; as also salt, sugar, sweet-meats, candles, dried meats, and hams. Rice, and all sorts of seed for puddings, should be closely covered to preserve them from insects; but even this will not prevent them from being affected by these destroyers, if they are long and carelessly kept.

3

Kitchen Equipment and Tools

The foodservice equipment located in the galley and dining areas at naval shore stations and aboard Navy ships is designed specifically for serving large quantities of food. To make sure of the safe, sanitary, and efficient operation of this equipment, it must be maintained in proper working order and used correctly. Before attempting to operate any foodservice equipment, you should observe the following general precautions:

— Check for and determine the location of emergency materials such as fire extinguishers, emergency switches, first aid boxes, and telephone emergency numbers to make sure they are available should an accident occur. Report any deficiencies or malfunctioning materials to the supervisor.

— Make sure the area around the equipment is clear of obstructions and thoroughly dry. All spills must be cleaned up immediately to ensure a clean, dry, nonslippery working surface.

— Make sure the working area has ample lighting.

— If there is any doubt about the operating procedures or safety precautions, report to the supervisor.

— No unauthorized personnel should attempt to operate equipment in any foodservice space.

— Be certain no loose gear is in the vicinity of moving parts of machines. Before starting, you should make sure all safety guards, screens, and devices are in place.

— When operating a machine, you should make sure you maintain a safe distance from all moving parts. Never use your hands or body to stop moving blades and parts even though power has been turned off.

— Never lean against a machine while it is operating.

— If ship movement is severe, exercise caution; if severe movement continues, nonessential machine operation should be discontinued and equipment turned off.

— Use safety equipment such as rubber protective gloves, safety goggles, and dip baskets while handling chemicals or hot water. Consult the material safety data sheets (MSDSs) for additional precautions before using cleaners and detergents.

— Keep your hands, body, and clothing away from moving machine parts.

— Never leave moving machinery unattended.

— Do not distract the attention of personnel who are operating the machines.

— Do not attempt to clean or service a machine while it is in operation. Before cleaning, adjusting, oiling, greasing, and so forth, you should be sure the power is turned off and the equipment is de-energized and properly tagged out of service.

— All repairs, tag-outs, and servicing should be made only by authorized personnel.

— Make sure safety devices such as safety interlocks on covers of vegetable peelers and bread slicer safety cutoffs are maintained in proper working condition at all times. If removed for any reason, such devices must be replaced before the machine is put into operation.

— Remove rings and watches and eliminate any loose clothing such as unbuttoned sleeve cuffs, oversized gloves, and ill-fitting coats or jackets.

— Make sure all permanently mounted equipments are hardwired.

— Make sure any rubber safety covers over electrical switches are in place and have no holes or cracks.

Types of Equipment

Foodservice equipment is used for the cooking and preparation of food and the cleaning of utensils and dinnerware. This consists of all equipment located in foodservice spaces like the general mess (GM), bakeshop, meat preparation room, private mess galleys, dining areas, and sculleries.

Numerous items of foodservice equipment such as vegetable peelers, meat choppers, dough mixers, and refrigerators are either driven by electric motors or are heated electrically (such as ranges, broilers, griddles, and fry kettles). Safety precautions must be observed around all electrical equipment to avoid injury from shock. Major cleaning requires the equipment to be tagged out according to the tag-out bill. Negligence in carrying out routine operating instructions and preventive maintenance introduces an undue health hazard among the people served.

Therefore, it is vital that the correct operating procedures be followed, that a cleaning schedule be carefully adhered to, and that the machine be given adequate preventive maintenance to make sure of satisfactory cleaning and sanitizing of eating utensils. It is necessary to know all the foodservice equipment needed, whether it is for cooking, serving, cleaning, mixing, cutting, or storing. Understanding their basic operation and cleaning is a must for every foodservice personnel.

Steam-Jacketed Kettles

There are two different types of steam-jacketed kettles in use afloat as well as ashore. It is important to know which type your command uses. The following are basic principles to follow for each type of kettle. Steam-jacketed kettle (steam supplied) : Steam is supplied to foodservice spaces for the use of the steam-jacketed kettles.

The foodservice division is required to make sure the operating procedures are closely monitored; the steam potential lethal instrument. To maintained properly, follow maintenance system (PMS) instructions. Steam-jacketed kettle can become a make sure the kettle is the required planned cards and operating (electric): Steam is internally supplied through a sealed "vacuum" system.

It is the responsibility of the galley watch captain to make sure the level of water does not go below the minimum level on the sight glass. To recharge the system you must add distilled water obtained from either the ship's distilling plant or from sources of supply. If tap water is used, it can cause a buildup of mineral deposits on the heating coils and decrease the effectiveness of the kettles.

Steam-jacketed kettles are used to prepare a variety of food items such as soups, sauces, vegetables, meat, and beverages. This equipment is very important and should be handled with great care. The kettles vary in size from 5 to 80 gallons.

Approximately the lower two-thirds of each kettle is surrounded by a jacket that is offset from the main kettle body to provide space for steam to circulate and heat the contents of the kettle. The kettles are permanently mounted on a pedestal or three legs and have a hinged lid or cover.

They also have a tube at the bottom of the kettle with a faucet at the outer end for drawing liquids instead of dipping them out, and a steam inlet connection, a steam outlet connection, and a safety valve. Some steam-jacketed kettles (or trunnions) have a handle on the side making it possible to tilt the kettle and pour contents into a service container. This type of kettle is usually used to prepare gravies and sauces.

Kettles now in use are made of three types of material: corrosion-resisting steel, aluminum, and single-clad corrosion-resisting steel. Never fill the kettle completely full. When the lid is closed while cooking, make sure you are extremely careful in opening the lid because hot steam trapped in the kettle could burst out and cause a serious injury. If it is necessary to stir the contents, use a metal paddle; never leave the paddle in the kettle while cooking.

Operation

The kettles are constructed to operate on a maximum steam pressure of 45 pounds per square inch. When the pressure in the galley steam line exceeds 45 psi, a pressure regulating valve (safety valve) installed in the steam line leading to the kettles is set to release pressure at 45 psi. Do not tamper with the safety valve or tie it closed. It is there to prevent the kettle from exploding.

When operating a cold kettle, turn the steam on gradually, allowing the shell to become thoroughly warm before full pressure is applied. After the shell has become warm, and before applying full pressure, open the safety valve by pulling the lever. Opening the safety valve when enough pressure is within the shell removes air from within the jacket and prevents the kettle from becoming air-bound.

Cleaning

Kettles (or coppers) must be cleaned after each use. General cleaning instructions are as follows:

— *Rinse kettle immediately after cooking*: Open draft faucet and flush with water.

— *Soak*: Close drain valve. Fill with water above cooking level. If greasy, apply heat. Use a scrub brush to loosen food particles. Drain soak water.

— *Refill and clean*: Add detergent, using 1 ounce to 1 gallon of water. Clean interior, hinges, under surfaces of lids, and frame with brush. Drain. Flush out.

— *Remove drain-off faucet and fittings and disassemble drain line*: Scrub draw off faucet and fittings with a flexible-handled brush. Pull back and forth through tube under running hot water. Thoroughly clean in detergent water. Carefully rinse with 180°F water to sanitize. Drain valves and tubing should also be cleaned and sanitized in a similar way.

— *Scrub exterior and frame*: Use hot detergent water and brush.

— *Resterilize interior*: Before using kettle, you should carefully rinse with 180°F water.

The above procedures are recommended for stainless steel kettles. If metals are aluminum, brightening or whitening is required. Boil with vinegar water for a short time period or use a product recommended for cleaning aluminum following the manufacturer's directions. Do not use caustic cleaners or steel pads. If kettles are stainless steel, clean as directed earlier. Make sure the safety valve is in proper working order before using a kettle.

Electric Griddle

The griddle consists of cooking surfaces of various sizes up to 34 inches deep by 72 inches wide. Each has a readily removable grease receptacle in the front of the griddle and a splash guard at least 3 inches high at the rear of the griddle which is tapered at the sides. All thermostat dial knobs are conveniently located on the front panel. Each thermostat dial knob has a signal light that indicates the griddle is turned on until the griddle has reached the dialed temperature.

Operation

To operate an electric griddle, proceed as follows:

— Carefully read the operating instructions posted near the griddle.

— Preheat the griddle by turning the thermostat dial knob to the recommended preheating temperature according to the manufacturer's technical manual.

— Set the thermostat dial knobs at the desired temperature listed on the recipe card of the food to be grilled. A red light will turn on automatically when the griddle dial is initially set and will turn off when the the griddle has reached the dialed temperature. The signal will flash on and off during the cooking process to show the correct temperature is being maintained. You are now ready to load the griddle.

— Turn the griddle off or to the lowest temperature setting during idle periods.

Care and Cleaning

Keep the cooking surface scraped and wiped clean at all times. The grease gutters should always be kept clean to help in draining off excess grease and thereby reduce smoke. The grease receptacle should be emptied frequently and thoroughly cleaned at the end of the workday. Before starting the griddle cleaning procedure, always make sure the electrical power is turned off at the main power panel and the correct tag-out procedures have been followed. The cooking surface of most griddles can be satisfactorily cleaned with a pumice stone. Never use water.

However, before cleaning, you should read the manufacturer's recommended cleaning instructions for that particular griddle surface. After each thorough cleaning, the griddle should be seasoned. Seasoning is done by preheating the griddle to 400°F. When the signal light goes off, spread a light film of cooking oil or fat over the entire surface of the griddle. In 2 minutes, wipe the surface clean of excess oil. Repeat this operation. The griddle is now ready for use.

Tilting Skillet

Tilting skillets are large frying pans with deep sides and an attached lid. They are used to grill, fry, simmer, and braise large quantities of food. They can be mounted on a wall or on a stand and can be tilted at least 90 degrees from the normal horizontal position for emptying cooked foods and cleaning. Skillets are either gas or electric, have an electric thermostat, and have a temperature range of 100°F to 450°F. There is also a secondary thermostat that is a high-limit cutoff that disables the power circuit when the temperature exceeds 460°F.

Gas skillets are also furnished with a pressure regulator, connector, quick-disconnect, and a 100-percent shutoff device for the pilot (automatic ignition of gas). Most skillets will also have a faucet directly attached to the skillet to aid in cooking and cleaning.

Operation

The skillet is heated from the bottom by either resistant

heating elements or a series of gas burners. Usually, the tilting mechanism can be locked in any position. On some models, the tilting feature may have a safety switch to be engaged if the skillet is hot or on. If the skillet is provided with a faucet, it may be connected directly to a water supply.

Care in Cleaning

The tilting skillet should be cleaned after each use. Before cleaning you must turn off the heating element and scrape off the hardened food from the inside of the skillet with a spatula or scraper and flush down the sediment with a small amount of water. If the skillet has become very dirty, fill it to the level with hot water containing a mild hand-dishwashing detergent.

Turn on the heating element and allow the water to come to a boil. Boil the water for at least 5 to 10 minutes. Turn off the heating element, drain, rinse with warm vinegar water, then rinse thoroughly with clear water, and dry the skillet well. Clean the outside of the skillet with a grease-cutting detergent. Do not leave heating element turned on when the skillet is empty.

Deep-Fat Fryer

Sizes of deep-fat fryers are expressed in the number of pounds of french fries that can be cooked in an hour and range from 30 to 125 pounds. Some deep-fat fryers are manually loaded. Others have automatic basket lowering and raising capabilities controlled by a timer.

Operation of machine

Before filling the deepfat fryer, you should always check three things:

— The Master switch must be in the OFF position.

— Thermostatic switch must be in the OFF position.

— Drain valve must be closed tightly. Fill the fryer with fat using the amount specified in technical manual furnished with the fryer.

Fats should be kept at least 2 inches below the fryer top. If possible, the fat should be heated and melted before placing it in the fry kettle. Cold solid fat may have moisture pockets that will explode, casting hot melted fat over a wide area. The temperature should not be more than 200°F while the fat is melting. Also, if the cold fat is not uniformly distributed around the heating element, the bare portions may heat up to a point where a sudden splash of fat on the overheated element will cause the fat to ignite.

Fat ignites at 475°F. The fat should cover the uppermost coil at all times when the deep-fat fryer is in operation so as not to overheat the element and cause a fire. After the fat has been added, operate the deep-fat fryer as follows:

— Turn on the master switch located outside the galley.

— Set the thermostat at the cooking temperature prescribed in the Armed Forces Recipe Service (AFRS), NAVSUP P-7, for the recipe you are using.

— Check the temperature of the fat with a hand thermometer frequently during the cooking process. Compare this hand reading with the thermostat reading to determine if the thermostat is accurate. The temperature should never, under any circumstances, go above 400°F. A safety requirement on all Navy fryers includes a second or over-temperature thermostat. This is a nonadjustable, manual, resetting type installed to limit the maximum temperature to 460°F. In case of failure of the adjustable automatic thermostat, the over-temperature thermostat disconnects the electric power to the heater elements.

— Have foods as free from moisture as possible before frying. Excess moisture causes the fat to foam, sputter, and boil over. It also causes fat to break down and its useful life is shortened.

— Do not fry bacon in the deep-fat fryer, as the fat from the bacon causes the fat level to rise above the safe level. It also contains salt that will shorten the life of the fat.

— Follow instructions furnished with the fryer. Do not exceed the capacity of the fryer indicated on the instruction plate.

— Never let the fat level fall below the point marked in the fat container, and never leave the deep-fat fryer unattended while in use.

— In the event a fire should occur in the deep-fat fryer, do not attempt to smother the fire with a cover of any sort. Call the emergency number for reporting a fire at your command and shut off the electrical source, which is the main power switch outside the space, to the fryer. If the fryer is provided with an automatic fire extinguishing unit and does not set off automatically, pull the manual release. If that does not function, use PKP portable extinguishers.

Cleaning

Under any circumstances, do not use water to extinguish the fire. The deep-fat fryer should be cleaned after each use. Before cleaning the deep-fat fryer, you must turn off the heating element and allow the fat to cool to about 150°F.

Drain the fat out of the fryer. Then remove the basket support screen, scrape off the oxidized fat from the sides of the kettle with a spatula or scraper, and flush down the sediment with a small amount of fat. If the kettle has become very dirty, fill it to the level with hot water containing dishwashing machine detergent. Turn on the heating element and allow the water to come to a boil. Boil the water for at least 5 to 10 minutes.

Turn off the heating element, drain, rinse with warm vinegar water, then rinse thoroughly with clear water, and dry the fryer well. Clean the outside of the fry kettle with a grease solvent. Do not leave heating element turned on when the deep-fat fryer is empty.

Electric Oven

Electric ovens have two to six compartments with two heating units in each compartment, one located below the bottom deck of the compartment. Each heating unit is controlled by a separate three-heat switch, and the temperature of each section is regulated by a thermostat.

Operation

The oven should be preheated before it is used by turning both upper and lower units to high until the desired temperature is reached. Then, the thermostat control will automatically cut off the current and will supply only enough heat to keep the temperature constant. After the oven has been heated, set the two three-heat oven switches at the top and bottom to the heat setting necessary to bake the product. In roasting meat, avoid spilling grease on the heating elements or thermostat, as damage to this equipment may result.

Care and Cleaning

Turn off heat. Scrape interior. Sprinkle salt on hardened spillage on oven floor. Turn thermostat to 500°F. When spillage has carbonized completely, turn off oven and let it cool thoroughly. Scrape the floor with a long-handled metal scraper. Use a metal sponge or hand scraper on inside of doors, including handles and edges.

Brush out scraped carbon and loose foods. Begin with the top deck if stacked. Brush out with a stiff-bristled brush and use a dustpan to collect. Wash doors with hot detergent solution on enameled surfaces only, rinse, and wipe dry. Brush combustion chamber using a small broom, and brush to clean everyday. Wash top, back, hinges, and feet with warm hand-detergent solution, rinse, and wipe dry. Clean and polish stainless steel exterior.

Convection Oven

A convection oven has a blower fan that circulates hot air throughout the oven, eliminating cold spots and promoting rapid cooking. Overall, cooking temperatures in convection ovens are lower and cooking time is shorter than in conventional ovens. The size, thickness, type of food, and the amount loaded into the oven at one time will influence the cooking time.

General Operation

The general operating procedures for convection ovens are as follows:

— Select and make the proper rack arrangement for the product to be cooked.

— Turn or push the main power switch on (gas oven-turn burner valve on).. Set the thermostat to the recommended temperature. The thermostat signal light will light when the power goes on. If possible, adjust the fan speed on the two-speed blower.

— Preheat oven until the thermostat signal light goes out indicating that the oven has reached the desired temperature. The oven should preheat to 350°F within 10 to 15 minutes.

— Open the oven doors and load the oven quickly to prevent excessive loss of heat. Load the oven from the top, centering the pans on the rack toward the front of the oven. Place partial loads in the center of the oven. Allow 1 to 2 inches of space between the pans and along the oven sides to permit good air circulation. Remember-overloading is the major cause of nonuniform baking and roasting.

— Close the oven doors and set the timer for the desired cooking time. Check periodically until the product is ready for removal.

Temperature Settings: Follow the recommended temperature guidelines provided either in the manufacturer's operating manual or those furnished in the AFRS, NAVSUP P-7, or reduce the temperatures specified on the recipe cards by 50°F.

If food is cooked around the edges, but the center is still raw or not thoroughly cooked, or if there is too much color variation (some is normal), reduce the heat by 15°F to 25°F and return food to the oven. If necessary, continue to reduce the heat on successive loads until the desired results are achieved. Record the most successful temperature on the recipe card for future reference.

Time Settings: Follow the recommended times provided in the manufacturer's operating manual, or follow the guidelines in the AFRS. Check progress halfway through the cooking cycle since time will vary with the quality of food loaded, the temperature, and the type of pan used. Remember, the use of meat thermometers for roasting and the visual examination of baked products are the most accurate methods of determining the desired cooking times, both in convection and conventional ovens.

Vent Damper Control Setting: The vent damper control is located on or near the control panel. The damper should be kept closed for most foods of low moisture content such as roasts. Leaving the vent open during roasting will produce a dry meat and result in excessive shrinkage. The damper should be kept open when baking items with high moisture content (cakes, muffins, yeast bread, and so forth). Leaving the damper closed throughout a baking cycle will produce cakes that are too moist and ones that will not rise. A "cloud" of water droplets on the oven window indicates excessive moisture that should be vented out of the oven through the open damper.

Interior Oven Lights: Turn on lights only when loading, unloading, or checking the product. The continual burning of lights will result in a shortened bulb life.

Timer: The oven timer will ring only as a reminder; it has no control over the functioning of the oven. To assure proper operation, you should wind the timer to the maximum setting, then turn it back to the setting desired for the particular product.

Care and Cleaning

Keep the inside of the oven and racks clean. If food particles or carbon accumulates so that doors cannot be tightly closed, heat is wasted and the oven will not operate properly. Poorly closed doors permit a constant escape of steam and vapor around the door. The vapor will condense and deteriorate the finish around the oven front and door lining.

The rule for all electrical appliances is to make sure the proper tag-out procedures have been followed. When cleaning the interior of the oven, it is important to bear in mind that the aluminum coating, though tightly adherent, is still a coating. To preserve the coating and to make maintenance easier, clean the interior daily when the oven is cold with a mild detergent or soap and water.

This will prevent food and dirt from "baking on" and will frequently be all the cleaning that is necessary. If soil resists soap and water cleaning, use a wooden tool to loosen spillage from the cold oven. Follow with a nonetching cleaner that is specifically recommended for aluminized steel. Use clear water to rinse; dry with a soft clean cloth. Avoid using wire brushes and caustic solutions such as lye, soda ash, or ammonia.

When the oven liner features stainless steel the following rules apply: In general, the principles detailed previously apply. Soap or detergent and water will usually take care of routine cleaning. Drying should be done with a soft clean cloth. For burnt-on foods and grease that resist simple soap and water cleaning, an abrasive cleaner mixed into a paste may be used. Apply with a sponge, always rubbing with the grain. This treatment is usually effective for heat tint (slightly darkened areas caused by oxidation). Again, remember to rub in the direction of the polish lines. Rinse with clear water and dry with a soft cloth.

When Teflon panels are featured, the following rules apply: To protect the easy-care properties of Teflon-coated oven panels, frequent cleaning, dependent on oven usage, is recommended. Panels should be cleaned as soon as soil begins to turn brown. This will minimize the possibility of Teflon discoloration. Do not use sharp instruments, abrasive materials, or oven cleaners on a Teflon surface, otherwise the warranty is void. Should the surface be accidently scratched, the performance and cleanability features would be adversely affected. To clean the Teflon panels, remove panels and wash thoroughly with hot sudsy water using a sponge or web pad that is supplied with the oven. Do not use harsh abrasives. Rinse well and dry. Between these cleanings, everyday oven spatters can be easily sponged off with a sudsy sponge or a cloth, rinsed, and dried.

With Teflon, there is never a need for oven cleaner. The step-by-step sequence for removing panels is as follows:

— Remove tray racks by pulling straight out.

— Remove right and left rack guides by lifting straight out. Right- and left-hand panels may now be removed by moving toward the center and pulling out.

— To avoid scratching, do not rest panels on bottom panel.

— Remove bottom panel by pulling straight out.

— Remove blower baffle by lifting straight up and pulling out toward the front.

— Care should be exercised to clear brackets on the side.

— Blower wheel can now be cleaned in place.

— Top panel and interior door panels can be cleaned while in place.

— If removal of top panel is desired, unscrew three screws from the front top edge of top and two screws from rear flange of top.

— Slide out toward front. To reassemble, reverse these procedures.

To keep the stainless steel front bright and gleaming at all times, just clean it regularly with a damp cloth and polish with a soft dry cloth. To remove discolorations that may have formed when regular cleaning was neglected, use any detergent or plain soap and water. Wash all exterior surfaces daily.

Use a cloth wet with warm water and a mild soap or detergent. Where surfaces have been polished, rub lightly with a cloth-hard rubbing will remove polish. Follow with a clean damp cloth, then dry. This simple beauty treatment not only keeps your equipment dirt-free and sparkling, but virtually eliminates the danger of grease accumulation that may form a stubborn stain if left on too long.

Most convection ovens are equipped with an electric interlock that energizes/de-energizes both the heating elements and the fan motor when the doors are closed/open. Therefore, the heating elements and fan will not operate independently and will only operate with the doors closed. Some convection ovens are equipped with single-speed fan motors while others are equipped with two-speed fan motors. This information is particularly important to note when baking cakes, muffins, meringue or custard pies, or similar products, and when oven-frying bacon.

High-speed air circulation may cause damage to the food or blow melted fat throughout the oven. Read the manufacturers' manuals and determine exactly what features you have and then, for the previous products, proceed as follows:

— *On two-speed interlocked fan motor*: set fan speed to low.

— *On single-speed interlocked fan motor*: preheat oven 50°F higher than the recommended cooking temperature. Load oven quickly, close doors, and reduce thermostat to recommended cooking temperature.

— *On single-speed independent fan motor*: preheat oven 25°F above temperature specified in recipe. Turn the fan off. Reduce heat 25°F. Load oven quickly and close doors. Turn fan on after 7 to 10 minutes and keep it on for remaining cooking time.

Electric Ranges

Electric ranges are normally found in private messes, small

ships, and submarines. descriptions and uses will now be explained.

Type S : Type S is found on submarines. Range The type S is a compact galley unit consisting of a griddle on the left side and hot plates on the right side. A two-compartment oven section makes up the body of the range. Dial temperature control knobs are mounted on the body directly adjacent to each section. The temperature control knobs for the ovens are located directly to the right of each oven compartment.

Type C : Type C is found on small ships and private messes where small galleys with limited space are found. This type of range consists of a griddle on the left side and hot plates on the right side with a single oven located in the body of the range. This type of range is also available with a single griddle top and single oven compartment. Dial temperature control knobs are mounted on the body directly adjacent to each section. Control knobs for the oven compartment are located to the right of the oven compartment.

Operation of surface units

When operating the surface unit, use the control knob or thermostat setting at maximum heat only to heat food to cooking temperature or to bring water to a boil, then reduce the control knob setting to the heat required by the food being cooked. Using more heat than necessary is not only a waste of power but produces inferior food. Do not leave the surface unit turned on when not in use. When steaming food, keep cooking utensils covered. The food will stick and burn if left uncovered and power will be wasted.

Care and Cleaning

Keep the range surface units clean and avoid spilling grease under the edges of the hot plates. Remove and clean drip pans after each use. To clean the surface units follow the cleaning procedures used for griddles and the manufacturer's technical manual for your range. To clean the oven compartment use the procedures recommended by the manufacturer's technical manual or the cleaning procedures posted near the range.

Electric Food Mixer

Electric food mixers are used for an infinite number of jobs including beating batters for cakes, mixing bread dough, beating eggs, and mashing and whipping potatoes.

Sizes and Attachments: Food-mixing machines are furnished in 20-, 60-, 80-, 110-, and 140-quart sizes with the necessary attachments, paddles, and beaters. The wire whip is used for eggs, cream, and lightweight mixing; the flat beater for cake batters and mediumweight mixing; the dough hook for mixing bread dough; and the wire beater for medium-stiff dough.

One part of the machine revolves through the use of a set of transmissions and differential gears. Various shaped paddles and mixers can be attached to this revolving unit. The lower part of the mixer contains two extended, adjustable arms. A bowl, containing the foods to be mixed, is placed on these arms and the arms are then moved up so the paddles will revolve throughout the mixture. The machines have either three or four speeds. Usually they have an attachment hub that can be used for a vegetable slicer, juicer, and meat grinder.

Operation

Before operating the machine make sure the bowl, paddles, and beaters are thoroughly clean. If necessary, wash them in hot soapy water and rinse with hot water (170°F). Place the ingredients in the bowl as specified on the AFRS recipe card.

Do not fill the bowl more than half full. Place the bowl on a castered dolly when moving across the deck. Insert the bowl in the mixing machine, making sure the bowl ears are on the supporting pins and both sides are locked in place. Select the proper attachment machine.

The L-shaped notch in and place it in the the beater is to be inserted over the pin in the shaft. On the smaller models the shaft will be grooved. The attachment is inserted into these grooves and slipped into the lock. Raise the bowl to the proper height by turning the wheel or crank.

Start the motor at no load and with clutch release shift to low speed; release the clutch each time the speed is changed. The speed to be used is indicated on the recipe card and on the instructions furnished by the manufacturer.

Watch mixing times and mixing speeds carefully. Often blended ingredients revert to separate ingredients if mixed too long or at an improper speed. If, during the process of mixing, some of the batter has piled up on the sides of the bowl, stop the machine. Using a long-handled spoon or spatula, scrape down the sides of the bowl.

Never put spoons, spatulas, or your hands in the bowl while the machine is in operation. When the mixing is completed, move the control switch to the OFF position and stop the motor. Lower the bowl by the lever with which you raised it and remove the beater by turning the sleeve to the left. Remove any food left on the beater with a spatula. Then, place the bowl on the castered dolly and move it to the place of use.

Care and Cleaning

The electric mixer, beaters, whips, and bowls all require care. Beaters, paddles, and bowls should be washed immediately after each use. Use hot soapy water and rinse with hot water (170°F). Hang beaters and paddles upside down to air dry. Clean the body of the machine after each meal. Use a damp cloth or wash with water as necessary for proper sanitation. Be sure the beater shaft is free of all dirt and food particles. The motor and mechanical parts of the mixer should be inspected and maintained by the engineering department once a week.

Electric Meat-Slicing Machine

The meat-slicing machine is motor operated and is used for slicing hard or soft foods such as roasts, cheese, bacon, luncheon meats, and ham. The machine has a carriage on which the meat is placed. A swiftly revolving disk knife slices the meat as the carriage is moved across the face of the revolving knife.

Operating the Meat slicer

Meat slicers may be either manual or automatic feed. To use the slicer, place the meat on the carriage and adjust the clamp to hold the meat firmly. Next, set the dial for the desired thickness of the slices. Set the machine on automatic or manual. Turn on power to the machine. If manual mode was selected, move carriage back and forth with the hand lever.

The meat-slicing machine must be hardwired (permanently attached) and have a backup electric switch. The switch will be equipped with a guard to prevent accidental starting. The meat slicer is a very dangerous piece of equipment. Never operate it with the blade guard off or put your hands anywhere near the blade while the blade is turning. The blade is very sharp, so extreme caution should be used when sharpening or cleaning it.

Clean the knife and the body of the slicer by following the manufacturer's recommended cleaning instructions or the instructions posted by the machine. Reassemble the slicer immediately so that the bare blade will not be exposed and apply a thin coating of salad oil on the blade. Do not forget to clean the counter top under the slicer.

Steamers

Steamers are used for steaming fish, fruit, meat, poultry, and vegetables. Most steamers used in the Navy consist of a three door, three-compartment unit. Each unit has one or two perforated pans or baskets.

Operation

When operating steamers, you are not limited to the use of pans and baskets furnished with them. If juices are to be saved, you should cook in leakproof solid pans of a suitable size. Pans should not be overloaded; steam circulates best when pans are about three-fourths full. Different foods may be cooked in the same steam compartment without mixing flavors or affecting the taste of the different foods. Onions and pudding placed in individual pans may be cooked in the same steam compartment without a transfer of flavor.

After the food has been placed in the steamer, close the compartment door securely. If the steam supply is controlled separately, open the steam valve slowly by turning the valve wheel counterclockwise after the door is latched. Then observe the middle indicator on the pressure gauge, which should be in the range of 5 to 7 psi. Turn the valve wheel clockwise to reduce steam pressure if it is above 7 psi.

Watch your cooking time closely and avoid spoiling food by overcooking. Less time is required for steam pressure cooking than for boiling food in water; the temperature of steam at 7 psi is 233°F and the boiling temperature of water is 212°F. After cooking has been completed, turn off the steam supply by turning the valve wheel clockwise on separately controlled units, or by unlatching the compartment door of the latch-controlled steam supply.

You can relieve the steam pressure by operating the lever of the safety valve, if one is provided; otherwise, wait 2 minutes before you open the door to the full OPEN position. The gauge should read 0 psi before the door is opened.

Care and Cleaning

Occasionally, when you examine the drainpipe for steam-condensate drip, none will appear after a few minutes of steamer operation. When this is the case, turn off the steam supply by unlatching the door or closing the valve, as necessary. The fault normally is stoppage in the trap, strainer, or drainpipe. To eliminate this condition, close the steam valve, remove the steam-trap strainer basket, and clean it by scraping out the solids and washing the basket until the mesh or perforations are open and clear.

Clean the pipe connection in the steamer compartment, reassemble the strainer, and repeat the pressure cooking. If there is still no drip, the steam trap is at fault, so report this to the engineer officer via the chain of command. After each meal, the steamer should be brush- scrubbed, washed clean with hot soapy water, and rinsed with hot water (170°F) and allowed to air dry.

High-Compression Steamer

The high-compression steamer is a modular unit that is used to defrost and cook food by using high-velocity steam. When steam enters the unit, it is piped to a jet box from which it is jetted directly onto the frozen food at approximately 200 miles per hour (mph). The steam gains the high velocity by being forced through a series of small perforations.

Operation

Check the steam supply gauge; 15 psi is needed for proper operation. Insert foods into the cooking chamber; then place the frozen food directly under the jet box; close and seal the door. Select the time (from 5 to 60 minutes) for the food to be cooked. Turn the selector switch to 60 minutes and then back to the desired cooking time. The pilot light indicates that cooking is in progress. Food is defrosted and cooked auto-matically.

The pressure gauge rises to approximately 5 psi and increases to 15 psi after 2 minutes, where it will stay until cooking has been completed. The door must be kept locked until the cooking cycle has been completed. All steam will exhaust automatically and the buzzer will sound when the cooking cycle has been completed.

Care and Cleaning

The steamer should be cleaned at the end of each day that it has been used. To clean the jet steamer, remove the jet plate, pan supports, and door, including the gasket around the door, and wash in warm soapy water. Rinse well in warm water. Scrub the interior of the cylinder with warm soapy water and rinse well.

The door gasket must be kept clean at all times. With normal closing and locking of the door assembly, a steamtight seal should be made between the door gasket and the door opening. This seal cannot be maintained if particles of foreign matter are allowed to accumulate upon either of the contacting surfaces. If leakage of steam occurs, the door assembly is improperly adjusted and a readjustment must be made to the adjustment screw.

Ventilator Hoods

Ventilator hoods, like people, come in a variety of shapes, sizes, and appearances, and vary in their effectiveness from barely acceptable to highly efficient. The filter-type hoods fall into the barely acceptable category, and the filterless grease extractors-mostly known as Gaylord ventilators-are the most efficient. Filter- type hoods are the hardest to keep clean and are gradually being re-placed as funds allow.

They generally have no built-in fire protection system. If the filters are not replaced after cleaning, a buildup of grease deposits in the exhaust duct system could lead to a fire! Depending upon the type of fumes exhausted and the amount of use, the filter should be removed and washed in the dishwasher or deep sink daily, or no less than once a week.

The hood chamber behind the filters should be cleaned while the filters are out and you should be sure the filters are then put back. Also, remember, with all ventilators, to remove the access cover plates on the exhaust ducts, inspect for grease buildup in the ducts, and clean as necessary. The hood, generally referred to as the Gaylord (named after the original manufacturer), is the type that uses an arrangement of internal baffles to cause the exhaust air to quickly change direction several times before it enters the exhaust duct.

In so doing, the air slings the grease out into the grease trough that is built into the bottom part of the hood. This action is what gives the hood the name of centrifugal grease extractor. Other than the air, the only moving part in this system is the fire damper that is spring-loaded to close the throat or inlet air slot in case of fire, and this damper, when open, also serves as the first of the air baffles. All the action up to this point is carried out automatically by the hood as long as the exhaust blower is operating correctly.

Another automatic feature is the fire-sensing thermostat located in the exhaust ductwork close to the hood. From the outside, this looks like an aluminum box about 2 1/2 inches wide by 4 inches long by 1 1/2 inches deep. On the back of this, and projecting inside the duct, is a thermostat probe that is constantly checking air temperature in the exhaust duct. If a fire starts, and the air going by the thermostat reaches 250°F, the thermostat switch operates a magnetic trip inside the fire damper control box (the one with the plunger mounted above the hood), the fire damper slams shut, and the blower shuts down.

In later model hoods with automatic cleaning (more about this later), this condition also will cause the automatic water washdown system to come on and spray water into the hood until the temperature at the thermostat is less than 250°F. On earlier models, the water or steam must be turned on manually. All shipboard model grease extractor hoods are fail-safe in that power failure or thermostat failure will cause the fire damper to close of cleaning systems, all having a look-alike appearance but slightly different in method:

— Steam cleaning (manual)

— Hot water cleaning (manual)

— Detergent washdown system (automatic and manual)

In both steam cleaning and hot water cleaning, you must shut off the exhaust blower motor at the control panel, turn on the steam or hot water valve in the line leading to the upper part of the hood and allow it to run for 5 minutes or more, depending on how dirty the inside of the hood gets. If hot water is used, the temperature should be between 130°F and 180°F, and the closer to 180°F the better.

After shutting off the steam or water, open the inspection doors on the ventilator and see if the grease and dirt have been flushed away. If the entire hood interior is still dirty, you need to leave the valve open longer. If only a certain area is dirty, you may have a clogged spray nozzle. Clean the hole in the nozzle with a small piece of wire.

During the washdown, watch the drain line from the bottom of the hood. It should run freely and should be dumping through an air gap to a deck drain. No shutoff valves are allowed in the drain line and the line should never be directly connected to a drain. Otherwise, a stopped-up drain could allow sewage to backup into the hood and spill into food and food equipment. Hand-clean all exposed surfaces of the hood including the front surface of the fire damper baffle.

Watch your fingers when cleaning the damper. If the damper is accidently tripped, it could pinch your fingers against the back of the hood. Automatic cleaning is a timed, push-button cleaning system. A dishwasher scrubbing action with detergent and hot water is obtained by directed spray nozzle action. The nozzles are located on 8- to 10-inch centers on the cleaning pipes mounted on the interior back wall of the ventilator.

The cleaning cycle is activated each time the blower serving the ventilator is stopped by pushing the STOP button on the exhaust control and cleaning station. This shuts off the blower and releases detergent and hot water into the ventilator for a preselected and preset time on the adjustable timer in the exhaust control and cleaning station. After the cleaning cycle has been completed, follow the same steps as previously explained in manual cleaning, except clean the detergent tank and refill, if needed, with the correct detergent.

Note that the timer for the automatic wash cycle is located in the stainless steel cabinet that houses the exhaust control and cleaning station. The length of the automatic wash cycle is adjustable and should be adjusted for the minimum time that will satisfactorily clean the hood. This will conserve utilities and detergent. The hot water shutoff valve, usually located in the cleaning station cabinet, should always be left on unless plumbing repairs are necessary.

On some ships, where low water pressure or the amount of hot water available is a problem and where all galley hoods are connected to a single automatic wash system, installing activities have found it necessary to install individual shutoff valves in the hot water/detergent line at each ventilator hood. In these cases, be sure only the valve at the hood to be cleaned is turned on. If you have an arrangement like this, for fire protection purposes, leave the valve to the hood serving deep-fat fryers turned on and all others off, except when they are actually being washed. Directions for priming the detergent pump are located most often on the inside of the door. Motor bearings on the detergent pump should be oiled once every 6 months.

Dough Trough

A dough trough is the container in which dough is placed during the fermentation period. It is an oblong boxlike trough of steel construction equipped with four casters to permit easy movement in the bakeshop area. Dough troughs are of various lengths and are designed to hold approximately 90 pounds of dough to a foot, or 50 pounds of flour to a foot. If the trough is too long for the amount of dough to be fermented properly, dam boards maybe inserted so that the correct amount of space is available.

Dough Proofers

Dough proofers or fermentation rooms are used for conditioning dough and cooling baked bread. The air temperature and air moisture (humidity) in a dough proofer are kept at preset levels by automatic controls. Dough proofers are thermally insulated enclosures and vary in size from a small box with shelving to a room with space for many portable bread racks.

The dough proofer is heated by steam coils or electric heating elements located inside the enclosure, or by self-contained air-conditioning units connected to the proofer by air ducts. For shipboard use, steam-heated dough proofers are furnished in various sizes; the number and size of the proofers depend on the capacity of the bake ovens installed in the bakery on board ship.

Operation

The operation of all dough proofers is basically the same regardless of the size of the proofer. Air within a proofer should be kept at a preset temperature and moisture level. Dough proofers require at least 1 hour to attain the proper atmosphere; the unit should be started well in advance of anticipated use. The time and temperature used to proof bread dough in the proofer should be as specified on the recipe card.

Turn the steam valve on full and open the petcock to provide the necessary amount of steam for humidity. Adjust the steam inlet valve to obtain the desired temperature. When the temperature and humidity are correct, place the pans of dough into the proofer and close the door. Watch the time closely and test the dough periodically by pressing the fingers into it.

If the depression is filled by rising dough, fermentation is progressing properly. To reduce fermentation, cover the bread pans with cloths and reduce the proofer temperature. At no time should there be more than 35 pounds of steam pressure allowed to pass through the steam coils of the proofer. Drain the condensation from the drip pan at regular intervals by opening the petcock.

Care and Cleaning

Proofers should be maintained in a safe, sanitary, dust-free, rust-free, nonleaking, and economical operating condition. The enclosures and accessories should be kept free of flies, ants, cockroaches, mice, and rats. Clean the floor, walls, top, and inside of the door. Scrape sides, corners, and guide rails with a putty knife. Scrub the floor with along-handled scrub brush and hot machine-detergent solution; rinse and dry. Wipe guide rails and ledges thoroughly. Remove and clean water pan; rinse and wipe dry. Scrub exterior and underneath if space permits; flush with hot water.

Bread Slicer

The bread slicer is a machine with small thin blades. The platform on which the bread is placed is at about a 45-degree angle so that the weight of the bread will force the loaf down on the cutting blade when the machine is turned on. The cutting blades are attached to a cam shaft that has half the blades going in one direction and the other half going in the opposite direction. The reason for this is so that it will not tear the loaf while it is being sliced. Never use your hand to push the load through the machine.

Vegetable Peelers

Vegetable peelers have capacities of 10, 15, 30, or 50 pounds and have a cylindrical hopper with an abrasive-covered wall and an abrasive-covered rotary disk in the bottom. The disk has a wavy surface. This surface agitates the vegetables in such a manner that they continually present new surfaces for action by the abrasive material.

Operation

Before loading the machine, sort the vegetables so that those in any one load are of the same size and free of stones, sticks, and other hard objects. The machine should be started and the water turned into it before any vegetables are added. Do not overload the machine. The quantity of vegetables loaded should not exceed approximately 66 percent of the total hopper capacity.

A larger quantity will not be thoroughly agitated. If the abrasive surfaces of the machine are kept reasonably clean, a load of vegetables should be satisfactorily peeled in about 1 minute. Deep eyes or depressions in potatoes should be removed and the peeling finished with a hand peeler or small knife. It is wasteful to allow vegetables to remain in the machine longer than necessary because valuable nutrients will be lost

Cleaning

At the end of each day's use, secure the power and dismantle the machine. Lift the cover off and take out the abrasive disks; remove the peel trap and strainers; wash the removable parts, the interior, and the exterior of the machine with hot soapy water, and rinse with hot water (170°F). Be sure all food particles are washed out. Allow all parts to air dry before reassembling the unit.

Electric Vegetable Cutters

Vegetable cutters are machines that, without the use of attachments or removable parts, make three classes of cuts of vegetables-shredded, sliced, and grated. A dial control on the side of the machine allows instant changing of the thickness of the cut, even while the machine is in operation.

The entire front of the machine swings open to provide complete access to the interior for the purpose of cleaning and changing the blade. The machine should be washed with hot water immediately after it is used. The knurled knob holds the front of the machine securely when it is in operation. Clean and scrub the knives and bowl with hot, soapy water and a very stiff brush. Rinse them well with hot water (170°F) and allow them to air dry thoroughly before reassembling.

Vegetable Cutter And Slicer

The vegetable cutter and slicer is used to cut vegetables that are to be used for cooking and for salads. The machine may be used to do as many as three different cutting jobs at once. It maybe used for slicing either bias or horizontal french fries and julienne strips, and for coarse and fine chopping. The machine has a slicer adjustment for thicknesses up to one-fourth of an inch.

The adjustment can be made while the machine is in motion. To make french fries or diced potatoes, the potatoes must be sized so that they will go into the machine. When the machine is turned on, put a pan underneath the outlet to catch the water and vegetable particles and flush with water. This should be done after each use

At the end of the day disassemble the machine and thoroughly clean the cutting plates and disks. Carefully inspect each part for strings of vegetables that may not have washed off. This machine has parts that must be oiled daily to prolong the life and efficiency of the machine.

Meat Saw

Electric sawing machines are used mainly for cutting chilled, frozen, and smoked meats into steaks and chops. It is important to know that meat can be cut more uniformly by machine when there is still some frost in the boneless piece. The saw is made to revolve by a mechanical arrangement of two wheels and an electric motor. The table on which the meat is laid is constructed so that you can cut the meat to any desired size. The saw blades themselves are five-eighths of an inch wide and about 10 feet long.

Operation

Before operating the saw, you must tighten the blade using only one hand to apply just enough tension to keep it from slipping. Feed the meat straight through giving the blade a chance to cut. Do not force. Use only sharp blades. Dull blades may heat up, twist, and break. The electric meat cutter is a dangerous piece of equipment. A great deal of care is necessary to avoid injury when you operate this machine.

There are seven safety precautions that should be observed when you are operating the meat saw:

— Always wear safety glasses or impact goggles when using the saw.

— Before you cut the meat, make sure the right amount of tension is on the saw blade.

— There should be no flexibility whatsoever.

— The feel of the saw blade will be solid when the right amount of tension is applied.

— Meat being sawed should be placed firmly against the sliding tray guide with enough pressure to maintain a uniform thickness of the slices.

— Never use unnecessary force when cutting (sawing) meat. It is possible to break the blade and cause serious injury to yourself or others from flying pieces of metal.

— Always make sure the guide is securely tightened after the adjustment for the thickness of the meat slices has been determined.

Set the blade guide 2 inches above the meat.

— Always keep your hands on the part of the meat that is most distant from the saw blade.

— Make sure the blade guard is in place at all times except when cleaning.

Care and Cleaning

The revolving wheels have grease chambers. Pack them frequently. Keep the machine clean. Oil it at least once a week. Always wash and sanitize the machine properly after each use or after every 4 hours of continued use. Use hot soapy water to wash the machine and rinse it with hot water (170°F). Do not drip water on the electric motor.

Meat Chopper

The electric meat chopper is used to chop or grind all meats (cooked or raw) and to prepare bread crumbs from leftover bread and toast. The meat chopper is portable and maybe placed where it is needed most. It should be placed on a sturdy stand within easy reach of an electric outlet.

Operation

Usually a 3/8-inch plate is used for grinding meat. The use of a 3/16-inch plate for such grinding puts too much pressure on the grinder. The cutting edge of the knife must go next to the plate. Never forcibly tighten the adjustment ring on the chopping end, but tighten it snugly. Excess pressure will wear the chopper parts. Start the motor, then feed the material into the chopper. Turn the motor off after the material is ground. Feed the material into the machine with the tools intended for that purpose-never with your hands.

Care and Cleaning

After meat has been chopped, take the grinder apart and wash each part thoroughly with soap and water, rinse with hot water (170°F), and allow to air dry. Do not allow food to dry on the surfaces of the chopper before you wash it. A grinder can be a breeding place for bacteria that might cause food poisoning. Great care should be exercised in keeping the parts of the grinder free from contamination.

Knives and plates should be sharpened before they get dull, but do not attempt this yourself. The engineering department should be consulted. It is a good idea to keep the same knife and plate together as they wear to fit each other. Tie them together with a cord after they are used so they will not be mislaid.

Keep the motor dry. Do not grind juicy foods, such as onions, because the juice will be forced back into the gear housing, causing a loss of oil and consequent wearing of gears. If you are grinding foods such as crackers, grind a very small amount at a time or the machine will jam. When the chopper is hot, do not run raw meat through it. Remember that bits of bones can break the warm gears and knives.

Meat Tenderizer

The meat tenderizer is used to tenderize all sorts of tough meats. The machine is about 20 inches long and about 1 foot wide. To operate, turn the motor on, insert the meat to be tenderized into the opening at the top of the machine. The meat will pass through two sets of revolving rollers that contain many small blades and will be made tender. If further tenderizing is required, insert the meat again after first giving it a one-quarter turn (90 degrees).

Meat-tenderizing machines are equipped with a safety device that automatically stops the machine when the cover (shield) is raised. Never attempt to raise the top with the machine running or to operate the machine with the cover raised because of the danger of catching your fingers in the machine. Take the machine apart and clean it after each use. Oil the parts often.

Knives

Many different sizes and shapes of knives are required for meat-cutting jobs. You must understand which knife to use for each job and make sure to use it for the job it was intended. You should never use the thin-bladed knife that is designed for carving cooked meats to bone a roast. It is quicker and more efficient to use the boning knife that has a stiff, narrow, short blade to cut close around bones. The knives with the long, wide blades are used to cut steaks and roasts before they are cooked.

Sharpening Knives: To get the most use out of the knives in the galley, they must be sharp. A dull knife is a hazard and makes extra work for you. A boning knife has a comparatively narrow bevel and will stand more hard use than a steak knife that has a wide bevel and a thin edge. But no matter what tool you use, you cannot do a good job unless the tool is sharp.

The butcher's steel is used only to keep the edges of knives straight and not to sharpen them. Nor should you sharpen knives on a power- or hand-driven stone, since this removes the temper from the cutting edge. The best things to use for sharpening are a waterstone and a carborundum oilstone.

If you use the entire stone when sharpening tools the stone will not hollow out at any one point. Draw the full blade, from heel to tip, across the length of the stone and then turn the knife over and pull it back from the opposite end of the stone. This sharpens the knife evenly and smoothly and causes the stone to wear uniformly. Always clean the blade and handle thoroughly after sharpening.

Steeling: In steeling, there is a definite technique. Specific types of steels should be used to true certain edges. Never use a rough steel. A smooth steel should be used to keep the blade in perfect condition and to maintain a keen edge. The steel should have good magnetism in order to hold steel particles. The easiest and most effective methods of steeling a knife are as follows:

— Hold the steel firmly in the left hand, thumb on the top of the handle under the guard, with the point upward and slightly away from the body.

— Place the heel of the blade against the top side of the tip of the steel. The steel and the blade should meet at an angle of about 25 degrees.

— With a quick swinging motion bring the blade down across the steel toward the left hand. This should pass the entire edge lightly over the steel.

— Bring the knife into position again but with the blade against the bottom side of the steel. Then, repeat the same motion of passing the blade over the steel.

— Repeat the motion, alternating the knife from side to side; a dozen strokes will true the edge. Steel your knives as often as necessary to keep their edges straight.

Care of Knives: Never throw knives into a drawer with other cutlery or tools. It is a good idea to have a knife rack for each watch fastened to some convenient place in the galley. Do not use knives to open cans, cut wire bands, or open cases of foodstuffs.

Dishwashing Machines

Proper operation and care of dishwashing machines are vital to the sanitation, safety, and efficiency of your activity, so you must know your machines and follow directions for their use and maintenance. Dishwashing machines used in the Navy are classified as one-tank, two-tank or three-tank machines. The three-tank machine is a fully automatic, continuous racking machine that scrapes, brushes, and provides two rinses. It is used at major recruit installations and other large activities.

Single-tank Dishwashing Machine: Single-tank machines are used in small ships or small messes whereby installation of larger dishwashing machines is not feasible and practical. Wash and rinse sprays are controlled separately by automatic, self-opening, and self-closing valves in the automatic machine, or by handles in the manually operated machine.

The automatic machine provides for a 40-second wash and a 10-second rinse; for manually operated machines, wash and rinse intervals are controlled by the operator who should allow a 40-second wash and a 10-second rinse. To control the bacteria to a satisfactory minimum in single-tank machines, it is necessary that the temperature of the wash water in the tank be 140°F to 160°F.

Therefore, a thermostat is provided in the automatic machines to prevent operation when the temperature of the water falls below 140°F. Rinsing is done by means of spraying hot water on the dishes from an outside source and is controlled by an adjustable automatic steam-mixing valve that maintains the temperature of the rinse water between 180°F to 195°F.

Double-tank Method

Double-tank machines are available with several different capacities and are used when more than 150 persons are to be served. These machines are provided with separate wash and rinse tanks. They also have a final rinse of hot water that is sprayed on the dishes from an outside source. This spray is opened by the racks passing through the machine.

The spray automatically closes when the rinse cycle is completed. The final rinse is controlled by an adjustable automatic steam-mixing valve that maintains the temperature between 180°F to 195°F. Double-tank machines are also equipped with a thermostatically operated switch in the rinse tank that prevents operation of the machine if the temperature of the rinse water falls below 180°F. The racks pass through the machine automatically by means of conveyor chains. The two-tank dishwashing machine should be timed so that the utensils are exposed to the machine sprays for not less than 40 seconds (20-second wash, 20-second rinse).

Triple-tank dishwashing machines

Some shore activities have triple-tank dishwashing machines installed. The procedures of operation are basically the same as with double-tank machines with the following exceptions:

— The dishwashing machine consists of prewash, wash, and rinse sections with a final rinse.

— Refer to the manufacturer's operating and instruction manual for the preset temperatures of the prewash, wash, and rinse sections. The final rinse should always remain the same (180°F to 195°F).

Operating Dishwasher: The first thing you should do is to read and become familiar with the operating instructions included on the instruction plate that is mounted on the hood of the machine you are operating. Always follow these instructions. Otherwise, you may damage the equipment or injure yourself and others. The following detailed instructions are given for double-tank machines since most machines in service are of this type. These directions are also generally applicable to single-tank units, except for wash and rinse time intervals and temperatures.

— Inspect the machine to make sure the scrap screens are in place, spray arms are capped and adjusted so that the spray hits the utensils directly, and splash curtains are in place and not hanging closer than 5 inches to the conveyor.

— Close the drain valves to the wash and rinse sections of the machine. Open the hot water fill valves and fill the tanks to the full mark on the water level indicator.

— Open the steam valves and allow the temperature of the water to reach 180°F. Adjust the mixing valve to the HOT position to maintain a temperature range of 180°F to 195°F. On machines with hot water booster heaters installed, open the hot water and steam valve to the booster heater.

— On machines without automatic detergent dispensers, add the prescribed amount of detergent.

— Push the START button to start the pumps and conveyor and run the machine for 2 minutes to thoroughly mix the detergent and bring the temperature of the wash tank up to 140°F or above.

— Look inside the ends of the machine to make sure the power sprays are operating properly.

— During the operation of the machine keep a close check on the temperature gauges and make sure they are within the following temperature ranges:

1 1 8. Wash: 140°F - 160°F

Rinse: 180°F-195°F

Final rinse: 180°F - 195°F

— Place the dishrack on the conveyor carefully and allow the conveyor to push the rack through the machine. If the conveyor is properly set, the utensils will receive a 20-second wash and a 20-second rinse

— As the dishrack approaches the end of the machine, it will pass a lever that will actuate the final rinse. Observe the final rinse temperature gauge for correct temperature (180°F- 195°F).

— Allow all dinnerware and silverware to air dry for at least 1 minute after passing through the machine.

— Place the clean, air-dried dinnerware and trays bottom side up in a clean storage cabinet or dispenser.

— Place an empty cylinder over clean, air-dried silverware; invert and place in a clean storage cabinet.

— For every 30 to 45 minutes of continuous machine operation, the wash tank should be drained and the scrap trays cleaned.

Check the machine temperatures frequently using a pocket thermometer (0°F-200°F) to assure the accuracy of the temperature gauges. The washing of silverware is often unsatisfactory because too much silverware is placed in the rack to be thoroughly cleaned. The proper procedure for washing the silverware is to sort the silver and place 15 to 20 pieces in each cylinder-shaped compartment; run the silverware through the dishwashing machine with the service end up. When the wash-rinse cycle is complete, the sanitized silver should be stored by inverting it in the cylinder-shaped containers; thereby the washing and sanitizing is done without having to touch the utensils.

Cleaning Dishwashing Machine: The dishwashing machine must be thoroughly cleaned after each meal or use. The following procedures are to be followed:

— Turn the machine off.

— Secure the steam and hot water valves to the final rinse mixing valve, or the steam and hot water valves to the hot water booster heater.

— Add 3/4 to 1 1/2 cups of dishwashing machine detergent to the rinse tank, depending on the capacity of the rinse tank.

— Turn the machine on and allow it to operate for 5 minutes.

— Turn the machine off and secure the steam valve to the rinse tank

— Open the drain valves to the wash and rinse tanks; open the doors and allow the machine to cool.

— Remove the doors, scrap screens, metal frames, wash and rinse spray arms, pump intake strainer, drain strainer, and splash curtains. Wash thoroughly in the utensils wash sink and rinse.

— Using hand-dishwashing detergent and water with a nylon-bristled brush, thoroughly clean the inside and outside of the machine. Rinse with clean water to remove all loosened dirt and detergent.

— Reassemble the machine, close the drain valve to the wash and rinse tanks.

— Fill the tanks one-half full of water, open the steam valve to the rinse tank and allow the temperature to reach 180°F.

— Turn the machine on and operate for 5 minutes without detergent.

— Turn the machine off, close the steam valve to the rinse tank, and open the drain valves to the wash and rinse tanks.

Descaling Dishwashing Machines

The interior of the dishwashing machine and manifold(s) should be inspected monthly the for accumulation of calcium or lime deposits. If deposits are evident, the machine must be descaled. Descaling the machine should be a part of the PMS and is the responsibility of the foodservice division. The descaling operation must be closely supervised from start to finish, and personnel must wear face shields, chemical safety goggles, rubber gloves, and rubber aprons when handling acid. These descaling procedures should be followed:

— Drain wash/rinse tanks, if applicable.

— Install overflow pipes, scrap trays, screens, spray manifolds (except final rinse), and curtains (inlet and discharge ends only). Place final rinse spray manifold on top of scrap tray in wash tank.

— Shut drain valves.

— Fill tanks to within 2 inches of top of overflow pipes with clean hot water.

— Add 7 fluid ounces of orthophosphoric acid and 1 fluid ounce of rinse additive for each gallon of water per tank. These items can be obtained through the supply system.

— Complete filling the tanks and close the doors.

— Start the machine and operate for 1 hour maintaining normal operating temperatures (150°F- 160°F wash and 180°F-195°F rinse).

— Stop the machine and open the drain valves. Completely drain acid solution from machine.

— Inspect the interior of the machine. All the parts should be free of calcium or lime deposits and metal should be shiny.

— Repeat steps 3 through 8 if necessary.

— Close drain valves and fill tanks with clean hot water. Add 2 cups of dishwashing compound per tank.

— Close doors, start machine, and operate for 5 minutes at operating temperatures.

— Stop machine and completely drain tanks.

— Refill and flush tanks with clean water to remove all traces of acid and detergent.

Garbage grinder

Garbage grinders are found in sculleries and deep sinks. They are used to dispose of food from plates, unused food items, and other wet garbage. Always read the operating instructions posted near the grinder before using. To clean the tank, dump a bucket of strong, hot detergent solution into the tank and scrub the interior. Rinse by flushing the interior walls with hot water. Clean exterior by scrubbing with hot detergent solution, then rinse.

Steam table

Steam tables are used for serving hot foods. There are several types: (a) those with water compartments heated by steam coils at 40 psi of pressure or less; (b) those with steam-heated water compartments and dish warmers; (c) those with water compartments heated by immersion-electric heating elements; and (d) dish warmers. Most steam tables used in general and private messes today are immersion-electric heating element types.

Operation: Do not overload food pans. An excessive amount of food makes it difficult to maintain the correct water compartment temperature which is between 180°F to 200°F. If, on the other hand, water in the steam table is allowed to become hotter than 200°F, the food will dry rapidly and continue cooking from the excess heat. You can correct this by adding more water to reduce the heat.

Because food tastes best if served within 30 minutes (preferably within 15 minutes) after being placed on the steam table, do not place food pans on the steam table too early. Care and Cleaning After each meal, drain the steam table, wash the tanks with hot soapy water, and rinse with very hot fresh water of at least 180°F. Wash the top and front of the steam table to make it bright, clean, and sterile; then wipe it dry with a clean cloth.

Electric toasters

Electric toasters used in the galley and dining area are the intermittent and rotary types. The intermittent type is composed of chrome-plated steel and has a vertical oven with two to four openings for inserting the bread slices. The continuous type has a chrome-plated heavy-duty conveyor with motor-driven trays for the bread. Rotary toasters are cleaned by first disconnecting the power.

After toaster is cooled, remove pan, slide, and baskets. Use soft brush to remove crumbs from front surface and behind bread racks. Wipe clean frame as far as is accessible with warm hand-detergent solution. Use a nonabrasive cleaner to remove stubborn spots. Clean baskets by boiling in hot detergent water. rinse, and air dry. Then, clean and replace all parts.

Shaper, Potato Mix (Extractor)

Potato shapers are used to reconstitute dehydrated potatoes into formed french fries. They are available with optional shaping heads and a conveyor. Some of the shaper accessories are dicers, onion rings, steak fries, shoestrings, and hash-browns. Follow the manufacturer's instructions and procedures of operation and cleaning of this equipment.

Refrigerators

Refrigerators are designed for storing foods for short periods of time. Most refrigerators installed aboard ship have movable bars that fit in front of each shelf to keep the contents of the refrigerator from moving or falling out when the door is opened. At sea, food must be stored in such a way that it will not move around when the ship rolls. To keep a refrigerator operating at top efficiency, three things are important:

— Keep it clean.

— Do not overload it.

— Defrost it regularly and properly.

Defrosting

You may defrost the refrigerator on a schedule or when the frost accumulation requires it. The number of times that a refrigerator requires defrosting depends, of course, on the rate at which frost builds up on the cooling unit. Ice formations should never be more than one-fourth of an inch thick because ice and frost act as insulators and reduce efficiency. Defrosting is done by turning off the refrigerator; removing all food, and blocking the doors open. Defrosting may be speeded up, however, by placing pans of hot water in the freezer compartment. Do not scrape or chip the ice from the cooling coils as they are easily damaged, and do not pour hot water over the ice accumulation to melt it.

Cleaning the Refrigerator

A refrigerator that is not thoroughly clean will quickly develop a bad odor and the foods in it will spoil. Cleanliness avoids the growth of mold and bacteria that often cause food poisoning. A refrigerator should be cleaned at least once a week and after each defrosting. Never use a water hose in cleaning a refrigerator. Thefluid may seep into the insulation and cause permanent damage. The proper cleaning procedures are as follows:

— Wipe the gaskets around the door of the refrigerator to remove any oil or grease.

— Wash the inside surfaces and food shelves with a hot detergent solution of water.

— Rinse them with a warm solution of baking soda, using 1 tablespoon of soda to 4 quarts of water.

— Dry all surfaces thoroughly after flushing out the drain with hot water.

— Clean the outside with warm water, rinse, and dry.

Avoid overloading

Never overload a refrigerator. An overloaded refrigerator cuts down air circulation and is hard to clean. To prevent overloading, limit the amount of food you draw from bulk storage at any one time. When you draw food that must be kept in the refrigerator, do not ask for more than you can store in your ready-service refrigerator.

Refrigerated Salad Bar

Mechanically refrigerated self-service cold food counters with refrigerated (salad bars) storage compartments are procured in various sizes from three- to six-pan compartment capacity with either a single door or double doors underneath storage areas.

Operation: Usually the refrigeration to the top section of the salad bar is controlled by a separate switch. This switch should be turned on approximately 1 hour before putting the salads on the salad bar to allow the temperature to drop below 40°F.

Defrosting and Cleaning: The refrigerated salad bar should be defrosted and thoroughly cleaned after each meal. Steps in defrosting and cleaning are as follows:

— Turn off the switch of the top unit and allow it to defrost freely. Do not use any metal objects to remove ice as it may puncture the coils.

— To clean, remove all inserts of salad and dressings and return them to the vegetable preparation room.

— Discard the ice.

— Using the two-pan method, you should clean and rinse the salad bar and allow it to air dry. Special attention should be given to the drain to make sure it is free of food particles and is draining properly.

— To clean the storage section of refrigerated salad bars, follow the same procedures as for the top unit, paying particular attention to the drains and door gaskets.

— Clean the sneeze shield, legs, and metal frame.

— Clean the exterior of the salad bar as recommended by the manufacturer's technical manual.

Refrigerated milk dispensers

Refrigerated milk dispensers are used to dispense bulk milk. They are available with one, two, or three dispensing units. The size of the mess and the number of personnel fed will determine which milk dispensing unit is installed.

Operation of the Milk Dispenser: Before loading the machine, you should make sure the temperature range is from 32°F to 40°F. Fill the milk dispenser. Cut the milk dispensing tubes with a clean, sharp, disposable plastic knife at a point one-fourth of an inch below the dispensing valve opening.

Care and Cleaning: After each meal, clean the exterior with a mild solution of hot detergent water, making sure the base of the machine around the legs, metal seams, and the edges under the dispenser opening and door are thoroughly cleaned. Remove and disassemble the metal dispensing valve and run it through the dishwashing machine. Defrost the milk dispenser when the ice reaches a thickness of one-fourth of an inch using the procedures that follow:

— Remove milk containers and place them under refrigeration while defrosting.

— Turn off electric power supply; open the door and allow the machine to defrost freely.

— Do not use metal objects to dislodge ice.

— After defrosting, clean the interior of the machine using the two-pan method. One pan contains 2 tablespoons of liquid detergent to each gallon of hot water which is applied .with a nylon-bristled brush. Pan number two contains hot clean water or a sanitizing solution which is applied with a clean sponge.

— Special attention should be given to the door gaskets to prevent damage and deterioration.

— After defrosting, cleaning, and wiping dry, you should turn the electric supply back on.

Soft-Serve Ice-Cream Machine

This machine is usually located in the messing area and the patrons serve themselves. The MSs are responsible for preparing the ice-cream mix and cleaning and sanitizing the machine. It is a must that the machine be sanitized before and after each use. Follow the procedures of operation according to the technical manual or the operation procedures posted next to the machine.

Cleaning After Each Use: Soft-serve ice-cream machines are very susceptible to a rapid bacterial growth of even a little amount of ice-cream mix left in the machine or on any area the mix contacted. Therefore, following the procedures in cleaning the machine are very important. The procedures are as follows:

— Empty freezer and flush with cold water until water runs clear.

— Rinse again with warm water (120°F).

— Place 1 gallon of hand-dishwashing detergent and water (140°F) solution into the hopper. Move the switch to the WASH position and operate for 2 minutes. Draw off water solution.

— Rinse the interior of the machine with clean water.

— Remove all detachable parts, freezer door assembly, and drawoff plunger, beater, blades, and beater drive shaft, mix feed assembly, and hopper cover assembly.

— Wash all parts in detergent solution and brush all surfaces. Brush inside of freezing cylinder; pay particular attention to the back wall and shaft connection. Rinse all parts thoroughly and allow them to air dry.

— Store all clean parts in a clean storage area until next use.

Sanitize machine before

Use Prepare sanitizing solution according to package directions on calcium hypochlorite or disinfectant foodservice. Wear disposable gloves when assembling the machine. Dip each part in solution as machine is assembled. Pour remaining solution into the hopper and brush solution over entire inside and lid. Let the machine runs for 1 minute to allow the solution to run through the mixer. Drain completely and the machine is ready for use.

Coffee Makers

Coffee makers used in the GM are normally electric and may be of different types. The automatic twin coffee urn and the automatic coffee maker are the types used most often in general and private messes.

Operation of the Automatic Twin Coffee Urn

To brew coffee, turn thermostat dial to the BREW position. Observe dial thermometer on front of the urn. When brewing temperature is at the high end of brew zone on dial, the urn is ready to brew coffee. Place paper filter or muslin leecher bag in brew basket.

Place desired amount of coffee in filter (use urn grind coffee in 3-gallon urn and regular grind in larger urns), replace cover, and place brew basket in position over coffee liner. When using muslin bag, be sure bag is soaked with cold water before using, and, if a new bag, be sure to wash out all sizing with warm water. Swing spray arm from the PARK position over brew basket and center spray nozzle over brew basket.

Push timer knob. After the timer has completed its cycle, the orange brewing light will go out, showing that the proper amount of water has been sprayed. Within 3 minutes the brew basket with spent coffee grounds should be removed from urn. To do so, swing spray arm back to center PARK position. The spray arm should always be parked in this center position so expansion drippage will go back into tank.

Do not leave the brew basket in liner over 5 minutes, if possible. Remove cover and brew basket and then always replace cover over coffee liner. Rinse out muslin leecher bag and store in cold water until ready to use. Keep the thermostat dial at the HOLD position during all standby periods so that the urn is ready to brew coffee at any time, with no waiting. Merely turn thermostat to the BREW position so the pilot light lights up during brewing.

During shutoff periods, turn thermostat to off. After all night or weekend shutoff, a minimum of at least 55 minutes is required to obtain the proper brewing temperature. On twin models, water for tea may be drawn from center faucet. Manual refill is required unless equipped with auto refill.

Care and Cleaning of a coffee urn

The procedures used in caring for and cleaning a coffee urn are as follows:

— Always rinse urn immediately after each use.

— Add small quantity of hot water, brush sides, and rinse with hot water until it runs clean. Urn is now ready for next batch.

— At end of each day clean and brush urn several times and then rinse thoroughly with hot water.

— Remove cleanout cap at end of coffee faucet (or take apart faucets that have no caps) and scrub pipe leading to center of urn. Clean urn gauge glass with brush and urn cleaner. Rinse thoroughly.

— Scrub the faucet and then rinse it thoroughly with hot water.

— Place a gallon or more of fresh water in urn until next use.

— Remove cover and clean. Replace cover and leave partly open.

— Always remember to empty and rinse the urn with hot water before using again.

Destaining a coffee urn

The procedures for destaining coffee urns are as follows:

— Fill urn with destaining compound solution. Fill urn with water 175°F. Add destaining compound (stain remover, tableware, in this ratio: 2 tablespoons per 5 gallons of water or as directed by manufacturer).

— Draw off mixture and repour. Open spigot and draw off 1 gallon; thoroughly remix to allow mixture to come into faucet. Allow solution to stand for 1 hour at 170°F to 180°F. Stir occasionally.

— Scrub urn liner and gauge glass. Use long-handled brush to loosen scales.

— Clean faucet. Take faucet valve apart and clean all components. Soak in hot water until reassembled.

— Rinse and reassemble faucet valve. Rinse urn liner three or four times carefully with hot water. Repeat until all traces of compound are removed.

Operation and care of an automatic coffee maker

The automatic coffee maker is designed to brew fresh coffee under strict, sanitary conditions. Each coffee maker is made in units, and each unit may contain four or five burners set in a single or double deck. The coffee maker has the ON/OFF switches and the head control switches on the front. Glass or metal bowl containers are supplied for the actual brewing of the coffee.

Automatic coffee makers let you pour fresh water into a reservoir at the top of the device to obtain the same amount of hot coffee. In some models, gravity displacement of preheated hot water by cold water is the working rule. In others, water is brought to a boil before brewing a batch of coffee. In using an automatic coffee maker, there are two phases in making coffee, preheating and brewing. The preheating phase consists of the following steps. Slide the brewing chamber under the spray head and place an empty decanter under it.

Then open the top cover and pour two decanters of cold water in the reservoir. Replace cover. Make sure to plug into electric outlet of the correct voltage (specified on the nameplate of device). It should be noted that the two decanters of cold water should be poured in before connecting the plug. Preheat time is usually 18 minutes, and a signal light will turn on when the water reaches the proper brewing temperature.

Brewing good coffee requires skill, technique, and the experience of the skilled foodservice specialist. To properly brew coffee, remove the brewing chamber and place one paper filter in it. Add required amount of the recommended coffee grind. Check to be sure the coffee is evenly leveled before replacing brewing chamber. After the preheating phase, add a decanter of cold water to the reservoir. Coffee will immediately start to brew and flow into the decanter under the brewing chamber.

When the flow stops, you are ready to serve. The simple care of your equipment makes an important contribution to the excellence of your coffee service and efficient use of energy. All parts of the brewer that come into contact with the coffee and coffee vapor should be kept immaculately clean. Decanters, for example, should be thoroughly cleansed and rinsed free of detergent after each use. Spray heads should be checked regularly for traces of lime or other deposits in or around the holes.

It is important to keep them clean. Paper filters should never be reused as they can pick up odors from other foods. Discard after each brewing process. Be careful where you store them. Cloth filters should be rinsed after each brew and stored overnight in a vessel of fresh cold water. Replace cloth filters often to ensure good-tasting coffee. A simple sniff test should tell you when it is time to change.

New cloth filters should be cleaned and rinsed in very hot water to remove sizing (starch) and cloth odors. Do not use soap, bleaches, or detergents since they transfer flavors. If you brew in sealed filter bags with a stainless steel filter screen, rinse out the holding cartridge and screen daily. Once a week soak the screen overnight in a solution of urn cleaner and rinse thoroughly before reusing.

Iced Tea Dispenser

The iced tea dispenser is used with instant powdered tea and provides a convenient method of serving iced tea at meals.

Operation: Instant tea comes in a sealed jar, ready for use in the dispenser. To get the machine in operation use the following procedures:

— Remove lid and seal from instant tea jar.

— Replace with dispensing funnel by screwing it on firmly.

— Do not touch internal components of funnel assembly. Insert jar and funnel in tea dispenser. It is now ready for operation.

— To operate, fill a glass with ice and place it directly under the spout. Press the glass lightly against the actuator and hold until glass is filled.

The tea dispenser is preset to produce a beverage suitable for the average consumer but can be adjusted to produce stronger or weaker tea.

Cleaning: Remove bottle and funnel assembly by sliding straight out of coil shield hole, then remove funnel assembly from jar. Using the two-pan method, wipe the exterior components. Empty the drip pans. Wash the drip pan and the grill with mild detergent and warm water. Do not soak plastic parts in hot water or wash in dishwashing machine. To prevent gumming of the instant tea dispenser, make sure all component parts are thoroughly dry before inserting anew bottle of tea. The machine should be cleaned after each meal.

Noncarbonated Beverage Dispenser

Noncarbonated beverage dispensers are usually located in the dining area to dispense fruit juices, lemonade, iced tea, and other popular beverages. These dispensers have a self-contained refrigeration unit and a circulating pump to keep the beverages thoroughly mixed and to promote uniform cooling. The beverages are dispensed from a clear plastic tank.

Operation: Fill the tank well in advance of the meal to assure a properly chilled beverage. To facilitate chilling, beverages should be prepared in advance and prechilled. Ice should not be used to chill the beverage at the time of preparation. As a beverage is being dispensed, make sure to empty and clean the drip pans as necessary and wipe up any spillage immediately. Turn off the refrigeration unit and circulating pump when the machine is not in use or the tank is empty.

Cleaning: The dispenser should be disassembled and thoroughly cleaned after each meal or when used. Use the following procedures:

— Turn off the electric power supply to the machine.

— Drain the beverage from the dispenser.

— Disassemble the dispenser. Clean the exterior of the exposed dispenser using the two-pan method. Make sure the base of the dispenser (legs) and the dispensing valve openings are also cleaned.

— Wash the removed items in warm detergent and water, rinse with clear hot water to remove all traces of detergent, place in a sanitizing solution, and allow to air dry. Do not use any abrasive cleaners and do not place in the dishwashing machine. Reassemble the dispenser after it has air dried. An extensive weekly cleaning at the base of the dispenser should be done that includes vacuuming inside the unit and wiping the exposed areas of the dispenser. Make sure the power is off and exercise extreme caution when doing this procedure.

— Bulk Ice-Making Machine

— This machine requires little maintenance by foodservice personnel, but should be closely monitored

Ice is easily contaminated; therefore, the following strict measures should be taken: . Only authorized personnel should have access to the machine. The ice bin should be locked. . The ice scoop should be stored dry outside the ice bin or inside the bin at a height above maximum ice level. A monthly cleaning is required. Thoroughly clean the interior of the bin with a mild detergent and water solution using a nylon-bristled brush, then flush with clean water until all traces of detergent have been removed. Adequate rinsing with water containing 2-ppm chlorine should be used to eliminate bad odors and the accumulation of film deposits from detergents.

Ice-Dispensing machine

These machines are highly appreciated by the dining patrons, particulary during the hot months of the year. It is recommended that the machine be secured except during meals to make sure a sufficient supply of ice is available. If the machine becomes empty during service, it should be immediately disconnected or turned off to prevent damage to the dispensing assembly.

To clean the machine without disassembling the unit, you must shut off water, then pour 1 quart of mild detergent solution slowly into water reservoir and let ice form from cleaning solution. Discard ice and shut off the machine. Flush the ice-making system by adding 1 quart of clean water to the reservoir. Discard the ice. Wash down the storage bin with a mild detergent solution and rinse thoroughly with clean water containing 2-ppm chlorine. Areas in and around motor, insulation panels, and condenser coils should be vacuumed to free them of lint and dust. Periodic weekly checks for cockroach infestation should be made.

Bench-Type Can Opener

Can openers are often neglected in foodservice. They are used so much that when neglected they could be a ready source of food contamination. Therefore, keeping them in good operating condition and in a high degree of cleanliness is a must. You must clean the shaft daily and after every use. Simply, lift the vertical shaft out of the base and then soak in hot detergent solution of 1 ounce to 1 gallon of water. Scrub with a stiff-bristled brush. Rinse under hot running water. Let it air-dry. The equipment is now ready for reuse or storing in clean drawer.

4

Fish Recipes

The average costs which will be found appended to each recipe, must be understood as about the average price for the different kinds of fish, when the market is supplied upon an average, and when the various sorts are of an average size and quality. A proof of freshness and goodness in most fishes, is their being covered with scales; for, if deficient in this respect, it is a sign of their being stale, or having been ill-used.

Various Modes of Cooking Fish

Fried Anchovies

Ingredients: 1 tablespoonful of oil, 1/2 a glass of white wine, sufficient flour to thicken; 12 anchovies.

Mode: Mix the oil and wine together, with sufficient flour to make them into a thickish paste; cleanse the anchovies, wipe them, dip them in the paste, and fry of a nice brown colour.

Anchovy Butter or Paste

Ingredients: 2 dozen anchovies, 1/2 lb. of fresh butter.

Mode: Wash the anchovies thoroughly; bone and dry them, and pound them in a mortar to a paste. Mix the butter gradually with them, and rub the whole through a sieve. Put it by in small pots for use, and carefully exclude the air with a bladder, as it soon changes the colour of anchovies, besides spoiling them.

Barbel

Ingredients: 1/2 pint of port wine, a saltspoonful of salt, 2 tablespoonfuls of vinegar, 2 sliced onions, a faggot of sweet herbs, nutmeg and mace to taste, the juice of a lemon, 2 anchovies; 1 or 2 barbels, according to size.

Mode: Boil the barbels in salt and water till done; pour off some of the water, and, to the remainder, put the ingredients mentioned above. Simmer gently for 1/2 hour, or rather more, and strain. Put in the fish; heat it gradually; but do not let it boil, or it will be broken.

Brill

Ingredients: 1/4 lb. of salt to each gallon of water; a little vinegar.

Mode: Clean the brill, cut off the fins, and rub it over with a little lemon-juice, to preserve its whiteness. Set the fish in sufficient cold water to cover it; throw in salt, in the above proportions, and a little vinegar, and bring it gradually to boil; simmer very gently till the fish is done, which will be in about 10 minutes; but the time for boiling, of course, depends entirely on the size of the fish. Serve it on a hot napkin, and garnish with cut lemon, parsley, horseradish, and a little lobster coral sprinkled over the fish. Send lobster or shrimp sauce and plain melted butter to table with it.

Codfish

Cod may be boiled whole; but a large head and shoulders are quite sufficient for a dish, and contain all that is usually helped, because, when the thick part is done, the tail is insipid and overdone. The latter, cut in slices, makes a very good dish for frying; or it may be salted down and served with egg sauce and parsnips. Cod, when boiled quite fresh, is watery; salting a little, renders it firmer.

Cod Tribe

The Jugular, characterized by bony gills, and ventral fins before the pectoral ones, commences the second of the Linnaean orders of fishes, and is a numerous tribe, inhabiting only the depths of the ocean, and seldom visiting the fresh waters. They have a smooth head, and the gill membrane has seven rays. The body is oblong, and covered with deciduous scales. The fins are all inclosed in skin, whilst their rays are unarmed. The ventral fins are slender, and terminate in a point. Their habits are gregarious, and they feed on smaller fish and other marine animals.

Cod's Head and Shoulders

Ingredients: Sufficient water to cover the fish; 5 oz. of salt to each gallon of water.

Mode: Cleanse the fish thoroughly, and rub a little salt over the thick part and inside of the fish, 1 or 2 hours before dressing it, as this very much improves the flavour. Lay it in the fish-kettle, with sufficient cold water to cover it. Be very particular not to pour the water on the fish, as it is liable to break it, and only keep it just simmering. If the water should boil away, add a little by pouring it in at the side of the kettle, and not on the fish. Add salt in the above proportion, and bring it gradually to a boil. Skim very carefully, draw it to the side of the fire, and let it gently simmer till done. Take it out and drain it; serve on a hot napkin, and garnish with cut lemon, horseradish, the roe and liver.

Salt-Fish

Ingredients: Sufficient water to cover the fish.

Mode: Wash the fish, and lay it all night in water, with a 1/4 pint of vinegar. When thoroughly soaked, take it out, see that it is perfectly clean, and put it in the fish-kettle with sufficient cold water to cover it. Heat it gradually, but do not let it boil much, or the fish will be hard. Skim well, and when done, drain the fish and put it on a napkin garnished with hard-boiled eggs cut in rings.

Cod Sounds, En Poule

Ingredients: For forcemeat, 12 chopped oysters, 3 chopped anchovies, 1/4 lb. of bread crumbs, 1 oz. of butter, 2 eggs; seasoning of salt, pepper, nutmeg, and mace to taste; 4 cod sounds.

Mode: Make the forcemeat by mixing the ingredients well together. Wash the sounds, and boil them in milk and water for 1/2 an hour; take them out and let them cool. Cover each with a layer of forcemeat, roll them up in a nice form, and skewer them. Rub over with lard, dredge with flour, and cook them gently before the fire in a Dutch oven.

Cod Pie

Ingredients: Any remains of cold cod, 12 oysters, sufficient melted butter to moisten it; mashed potatoes enough to fill up the dish.

Mode: Flake the fish from the bone, and carefully take away all the skin. Lay it in a pie-dish, pour over the melted butter and oysters (or oyster sauce, if there is any left), and cover with mashed potatoes. Bake for 1/2 an hour, and send to table of a nice brown colour.

Curried Cod

Ingredients: 2 slices of large cod, or the remains of any cold fish; 3 oz. of butter, 1 onion sliced, a teacupful of white stock, thickening of butter and flour, 1 small teaspoonful of curry-powder, 1/4 pint of cream, salt and cayenne to taste.

Mode: Flake the fish, and fry it of a nice brown colour with the butter and onions; put this in a stewpan, add the stock and thickening, and simmer for 10 minutes. Stir the curry-powder into the cream; put it, with the seasoning, to the other ingredients; give one boil, and serve.

Cod A La Creme

Ingredients: 1 large slice of cod, 1 oz. of butter, 1 chopped shalot, a little minced parsley, 1/4 teacupful of white stock, 1/4 pint of milk or cream, flour to thicken, cayenne and lemon-juice to taste, 1/4 teaspoonful of powdered sugar.

Mode: Boil the cod, and while hot, break it into flakes; put the butter, shalot, parsley, and stock into a stewpan, and let them boil for 5 minutes. Stir in sufficient flour to thicken, and pour to it the milk or cream. Simmer for 10 minutes, add the cayenne and sugar, and, when liked, a little lemon-juice. Put the fish in the sauce to warm gradually, but do not let it boil. Serve in a dish garnished with croûtons.

Cod A La Bechamel

Ingredients: Any remains of cold cod, 4 tablespoonfuls of béchamel, 2 oz. butter; seasoning to taste of pepper and salt; fried bread, a few bread crumbs.

Mode: Flake the cod carefully, leaving out all skin and bone; put the béchamel in a stewpan with the butter, and stir it over the fire till the latter is melted; add seasoning, put in the fish, and mix it well with the sauce. Make a border of fried bread round the dish, lay in the fish, sprinkle over with bread crumbs, and baste with butter. Brown either before the fire or with a salamander, and garnish with toasted bread cut in fanciful shapes.

Cod A La Maitre D'hotel

Ingredients: 2 slices of cod, 1/4 lb. of butter, a little chopped shalot and parsley; pepper to taste, 1/4 teaspoonful of grated nutmeg, or rather less, when the flavour is not liked; the juice of 1/4 lemon.

Mode: Boil the cod, and either leave it whole, or, what is still better, flake it from the bone, and take off the skin. Put it into a stewpan with the butter, parsley, shalot, pepper, and nutmeg. Melt the butter gradually, and be very careful that it does not become like oil. When all is well mixed and thoroughly hot, add the lemon-juice, and serve.

To Dress Crab

Ingredients: 1 crab, 2 tablespoonfuls of vinegar, 1 ditto of oil; salt, white pepper, and cayenne, to taste.

Mode: Empty the shells, and thoroughly mix the meat with the above ingredients, and put it in the large shell. Garnish with slices of cut lemon and parsley. The quantity of oil may be increased when it is much liked.

To Choose Crab: The middle-sized crab is the best; and the crab, like the lobster, should be judged by its weight; for if light, it is watery.

Hot Crab

Ingredients: 1 crab, nutmeg, salt and pepper to taste, 3 oz. of butter, 1/4 lb. of bread crumbs, 3 tablespoonfuls of vinegar.

Mode: After having boiled the crab, pick the meat out from the shells, and mix with it the nutmeg and seasoning. Cut up the butter in small pieces, and add the bread crumbs and vinegar. Mix altogether, put the whole in the large shell, and brown before the fire or with a salamander.

Crayfish

Crayfish should be thrown into boiling water, to which has been added a good seasoning of salt and a little vinegar. When done, which will be in 1/4 hour, take them out and drain them. Let them cool, arrange them on a napkin, and garnish with plenty of double parsley.

Potted Crayfish

Ingredients: 100 crayfish; pounded mace, pepper and salt to taste, 2 oz. butter.

Mode: Boil the fish in salt and water; pick out all the meat and pound it in a mortar to a paste. Whilst pounding, add the butter gradually, and mix in the spice and seasoning. Put it in small pots, and pour over it clarified butter, carefully excluding the air.

John Dory

Ingredients: 1/4 lb. of salt to each gallon of water.

Mode: This fish, which is esteemed by most people a great delicacy, is dressed in the same way as a turbot, which it resembles in firmness, but not in richness. Cleanse it thoroughly and cut off the fins; lay it in a fish-kettle, cover with cold water, and add salt in the above proportion. Bring it gradually to a boil, and simmer gently for 1/4 hour, or rather longer, should the fish be very large. Serve on a hot napkin, and garnish with cut lemon and parsley. Lobster, anchovy, or shrimp sauce, and plain melted butter, should be sent to table with it.

Doru, or John Dory

This fish is of a yellowish golden colour, and is, in general, rare, although it is sometimes taken in abundance on the Devon and Cornish coasts. It is highly esteemed for the table, and its flesh, when dressed, is of a beautiful clear white. When fresh caught, it is tough, and, being a ground fish, it is not the worse for being kept two, or even three days before it is cooked.

Boiled Eels

Ingredients: 4 small eels, sufficient water to cover them; a large bunch of parsley.

Mode: Choose small eels for boiling; put them in a stewpan with the parsley, and just sufficient water to cover them; simmer till tender. Take them out, pour a little parsley and butter over them, and serve some in a tureen.

Eel Tribe

The Apodal, or bony-gilled and ventral-finned fish, of which the eel forms the first Linnaean tribe, in their general aspect and manners, approach, in some instances, very nearly to serpents. They have a smooth head and slippery skin, are in general naked, or covered with such small, soft, and distant scales, as are scarcely visible. Their bodies are long and slender, and they are supposed to subsist entirely on animal substances. There are about nine species of them, mostly found in the seas. One of them frequents our fresh waters, and three of the others occasionally pay a visit to our shores.

Fried Eels

Ingredients: 1 lb. of eels, 1 egg, a few bread crumbs, hot lard.

Mode: Wash the eels, cut them into pieces 3 inches long, trim and wipe them very dry; dredge with flour, rub them over with egg, and cover with bread crumbs; fry of a nice brown in hot lard. If the eels are small, curl them round, instead of cutting them up. Garnish with fried parsley.

Eel Pie

Ingredients: 1 lb. of eels, a little chopped parsley, 1 shalot; grated nutmeg; pepper and salt to taste; the juice of 1/2 a lemon, small quantity of forcemeat, 1/4 pint of béchamel; puff paste.

Mode: Skin and wash the eels, cut them into pieces 2 inches long, and line the bottom of the pie-dish with forcemeat. Put in the eels, and sprinkle them with the parsley, shalots, nutmeg, seasoning, and lemon-juice, and cover with puff-paste. Bake for 1 hour, or rather more; make the béchamel hot, and pour it into the pie.

Collared Eel

Ingredients: 1 large eel; pepper and salt to taste; 2 blades of mace, 2 cloves, a little allspice very finely pounded, 6 leaves of sage, and a small bunch of herbs minced very small.

Mode: Bone the eel and skin it; split it, and sprinkle it over with the ingredients, taking care that the spices are very finely pounded, and the herbs chopped very small. Roll it up and bind with a broad piece of tape, and boil it in water, mixed with a little salt and vinegar, till tender. It may either be served whole or cut in slices; and when cold, the eel should be kept in the liquor it was boiled in, but with a little more vinegar put to it.

Haunts of The Eel

These are usually in mud, among weeds, under roots or stumps of trees, or in holes in the banks or the bottoms of rivers. Here they often grow to an enormous size, sometimes weighing as much as fifteen or sixteen pounds. They seldom come forth from their hiding-places except in the night; and, in winter, bury themselves deep in the mud, on account of their great susceptibility of cold.

Eels A La Tartare

Ingredients: 2 lbs. of eels, 1 carrot, 1 onion, a little flour, 1 glass of sherry; salt, pepper, and nutmeg to taste; bread crumbs, 1 egg, 2 tablespoonfuls of vinegar.

Mode: Rub the butter on the bottom of the stewpan; cut up the carrot and onion, and stir them over the fire for 5 minutes; dredge in a little flour, add the wine and seasoning, and boil for 1/2 an hour. Skin and wash the eels, cut them into pieces, put them to the other ingredients, and simmer till tender. When they are done, take them out, let them get cold, cover them with egg and bread crumbs, and fry them of a nice brown. Put them on a dish, pour sauce piquante over, and serve them hot.

Fish and Oyster Pie

Ingredients: Any remains of cold fish, such as cod or haddock; 2 dozen oysters, pepper and salt to taste, bread crumbs sufficient for the quantity of fish; 1/2 teaspoonful of grated nutmeg, 1 teaspoonful of finely-chopped parsley.

Mode: Clear the fish from the bones, and put a layer of it in a pie-dish, which sprinkle with pepper and salt; then a layer of bread crumbs, oysters, nutmeg, and chopped parsley. Repeat this till the dish is quite full. You may form a covering either of bread crumbs, which should be browned, or puff-paste, which should be cut into long strips, and laid in cross-bars over the fish, with a line of the paste first laid round the edge. Before putting on the top, pour in some made melted butter, or a little thin white sauce, and the oyster-liquor, and bake.

Fish Cake

Ingredients: The remains of any cold fish, 1 onion, 1 faggot of sweet herbs; salt and pepper to taste, 1 pint of water, equal quantities of bread crumbs and cold potatoes, 1/2 teaspoonful of parsley, 1 egg, bread crumbs.

Mode: Pick the meat from the bones of the fish, which latter put, with the head and fins, into a stewpan with the water; add pepper and salt, the onion and herbs, and stew slowly for gravy about 2 hours; chop the fish fine, and mix it well with bread crumbs and cold potatoes, adding the parsley and seasoning; make the whole into a cake with the white of an egg, brush it over with egg, cover with bread crumbs, and fry of a light brown; strain the gravy, pour it over, and stew gently for 1/4 hour, stirring it carefully once or twice. Serve hot, and garnish with slices of lemon and parsley.

Boiled Flounders

Ingredients: Sufficient water to cover the flounders, salt in the proportion of 6 oz. to each gallon, a little vinegar.

Mode: Pat on a kettle with enough water to cover the flounders, lay in the fish, add salt and vinegar in the above proportions, and when it boils, simmer very gently for 5 minutes. They must not boil fast, or they will break. Serve with plain melted butter, or parsley and butter.

Fried Flounders

Ingredients: Flounders, egg, and bread crumbs; boiling lard.

Mode: Cleanse the fish, and, two hours before they are wanted, rub them inside and out with salt, to render them firm; wash and wipe them very dry, dip them into egg, and sprinkle over with bread crumbs; fry them in boiling lard, dish on a hot napkin, and garnish with crisped parsley.

Gudgeons

Ingredients: Egg and bread crumbs sufficient for the quantity of fish; hot lard.

Mode: Do not scrape off the scales, but take out the gills and inside, and cleanse thoroughly; wipe them dry, flour and dip them into egg, and sprinkle over with bread crumbs. Fry of a nice brown.

Baked Haddocks

Ingredients: A nice forcemeat, butter to taste, egg and bread crumbs.

Mode: Scale and clean the fish, without cutting it open much; put in a nice delicate forcemeat, and sew up the slit. Brush it over with egg, sprinkle over bread crumbs, and baste frequently with butter. Garnish with parsley and cut lemon, and serve with a nice brown gravy, plain melted butter, or anchovy sauce. The egg and bread crumbs can be omitted, and pieces of butter placed over the fish.

Boiled Haddock

Ingredients: Sufficient water to cover the fish; 1/4 lb. of salt to each gallon of water.

Mode: Scrape the fish, take out the inside, wash it thoroughly, and lay it in a kettle, with enough water to cover it and salt in the above proportion. Simmer gently from 15 to 20 minutes, or rather more, should the fish be very large. For small haddocks, fasten the tails in their mouths, and put them into boiling water. 10 to 15 minutes will cook them. Serve with plain melted butter, or anchovy sauce.

Dried Haddock

Dried haddock should be gradually warmed through, either before or over a nice clear fire. Rub a little piece of butter over, just before sending it to table.

Ingredients: 1 large thick haddock, 2 bay-leaves, 1 small bunch of savoury herbs, not forgetting parsley, a little butter and pepper; boiling water.

Mode: Cut up the haddock into square pieces, make a basin hot by means of hot water, which pour out. Lay in the fish, with the bay-leaves and herbs; cover with boiling water; put a plate over to keep in the steam, and let it remain for 10 minutes. Take out the slices, put them in a hot dish, rub over with butter and pepper, and serve.

Red Herrings, or Yarmouth Bloaters

The best way to cook these is to make incisions in the skin across the fish, because they do not then require to be so long on the fire, and will be far better than when cut open. The hard roe makes a nice relish by pounding it in a mortar, with a little anchovy, and spreading it on toast. If very dry, soak in warm water 1 hour before dressing.

Baked White Herrings

Ingredients: 12 herrings, 4 bay-leaves, 12 cloves, 12 allspice, 2 small blades of mace, cayenne pepper and salt to taste, sufficient vinegar to fill up the dish.

Mode: Take the herrings, cut off the heads, and gut them. Put them in a pie-dish, heads and tails alternately, and, between each layer, sprinkle over the above ingredients. Cover the fish with the vinegar, and bake for 1/2 hour, but do not use it till quite cold. The herrings may be cut down the front, the backbone taken out, and closed again. Sprats done in this way are very delicious.

Kegeree

Ingredients: Any cold fish, 1 teacupful of boiled rice, 1 oz. of butter, 1 teaspoonful of mustard, 2 soft-boiled eggs, salt and cayenne to taste.

Mode: Pick the fish carefully from the bones, mix with the other ingredients, and serve very hot. The quantities may be varied according to the amount of fish used.

Hot Lobster

Ingredients: 1 lobster, 2 oz. of butter, grated nutmeg; salt, pepper, and pounded mace, to taste; bread crumbs, 2 eggs.

Mode: Pound the meat of the lobster to a smooth paste with the butter and seasoning, and add a few bread crumbs. Beat the eggs, and make the whole mixture into the form of a lobster; pound the spawn, and sprinkle over it. Bake 1/4 hour, and just before serving, lay over it the tail and body shell, with the small claws underneath, to resemble a lobster.

Lobster Salad

Ingredients: 1 hen lobster, lettuces, endive, small salad (whatever is in season), a little chopped beetroot, 2 hard-boiled eggs, a few slices of cucumber. For dressing, equal quantities of oil and vinegar, 1 teaspoonful of made mustard, the yolks of 2 eggs; cayenne and salt to taste; 3 teaspoonful of anchovy sauce. These ingredients should be mixed perfectly smooth, and form a creamy-looking sauce.

Mode: Wash the salad, and thoroughly dry it by shaking it in a cloth. Cut up the lettuces and endive, pour the dressing on them, and lightly throw in the small salad. Mix all well together with the pickings from the body of the lobster; pick the meat from the shell, cut it up into nice square pieces, put half in the salad, the other half reserve for garnishing.

Separate the yolks from the whites of 2 hard-boiled eggs; chop the whites very fine, and rub the yolks through a sieve, and afterwards the coral from the inside. Arrange the salad lightly on a glass dish, and garnish, first with a row of sliced cucumber, then with the pieces of lobster, the yolks and whites of the eggs, coral, and beetroot placed alternately, and arranged in small separate bunches, so that the colours contrast nicely.

Lobster

Ingredients: 1 lobster, 4 tablespoonfuls of white stock, 2 tablespoonfuls of cream, pounded mace, and cayenne to taste; bread crumbs.

Mode: Pick the meat from the shell, and cut it up into small square pieces; put the stock, cream, and seasoning into a stewpan, add the lobster, and let it simmer gently for 6 minutes. Serve it in the shell, which must be nicely cleaned, and have a border of puff-paste; cover it with bread crumbs, place small pieces of butter over, and brown before the fire, or with a salamander.

Lobster Cutlets

Ingredients: 1 large hen lobster, 1 oz. fresh butter, 1/2 saltspoonful of salt, pounded mace, grated nutmeg, cayenne and white pepper to taste, egg, and bread crumbs.

Mode: Pick the meat from the shell, and pound it in a mortar with the butter, and gradually add the mace and seasoning, well mixing the ingredients; beat all to a smooth paste, and add a little of the spawn; divide the mixture into pieces of an equal size, and shape them like cutlets. They should not be very thick. Brush them over with egg, and sprinkle with bread crumbs, and stick a short piece of the small claw in the top of each; fry them of a nice brown in boiling lard, and drain them before the fire, on a sieve reversed; arrange them nicely on a dish, and pour béchamel in the middle, but not over the cutlets.

Dress Lobsters

When the lobster is boiled, rub it over with a little salad-oil, which wipe off again; separate the body from the tail, break off the great claws, and crack them at the joints, without injuring the meat; split the tail in halves, and arrange all neatly in a dish, with the body upright in the middle, and garnish with parsley.

Lobster Patties

Ingredients: Minced lobster, 4 tablespoonfuls of béchamel, 6 drops of anchovy sauce, lemon-juice, cayenne to taste.

Mode: Line the patty-pans with puff-paste, and put into each a small piece of bread: cover with paste, brush over with egg, and bake of a light colour. Take as much lobster as is required, mince the meat very fine, and add the above ingredients; stir it over the fire for 6 minutes; remove the lids of the patty-cases, take out the bread, fill with the mixture, and replace the covers.

Potted Lobster

Ingredients: 2 lobsters; seasoning to taste, of nutmeg, pounded mace, white pepper, and salt; 1/4 lb. of butter, 3 or 4 bay-leaves.

Mode: Take out the meat carefully from the shell, but do not cut it up. Put some butter at the bottom of a dish, lay in the lobster as evenly as possible, with the bay-leaves and seasoning between. Cover with butter, and bake for 3/4 hour in a gentle oven. When done, drain the whole on a sieve, and lay the pieces in potting-jars, with the seasoning about them. When cold, pour over it clarified butter, and, if very highly seasoned, it will keep some time.

Baked Mackerel

Ingredients: 4 middling-sized mackerel, a nice delicate forcemeat, 3 oz. of butter; pepper and salt to taste.

Mode: Clean the fish, take out the roes, and fill up with forcemeat, and sew up the slit. Flour, and put them in a dish, heads and tails alternately, with the roes; and, between each layer, put some little pieces of butter, and pepper and salt. Bake for 1/2 an hour, and either serve with plain melted butter or a maître d'hôtel sauce.

Boiled Mackerel

Ingredients: 1/4 lb. of salt to each gallon of water.

Mode: Cleanse the inside of the fish thoroughly, and lay it in the kettle with sufficient water to cover it with salt as above; bring it gradually to boil, skim well, and simmer gently till done; dish them on a hot napkin, heads and tails alternately, and garnish with fennel. Fennel sauce and plain melted butter are the usual accompaniments to boiled mackerel; but caper or anchovy sauce is sometimes served with it.

Broiled Mackerel

Ingredients: Pepper and salt to taste, a small quantity of oil.

Mode: Mackerel should never be washed when intended to be broiled, but merely wiped very clean and dry, after taking out the gills and insides. Open the back, and put in a little pepper, salt, and oil; broil it over a clear fire, turn it over on both sides, and also on the back. When sufficiently cooked, the flesh can be detached from the bone, which will be in about 15 minutes for a small mackerel. Chop a little parsley, work it up in the butter, with pepper and salt to taste, and a squeeze of lemon-juice, and put it in the back. Serve before the butter is quite melted, with a maître d'hôtel sauce in a tureen.

Grey Mullet

Ingredients: 1/4 lb. of salt to each gallon of water.

Mode: If the fish be very large, it should be laid in cold water, and gradually brought to a boil; if small, put it in boiling water, salted in the above proportion. Serve with anchovy sauce and plain melted butter.

Red Mullet

Ingredients: Oiled paper, thickening of butter and flour, 1/2 teaspoonful of anchovy sauce, 1 glass of sherry; cayenne and salt to taste.

Mode: Clean the fish, take out the gills, but leave the inside, fold in oiled paper, and bake them gently. When done, take the liquor that flows from the fish, add a thickening of butter kneaded with flour; put in the other ingredients, and let it boil for 2 minutes. Serve the sauce in a tureen, and the fish, either with or without the paper cases.

Fried Oysters

Ingredients: 3 dozen oysters, 2 oz. butter, 1 tablespoonful of ketchup, a little chopped lemon-peel, 1/2 teaspoonful of chopped parsley.

Mode: Boil the oysters for 1 minute in their own liquor, and drain them; fry them with the butter, ketchup, lemon-peel, and parsley; lay them on a dish, and garnish with fried potatoes, toasted sippets, and parsley. This is a delicious delicacy, and is a favourite Italian dish.

Scalloped Oysters

Ingredients: Oysters, say 1 pint, 1 oz. butter, flour, 2 tablespoonfuls of white stock, 2 tablespoonfuls of cream; pepper and salt to taste; bread crumbs, oiled butter.

Mode: Scald the oysters in their own liquor, take them out, beard them, and strain the liquor free from grit. Put 1 oz. of batter into a stewpan; when melted, dredge in sufficient flour to dry it up; add the stock, cream, and strained liquor, and give one boil. Put in the oysters and seasoning; let them gradually heat through, but not boil. Have ready the scallop-shells buttered; lay in the oysters, and as much of the liquid as they will hold; cover them over with bread crumbs, over which drop a little oiled butter. Brown them in the oven, or before the fire, and serve quickly, and very hot.

Prepare the oysters as in the preceding recipe, and put them in a scallop-shell or saucer, and between each layer sprinkle over a few bread crumbs, pepper, salt, and grated nutmeg; place small pieces of butter over, and bake before the fire in a Dutch oven. Put sufficient bread crumbs on the top to make a smooth surface, as the oysters should not be seen.

Oysters Fried in Batter

Ingredients: 1/2 pint of oysters, 2 eggs, 1/2 pint of milk, sufficient flour to make the batter; pepper and salt to taste; when liked, a little nutmeg; hot lard.

Mode: Scald the oysters in their own liquor, beard them, and lay them on a cloth, to drain thoroughly. Break the eggs into a basin, mix the flour with them, add the milk gradually, with nutmeg and seasoning, and put the oysters in the batter. Make some lard hot in a deep frying-pan, put in the oysters, one at a time; when done, take them up with a sharp-pointed skewer, and dish them on a napkin. Fried oysters are frequently used for garnishing boiled fish, and then a few bread crumbs should be added to the flour.

Boiled Perch

Ingredients: 1/4 lb. of salt to each gallon of water.

Mode: Scale the fish, take out the gills and clean it thoroughly; lay it in boiling water, salted as above, and simmer gently for 10 minutes. If the fish is very large, longer time must be allowed. Garnish with parsley, and serve with plain melted butter, or Dutch sauce. Perch do not preserve so good a flavour when stewed as when dressed in any other way.

Fried Perch

Ingredients: Egg and bread crumbs, hot lard.

Mode: Scale and clean the fish, brush it over with egg, and cover with bread crumbs. Have ready some boiling lard; put the fish in, and fry a nice brown. Serve with plain melted butter or anchovy sauce.

Boiled Pike

Ingredients: 1/4 lb. of salt to each gallon of water; a little vinegar.

Mode: Scale and clean the pike, and fasten the tail in its mouth by means of a skewer. Lay it in cold water, and when it boils, throw in the salt and vinegar. The time for boiling depends, of course, on the size of the fish; but a middling-sized pike will take about 1/2 an hour. Serve with Dutch or anchovy sauce, and plain melted butter.

Baked Pike

Ingredients: 1 or 2 pike, a nice delicate stuffing, 1 egg, bread crumbs, 1/4 lb. butter.

Mode: Scale the fish, take out the gills, wash, and wipe it thoroughly dry; stuff it with forcemeat, sew it up, and fasten the tail in the mouth by means of a skewer; brush it over with egg, sprinkle with bread crumbs, and baste with butter, before putting it in the oven, which must be well heated. When the pike is of a nice brown colour, cover it with buttered paper, as the outside would become too dry. If 2 are dressed, a little variety may be made by making one of them green with a little chopped parsley mixed with the bread crumbs. Serve anchovy or Dutch sauce, and plain melted butter with it.

Fried Plaice

Ingredients: Hot lard, or clarified dripping; egg and bread crumbs.

Mode: This fish is fried in the same manner as soles. Wash and wipe them thoroughly dry, and let them remain in a cloth until it is time to dress them. Brush them over with egg, and cover with bread crumbs mixed with a little flour. Fry of a nice brown in hot dripping or lard, and garnish with fried parsley and cut lemon. Send them to table with shrimp-sauce and plain melted butter.

Stewed Plaice

Ingredients: 4 or 5 plaice, 2 onions, 1/2 oz. ground ginger, 1 pint of lemon-juice, 1/4 pint water, 6 eggs; cayenne to taste.

Mode: Cut the fish into pieces about 2 inches wide, salt them, and let them remain 1/4 hour. Slice and fry the onions a light brown; put them in a stewpan, on the top of which put the fish without washing, and add the ginger, lemon-juice, and water. Cook slowly for 1/2 hour, and do not let the fish boil, or it will break. Take it out, and when the liquor is cool, add 6 well-beaten eggs; simmer till it thickens, when pour over the fish, and serve.

Boil Prawns or Shrimps

Ingredients: 1/4 lb. salt to each gallon of water.

Mode: Prawns should be very red, and have no spawn under the tail; much depends on their freshness and the way in which they are cooked. Throw them into boiling water, salted as above, and keep them boiling for about 7 or 8 minutes. Shrimps should be done in the same way; but less time must be allowed. It may easily be known when they are done by their changing colour. Care should be taken that they are not over-boiled, as they then become tasteless and indigestible.

BOILED SALMON

Ingredients: 6 oz. of salt to each gallon of water,-- sufficient water to cover the fish.

Mode: Scale and clean the fish, and be particular that no blood is left inside; lay it in the fish-kettle with sufficient cold water to cover it, adding salt in the above proportion. Bring it quickly to a boil, take off all the scum, and let it simmer gently till the fish is done, which will be when the meat separates easily from the bone. Experience alone can teach the cook to fix the time for boiling fish; but it is especially to be remembered, that it should never be underdressed, as then nothing is more unwholesome. Neither let it remain in the kettle after it is sufficiently cooked, as that would render it insipid, watery, and colourless.

Drain it, and if not wanted for a few minutes, keep it warm by means of warm cloths laid over it. Serve on a hot napkin, garnish with cut lemon and parsley, and send lobster or shrimp sauce, and plain melted butter to table with it. A dish of dressed cucumber usually accompanies this fish.

Salmon and Caper Sauce

Ingredients: 2 slices of salmon, 1/4 lb. batter, 1/2 teaspoonful of chopped parsley, 1 shalot; salt, pepper, and grated nutmeg to taste.

Mode: Lay the salmon in a baking-dish, place pieces of butter over it, and add the other ingredients, rubbing a little of the seasoning into the fish; baste it frequently; when done, take it out and drain for a minute or two; lay it in a dish, pour caper sauce over it, and serve. Salmon dressed in this way, with tomato sauce, is very delicious.

Collared Salmon

Ingredients: A piece of salmon, say 3 lbs., a high seasoning of salt, pounded mace, and pepper; water and vinegar, 3 bay-leaves.

Mode: Split the fish; scale, bone, and wash it thoroughly clean; wipe it, and rub in the seasoning inside and out; roll it up, and bind firmly; lay it in a kettle, cover it with vinegar and water (1/3 vinegar, in proportion to the water); add the bay-leaves and a good seasoning of salt and whole pepper, and simmer till done. Do not remove the lid. Serve with melted butter or anchovy sauce. For preserving the collared fish, boil up the liquor in which it was cooked, and add a little more vinegar. Pour over when cold.

Pickled Salmon

Ingredients: Salmon, 1/2 oz. of whole pepper, 1/2 oz. of whole allspice, 1 teaspoonful of salt, 2 bay-leaves, equal quantities of vinegar and the liquor in which the fish was boiled.

Mode: After the fish comes from table, lay it in a nice dish with a cover to it, as it should be excluded from the air, and take away the bone; boil the liquor and vinegar with the other ingredients for 10 minutes, and let it stand to get cold; pour it over the salmon, and in 12 hours this will be fit for the table.

Potted Salmon

Ingredients: Salmon; pounded mace, cloves, and pepper to taste; 3 bay-leaves, 1/4 lb. butter.

Mode: Skin the salmon, and clean it thoroughly by wiping with a cloth (water would spoil it); cut it into square pieces, which rub with salt; let them remain till thoroughly drained, then lay them in a dish with the other ingredients, and bake. When quite done, drain them from the gravy, press into pots for use, and, when cold, pour over it clarified butter.

An Aversion in the Salmon: The salmon is said to have an aversion to anything red; hence, fishermen engaged in catching it do not wear jackets or caps of that colour. Pontoppidan also says, that it has an abhorrence of carrion, and if any happens to be thrown into the places it haunts, it immediately forsakes them. The remedy adopted for this in Norway, is to throw into the polluted water a lighted torch. As food, salmon, when in perfection, is one of the most delicious and nutritive of our fish.

5

Various Modes of Cooking Meat

The gradual progress of mankind in the art of cookery, the probability being, that the human race, for a long period, lived wholly on fruits. Man's means of attacking animals, even if he had the desire of slaughtering them, were very limited, until he acquired the use of arms. He, however, made weapons for himself, and, impelled by a carnivorous instinct, made prey of the animals that surrounded him. It is natural that man should seek to feed on flesh; he has too small a stomach to be supported alone by fruit, which has not sufficient nourishment to renovate him.

It is possible he might subsist on vegetables; but their preparation needs the knowledge of art, only to be obtained after the lapse of many centuries. Man's first weapons were the branches of trees, which were succeeded by bows and arrows, and it is worthy of remark, that these latter weapons have been found with the natives of all climates and latitudes. It is singular how this idea presented itself to individuals so differently placed.

Brillat Savarin says, that raw flesh has but one inconvenience,-from its viscousness it attaches itself to the teeth. He goes on to say, that it is not, however, disagreeable; but, when seasoned with salt, that it is easily digested. He tells a story of a Croat captain, whom he invited to dinner in 1815, during the occupation of Paris by the allied troops. This officer was amazed at his host's preparations, and said, "When we are campaigning, and get hungry, we knock over the first animal we find, cut off a steak, powder it with salt, which we always have in the sabretasche, put it under the saddle, gallop over it for half a mile, and then dine like princes." Again, of the huntsmen of Dauphiny it is said, that when they are out shooting in September, they take with them both pepper and salt. If they kill a very fat bird, they pluck and season it, and, after carrying it some time in their caps, eat it. This, they declare, is the best way of serving it up.

Subsequently to the Croat Mode, which, doubtless, was in fashion in the earlier ages of the world, fire was discovered. This was an accident; for fire is not, although we are accustomed to call it so, an element, or spontaneous. Many savage nations have been found utterly ignorant of it, and many races had no other way of dressing their food than by exposing it to the rays of the sun.

The inhabitants of the marian islands, which were discovered in 1521, had no idea of fire. Never was astonishment greater than theirs when they first saw it, on the descent of Magellan, the navigator, on one of their isles. At first they thought it a kind of animal, that fixed itself to and fed upon wood. Some of them, who approached too near, being burnt, the rest were terrified, and durst only look upon it at a distance. They were afraid, they said, of being bit, or lest that dreadful animal should wound with his violent respiration and dreadful breath; for these were the first notions they formed of the heat and flame. Such, too, probably, were the notions the Greeks originally formed of them.

Fire having been discovered, mankind endeavoured to make use of it for drying, and afterwards for cooking their meat; but they were a considerable time before they hit upon proper and commodious methods of employing it in the preparation of their food.

Meat, then, placed on burning fuel was found better than when raw: it had more firmness, was eaten with less difficulty, and the ozmazome being condensed by the carbonization, gave it a pleasing perfume and flavour. Still, however, the meat cooked on the coal would become somewhat befouled, certain portions of the fuel adhering to it. This disadvantage was remedied by passing spits through it, and placing it at a suitable height above the burning fuel. Thus grilling was invented; and it is well known that, simple as is this mode of cookery, yet all meat cooked in this way is richly and pleasantly flavoured.

In Homer's time, the, art of cookery had not advanced much beyond this; for we read in the "Iliad," how the great Achilles and his friend Patroclus regaled the three Grecian leaders on bread, wine, and broiled meat. It is noticeable, too, that Homer does not speak of boiled meat anywhere in his poems. Later, however, the Jews, coming out of their captivity in Egypt, had made much greater progress. They undoubtedly possessed kettles; and in one of these, Esau's mess of pottage, for which he sold his birthright, must have been prepared.

Having thus briefly traced a history of gastronomical progresses, we will now proceed to describe the various methods of cooking meat, and make a few observations on the chemical changes which occur in each of the operations.

In this country, plain boiling, roasting, and baking are the usual methods of cooking animal food. To explain the philosophy of these simple culinary operations, we must advert to the effects that are produced by heat on the principal constituents of flesh. When finely-chopped mutton or beef is steeped for some time in a small quantity of clean water, and then subjected to slight pressure, the juice of the meat is extracted, and there is left a white tasteless residue, consisting chiefly of muscular fibres. When this residue is heated to between 158° and 177° Fahrenheit, the fibres shrink together, and become hard and horny.

The influence of an elevated temperature on the soluble extract of flesh is not less remarkable. When the watery infusion, which contains all the savoury constituents of the meat, is gradually heated, it soon becomes turbid; and, when the temperature reaches 133°, flakes of whitish matter separate. These flakes are albumen, a substance precisely similar, in all its properties, to the white of egg. When the temperature of the watery extract is raised to 158°, the colouring matter of the blood coagulates, and the liquid, which was originally tinged red by this substance, is left perfectly clear, and almost colourless. When evaporated, even at a gentle heat, this residual liquid gradually becomes brown, and acquires the flavour of roast meat.

These interesting facts, discovered in the laboratory, throw a flood of light upon the mysteries of the kitchen. The fibres of meat are surrounded by a liquid which contains albumen in its soluble state, just as it exists in the unboiled egg. During the operation of boiling or roasting, this substance coagulates, and thereby prevents the contraction and hardening of the fibres. The tenderness of well-cooked meat is consequently proportioned to the amount of albumen deposited in its substance. Meat is underdone when it has been heated throughout only to the temperature of coagulating albumen: it is thoroughly done when it has been heated through its whole mass to the temperature at which the colouring matter of the blood coagulates: it is overdone when the heat has been continued long enough to harden the fibres.

The juice of flesh is water, holding in solution many substances besides albumen, which are of the highest possible value as articles of food. In preparing meat for the table, great care should be taken to prevent the escape of this precious juice, as the succulence and sapidity of the meat depend on its retention. The meat to be cooked should be exposed at first to a quick heat, which immediately coagulates the albumen on and near the surface. A kind of shell is thus formed, which effectually retains the whole of the juice within the meat.

During the operations of boiling, boasting, and baking, fresh beef and mutton, when moderately fat, lose, according to Johnston, on an average about-

	In boiling.	In baking.	In roasting.
4 lbs. of beef lose	1 lb.	1 lb. 3 oz.	1 lb. 5 oz.
4 lbs. of mutton lose	14 oz.	1 lb. 4 oz.	1 lb. 6 oz.

Baking

The difference between roasting meat and baking it, may be generally described as consisting in the fact, that, in baking it, the fumes caused by the operation are not carried off in the same way as occurs in roasting. Much, however, of this disadvantage is obviated by the improved construction of modern ovens, and of especially those in connection with the Leamington kitchener, of which we give an engraving here. With meat baked in the generality of ovens, however, which do not possess ventilators on the principle of this kitchener, there is undoubtedly a peculiar taste, which does not at all equal the flavour developed by roasting meat. The chemistry of baking may be said to be the same as that described in roasting.

Should the oven be very brisk, it will be found necessary to cover the joint with a piece of white paper, to prevent the meat from being scorched and blackened outside, before the heat can penetrate into the inside. This paper should be removed half an hour before the time of serving dinner, so that the joint may take a good colour.

By means of a jar, many dishes, which will be enumerated under their special heads, may be economically prepared in the oven. The principal of these are soup, gravies, jugged hare, beef tea; and this mode of cooking may be advantageously adopted with a ham, which has previously been covered with a common crust of flour and water.

All dishes prepared for baking should be more highly seasoned than when intended to be roasted. There are some dishes which, it may be said, are at least equally well cooked in the oven as by the roaster; thus, a shoulder of mutton and baked potatoes, a fillet or breast of veal, a sucking pig, a hare, well basted, will be received by connoisseurs as well, when baked, as if they had been roasted. Indeed, the baker's oven, or the family oven, may often, as has been said, be substituted for the cook and the spit with greater economy and convenience.

A baking-dish, of which we give an engraving, should not be less than 6 or 7 inches deep; so that the meat, which of course cannot be basted, can stew in its own juices. In the recipe for each dish, full explanations concerning any special points in relation to it will be given.

Boiling

Boiling, or the preparation of meat by hot water, though one of the easiest processes in cookery, requires skilful management. Boiled meat should be tender, savoury, and full of its own juice, or natural gravy; but, through the carelessness and ignorance of cooks, it is too often sent to table hard, tasteless, and innutritious. To insure a successful result in boiling flesh, the heat of the fire must be judiciously regulated, the proper quantity of water must be kept up in the pot, and the scum which rises to the surface must be carefully removed.

Many writers on cookery assert that the meat to be boiled should be put into cold water, and that the pot should be heated gradually; but Liebig, the highest authority on all matters connected with the chemistry of food, has shown that meat so treated loses some of its most nutritious constituents. "If the flesh," says the great chemist, "be introduced into the boiler when the water is in a state of brisk ebullition, and if the boiling be kept up for a few minutes, and the pot then placed in a warm place, so that the temperature of the water is kept at 158° to 165°, we have the united conditions for giving to the flesh the qualities which best fit it for being eaten."

When a piece of meat is plunged into boiling water, the albumen which is near the surface immediately coagulates, forming an envelope, which prevents the escape of the internal juice, and most effectually excludes the water, which, by mixing with this juice, would render the meat insipid. Meat treated thus is juicy and well-flavoured, when cooked, as it retains most of its savoury constituents. On the other hand, if the piece of meat be set on the fire with cold water, and this slowly heated to boiling, the flesh undergoes a loss of soluble and nutritious substances, while, as a matter of course, the soup becomes richer in these matters.

The albumen is gradually dissolved from the surface to the centre; the fibre loses, more or less, its quality of shortness or tenderness, and becomes hard and tough: the thinner the piece of meat is, the greater is its loss of savoury constituents. In order to obtain well-flavoured and eatable meat, we must relinquish the idea of making good soup from it, as that mode of boiling which yields the best soup gives the driest, toughest, and most vapid meat. Slow boiling whitens the meat; and, we suspect, that it is on this account that it is in such favour with the cooks.

The wholesomeness of food is, however, a matter of much greater moment than the appearance it presents on the table. It should be borne in mind, that the whiteness of meat that has been boiled slowly, is produced by the loss of some important alimentary properties.

The objections we have raised to the practice of putting meat on the fire in cold water, apply with equal force to the practice of soaking meat before cooking it, which is so strongly recommended by some cooks. Fresh meat ought never to be soaked, as all its most nutritive constituents are soluble in water. Soaking, however, is an operation that cannot be entirely dispensed with in the preparation of animal food. Salted and dried meats require to be soaked for some time in water before they are cooked.

For boiling meat, the softer the water is, the better. When spring water is boiled, the chalk which gives to it the quality of hardness, is precipitated. This chalk stains the meat, and communicates to it an unpleasant earthy taste. When nothing but hard water can be procured, it should be softened by boiling it for an hour or two before it is used for culinary purposes.

The fire must be watched with great attention during the operation of boiling, so that its heat may be properly regulated. As a rule, the pot should be kept in a simmering state; a result which cannot be attained without vigilance.

The temperature at which water boils, under usual circumstances, is 212° Fahr. Water does not become hotter after it has begun to boil, however long or with whatever violence the boiling is continued. This fact is of great importance in cookery, and attention to it will save much fuel. Water made to boil in a gentle way by the application of a moderate heat is just as hot as when it is made to boil on a strong fire with the greatest possible violence. When once water has been brought to the boiling point, the fire may be considerably reduced, as a very gentle heat will suffice to keep the water at its highest temperature.

The scum which rises to the surface of the pot during the operation of boiling must be carefully removed, otherwise it will attach itself to the meat, and thereby spoil its appearance. The cook must not neglect to skim during the whole process, though by far the greater part of the scum rises at first. The practice of wrapping meat in a cloth may be dispensed with if the skimming be skillfully managed. If the scum be removed as fast as it rises, the meat will be cooked clean and pure, and come out of the vessel in which it was boiled, much more delicate and firm than when cooked in a cloth.

When taken from the pot, the meat must be wiped with a clean cloth, or, what will be found more convenient, a sponge previously dipped in water and wrung dry. The meat should not be allowed to stand a moment longer than necessary, as boiled meat, as well as roasted, cannot be eaten too hot.

The time allowed for the operation of boiling must be regulated according to the size and quality of the meat. As a general rule, twenty minutes, reckoning from the moment when the boiling commences, may be allowed for every pound of meat. All the best authorities, however, agree in this, that the longer the boiling the more perfect the operation.

A few observations on the nutritive value of salted meat may be properly introduced in this place. Every housewife knows that dry salt in contact with fresh meat gradually becomes fluid brine. The application of salt causes the fibres of the meat to contract, and the juice to flow out from its pores: as much as one-third of the juice of the meat is often forced out in this manner. Now, as this juice is pure extract of meat, containing albumen, osmazome, and other valuable principles, it follows that meat which has been preserved by the action of salt can never have the nutritive properties of fresh meat.

The vessels used for boiling should be made of cast-iron, well tinned within, and provided with closely-fitting lids. They must be kept scrupulously clean, otherwise they will render the meat cooked in them unsightly and unwholesome. Copper pans, if used at all, should be reserved for operations that are performed with rapidity; as, by long contact with copper, food may become dangerously contaminated. The kettle in which a joint is dressed should be large enough to allow room for a good supply of water; if the meat be cramped and be surrounded with but little water, it will be stewed, not boiled.

In stewing, it is not requisite to have so great a heat as in boiling. A gentle simmering in a small quantity of water, so that the meat is stewed almost in its own juices, is all that is necessary. It is a method much used on the continent, and is wholesome and economical.

Two useful culinary vessels are represented above. One is a boiling-pot, in which large joints may be boiled; the other is a stewpan, with a closely-fitting lid, to which is attached a long handle; so that the cover can be removed without scalding the fingers.

The hot-plate is a modern improvement on the old kitchen ranges, being used for boiling and stewing. It is a plate of cast iron, having a closed fire burning beneath it, by which it is thoroughly well heated. On this plate are set the various saucepans, stewpans, &c.; and, by this convenient and economical method, a number of dishes may be prepared at one time. The culinary processes of braising and stewing are, in this manner, rendered more gradual, and consequently the substance acted on becomes more tender, and the gravy is not so much reduced.

Broiling

Generally speaking, small dishes only are prepared by this mode of cooking; amongst these, the beef-steak and mutton chop of the solitary English diner may be mentioned as celebrated all the world over. In order to succeed in a broil, the cook must have a bright, clear fire; so that the surface of the meat may be quickly heated. The result of this is the same as that obtained in roasting; namely, that a crust, so to speak, is formed outside, and thus the juices of the meat are retained. The appetite of an invalid, so difficult to minister to, is often pleased with a broiled dish, as the flavour and sapidity of the meat are so well preserved.

The utensils used for broiling need but little description. One point it is well to bear in mind, viz., that the gridiron should be kept in a direction slanting towards the cook, so that as little fat as possible may fall into the fire. It has been observed, that broiling is the most difficult manual office the general cook has to perform, and one that requires the most unremitting attention; for she may turn her back upon the stewpan or the spit, but the gridiron can never be left with impunity. The revolving gridiron, shown in the engraving, possesses some advantages of convenience, which will be at once apparent.

Frying

This very favourite mode of cooking may be accurately described as boiling in fat or oil. Substances dressed in this way are generally well received, for they introduce an agreeable variety, possessing, as they do, a peculiar flavour. By means of frying, cooks can soon satisfy many requisitions made on them, it being a very expeditious mode of preparing dishes for the table, and one which can be employed when the fire is not sufficiently large for the purposes of roasting and boiling. The great point to be borne in mind in frying, is that the liquid must be hot enough to act instantaneously, as all the merit of this culinary operation lies in the invasion of the boiling liquid, which carbonizes or burns, at the very instant of the immersion of the body placed in it.

It may be ascertained if the fat is heated to the proper degree, by cutting a piece of bread and dipping it in the frying-pan for five or six seconds; and if it be firm and of a dark brown when taken out, put in immediately what you wish to prepare; if it be not, let the fat be heated until of the right temperature. This having been effected, moderate the fire, so that the action may not be too hurried, and that by a continuous heat the juices of the substance may be preserved, and its flavour enhanced.

The philosophy of frying consists in this, that liquids subjected to the action of fire do not all receive the same quantity of heat. Being differently constituted in their nature, they possess different "capacities for caloric." Thus, you may, with impunity, dip your finger in boiling spirits of wine; you would take it very quickly from boiling brandy, yet more rapidly from water; whilst the effects of the most rapid immersion in boiling oil need not be told.

As a consequence of this, heated fluids act differently on the sapid bodies presented to them. Those put in water, dissolve, and are reduced to a soft mass; the result being bouillon, stock, &c. Those substances, on the contrary, treated with oil, harden, assume a more or less deep colour, and are finally carbonized. The reason of these different results is, that, in the first instance, water dissolves and extracts the interior juices of the alimentary substances placed in it; whilst, in the second, the juices are preserved; for they are insoluble in oil.

It is to be especially remembered, in connection with frying, that all dishes fried in fat should be placed before the fire on a piece of blotting-paper, or sieve reversed, and there left for a few minutes, so that any superfluous greasy moisture may be removed.

The utensils used for the purposes of frying are confined to frying-pans, although these are of various sizes; and, for small and delicate dishes, such as collops, fritters, pancakes, &c., the sauté pan, of which we give an engraving, is used.

COOKING BY GAS

Gas-cooking can scarcely now be considered a novelty,—many establishments, both small and large, have been fitted with apparatus for cooking by this mode, which undoubtedly exhibits some advantages. Thus the heat may be more regularly supplied to the substance cooking, and the operation is essentially a·clean one, because there can be no cinders or other dirt to be provided for. Some labour and attention necessary, too, with a coal fire or close stove, may be saved; and, besides this, it may, perhaps, be said that culinary operations are reduced, by this means, to something like a certainty.

There are, however, we think, many objections to this mode of cooking, more especially when applied to small domestic establishments. For instance, the ingenious machinery necessary for carrying it out, requires cooks perfectly conversant with its use; and if the gas, when the cooking operations are finished, be not turned off, there will be a large increase in the cost of cooking, instead of the economy which it has been supposed to bring. For large establishments, such as some of the immense London warehouses, where a large number of young men have to be catered for daily, it may be well adapted, as it is just possible that a slight increase in the supply of gas necessary for a couple of joints, may serve equally to cook a dozen dishes.

ROASTING

Of the various methods of preparing meat, roasting is that which most effectually preserves its nutritive qualities. Meat is roasted by being exposed to the direct influence of the fire. This is done by placing the meat before an open grate, and keeping it in motion to prevent the scorching on any particular part. When meat is properly roasted, the outer layer of its albumen is coagulated, and thus presents a barrier to the exit of the juice. In roasting meat, the heat must be strongest at first, and it should then be much reduced. To have a good juicy roast, therefore, the fire must be red and vigorous at the very commencement of the operation.

In the most careful roasting, some of the juice is squeezed out of the meat: this evaporates on the surface of the meat, and gives it a dark brown colour, a rich lustre, and a strong aromatic taste. Besides these effects on the albumen and the expelled juice, roasting converts the cellular tissue of the meat into gelatine, and melts the fat out of the fat-cells.

If a spit is used to support the meat before the fire, it should be kept quite bright. Sand and water ought to be used to scour it with, for brickdust and oil may give a disagreeable taste to the meat. When well scoured, it must be wiped quite dry with a clean cloth; and, in spitting the meat, the prime parts should be left untouched, so as to avoid any great escape of its juices.

Kitchens in large establishments are usually fitted with what are termed "smoke-jacks." By means of these, several spits, if required, may be turned at the same time. This not being, of course, necessary in smaller establishments, a roasting apparatus, more economical in its consumption of coal, is more frequently in use.

The bottle-jack, of which we here give an illustration, with the wheel and hook, and showing the precise manner of using it, is now commonly used in many kitchens. This consists of a spring inclosed in a brass cylinder, and requires winding up before it is used, and sometimes, also, during the operation of roasting. The joint is fixed to an iron hook, which is suspended by a chain connected with a wheel, and which, in its turn, is connected with the bottle-jack. Beneath it stands the dripping-pan, which we have also engraved, together with the basting-ladle, the use of which latter should not be spared; as there can be no good roast without good basting.

"Spare the rod, and spoil the child," might easily be paraphrased into "Spare the basting, and spoil the meat." If the joint is small and light, and so turns unsteadily, this may be remedied by fixing to the wheel one of the kitchen weights. Sometimes this jack is fixed inside a screen; but there is this objection to this apparatus,—that the meat cooked in it resembles the flavour of baked meat. This is derived from its being so completely surrounded with the tin, that no sufficient current of air gets to it. It will be found preferable to make use of a common meat-screen, such as is shown in the woodcut. This contains shelves for warming plates and dishes; and with this, the reflection not being so powerful, and more air being admitted to the joint, the roast may be very excellently cooked.

In stirring the fire, or putting fresh coals on it, the dripping-pan should always be drawn back, so that there may be no danger of the coal, cinders, or ashes falling down into it.

Under each particular recipe there is stated the time required for roasting each joint; but, as a general rule, it may be here given, that for every pound of meat, in ordinary-sized joints, a quarter of an hour may be allotted.

White meats, and the meat of young animals, require to be very well roasted, both to be pleasant to the palate and easy of digestion. Thus veal, pork, and lamb, should be thoroughly done to the centre.

Mutton and beef, on the other hand, do not, generally speaking, require to be so thoroughly done, and they should be dressed to the point, that, in carving them, the gravy should just run, but not too freely. Of course in this, as in most other dishes, the tastes of individuals vary; and there are many who cannot partake, with satisfaction, of any joint unless it is what others would call overdressed.

6

Preparation of Sauces and Gravies

The preparation and appearance of sauces and gravies are of the highest consequence, and in nothing does the talent and taste of the cook more display itself. Their special adaptability to the various viands they are to accompany cannot be too much studied, in order that they may harmonize and blend with them as perfectly, so to speak, as does a pianoforte accompaniment with the voice of the singer.

The general basis of most gravies and some sauces is the same stock as that used for soups; and, by the employment of these, with, perhaps, an additional slice of ham, a little spice, a few herbs, and a slight flavouring from some cold sauce or ketchup, very nice gravies may be made for a very small expenditure.

A milt (either of a bullock or sheep), the shank-end of mutton that has already been dressed, and the necks and feet of poultry, may all be advantageously used for gravy, where much is not required. It may, then, be established as a rule, that there exists no necessity for good gravies to be expensive, and that there is no occasion, as many would have the world believe, to buy ever so many pounds of fresh meat, in order to furnish an ever so little quantity of gravy.

Brown Sauces, generally speaking, should scarcely be so thick as white sauces; and it is well to bear in mind, that all those which are intended to mask the various dishes of poultry or meat, should be of a sufficient consistency to slightly adhere to the fowls or joints over which they are poured. For browning and thickening sauces, &c., browned flour may be properly employed.

Sauces should possess a decided character; and whether sharp or sweet, savoury or plain, they should carry out their names in a distinct manner, although, of course, not so much flavoured as to make them too piquant on the one hand, or too mawkish on the other.

Gravies and sauces should be sent to table very hot; and there is all the more necessity for the cook to see to this point, as, from their being usually served in small quantities, they are more liable to cool quickly than if they were in a larger body. Those sauces, of which cream or eggs form a component part, should be well stirred, as soon as these ingredients are added to them, and must never be allowed to boil; as, in that case, they would instantly curdle.

Although pickles may be purchased at shops at as low a rate as they can usually be made for at home, or perhaps even for less, yet we would advise all housewives, who have sufficient time and convenience, to prepare their own. The only general rules, perhaps, worth stating here,-- as in the recipes all necessary details will be explained, are, that the vegetables and fruits used should be sound, and not over ripe, and that the very best vinegar should be employed.

For forcemeats, special attention is necessary. The points which cooks should, in this branch of cookery, more particularly observe, are the thorough chopping of the suet, the complete mincing of the herbs, the careful grating of the bread-crumbs, and the perfect mixing of the whole.

These are the three principal ingredients of forcemeats, and they can scarcely be cut too small, as nothing like a lump or fibre should be anywhere perceptible. To conclude, the flavour of no one spice or herb should be permitted to predominate.

Anchovy Sauce for Fish

Ingredients.-4 anchovies, 1 oz. of butter, 1/2 pint of melted butter, cayenne to taste.

Mode.-Bone the anchovies, and pound them in a mortar to a paste, with 1 oz. of butter. Make the melted butter hot, stir in the pounded anchovies and cayenne; simmer for 3 or 4 minutes; and if liked, add a squeeze of lemon-juice. A more general and expeditious way of making this sauce is to stir in 1-1/2 tablespoonfuls of anchovy essence to 1/2 pint of melted butter, and to add seasoning to taste. Boil the whole up for 1 minute, and serve hot.

Anchovy Butter

Cayenne.-This is the most acrid and stimulating spice with which we are acquainted. It is a powder prepared from several varieties of the capsicum annual East-India plants, of which there are three so far naturalized in this country as to be able to grow in the open air: these are the Guinea, the Cherry, and the Bell pepper. All the pods of these are extremely pungent to the taste, and in the green state are used by us as a pickle. When ripe, they are ground into cayenne pepper, and sold as a condiment. The best of this, however, is made in the West Indies, from what is called the Bird pepper, on account of hens and turkeys being extremely partial to it. It is imported ready for use.

Of the capiscum species of plants there are five; but the principal are,-1. Capsicum annuum, the common longpodded capsicum, which is cultivated in our gardens, and of which there are two varieties, one with red, and another with yellow fruit. 2. Capsicum baccatum, or bird pepper, which rises with a shrubby stalk four or five feet high, with its berries growing at the division of the branches: this is small, oval-shaped, and of a bright-red colour, from which, as we have said, the best cayenne is made. 3. Capsicum grossum, the bell-pepper: the fruit of this is red, and is the only kind fit for pickling.

Apple Sauce for Geese, Pork, &c.

Ingredients.-6 good-sized apples, sifted sugar to taste, a piece of butter the size of a walnut, water.

Mode.-Pare, core, and quarter the apples, and throw them into cold water to preserve their whiteness. Put them in a saucepan, with sufficient water to moisten them, and boil till soft enough to pulp. Beat them up, adding sugar to taste, and a small piece of butter This quantity is sufficient for a good-sized tureen.

Brown Apple Sauce

Ingredients.-6 good-sized apples, 1/2 pint of brown gravy, cayenne to taste.

Mode. Put the gravy in a stewpan, and add the apples, after having pared, cored, and quartered them. Let them simmer gently till tender; beat them to a pulp, and season with cayenne. This sauce is preferred by many to the preceding.

Asparagus Sauce

Ingredients.-1 bunch of green asparagus, salt, 1 oz. of fresh butter, 1 small bunch of parsley, 3 or 4 green onions, 1 large lump of sugar, 4 tablespoonfuls of sauce tournée.

Mode.-Break the asparagus in the tender part, wash well, and put them into boiling salt and water to render them green. When they are tender, take them out, and put them into cold water; drain them on a cloth till all moisture is absorbed from them. Put the butter in a stewpan, with the parsley and onions; lay in the asparagus, and fry the whole over a sharp fire for 5 minutes. Add salt, the sugar and sauce tournée, and simmer for another 5 minutes. Rub all through a tammy, and if not a very good colour, use a little spinach green. This sauce should be rather sweet.

Aspic, or Ornamental Savoury Jelly

Ingredients.-4 lbs. of knuckle of veal, 1 cow-heel, 3 or 4 slices of ham, any poultry trimmings, 2 carrots, 1 onion, 1 faggot of savoury herbs, 1 glass of sherry, 3 quarts of water; seasoning to taste of salt and whole white pepper; 3 eggs.

Mode.-Lay the ham on the bottom of a stewpan, cut up the veal and cow-heel into small pieces, and lay them on the ham; add the poultry trimmings, vegetables, herbs, sherry, and water, and let the whole simmer very gently for 4 hours, carefully taking away all scum that may rise to the surface; strain through a fine sieve, and pour into an earthen pan to get cold. Have ready a clean stewpan, put in the jelly, and be particular to leave the sediment behind, or it will not be clear. Add the whites of 3 eggs, with salt and pepper, to clarify; keep stirring over the fire, till the whole becomes very white; then draw it to the side, and let it stand till clear. When this is the case, strain it through a cloth or jelly-bag, and use it for moulding poultry, etc. Tarragon vinegar may be added to give an additional flavour.

White Pepper.-This is the produce of the same plant as that which produces the black pepper, from which it is manufactured by steeping this in lime and water, and rubbing it between the hands till the coats come off. The best berries only will bear this operation; hence the superior qualities of white pepper fetch a higher price than those of the other. It is less acrid than the black, and is much prized among the Chinese. It is sometimes adulterated with rice-flour, as the black is with burnt bread. The berries of the pepper-plant grow in spikes of from twenty to thirty, and are, when ripe, of a bright-red colour. After being gathered, which is done when they are green, they are spread out in the sun, where they dry and become black and shrivelled, when they are ready for being prepared for the market.

BECHAMEL, OR FRENCH WHITE SAUCE

Ingredients.-1 small bunch of parsley, 2 cloves, 1/2 bay-leaf, 1 small faggot of savoury herbs, salt to taste; 3 or 4 mushrooms, when obtainable; 2 pints of white stock, 1 pint of cream, 1 tablespoonful of arrowroot.

Mode.-Put the stock into a stewpan, with the parsley, cloves, bay-leaf, herbs, and mushrooms; add a seasoning of salt, but no pepper, as that would give the sauce a dusty appearance, and should be avoided. When it has boiled long enough to extract the flavour of the herbs, etc., strain it, and boil it up quickly again, until it is nearly half-reduced. Now mix the arrowroot smoothly with the cream, and let it simmer very gently for 5 minutes over a slow fire; pour to it the reduced stock, and continue to simmer slowly for 10 minutes, if the sauce be thick.

If, on the contrary, it be too thin, it must be stirred over a sharp fire till it thickens. This is the foundation of many kinds of sauces, especially white sauces. Always make it thick, as you can easily thin it with cream, milk, or white stock.

The Clove.-The clove-tree is a native of the Molucca Islands, particularly Amboyna, and attains the height of a laurel-tree, and no verdure is ever seen under it. From the extremities of the branches quantities of flowers grow, first white; then they become green, and next red and hard, when they have arrived at their clove state. When they become dry, they assume a yellowish hue, which subsequently changes into a dark brown.

As an aromatic, the clove is highly stimulating, and yields an abundance of oil. There are several varieties of the clove; the best is called the royal clove, which is scarce, and which is blacker and smaller than the other kinds. It is a curious fact, that the flowers, when fully developed, are quite inodorous, and that the real fruit is not in the least aromatic. The form is that of a nail, having a globular head, formed of the four petals of the corolla, and four leaves of the calyx not expanded, with a nearly cylindrical germen, scarcely an inch in length, situate below.

Bechamel Maigre, or Without Meat.

Ingredients.-2 onions, 1 blade of mace, mushroom trimmings, a small bunch of parsley, 1 oz. of butter, flour, 1/2 pint of water, 1 pint of milk, salt, the juice of 1 lemon, 2 eggs.

Mode.-Put in a stewpan the milk, and 1/2 pint of water, with the onions, mace, mushrooms, parsley, and salt. Let these simmer gently for 20 minutes. In the mean time, rub on a plate 1 oz. of flour and butter; put it to the liquor, and stir it well till it boils up; then place it by the side of the fire, and continue stirring until it is perfectly smooth. Now strain it through a sieve into a basin, after which put it back in the stewpan, and add the lemon-juice. Beat up the yolks of the eggs with about 4 dessertspoonfuls of milk; strain this to the sauce, keep stirring it over the fire, but do not let it boil, lest it curdle.

This is a good sauce to pour over boiled fowls when they are a bad colour.

Pickled Beetroot

Ingredients.-Sufficient vinegar to cover the beets, 2 oz. of whole pepper, 2 oz. of allspice to each gallon of vinegar.

Mode.-Wash the beets free from dirt, and be very careful not to prick the outside skin, or they would lose their beautiful colour. Put them into boiling water, let them simmer gently, and when about three parts done, which will be in 1-1/2 hour, take them out and let them cool. Boil the vinegar with pepper and allspice, in the above proportion, for ten minutes, and when cold, pour it on the beets, which must be peeled and cut into slices about 1/2 inch thick. Cover with bladder to exclude the air, and in a week they will be fit for use.

Black Pepper.-This well-known aromatic spice is the fruit of a species of climbing vine, and is a native of the East Indies, and is extensively cultivated in Malabar and the eastern islands of Borneo, Sumatra, and Java, and others in the same latitude. It was formerly confined to these countries, but it has now been introduced to Cayenne.

It is generally employed as a condiment; but it should never be forgotten, that, even in small quantities, it produces detrimental effects on inflammatory constitutions. Dr. Paris, in his work on Diet, says, "Foreign spices were not intended by Nature for the inhabitants of temperate climes; they are heating, and highly stimulant. I am, however, not anxious to give more weight to this objection than it deserves. Man is no longer the child of Nature, nor the passive inhabitant of any particular region. He ranges over every part of the globe, and elicits nourishment from the productions of every climate. Nature is very kind in favouring the growth of those productions which are most likely to answer our local wants. Those climates, for instance, which engender endemic diseases, are, in general, congenial to the growth of plants that operate as antidotes to them. But if we go to the East for tea, there is no reason why we should not go to the West for sugar. The dyspeptic invalid, however, should be cautious in their use; they may afford temporary benefit, at the expense of permanent mischief.

It has been well said, that the best quality of spices is to stimulate the appetite, and their worst to destroy, by insensible degrees, the tone of the stomach. The intrinsic goodness of meats should always be suspected when they require spicy seasonings to compensate for their natural want of sapidity." The quality of pepper is known by rubbing it between the hands: that which withstands this operation is good, that which is reduced to powder by it is bad. The quantity of pepper imported into Europe is very great.

Benton Sauce

Ingredients.-1 tablespoonful of scraped horseradish, 1 teaspoonful of made mustard, 1 teaspoonful of pounded sugar, 4 tablespoonfuls of vinegar.

Mode.-Grate or scrape the horseradish very fine, and mix it with the other ingredients, which must be all well blended together; serve in a tureen. With cold meat, this sauce is a very good substitute for pickles.

Bread Sauce

Ingredients.-1 pint of milk, 3/4 of the crumb of a stale loaf, 1 onion; pounded mace, cayenne, and salt to taste; 1 oz. of butter.

Mode.-Peel and quarter the onion, and simmer it in the milk till perfectly tender. Break the bread, which should be stale, into small pieces, carefully picking out any hard outside pieces; put it in a very clean saucepan, strain the milk over it, cover it up, and let it remain for an hour to soak. Now beat it up with a fork very smoothly, add a seasoning of pounded mace, cayenne, and salt, with 1 oz. of butter; give the whole one boil, and serve. To enrich this sauce, a small quantity of cream may be added just before sending it to table.

BROWNING FOR GRAVIES AND SAUCES.

The browning for soups answers equally well for sauces and gravies, when it is absolutely necessary to colour them in this manner; but where they can be made to look brown by using ketchup, wine, browned flour, tomatoes, or any colour sauce, it is far preferable. As, however, in cooking, so much depends on appearance, perhaps it would be as well for the inexperienced cook to use the artificial means. When no browning is at hand, and you wish to heighten the colour of your gravy, dissolve a lump of sugar in an iron spoon over a sharp fire; when it is in a liquid state, drop it into the sauce or gravy quite hot. Care, however, must be taken not to put in too much, as it would impart a very disagreeable flavour.

BEURRE NOIR, OR BROWNED BUTTER

Ingredients.-1/4 lb. of butter, 1 tablespoonful of minced parsley, 3 tablespoonfuls of vinegar, salt and pepper to taste.

Mode.-Put the butter into a fryingpan over a nice clear fire, and when it smokes, throw in the parsley, and add the vinegar and seasoning. Let the whole simmer for a minute or two, when it is ready to serve. This is a very good sauce for skate.

Clarified Butter

Put the butter in a basin before the fire, and when it melts, stir it round once or twice, and let it settle. Do not strain it unless absolutely necessary, as it causes so much waste. Pour it gently off into a clean dry jar, carefully leaving all sediment behind. Let it cool, and carefully exclude the air by means of a bladder, or piece of wash-leather, tied over. If the butter is salt, it may be washed before melting, when it is to be used for sweet dishes.

MELTED BUTTER

Ingredients.-1/4 lb. of butter, a dessertspoonful of flour, 1 wineglassful of water, salt to taste.

Mode.-Cut the butter up into small pieces, put it in a saucepan, dredge over the flour, and add the water and a seasoning of salt; stir it one way constantly till the whole of the ingredients are melted and thoroughly blended. Let it just boil, when it is ready to serve. If the butter is to be melted with cream, use the same quantity as of water, but omit the flour; keep stirring it, but do not allow it to boil.

MELTED BUTTER (THE FRENCH SAUCE BLANCHE).

Ingredients.-1/4 lb. of fresh butter, 1 tablespoonful of flour, salt to taste, 1/2 gill of water, 1/2 spoonful of white vinegar, a very little grated nutmeg.

Mode.-Mix the flour and water to a smooth batter, carefully rubbing down with the back of a spoon any lumps that may appear. Put it in a saucepan with all the other ingredients, and let it thicken on the fire, but do not allow it to boil, lest it should taste of the flour.

THICKENED BUTTER

Ingredients.-1/4 pint of melted butter, the yolks of 2 eggs, a little lemon-juice.

Mode.-Make the butter quite hot, and be careful not to colour it. Well whisk the yolks of the eggs, pour them to the butter, beating them all the while. Make the sauce hot over the fire, but do not let it boil; add a squeeze of lemon-juice.

Melted Butter Made With Milk.

Ingredients.-1 teaspoonful of flour, 2 oz. butter, 1/3 pint of milk, a few grains of salt.

Mode.-Mix the butter and flour smoothly together on a plate, put it into a lined saucepan, and pour in the milk. Keep stirring it one way over a sharp fire; let it boil quickly for a minute or two, and it is ready to serve. This is a very good foundation for onion, lobster, or oyster sauce: using milk instead of water makes it look so much whiter and more delicate.

Caper Sauce for Boiled Mutton

Ingredients.-1/2 pint of melted butter, 3 tablespoonfuls of capers or nasturtiums, 1 tablespoonful of their liquor.

Mode.-Chop the capers twice or thrice, and add them, with their liquor, to 1/2 pint of melted butter, made very smoothly; keep stirring well; let the sauce just simmer, and serve in a tureen. Pickled nasturtium-pods are fine-flavoured, and by many are eaten in preference to capers. They make an excellent sauce.

Caper Sauce for Fish.

Ingredients.-1/2 pint of melted butter, 3 dessertspoonfuls of capers, 1 dessertspoonful of their liquor, a small piece of glaze, if at hand (this may be dispensed with), 1/4 teaspoonful of salt, ditto of pepper, 1 tablespoonful of anchovy essence.

Mode.-Cut the capers across once or twice, but do not chop them fine; put them in a saucepan with 1/2 pint of good melted butter, and add all the other ingredients. Keep stirring the whole until it just simmers, when it is ready to serve.

Capers

These are the unopened buds of a low trailing shrub, which grows wild among the crevices of the rocks of Greece, as well as in northern Africa: the plant, however, has come to be cultivated in the south of Europe. After being pickled in vinegar and salt, they are imported from Sicily, Italy, and the south of France. The best are from Toulon.

Ingredients.-1/2 pint of melted butter, 2 tablespoonfuls of cut parsley, 1/2 teaspoonful of salt, 1 tablespoonful of vinegar.

Mode.-Boil the parsley slowly to let it become a bad colour; cut, but do not chop it fine. Add it to 1/2 pint of smoothly-made melted butter, with salt and vinegar in the above proportions. Boil up and serve.

Pickled Capsicums

Ingredients.-Vinegar, 1/4 oz. of pounded mace, and 1/4 oz. of grated nutmeg, to each quart; brine.

Mode.-Gather the pods with the stalks on, before they turn red; slit them down the side with a small-pointed knife, and remove the seeds only; put them in a strong brine for 3 days, changing it every morning; then take them out, lay them on a cloth, with another one over them, until they are perfectly free from moisture. Boil sufficient vinegar to cover them, with mace and nutmeg in the above proportions; put the pods in a jar, pour over the vinegar when cold, and exclude them from the air by means of a wet bladder tied over.

Celery Sauce

Ingredients.-4 heads of celery, 1/2 pint of melted butter, made with milk, 1 blade of pounded mace; salt and white pepper to taste.

Mode.-Wash the celery, boil it in salt and water till tender, and cut it into pieces 2 inches long; make 1/2 pint melted butter; put in the celery, pounded mace, and seasoning; simmer for three minutes, when the sauce will be ready to serve.

Bengal Recipe for Making Mango Chetney

Ingredients.-1-1/2 lbs. of moist sugar, 3/4 lb. of salt, 1/4 lb. of garlic, 1/4 lb. of onions, 3/4 lb. of powdered ginger, 1/4 lb. of dried chilies, 3/4 lb. of mustard-seed, 3/4 lb. of stoned raisins, 2 bottles of best vinegar, 30 large unripe sour apples.

Mode.-The sugar must be made into syrup; the garlic, onions, and ginger be finely pounded in a mortar; the mustard-seed be washed in cold vinegar, and dried in the sun; the apples be peeled, cored, and sliced, and boiled in a bottle and a half of the vinegar. When all this is done, and the apples are quite cold, put them into a large pan, and gradually mix the whole of the rest of the ingredients, including the remaining half-bottle of vinegar. It must be well stirred until the whole is thoroughly blended, and then put into bottles for use. Tie a piece of wet bladder over the mouths of the bottles, after they are well corked. This chetney is very superior to any which can be bought, and one trial will prove it to be delicious.

Note.-This recipe was given by a native to an English lady, who had long been a resident in India, and who, since her return to her native country, has become quite celebrated amongst her friends for the excellence of this Eastern relish.

Garlic.-The smell of this plant is generally considered offensive, and it is the most acrimonious in its taste of the whole of the alliaceous tribe. In 1548 it was introduced to England from the shores of the Mediterranean, where it is abundant, and in Sicily it grows naturally. It was in greater repute with our ancestors than it is with ourselves, although it is still used as a seasoning herb. On the continent, especially in Italy, it is much used, and the French consider it an essential in many made dishes.

Crab Sauce for Fish

Ingredients.-1 crab; salt, pounded mace, and cayenne to taste; 1/2 pint of melted butter made with milk.

Mode.-Choose a nice fresh crab, pick all the meat away from the shell, and cut it into small square pieces. Make 1/2 pint of melted butter, put in the fish and seasoning; let it gradually warm through, and simmer for 2 minutes. It should not boil.

Cucumber Sauce

Ingredients.-3 or 4 cucumbers, 2 oz. of butter, 6 tablespoonfuls of brown gravy.

Mode.-Peel the cucumbers, quarter them, and take out the seeds; cut them into small pieces; put them in a cloth, and rub them well, to take out the water which hangs about them. Put the butter in a saucepan, add the cucumbers, and shake them over a sharp fire until they are of a good colour. Then pour over it the gravy, mix this with the cucumbers, and simmer gently for 10 minutes, when it will be ready to serve.

Pickled Cucumbers

Ingredients.-1 oz. of whole pepper, 1 oz. of bruised ginger; sufficient vinegar to cover the cucumbers.

Mode.—Cut the cucumbers in thick slices, sprinkle salt over them, and let them remain for 24 hours. The next day, drain them well for 6 hours, put them into a jar, pour boiling vinegar over them, and keep them in a warm place. In a short time, boil up the vinegar again, add pepper and ginger in the above proportion, and instantly cover them up. Tie them down with bladder, and in a few days they will be fit for use.

Long Pepper.—This is the produce of a different plant from that which produces the black, it consisting of the half-ripe flower-heads of what naturalists call Piper longum and chaba. It is the growth, however, of the same countries; indeed, all the spices are the produce of tropical climates only. Originally, the most valuable of these were found in the Spice Islands, or Moluccas, of the Indian Ocean, and were highly prized by the nations of antiquity. The Romans indulged in them to a most extravagant degree. The long pepper is less aromatic than the black, but its oil is more pungent.

Cucumber Sauce, White

Ingredients.—3 or four cucumbers, 1/2 pint of white stock, cayenne and salt to taste, the yolks of 3 eggs.

Mode.— Cut the cucumbers into small pieces, after peeling them and taking out the seeds. Put them in a stewpan with the white stock and seasoning; simmer gently till the cucumbers are tender, which will be in about 1/4 hour. Then add the yolks of the eggs well beaten; stir them to the sauce, but do not allow it to boil, and serve very hot.

Cucumber Vinegar

Ingredients.-10 large cucumbers, or 12 smaller ones, 1 quart of vinegar, 2 onions, 2 shalots, 1 tablespoonful of salt, 2 tablespoonfuls of pepper, 1/4 teaspoonful of cayenne.

Mode.-Pare and slice the cucumbers, put them in a stone jar or wide-mouthed bottle, with the vinegar; slice the onions and shalots, and add them, with all the other ingredients, to the cucumbers. Let it stand 4 or 5 days, boil it all up, and when cold, strain the liquor through a piece of muslin, and store it away in small bottles well sealed. This vinegar is a very nice addition to gravies, hashes, &e., as well as a great improvement to salads, or to eat with cold meat.

Custard Sauce for Sweet Puddings or Tarts

Ingredients.-1 pint of milk, 2 eggs, 3 oz. of pounded sugar, 1 tablespoonful of brandy.

Mode.-Put the milk in a very clean saucepan, and let it boil. Beat the eggs, stir to them the milk and pounded sugar, and put the mixture into a jug. Place the jug in a saucepan of boiling water; keep stirring well until it thickens, but do not allow it to boil, or it will curdle. Serve the sauce in a tureen, stir in the brandy, and grate a little nutmeg over the top. This sauce may be made very much nicer by using cream instead of milk; but the above recipe will be found quite good enough for ordinary purposes.

Dutch Sauce for Fish

Ingredients.-1/2 teaspoonful of flour, 2 oz. of butter, 4 tablespoonfuls of vinegar, the yolks of 2 eggs, the juice of 1/2 lemon; salt to taste.

Mode.-Put all the ingredients, except the lemon-juice, into a stew-pan; set it over the fire, and keep continually stirring. When it is sufficiently thick, take it off, as it should not boil. If, however, it happens to curdle, strain the sauce through a tammy, add the lemon-juice, and serve. Tarragon vinegar may be used instead of plain, and, by many, is considered far preferable.

Green Dutch Sauce, or Hollandaise Verte

Ingredients.-6 tablespoonfuls of Béchamel, seasoning to taste of salt and cayenne, a little parsley-green to colour, the juice of 1/2 a lemon.

Mode.-Put the Béchamel into a saucepan with the seasoning, and bring it to a boil. Make a green colouring by pounding some parsley in a mortar, and squeezing all the juice from it. Let this just simmer, when add it to the sauce. A moment before serving, put in the lemon-juice, but not before; for otherwise the sauce would turn yellow, and its appearance be thus spoiled.

To Pickle Eggs

Ingredients.-16 eggs, 1 quart of vinegar, 1/2 oz. of Black pepper, 1/2 oz. of Jamaica pepper, 1/2 oz. of ginger.

Mode.-Boil the eggs for 12 minutes, then dip them into cold water, and take off the shells. Put the vinegar, with the pepper and ginger, into a stewpan, and let it simmer for 10 minutes. Now place the eggs in a jar, pour over them the vinegar, &c., boiling hot, and, when cold, tie them down with bladder to exclude the air. This pickle will be ready for use in a month.

Egg Balls for Soups and Made Dishes

Ingredients.- 8 eggs, a little flour; seasoning to taste of salt.

Mode.-Boil 6 eggs for 20 minutes, strip off the shells, take the yolks and pound them in a mortar. Beat the yolks of the other 2 eggs; add them, with a little flour and salt, to those pounded; mix all well together, and roll into balls. Boil them before they are put into the soup or other dish they may be intended for.

Egg Sauce for Salt Fish

Ingredients.-4 eggs, 1/2 pint of melted butter, when liked, a very little lemon-juice.

Mode.-Boil the eggs until quite hard, which will be in about 20 minutes, and put them into cold water for 1/2 hour. Strip off the shells, chop the eggs into small pieces, not, however, too fine. Make the melted butter very smoothly, and, when boiling, stir in the eggs, and serve very hot. Lemon-juice may be added at pleasure.

Epicurean Sauce for Steaks, Chops, Gravies, or Fish

Ingredients.-1/4 pint of walnut ketchup, 1/4 pint of mushroom ditto, 2 tablespoonfuls of Indian soy, 2 tablespoonfuls of port wine; 1/4 oz. of white pepper, 2 oz. of shalots, 1/4 oz. of cayenne, 1/4 oz. of cloves, 3/4 pint of vinegar.

Mode.-Put the whole of the ingredients into a bottle, and let it remain for a fortnight in a warm place, occasionally shaking up the contents. Strain, and bottle off for use. This sauce will be found an agreeable addition to gravies, hashes, stews, &c.

Espagnole, or Brown Spanish Sauce

Ingredients.-2 slices of lean ham, 1 lb. of veal, 1-1/2 pint of white stock, 2 or 3 sprigs of parsley, 1/2 a bay-leaf, 2 or 3 sprigs of savoury herbs, 6 green onions, 3 shalots, 2 cloves, 1 blade of mace, 2 glasses of sherry or Madeira, thickening of butter and flour.

Mode.-Cut up the ham and veal into small square pieces, and put them into a stewpan. Moisten these with 1/2 pint of the stock, and simmer till the bottom of the stewpan is covered with a nicely-coloured glaze, when put in a few more spoonfuls to detach it. Add the remainder of the stock, with the spices, herbs, shalots, and onions, and simmer very gently for 1 hour. Strain and skim off every particle of fat, and when required for use, thicken with butter and flour, or with a little roux. Add the wine, and, if necessary, a seasoning of cayenne; when it will be ready to serve.

Fish Sauce

Ingredients.-1-1/2 oz. of cayenne, 2 tablespoonfuls of walnut ketchup, 2 tablespoonfuls of soy, a few shreds of garlic and shalot, 1 quart of vinegar.

Mode.-Put all the ingredients into a large bottle, and shake well every day for a fortnight. Keep it in small bottles well sealed, and in a few days it will be fit for use.

Forcemeat for Pike, Carp, Haddock, and Various Kinds of Fish

Ingredients.-1 oz. of fresh butter, 1 oz. of suet, 1 oz. of fat bacon, 1 small teaspoonful of minced savoury herbs, including parsley; a little onion, when liked, shredded very fine; salt, nutmeg, and cayenne to taste; 4 oz. of bread crumbs, 1 egg.

Mode.-Mix all the ingredients well together, carefully mincing them very finely; beat up the egg, moisten with it, and work the whole very smoothly together. Oysters or anchovies may be added to this forcemeat, and will be found a great improvement.

Forcemeat for Veal, Turkeys, Fowls, Hare, &c.

Ingredients.-2 oz. of ham or lean bacon, 1/4 lb. of suet, the rind of half a lemon, 1 teaspoonful of minced parsley, 1 teaspoonful of minced sweet herbs; salt, cayenne, and pounded mace to taste; 6 oz. of bread crumbs, 2 eggs.

Mode.-Shred the ham or bacon, chop the suet, lemon-peel, and herbs, taking particular care that all be very finely minced; add a seasoning to taste, of salt, cayenne, and mace, and blend all thoroughly together with the bread crumbs, before wetting. Now beat and strain the eggs, work these up with the other ingredients, and the forcemeat will be ready for use. When it is made into balls, fry of a nice brown, in boiling lard, or put them on a tin and bake for 1/2 hour in a moderate oven. As we have stated before, no one flavour should predominate greatly, and the forcemeat should be of sufficient body to cut with a knife, and yet not dry and heavy. For very delicate forcemeat, it is advisable to pound the ingredients together before binding with the egg; but for ordinary cooking, mincing very finely answers the purpose.

Forcemeat for Baked Pike

Ingredients.-3 oz. of bread crumbs, 1 teaspoonful of minced savoury herbs, 8 oysters, 2 anchovies (these may be dispensed with), 2 oz. of suet; salt, pepper, and pounded mace to taste; 6 tablespoonfuls of cream or milk, the yolks of 2 eggs.

Mode.-Beard and mince the oysters, prepare and mix the other ingredients, and blend the whole thoroughly together. Moisten with the cream and eggs, put all into a stewpan, and stir it over the fire till it thickens, when put it into the fish, which should have previously been cut open, and sew it up.

Soyer's Recipe for Forcemeats

Take a pound and a half of lean veal from the fillet, and cut it in long thin slices; scrape with a knife till nothing but the fibre remains; put it in a mortar, pound it 10 minutes, or until in a purée; pass it through a wire sieve (use the remainder in stock); then take 1 pound of good fresh beef suet, which skin, shred, and chop very fine; put it in a mortar and pound it; then add 6 oz. of panada (that is, bread soaked in milk and boiled till nearly dry) with the suet; pound them well together, and add the veal; season with a teaspoonful of salt, a quarter one of pepper, half that of nutmeg; work all well together; then add four eggs by degrees, continually pounding the contents of the mortar. When well mixed, take a small piece in a spoon, and poach it in some boiling water; and if it is delicate, firm, and of a good flavour, it is ready for use.

Fried Bread Crumbs

Cut the bread into thin slices, place them in a cool oven overnight, and when thoroughly dry and crisp, roll them down into fine crumbs. Put some lard, or clarified dripping, into a frying-pan; bring it to the boiling-point, throw in the crumbs, and fry them very quickly. Directly they are done, lift them out with a slice, and drain them before the fire from all greasy moisture. When quite crisp, they are ready for use. The fat they are fried in should be clear, and the crumbs should not have the slightest appearance or taste of having been, in the least degree, burnt.

Pickled Gherkins

Ingredients.-Salt and water, 1 oz. of bruised ginger, 1/2 oz. of whole black pepper, 1/4 oz. of whole allspice, 4 cloves, 2 blades of mace, a little horseradish. This proportion of pepper, spices, &c., for 1 quart of vinegar.

Mode.-Let the gherkins remain in salt and water for 3 or 4 days, when take them out, wipe perfectly dry, and put them into a stone jar. Boil sufficient vinegar to cover them, with spices and pepper, &c., in the above proportion, for 10 minutes; pour it, quite boiling, over the gherkins, cover the jar with vine-leaves, and put over them a plate, setting them near the fire, where they must remain all night.

Next day drain off the vinegar, boil it up again, and pour it hot over them. Cover up with fresh leaves, and let the whole remain till quite cold. Now tie down closely with bladder to exclude the air, and in a month or two, they will be fit for use.

Glaze for Covering Cold Hams, Tongues, &c.

We may remark at the outset, that unless glaze is wanted in very large quantities, it is seldom made expressly. Either of the stocks mentioned above, boiled down and reduced very considerably, will be found to produce a very good glaze. Put the stock into a stewpan, over a nice clear fire; let it boil till it becomes somewhat stiff, when keep stirring, to prevent its burning.

The moment it is sufficiently reduced, and comes to a glaze, turn it out into the glaze-pot, of which we have here given an engraving. As, however, this is not to be found in every establishment, a white earthenware jar would answer the purpose; and this may be placed in a vessel of boiling water, to melt the glaze when required. It should never be warmed in a saucepan, except on the principle of the bain marie, lest it should reduce too much, and become black and bitter. If the glaze is wanted of a pale colour, more veal than beef should be used in making the stock; and it is as well to omit turnips and celery, as these impart a disagreeable bitter flavour.

Gravy for Roast Meat

Ingredients.-Gravy, salt.

Mode.-Put a common dish with a small quantity of salt in it under the meat, about a quarter of an hour before it is removed from the fire. When the dish is full, take it away, baste the meat, and pour the gravy into the dish on which the joint is to be served.

Indian Curry-Powder

Ingredients.-1/4 lb. of coriander-seed, 1/4 lb. of turmeric, 2 oz. of cinnamon-seed, 1/2 oz. of cayenne, 1 oz. of mustard, 1 oz. of ground ginger, 1/2 ounce of allspice, 2 oz. of fenugreek-seed.

Mode.-Put all the ingredients in a cool oven, where they should remain one night; then pound them in a mortar, rub them through a sieve, and mix thoroughly together; keep the powder in a bottle, from which the air should be completely excluded.

Note.-We have given this recipe for curry-powder, as some persons prefer to make it at home; but that purchased at any respectable shop is, generally speaking, far superior, and, taking all things into consideration, very frequently more economical.

Indian Mustard

Ingredients.-1/4 lb. of the best mustard, 1/4 lb. of flour, 1/2 oz. of salt, 4 shalots, 4 tablespoonfuls of vinegar, 4 tablespoonfuls of ketchup, 1/4 bottle of anchovy sauce.

Mode.-Put the mustard, flour, and salt into a basin, and make them into a stiff paste with boiling water. Boil the shalots with the vinegar, ketchup, and anchovy sauce, for 10 minutes, and pour the whole, boiling, over the mixture in the basin; stir well, and reduce it to a proper thickness; put it into a bottle, with a bruised shalot at the bottom, and store away for use. This makes an excellent relish, and if properly prepared will keep for years.

Indian Pickle

Ingredients.-To each gallon of vinegar allow 6 cloves of garlic, 12 shalots, 2 sticks of sliced horseradish, 1/4 lb. of bruised ginger, 2 oz. of whole black pepper, 1 oz. of long pepper, 1 oz. of allspice, 12 cloves, 1/4 oz. of cayenne, 2 oz. of mustard-seed, 1/4 lb. of mustard, 1 oz. of turmeric; a white cabbage, cauliflowers, radish-pods, French beans, gherkins, small round pickling-onions, nasturtiums, capsicums, chilies, &c.

Mode.-Cut the cabbage, which must be hard and white, into slices, and the cauliflowers into small branches; sprinkle salt over them in a large dish, and let them remain two days; then dry them, and put them into a very large jar, with garlic, shalots, horseradish, ginger, pepper, allspice, and cloves, in the above proportions. Boil sufficient vinegar to cover them, which pour over, and, when cold, cover up to keep them free from dust. As the other things for the pickle ripen at different times, they may be added as they are ready: these will be radish-pods, French beans, gherkins, small onions, nasturtiums, capsicums, chilies, &c. &c. As these are procured, they must, first of all, be washed in a little cold vinegar, wiped, and then simply added to the other ingredients in the large jar, only taking care that they are covered by the vinegar.

If more vinegar should be wanted to add to the pickle, do not omit first to boil it before adding it to the rest. When you have collected all the things you require, turn all out in a large pan, and thoroughly mix them.

Now put the mixed vegetables into smaller jars, without any of the vinegar; then boil the vinegar again, adding as much more as will be required to fill the different jars, and also cayenne, mustard-seed, turmeric, and mustard, which must be well mixed with a little cold vinegar, allowing the quantities named above to each gallon of vinegar. Pour the vinegar, boiling hot, over the pickle, and when cold, tie down with a bladder. If the pickle is wanted for immediate use, the vinegar should be boiled twice more, but the better way is to make it during one season for use during the next. It will keep for years, if care is taken that the vegetables are quite covered by the vinegar.

Indian Chetney Sauce

Ingredients.-8 oz. of sharp, sour apples, pared and cored; 8 oz. of tomatoes, 8 oz. of salt, 8 oz. of brown, sugar, 8 oz. of stoned raisins, 4 oz. of cayenne, 4 oz. of powdered ginger, 2 oz. of garlic, 2 oz. of shalots, 3 quarts of vinegar, 1 quart of lemon-juice.

Mode.-Chop the apples in small square pieces, and add to them the other ingredients. Mix the whole well together, and put in a well-covered jar. Keep this in a warm place, and stir every day for a month, taking care to put on the lid after this operation; strain, but do not squeeze it dry; store it away in clean jars or bottles for use, and the liquor will serve as an excellent sauce for meat or fish.

Seasonable.-Make this sauce when tomatoes are in full season, that is, from the beginning of September to the end of October.

Lemon Sauçe for Boiled Fowls

Ingredients.-1 small lemon, 3/4 pint of melted butter.

Mode.-Cut the lemon into very thin slices, and these again into very small dice. Have ready 3/4 pint of melted butter; put in the lemon; let it just simmer, but not boil, and pour it over the fowls.

Lemon White Sauce, for Fowls, Fricassees, &c.

Ingredients.-3/4 pint of cream, the rind and juice of 1 lemon, 1/2 teaspoonful of whole white pepper, 1 sprig of lemon thyme, 3 oz. of butter, 1 dessertspoonful of flour, 1 teacupful of white stock; salt to taste.

Mode.-Put the cream into a very clean saucepan (a lined one is best), with the lemon-peel, pepper, and thyme, and let these infuse for 1/2 hour, when simmer gently for a few minutes, or until there is a nice flavour of lemon. Strain it, and add a thickening of butter and flour in the above proportions; stir this well in, and put in the lemon-juice at the moment of serving; mix the stock with the cream, and add a little salt. This sauce should not boil after the cream and stock are mixed together.

Lemon Brandy

Ingredients.-1 pint of brandy, the rind of two small lemons, 2 oz. of loaf-sugar, 1/4 pint of water.

Mode.—Peel the lemons rather thin, taking care to have none of the white pith. Put the rinds into a bottle with the brandy, and let them infuse for 24 hours, when they should be strained. Now boil the sugar with the water for a few minutes, skim it, and, when cold, add it to the brandy. A dessertspoonful of this will be found an excellent flavouring for boiled custards.

Lemon Rind or Peel

This contains an essential oil of a very high flavour and fragrance, and is consequently esteemed both a wholesome and agreeable stomachic. It is used, as will be seen by many recipes in this book, as an ingredient for flavouring a number of various dishes. Under the name of CANDIED LEMON-PEEL, it is cleared of the pulp and preserved by sugar, when it becomes an excellent sweetmeat. By the ancient medical philosopher Galen, and others, it may be added, that dried lemon-peel was considered as one of the best digestives, and recommended to weak and delicate persons.

LIAISON OF EGGS FOR THICKENING SAUCES

Ingredients.-The yolks of 3 eggs, 8 tablespoonfuls of milk or cream.

Mode.-Beat up the yolks of the eggs, to which add the milk, and strain the whole through a hair-sieve. When the liaison is being added to the sauce it is intended to thicken, care must be exercised to keep stirring it during the whole time, or, otherwise, the eggs will curdle. It should only just simmer, but not boil.

LIVER AND PARSLEY SAUCE FOR POULTRY.

Ingredients.-The liver of a fowl, one tablespoonful of minced parsley, 1/2 pint of melted butter.

Mode.-Wash and score the liver, boil it for a few minutes, and mince it very fine; blanch or scald a small bunch of parsley, of which there should be sufficient when chopped to fill a tablespoon; add this, with the minced liver, to 1/2 pint of smoothly-made melted butter; let it just boil; when serve.

MIXED PICKLE

Ingredients.-To each gallon of vinegar allow 1/4 lb. of bruised ginger, 1/4 lb. of mustard, 1/4 lb. of salt, 2 oz. of mustard-seed, 1-1/2 oz. of turmeric, 1 oz. of ground black pepper, 1/4 oz. of cayenne, cauliflowers, onions, celery, sliced cucumbers, gherkins, French beans, nasturtiums, capsicums.

Mode.-Have a large jar, with a tightly-fitting lid, in which put as much vinegar as required, reserving a little to mix the various powders to a smooth paste. Put into a basin the mustard, turmeric, pepper, and cayenne; mix them with vinegar, and stir well until no lumps remain; add all the ingredients to the vinegar, and mix well. Keep this liquor in a warm place, and thoroughly stir every morning for a month with a wooden spoon, when it will be ready for the different vegetables to be added to it. As these come into season, have them gathered on a dry day, and, after merely wiping them with a cloth, to free them from moisture, put them into the pickle.

The cauliflowers, it may be said, must be divided into small bunches. Put all these into the pickle raw, and at the end of the season, when there have been added as many of the vegetables as could be procured, store it away in jars, and tie over with bladder. As none of the ingredients are boiled, this pickle will not be fit to eat till 12 months have elapsed. Whilst the pickle is being made, keep a wooden spoon tied to the jar; and its contents, it may be repeated, must be stirred every morning.

Mushroom Ketchup

Ingredients.-To each peck of mushrooms 1/2 lb. of salt; to each quart of mushroom-liquor 1/4 oz. of cayenne, 1/2 oz. of allspice, 1/2 oz. of ginger, 2 blades of pounded mace.

Mode.-Choose full-grown mushroom-flaps, and take care they are perfectly fresh-gathered when the weather is tolerably dry; for, if they are picked during very heavy rain, the ketchup from which they are made is liable to get musty, and will not keep long. Put a layer of them in a deep pan, sprinkle salt over them, and then another layer of mushrooms, and so on alternately.

Let them remain for a few hours, when break them up with the hand; put them in a nice cool place for 3 days, occasionally stirring and mashing them well, to extract from them as much juice as possible. Now measure the quantity of liquor without straining, and to each quart allow the above proportion of spices, &c. Put all into a stone jar, cover it up very closely, put it in a saucepan of boiling water, set it over the fire, and let it boil for 3 hours.

Have ready a nice clean stewpan; turn into it the contents of the jar, and let the whole simmer very gently for 1/2 hour; pour it into a jug, where it should stand in a cool place till the next day; then pour it off into another jug, and strain it into very dry clean bottles, and do not squeeze the mushrooms.

To each pint of ketchup add a few drops of brandy. Be careful not to shake the contents, but leave all the sediment behind in the jug; cork well, and either seal or rosin the cork, so as perfectly to exclude the air. When a very clear bright ketchup is wanted, the liquor must be strained through a very fine hair-sieve, or flannel bag, after it has been very gently poured off; if the operation is not successful, it must be repeated until you have quite a clear liquor. It should be examined occasionally, and if it is spoiling, should be reboiled with a few peppercorns.

Pickled Mushrooms

Ingredients.-Sufficient vinegar to cover the mushrooms; to each quart of mushrooms, 2 blades of pounded mace, 1 oz. of ground pepper, salt to taste.

Mode.-Choose some nice young button mushrooms for pickling, and rub off the skin with a piece of flannel and salt, and cut off the stalks; if very large, take out the red inside, and reject the black ones, as they are too old. Put them in a stewpan, sprinkle salt over them, with pounded mace and pepper in the above proportion; shake them well over a clear fire until the liquor flows, and keep them there until it is all dried up again; then add as much vinegar as will cover them; just let it simmer for 1 minute, and store it away in stone jars for use. When cold, tie down with bladder and keep in a dry place; they will remain good for a length of time, and are generally considered delicious.

TARTAR MUSTARD

Ingredients.-Horseradish vinegar, cayenne, 1/2 a teacupful of mustard.

Mode.-Have ready sufficient horseradish vinegar to mix with the above proportion of mustard; put the mustard in a cup, with a slight seasoning of cayenne; mix it perfectly smooth with the vinegar, adding this a little at a time; rub down with the back of a spoon any lumps that may appear, and do not let it be too thin. Mustard may be flavoured in various ways, with Tarragon, shalot, celery, and many other vinegars, herbs, spices, &c.; but this is more customary in France than in England, as there it is merely considered a "vehicle of flavours," as it has been termed.

FRENCH ONION SAUCE, OR SOUBISE

Ingredients.-1/2 pint of Béchamel, 1 bay-leaf, seasoning to taste of pounded mace and cayenne, 6 onions, a small piece of ham.

Mode.-Peel the onions and cut them in halves; put them in a stewpan, with just sufficient water to cover them, and add the bay-leaf, ham, cayenne, and mace; be careful to keep the lid closely shut, and simmer them until tender. Take them out and drain thoroughly; rub them through a tammy or sieve (an old one does for the purpose) with a wooden spoon, and put them to 1/2 pint of Béchamel; keep stirring over the fire until it boils, when serve. If it should require any more seasoning, add it to taste.

Pickled Onions

Ingredients.-1 gallon of pickling onions, salt and water, milk; to each 1/2 gallon of vinegar, 1 oz. of bruised ginger, 1/4 teaspoonful of cayenne, 1 oz. of allspice, 1 oz. of whole black pepper, 1/4 oz. of whole nutmeg bruised, 8 cloves, 1/4 oz. of mace.

Mode.-Gather the onions, which should not be too small, when they are quite dry and ripe; wipe off the dirt, but do not pare them; make a strong solution of salt and water, into which put the onions, and change this, morning and night, for 3 days, and save the last brine they were put in. Then take the outside skin off, and put them into a tin saucepan capable of holding them all, as they are always better done together. Now take equal quantities of milk and the last salt and water the onions were in, and pour this to them; to this add 2 large spoonfuls of salt, put them over the fire, and watch them very attentively. Keep constantly turning the onions about with a wooden skimmer, those at the bottom to the top, and vice versâ; and let the milk and water run through the holes of the skimmer. Remember, the onions must never boil, or, if they do, they will be good for nothing; and they should be quite transparent.

Keep the onions stirred for a few minutes, and, in stirring them, be particular not to break them. Then have ready a pan with a colander, into which turn the onions to drain, covering them with a cloth to keep in the steam. Place on a table an old cloth, 2 or 3 times double; put the onions on it when quite hot, and over them an old piece of blanket; cover this closely over them, to keep in the steam. Let them remain till the next day, when they will be quite cold, and look yellow and shrivelled; take off the shrivelled skins, when they should be as white as snow.

Put them in a pan, make a pickle of vinegar and the remaining ingredients, boil all these up, and pour hot over the onions in the pan. Cover very closely to keep in all the steam, and let them stand till the following day, when they will be quite cold. Put them into jars or bottles well bunged, and a tablespoonful of the best olive-oil on the top of each jar or bottle. Tie them down with bladder, and let them stand in a cool place for a month or six weeks, when they will be fit for use. They should be beautifully white, and eat crisp, without the least softness, and will keep good many months.

Pickled Red Cabbage

Ingredients.-Red cabbages, salt and water; to each quart of vinegar, 1/2 oz. of ginger well bruised, 1 oz. of whole black pepper, and, when liked, a little cayenne.

Mode.-Take off the outside decayed leaves of a nice red cabbage, cut it in quarters, remove the stalks, and cut it across in very thin slices. Lay these on a dish, and strew them plentifully with salt, covering them with another dish. Let them remain for 24 hours, turn into a colander to drain, and, if necessary, wipe lightly with a clean soft cloth. Put them in a jar; boil up the vinegar with spices in the above proportion, and, when cold, pour it over the cabbage. It will be fit for use in a week or two, and, if kept for a very long time, the cabbage is liable get soft and to discolour. To be really nice and crisp, and of a good red colour, it should be eaten almost immediately after it is made. A little bruised cochineal boiled with the vinegar adds much to the appearance of this pickle. Tie down with bladder, and keep in a dry place.

Pickled Walnuts

Ingredients.-100 walnuts, salt and water. To each quart of vinegar allow 2 oz. of whole black pepper, 1 oz. of allspice, 1 oz. of bruised ginger.

Mode.-Procure the walnuts while young; be careful they are not woody, and prick them well with a fork; prepare a strong brine of salt and water (4 lbs. of salt to each gallon of water), into which put the walnuts, letting them remain 9 days, and changing the brine every third day; drain them off, put them on a dish, place it in the sun until they become perfectly black, which will be in 2 or 3 days; have ready dry jars, into which place the walnuts, and do not quite fill the jars. Boil sufficient vinegar to cover them, for 10 minutes, with spices in the above proportion, and pour it hot over the walnuts, which must be quite covered with the pickle; tie down with bladder, and keep in a dry place. They will be fit for use in a month, and will keep good 2 or 3 years.

7

Production of Dishes from Milk, Butter, Cheese and Eggs

Milk is obtained only from the class of animals called Mammalia, and is intended by Nature for the nourishment of their young. The milk of each animal is distinguished by some peculiarities; but as that of the cow is by far the most useful to us in this part of the world, our observations will be confined to that variety. Milk, when drawn from the cow, is of a yellowish-white colour, and is the most yellow at the beginning of the period of lactation. Its taste is agreeable, and rather saccharine. The viscidity and specific gravity of milk are somewhat greater than that of water; but these properties vary somewhat in the milk procured from different individuals.

Milk which is carried to a considerable distance, so as to be much agitated, and cooled before it is put into pans to settle for cream, never throws up so much, nor such rich cream, as if the same milk had been put into pans directly after it was milked. Milk, considered as an aliment, is of such importance in domestic economy as to render all the improvements in its production extremely valuable. To enlarge upon the antiquity of its use is unnecessary; it has always been a favourite food in Britain. Although milk in its natural state be a fluid, yet, considered as an aliment, it is both solid and fluid: for no sooner does it enter the stomach, than it is coagulated by the gastric juice, and separated into curd and whey, the first of these being extremely nutritive.

Milk of the human subject is much thinner than cow's milk; Ass's milk comes the nearest to human milk of any other; Goat's milk is something thicker and richer than cow's milk; Ewe's milk has the appearance of cow's milk, and affords a larger quantity of cream; Mare's milk contains more sugar than that of the ewe; Camel's milk is used only in Africa; Buffalo's milk is employed in India.

From no other substance, solid or fluid, can so great a number of distinct kinds of aliment be prepared as from milk; some forming food, others drink; some of them delicious, and deserving the name of luxuries; all of them wholesome, and some medicinal: indeed, the variety of aliments that seems capable of being produced from milk, appears to be quite endless. In every age this must have been a subject for experiment, and every nation has added to the number by the invention of some peculiarity of its own.

Beckman, in his "History of Inventions," states that butter was not used either by the Greeks or Romans in cooking, nor was it brought upon their tables at certain meals, as is the custom at present. In England it has been made from time immemorial, though the art of making cheese is said not to have been known to the ancient Britons, and to have been learned from their conquerors. The taste of butter is peculiar, and very unlike any other fatty substance. It is extremely agreeable when of the best quality; but its flavour depends much upon the food given to the cows: to be good, it should not adhere to the knife.

Butter, with regard to its dietetic properties, may be regarded nearly in the light of vegetable oils and animal fats; but it becomes sooner rancid than most other fat oils. When fresh, it cannot but be considered as very wholesome; but it should be quite free from rancidity. If slightly salted when it is fresh, its wholesomeness is probably not at all impaired; but should it begin to turn rancid, salting will not correct its unwholesomeness. When salt butter is put into casks, the upper part next the air is very apt to become rancid, and this rancidity is also liable to affect the whole cask.

Cheese is the curd formed from milk by artificial coagulation, pressed and dried for use. Curd, called also casein and caseous matter, or the basis of cheese, exists in the milk, and not in the cream, and requires only to be separated by coagulation. The coagulation, however, supposes some alteration of the curd. By means of the substance employed to coagulate it, it is rendered insoluble in water. When the curd is freed from the whey, kneaded and pressed to expel it entirely, it becomes cheese. This assumes a degree of transparency, and possesses many of the properties of coagulated albumen. If it be well dried, it does not change by exposure to the air; but if it contain moisture, it soon putrefies. It therefore requires some salt to preserve it, and this acts likewise as a kind of seasoning. All our cheese is coloured more or less, except that made from skim milk. The colouring substances employed are arnatto, turmeric, or marigold, all perfectly harmless unless they are adulterated; and it is said that arnatto sometimes contains red lead.

There is only one opinion as to the nutritive properties of eggs, although the qualities of those belonging to different birds vary somewhat. Those of the common hen are most esteemed as delicate food, particularly when "new-laid." The quality of eggs depends much upon the food given to the hen. Eggs in general are considered most easily digestible when little subjected to the art of cookery. The lightest way of dressing them is by poaching, which is effected by putting them for a minute or two into brisk boiling water: this coagulates the external white, without doing the inner part too much.

Eggs are much better when new-laid than a day or two afterwards. The usual time allotted for boiling eggs in the shell is 3 to 3-3/4 minutes: less time than that in boiling water will not be sufficient to solidify the white, and more will make the yolk hard and less digestible: it is very difficult to guess accurately as to the time. Great care should be employed in putting them into the water, to prevent cracking the shell, which inevitably causes a portion of the white to exude, and lets water into the egg. Eggs are often beaten up raw in nutritive beverages.

Eggs are employed in a very great many articles of cookery, entrées, and entremets, and they form an essential ingredient in pastry, creams, flip, &c. It is particularly necessary that they should be quite fresh, as nothing is worse than stale eggs. Cobbett justly says, stale, or even preserved eggs, are things to be run from, not after. The Metropolis is supplied with eggs from all parts of the kingdom, and they are likewise largely imported from various places on the continent; as France, Holland, Belgium, Guernsey, and Jersey.

RECIPES FOR MILK, BUTTER, CHEESE AND EGGS.

Curds And Whey

Ingredients: A very small piece of rennet, 1/2 gallon of milk.

Mode: Procure from the butcher's a small piece of rennet, which is the stomach of the calf, taken as soon as it is killed, scoured, and well rubbed with salt, and stretched on sticks to dry. Pour some boiling water on the rennet, and let it remain for 6 hours; then use the liquor to turn the milk. The milk should be warm and fresh from the cow: if allowed to cool, it must be heated till it is of a degree quite equal to new milk; but do not let it be too hot. About a tablespoonful or rather more, would be sufficient to turn the above proportion of milk into curds and whey; and whilst the milk is turning, let it be kept in rather a warm place.

Devonshire Cream

The milk should stand 24 hours in the winter, half that time when the weather is very warm. The milkpan is then set on a stove, and should there remain until the milk is quite hot; but it must not boil, or there will be a thick skin on the surface. When it is sufficiently done, the undulations on the surface look thick, and small rings appear. The time required for scalding cream depends on the size of the pan and the heat of the fire; but the slower it is done, the better. The pan should be placed in the dairy when the cream is sufficiently scalded, and skimmed the following day. This cream is so much esteemed that it is sent to the London markets in small square tins, and is exceedingly delicious eaten with fresh fruit. In Devonshire, butter is made from this cream, and is usually very firm.

Devonshire Junket

Ingredients: To every pint of new milk allow 2 dessertspoonfuls of brandy, 1 dessertspoonful of sugar, and 1-1/2 dessertspoonful of prepared rennet; thick cream, pounded cinnamon, or grated nutmeg.

Mode: Make the milk blood-warm; put it into a deep dish with the brandy, sugar, and rennet; stir it altogether, and cover it over until it is set. Then spread some thick or clotted cream over the top, grate some nutmeg, and strew some sugar over, and the dish will be ready to serve.

Butter-Moulds

Butter-moulds, or wooden stamps for moulding fresh butter, are much used, and are made in a variety of forms and shapes. In using them, let them be kept scrupulously clean, and before the butter is pressed in, the interior should be well wetted with cold water; the butter must then be pressed in, the mould opened, and the perfect shape taken out. The butter may be then dished, and garnished with a wreath of parsley, if for a cheese course; if for breakfast, put it into an ornamental butter-dish, with a little water at the bottom, should the weather be very warm.

Curled Butter

Tie a strong cloth by two of the corners to an iron hook in the wall; make a knot with the other two ends, so that a stick might pass through. Put the butter into the cloth; twist it tightly over a dish, into which the butter will fall through the knot, so forming small and pretty little strings. The butter may then be garnished with parsley, if to serve with a cheese course; or it may be sent to table plain for breakfast, in an ornamental dish. Squirted butter for garnishing hams, salads, eggs, &c., is made by forming a piece of stiff paper in the shape of a cornet, and squeezing the butter in fine strings from the hole at the bottom. Scooped butter is made by dipping a teaspoon or scooper in warm water, and then scooping the butter quickly and thin. In warm weather, it would not be necessary to heat the spoon.

Fairy Butter

Ingredients: The yolks of 2 hard-boiled eggs, 1 tablespoonful of orange-flower water, 2 tablespoonfuls of pounded sugar, 1/4 lb. of good fresh butter.

Mode: Beat the yolks of the eggs smoothly in a mortar, with the orange-flower water and the sugar, until the whole is reduced to a fine paste; add the butter, and force all through an old but clean cloth by wringing the cloth and squeezing the butter very hard. The butter will then drop on the plate in large and small pieces, according to the holes in the cloth. Plain butter may be done in the same manner, and is very quickly prepared, besides having a very good effect.

Anchovy Butter.

Ingredients: To every lb. of butter allow 6 anchovies, 1 small bunch of parsley.

Mode: Wash, bone, and pound the anchovies well in a mortar; scald the parsley, chop it, and rub through a sieve; then pound all the ingredients together, mix well, and make the butter into pats immediately. This makes a pretty dish, if fancifully moulded, for breakfast or supper, and should be garnished with parsley.

Stilton Cheese

Stilton cheese, or British Parmesan, as it is sometimes called, is generally preferred to all other cheeses by those whose authority few will dispute. An artificial ripeness in Stilton cheese is sometimes produced by inserting a small piece of decayed Cheshire into an aperture at the top. From 3 weeks to a month is sufficient time to ripen the cheese. An additional flavour may also be obtained by scooping out a piece from the top, and pouring therein port, sherry, Madeira, or old ale, and letting the cheese absorb these for 2 or 3 weeks. But that cheese is the finest which is ripened without any artificial aid, is the opinion of those who are judges in these matters. In serving a Stilton cheese, the top of it should be cut off to form a lid, and a napkin or piece of white paper, with a frill at the top, pinned round. When the cheese goes from table, the lid should be replaced.

Cheese Sandwiches

Ingredients: Slices of brown bread-and-butter, thin slices of cheese.

Mode: Cut from a nice fat Cheshire, or any good rich cheese, some slices about 1/2 inch thick, and place them between some slices of brown bread-and-butter, like sandwiches. Place them on a plate in the oven, and, when the bread is toasted, serve on a napkin very hot and very quickly.

Cayenne Cheeses

Ingredients: 1/2 lb. of butter, 1/2 lb. of flour, 1/2 lb. of grated cheese, 1/3 teaspoonful of cayenne, 1/3 teaspoonful of salt; water.

Mode: Rub the butter in the flour; add the grated cheese, cayenne. and salt; and mix these ingredients well together. Moisten with sufficient water to make the whole into a paste; roll out, and cut into fingers about 4 inches in length. Bake them in a moderate oven a very light colour, and serve very hot.

Brillat Savarin's Fondue

Ingredients: Eggs, cheese, butter, pepper and salt.

Mode: Take the same number of eggs as there are guests; weigh the eggs in the shell, allow a third of their weight in Gruyère cheese, and a piece of butter one-sixth of the weight of the cheese. Break the eggs into a basin, beat them well; add the cheese, which should be grated, and the butter, which should be broken into small pieces.

Stir these ingredients together with a wooden spoon; put the mixture into a lined saucepan, place it over the fire, and stir until the substance is thick and soft. Put in a little salt, according to the age of the cheese, and a good sprinkling of pepper, and serve the fondue on a very hot silver or metal plate. Do not allow the fondue to remain on the fire after the mixture is set, as, if it boils, it will be entirely spoiled. Brillat Savarin recommends that some choice Burgundy should be handed round with this dish. We have given this recipe exactly as he recommends it to be made; but we have tried it with good Cheshire cheese, and found it answer remarkably well.

Pounded Cheese

Ingredients: To every lb. of cheese allow 3 oz. of fresh butter.

Mode: To pound cheese is an economical way of using it, if it has become dry; it is exceedingly good spread on bread, and is the best way of eating it for those whose digestion is weak. Cut up the cheese into small pieces, and pound it smoothly in a mortar, adding butter in the above proportion. Press it down into a jar, cover with clarified butter, and it will keep for several days. The flavour may be very much increased by adding mixed mustard (about a teaspoonful to every lb.), or cayenne, or pounded mace. Curry-powder is also not unfrequently mixed with it.

Pastry Ramakins

Ingredients: Any pieces of very good light puff-paste Cheshire, Parmesan, or Stilton cheese.

Mode: The remains or odd pieces of paste left from large tarts, &c. answer for making these little dishes. Gather up the pieces of paste, roll it out evenly, and sprinkle it with grated cheese of a nice flavour. Fold the paste in three, roll it out again, and sprinkle more cheese over; fold the paste, roll it out, and with a paste-cutter shape it in any way that may be desired. Bake the ramakins in a brisk oven from 10 to 15 minutes, dish them on a hot napkin, and serve quickly. The appearance of this dish may be very much improved by brushing the ramakins over with yolk of egg before they are placed in the oven. Where expense is not objected to, Parmesan is the best kind of cheese to use for making this dish.

Toasted Cheese, or Scotch Rare-Bit

Ingredients: A few slices of rich cheese, toast, mustard, and pepper.

Mode: Cut some nice rich sound cheese into rather thin slices; melt it in a cheese-toaster on a hot plate, or over steam, and, when melted, add a small quantity of mixed mustard and a seasoning of pepper; stir the cheese until it is completely dissolved, then brown it before the fire, or with a salamander. Fill the bottom of the cheese-toaster with hot water, and serve with dry or buttered toasts, whichever may be preferred. Our engraving illustrates a cheese-toaster with hot-water reservoir: the cheese is melted in the upper tin, which is placed in another vessel of boiling water, so keeping the preparation beautifully hot.

A small quantity of porter, or port wine, is sometimes mixed with the cheese; and, if it be not very rich, a few pieces of butter may be mixed with it to great advantage. Sometimes the melted cheese is spread on the toasts, and then laid in the cheese-dish at the top of the hot water. Whichever way it is served, it is highly necessary that the mixture be very hot, and very quickly sent to table, or it will be worthless.

Toasted Cheese, or Welsh Rare-Bit

Ingredients: Slices of bread, butter, Cheshire or Gloucester cheese, mustard, and pepper.

Mode: Cut the bread into slices about 1/2 inch in thickness; pare off the crust, toast the bread slightly without hardening or burning it, and spread it with butter. Cut some slices, not quite so large as the bread, from a good rich fat cheese; lay them on the toasted bread in a cheese-toaster; be careful that the cheese does not burn, and let it be equally melted. Spread over the top a little made mustard and a seasoning of pepper, and serve very hot, with very hot plates. To facilitate the melting of the cheese, it may be cut into thin flakes or toasted on one side before it is laid on the bread. As it is so essential to send this dish hot to table, it is a good plan to melt the cheese in small round silver or metal pans, and to send these pans to table, allowing one for each guest. Slices of dry or buttered toast should always accompany them, with mustard, pepper, and salt.

Scotch Woodcock

Ingredients: A few slices of hot buttered toast; allow 1 anchovy to each slice. For the sauce,—1/4 pint of cream, the yolks of 3 eggs.

Mode: Separate the yolks from the whites of the eggs; beat the former, stir to them the cream, and bring the sauce to the boiling-point, but do not allow it to boil, or it will curdle. Have ready some hot buttered toast, spread with anchovies pounded to a paste; pour a little of the hot sauce on the top, and serve very hot and very quickly.

Buttered Eggs

Ingredients: 4 new-laid eggs, 2 oz. of butter.

Mode: Procure the eggs new-laid if possible; break them into a basin, and beat them well; put the butter into another basin, which place in boiling water, and stir till the butter is melted. Pour that and the eggs into a lined saucepan; hold it over a gentle fire, and, as the mixture begins to warm, pour it two or three times into the basin, and back again, that the two ingredients may be well incorporated. Keep stirring the eggs and butter one way until they are hot, without boiling, and serve on hot buttered toast. If the mixture is allowed to boil, it will curdle, and so be entirely spoiled.

Fried Eggs

Ingredients: 4 eggs, 1/4 lb. of lard, butter or clarified dripping.

Mode: Place a delicately-clean frying-pan over a gentle fire; put in the fat, and allow it to come to the boiling-point. Break the eggs into cups, slip them into the boiling fat, and let them remain until the whites are delicately set; and, whilst they are frying, ladle a little of the fat over them. Take them up with a slice, drain them for a minute from their greasy moisture, trim them neatly, and serve on slices of fried bacon or ham; or the eggs may be placed in the middle of the dish, with the bacon put round as a garnish.

Oeufs Au Plat, or Au Miroir

Ingredients: 4 eggs, 1 oz. of butter, pepper and salt to taste.

Mode: Butter a dish rather thickly with good fresh butter; melt it, break the eggs into it the same as for poaching, sprinkle them with white pepper and fine salt, and put the remainder of the butter, cut into very small pieces, on the top of them. Put the dish on a hot plate, or in the oven, or before the fire, and let it remain until the whites become set, but not hard, when serve immediately, placing the dish they were cooked in on another. To hasten the cooking of the eggs, a salamander may be held over them for a minute; but great care must be taken that they are not too much done. This is an exceedingly nice dish, and one very easily prepared for breakfast.

Poached Eggs

Ingredients: Eggs, water. To every pint of water allow 1 tablespoonful of vinegar.

Mode: Eggs for poaching should be perfectly fresh, but not quite new-laid; those that are about 36 hours old are the best for the purpose. If quite new-laid, the white is so milky it is almost impossible to set it; and, on the other hand, if the egg be at all stale, it is equally difficult to poach it nicely. Strain some boiling water into a deep clean frying-pan; break the egg into a cup without damaging the yolk, and, when the water boils, remove the pan to the side of the fire, and gently slip the egg into it. Place the pan over a gentle fire, and keep the water simmering until the white looks nicely set, when the egg is ready. Take it up gently with a slice, cut away the ragged edges of the white, and serve either on toasted bread or on slices of ham or bacon, or on spinach, &c.

A poached egg should not be overdone, as its appearance and taste will be quite spoiled if the yolk be allowed to harden. When the egg is slipped into the water, the white should be gathered together, to keep it a little in form, or the cup should be turned over it for 1 minute. To poach an egg to perfection is rather a difficult operation; so, for inexperienced cooks, a tin egg-poacher may be purchased, which greatly facilitates this manner of dressing ecgs. Our illustration clearly shows what it is: it consists of a tin plate with a handle, with a space for three perforated cups. An egg should be broken into each cup, and the machine then placed in a stewpan of boiling water, which has been previously strained. When the whites of the eggs appear set, they are done, and should then be carefully slipped on to the toast or spinach, or with whatever they are served. In poaching eggs in a frying-pan, never do more than four at a time; and, when a little vinegar is liked mixed with the water in which the eggs are done, use the above proportion.

Poached Eggs, with Cream.

Ingredients: 1 pint of water, 1 teaspoonful of salt, 4 teaspoonfuls of vinegar, 4 fresh eggs, 1/2 gill of cream, salt, pepper, and pounded sugar to taste, 1 oz. of butter.

Mode: Put the water, vinegar, and salt into a frying-pan, and break each egg into a separate cup; bring the water, &c. to boil, and slip the eggs gently into it without breaking the yolks. Simmer them from 3 to 4 minutes, but not longer, and, with a slice, lift them out on to a hot dish, and trim the edges. Empty the pan of its contents, put in the cream, add a seasoning to taste of pepper, salt, and pounded sugar; bring the whole to the boiling-point; then add the butter, broken into small pieces; toss the pan round and round till the butter is melted; pour it over the eggs, and serve. To insure the eggs not being spoiled whilst the cream, &c., is preparing, it is a good plan to warm the cream with the butter, &c., before the eggs are poached, so that it may be poured over them immediately after they are dished.

8

Preserves, Confectionary, Ices and Dessert Dishes

All the means of preservation are put in practice occasionally for fruits and the various parts of vegetables, according to the nature of the species, the climate, the uses to which they are applied, &c. Some are dried, as nuts, raisins, sweet herbs, &c.; others are preserved by means of sugar, such as many fruits whose delicate juices would be lost by drying; some are preserved by means of vinegar, and chiefly used as condiments or pickles; a few also by salting, as French beans; while others are preserved in spirits. We have, however, in this place to treat of the best methods of preserving fruits.

Fruit is a most important item in the economy of health; the epicurean can scarcely be said to have any luxuries without it; therefore, as it is so invaluable, when we cannot have it fresh, we must have it preserved. It has long been a desideratum to preserve fruits by some cheap method, yet by such as would keep them fit for the various culinary purposes, as making tarts and other similar dishes.

The expense of preserving them with sugar is a serious objection; for, except the sugar is used in considerable quantities, the success is very uncertain. Sugar also overpowers and destroys the sub-acid taste so desirable in many fruits: these which are preserved in this manner are chiefly intended for the dessert.

Fruits intended for preservation should be gathered in the morning, in dry weather, with the morning sun upon them, if possible; they will then have their fullest flavour, and keep in good condition longer than when gathered at any other time. Until fruit can be used, it should be placed in the dairy, an ice-house, or a refrigerator. In an icehouse it will remain fresh and plump for several days. Fruit gathered in wet or foggy weather will soon be mildewed, and be of no service for preserves.

Having secured the first and most important contribution to the manufacture of preserves,-the fruit, the next consideration is the preparation of the syrup in which the fruit is to be suspended; and this requires much care. In the confectioner's art there is a great nicety in proportioning the degree of concentration of the syrup very exactly to each particular case; and they know this by signs, and express it by certain technical terms. But to distinguish these properly requires very great attention and considerable experience. The principal thing to be acquainted with is the fact, that, in proportion as the syrup is longer boiled, its water will become evaporated, and its consistency will be thicker. Great care must be taken in the management of the fire, that the syrup does not boil over, and that the boiling is not carried to such an extent as to burn the sugar.

The first degree of consistency is called the thread, which is subdivided into the little and great thread. If you dip the finger into the syrup and apply it to the thumb, the tenacity of the syrup will, on separating the finger and thumb, afford a thread, which shortly breaks: this is the little thread. If the thread, from the greater tenacity, and, consequently, greater strength of the syrup, admits of a greater extension of the finger and thumb, it is called the great thread. There are half a dozen other terms and experiments for testing the various thickness of the boiling sugar towards the consistency called caramel; but that degree of sugar-boiling belongs to the confectioner.

A solution of sugar prepared by dissolving two parts of double-refined sugar (the best sugar is the most economical for preserves) in one of water, and boiling this a little, affords a syrup of the right degree of strength, and which neither ferments nor crystallizes. This appears to be the degree called smooth by the confectioners, and is proper to be used for the purposes of preserves. The syrup employed should sometimes be clarified, which is done in the following manner:-Dissolve 2 lbs. of loaf sugar in a pint of water; add to this solution the white of an egg, and beat it well.

Put the preserving-pan upon the fire with the solution; stir it with a wooden spatula and, when it begins to swell and boil up, throw in some cold water or a little oil, to damp the boiling; for, as it rises suddenly, if it should boil over, it would take fire, being of a very inflammable nature. Let it boil up again; then take it off, and remove carefully the scum that has risen. Boil the solution again, throw in a little more cold water, remove the scum, and so on for three or four times successively; then strain it. It is considered to be sufficiently boiled when some taken up in a spoon pours out like oil.

Although sugar passes so easily into the state of fermentation, and is, in fact, the only substance capable of undergoing the vinous stage of that process, yet it will not ferment at all if the quantity be sufficient to constitute a very strong syrup: hence, syrups are used to preserve fruits and other vegetable substances from the changes they would undergo if left to themselves. Before sugar was in use, honey was employed to preserve many vegetable productions, though this substance has now given way to the juice of the sugar-cane.

The fruits that are the most fit for preservation in syrup are, apricots, peaches, nectarines, apples, greengages, plums of all kinds, and pears. As an example, take some apricots not too ripe, make a small slit at the stem end, and push out the stone; simmer them in water till they are softened and about half done, and afterwards throw them into cold water. When they have cooled, take them out and drain them. Put the apricots into the pie-serving-pan with sufficient syrup to cover them; let them boil up three or four times, and then skim them; remove them from the fire, pour them into an earthen pan, and let them cool till next day. Boil them up three days successively, skimming each time, and they will then be finished and in a state fit to be put into pots for use.

After each bailing, it is proper to examine into the state of the syrup when cold; if too thin, it will bear additional boiling; if too thick, it may be lowered with more syrup of the usual standard. The reason why the fruit is emptied out of the preserving-pan into an earthen pan is, that the acid of the fruit acts upon the copper, of which the preserving-pans are usually made. From this example the process of preserving fruits by syrup will be easily comprehended. The first object is to soften the fruit by blanching or boiling it in water, in order that the syrup by which it is preserved may penetrate through its substance.

Many fruits, when preserved by boiling, lose much of their peculiar and delicate flavour, as, for instance, pine-apples; and this inconvenience may, in some instances, be remedied by preserving them without heat. Cut the fruit in slices about one fifth of an inch thick, strew powdered loaf sugar an eighth of an inch thick on the bottom of a jar, and put the slices on it. Put more sugar on this, and then another layer of the slices, and so on till the jar is full. Place the jar with the fruit up to the neck in boiling water, and keep it there till the sugar is completely dissolved, which may take half an hour, removing the scum as it rises. Lastly, tie a wet bladder over the mouth of the jar, or cork and wax it.

Any of the fruits that have been preserved in syrup may be converted into dry preserves, by first draining them from the syrup, and then drying them in a stove or very moderate oven, adding to them a quantity of powdered loaf sugar, which will gradually penetrate the fruit, while the fluid parts of the syrup gently evaporate. They should be dried in the stove or oven on a sieve, and turned every six or eight hours, fresh powdered sugar being sifted over them every time they are turned. Afterwards, they are to be kept in a dry situation, in drawers or boxes. Currants and cherries preserved whole in this manner, in bunches, are extremely elegant, and have a fine flavour. In this way it is, also, that orange and lemon chips are preserved.

Marmalades, jams, and fruit pastes are of the same nature, and are now in very general request. They are prepared without difficulty, by attending to a very few directions; they are somewhat expensive, but may be kept without spoiling for a considerable time. Marmalades and jams differ little from each other: they are preserves of a half-liquid consistency, made by boiling the pulp of fruits, and sometimes part of the rinds, with sugar. The appellation of marmalade is applied to those confitures which are composed of the firmer fruits, as pineapples or the rinds of oranges; whereas jams are made of the more juicy berries, such as strawberries, raspberries, currants, mulberries, &c.

Fruit pastes are a kind of marmalades, consisting of the pulp of fruits, first evaporated to a proper consistency, and afterwards boiled with sugar. The mixture is then poured into a mould, or spread on sheets of tin, and subsequently dried in the oven or stove till it has acquired the state of a paste. From a sheet of this paste, strips may be cut and formed into any shape that may be desired, as knots, rings, &c. Jams require the same care and attention in the boiling as marmalade; the slightest degree of burning communicates a disagreeable empyreumatic taste, and if they are not boiled sufficiently, they will not keep. That they may keep, it is necessary not to be sparing of sugar. In all the operations for preserve-making, when the preserving-pan is used, it should not be placed on the fire, but on a trivet, unless the jam is made on a hot plate, when this is not necessary. If the pan is placed close on to the fire, the preserve is very liable to burn, and the colour and flavour be consequently spoiled.

Fruit jellies are compounds of the juices of fruits combined with sugar, concentrated, by boiling, to such a consistency that the liquid, upon cooling, assumes the form of a tremulous jelly. Before fruits are candied, they must first be boiled in syrup, after which they are taken out and dried on a stove, or before the fire; the syrup is then to be concentrated, or boiled to a candy height, and the fruit dipped in it, and again laid on the stove to dry and candy: they are then to be put into boxes, and kept dry. Conserves consist of fresh vegetable matters beat into a uniform mass with refined sugar, and they are intended to preserve the virtues and properties of recent flowers, leaves, roots, peels, or fruits, unaltered, and as near as possible to what they were when fresh gathered, and to give them an agreeable taste.

CONFECTIONARY

In speaking of confectionary, it should be remarked that all the various preparations above named come, strictly speaking, under that head; for the various fruits, flowers, herbs, roots, and juices, which, when boiled with sugar, were formerly employed in pharmacy as well as for sweetmeats, were called confections, from the Latin word conficere, 'to make up;' but the term confectionary embraces a very large class indeed of sweet food, many kinds of which should not be attempted in the ordinary cuisine. The thousand and one ornamental dishes that adorn the tables of the wealthy should be purchased from the confectioner: they cannot profitably be made at home. Apart from these, cakes, biscuits, and tarts, &c., the class of sweetmeats called confections may be thus classified:

1. Liquid confects, or fruits either whole or in pieces, preserved by being immersed in a fluid transparent syrup; as the liquid confects of apricots, green citrons, and many foreign fruits.
2. Dry confects are those which, after having been boiled in the syrup, are taken out and put to dry in an oven, as citron and orange-peel, &c.
3. Marmalade, jams, and pastes, a kind of soft compounds made of the pulp of fruits or other vegetable substances, beat up with sugar or honey; such as oranges, apricots, pears, &c.
4. Jellies are the juices of fruits boiled with sugar to a pretty thick consistency, so as, upon cooling, to form a trembling jelly; as currant, gooseberry, apple jelly, &c.
5. Conserves are a kind of dry confects, made by beating up flowers, fruits, &c., with sugar, not dissolved.
6. Candies are fruits candied over with sugar after having been boiled in the syrup.

Dessert Dishes

With moderns the dessert is not so profuse, nor does it hold the same relationship to the dinner that it held with the ancients,-the Romans more especially. On ivory tables they would spread hundreds of different kinds of raw, cooked, and preserved fruits, tarts and cakes, as substitutes for the more substantial comestibles with which the guests were satiated. The dessert certainly repays, in its general effect, the expenditure upon it of much pains; and it may be said, that if there be any poetry at all in meals, or the process of feeding, there is poetry in the dessert, the materials for which should be selected with taste, and, of course, must depend, in a great measure, upon the season.

The shape of the dishes varies at different periods, the prevailing fashion at present being oval and circular dishes on stems. The patterns and colours are also subject to changes of fashion; some persons selecting china, chaste in pattern and colour; others, elegantly-shaped glass dishes on stems, with gilt edges. The beauty of the dessert services at the tables of the wealthy tends to enhance the splendour of the plate. The general mode of putting a dessert on table, now the elegant tazzas are fashionable, is, to place them down the middle of the table, a tall and short dish alternately; the fresh fruits being arranged on the tall dishes, and dried fruits, bon-bons, &c., on small round or oval glass plates.

The garnishing needs especial attention, as the contrast of the brilliant-coloured fruits with nicely-arranged foliage is very charming. The garnish par excellence for dessert is the ice-plant; its crystallized dewdrops producing a marvellous effect in the height of summer, giving a most inviting sense of coolness to the fruit it encircles. The double-edged mallow, strawberry, and vine leaves have a pleasing effect; and for winter desserts, the bay, cuba, and laurel are sometimes used. In town, the expense and difficulty of obtaining natural foliage is great, but paper and composite leaves are to be purchased at an almost nominal price.

Mixed fruits of the larger sort are now frequently served on one dish. This mode admits of the display of much taste in the arrangement of the fruit: for instance, a pine in the centre of the dish, surrounded with large plums of various sorts and colours, mixed with pears, rosy-cheeked apples, all arranged with a due regard to colour, have a very good effect. Again, apples and pears look well mingled with plums and grapes, hanging from the border of the dish in a négligé sort of manner, with a large bunch of the same fruit lying on the top of the apples. A dessert would not now be considered complete without candied and preserved fruits and confections. The candied fruits may be purchased at a less cost than they can be manufactured at home.

Ices

Ices are composed, it is scarcely necessary to say, of congealed cream or water, combined sometimes with liqueurs or other flavouring ingredients, or more generally with the juices of fruits. At desserts, or at some evening parties, ices are scarcely to be dispensed with. The principal utensils required for making ice-creams are ice-tubs, freezing-pots, spaddles, and a cellaret. The tub must be large enough to contain about a bushel of ice, pounded small, when brought out of the ice-house, and mixed very carefully with either salt, nitre, or soda. The freezing-pot is best made of pewter. If it be of tin, as is sometimes the case, the congelation goes on too rapidly in it for the thorough intermingling of its contents, on which the excellence of the ice greatly depends. The spaddle is generally made of copper, kept bright and clean. The cellaret is a tin vessel, in which ices are kept for a short time from dissolving. The method to be pursued in the freezing process must be attended to.

When the ice-tub is prepared with fresh-pounded ice and salt, the freezing-pot is put into it up to its cover. The articles to be congealed are then poured into it and covered over; but to prevent the ingredients from separating and the heaviest of them from falling to the bottom of the mould, it is requisite to turn the freezing-pot round and round by the handle, so as to keep its contents moving until the congelation commences. As soon as this is perceived (the cover of the pot being occasionally taken off for the purpose of noticing when freezing takes place), the cover is immediately closed over it, ice is put upon it, and it is left in this state till it is served.

The use of the spaddle is to stir up and remove from the sides of the freezing pot the cream, which in the shaking may have washed against it, and by stirring it in with the rest, to prevent waste of it occurring. Any negligence in stirring the contents of the freezing-pot before congelation takes place, will destroy the whole: either the sugar sinks to the bottom and leaves the ice insufficiently sweetened, or lumps are formed, which disfigure and discolour it.

Recipes For Preserves, Confectionary, Etc.

To Make Syrup For Compotes, &c.

Ingredients: To every lb. of sugar allow 1-1/2 pint of water.

Mode: Boil the sugar and water together for 1/4 hour, carefully removing the scum as it rises: the syrup is then ready for the fruit. The articles boiled in this syrup will not keep for any length of time, it being suitable only for dishes intended to be eaten immediately. A larger proportion of sugar must be added for a syrup intended to keep.

To Clarify Sugar Or Syrup.

Ingredients: To every lb. of sugar allow 1/2 pint of water and 1/2 the white of an egg.

Mode: Put the sugar, water, and the white of the egg, which should, be well beaten, into a preserving-pan or lined saucepan; and do not put it on the fire till the sugar is dissolved. Then place it on the fire, and when it boils, throw in a teacupful of cold water, and do not stir the sugar after this is added. Bring it to the boiling-point again, and then place the pan by the side of the fire, for the preparation to settle. Remove all the scum, and the sugar will be ready for use. The scum should be placed on a sieve, so that what syrup runs from it may be boiled up again: this must also be well skimmed.

Apple Jam.

Ingredients: To every lb. of fruit weighed after being pared, cored, and sliced, allow 3/4 lb. of preserving-sugar, the grated rind of 1 lemon, the juice of 1/2 lemon.

Mode: Peel the apples, core and slice them very thin, and be particular that they are all the same sort. Put them into a jar, stand this in a saucepan of boiling water, and let the apples stew until quite tender. Previously to putting the fruit into the jar, weigh it, to ascertain the proportion of sugar that may be required. Put the apples into a preserving-pan, crush the sugar to small lumps, and add it, with the grated lemon-rind and juice, to the apples. Simmer these over the fire for 1/2 hour, reckoning from the time the jam begins to simmer properly; remove the scum as it rises, and when the jam is done, put it into pots for use. Place a piece of oiled paper over the jam, and to exclude the air, cover the pots with tissue-paper dipped in the white of an egg, and stretched over the top. This jam will keep good for a long time.

Apple Jelly.

Ingredients: To 6 lbs. of apples allow 3 pints of water; to every quart of juice allow 2 lbs. of loaf sugar;-- the juice of 1/2 lemon.

Mode: Pare, core, and cut the apples into slices, and put them into a jar, with water in the above proportion. Place them in a cool oven, with the jar well covered, and when the juice is thoroughly drawn and the apples are quite soft, strain them through a jelly-bag. To every quart of juice allow 2 lbs. of loaf sugar, which should be crushed to small lumps, and put into a preserving-pan with the juice. Boil these together for rather more than 1/2 hour, remove the scum as it rises, add the lemon-juice just before it is done, and put the jelly into pots for use. This preparation is useful for garnishing sweet dishes, and may be turned out for dessert.

Apricot Jam Or Marmalade

Ingredients: To every lb. of ripe apricots, weighed after being skinned and stoned, allow 1 lb. of sugar.

Mode: Pare the apricots, which should be ripe, as thinly as possible, break them in half, and remove the stones. Weigh the fruit, and to every lb. allow the same proportion of loaf sugar. Pound the sugar very finely in a mortar, strew it over the apricots, which should be placed on dishes, and let them remain for 12 hours. Break the stones, blanch the kernels, and put them with the sugar and fruit into a preserving-pan. Let these simmer very gently until clear; take out the pieces of apricot singly as they become so, and, as fast as the scum rises, carefully remove it. Put the apricots into small jars, pour over them the syrup and kernels, cover the jam with pieces of paper dipped in the purest salad-oil, and stretch over the top of the jars tissue-paper, cut about 2 inches larger and brushed over with the white of an egg: when dry, it will be perfectly hard and air-tight.

To Make Barley-Sugar.

Ingredients: To every lb. of sugar allow 1/2 pint of water, 1/2 the white of an egg.

Mode: Put the sugar into a well-tinned saucepan, with the water, and, when the former is dissolved, set it over a moderate fire, adding the well-beaten egg before the mixture gets warm, and stir it well together. When it boils, remove the scum as it rises, and keep it boiling until no more appears, and the syrup looks perfectly clear; then strain it through a fine sieve or muslin bag, and put it back into the saucepan. Boil it again like caramel, until it is brittle, when a little is dropped in a basin of cold water: it is then sufficiently boiled. Add a little lemon-juice and a few drops of essence of lemon, and let it stand for a minute or two. Have ready a marble slab or large dish, rubbed over with salad-oil; pour on it the sugar, and cut it into strips with a pair of scissors: these strips should then be twisted, and the barley-sugar stored away in a very dry place. It may be formed into lozenges or drops, by dropping the sugar in a very small quantity at a time on to the oiled slab or dish.

Carrot Jam to Imitate Apricot Preserve.

Ingredients: Carrots; to every lb. of carrot pulp allow 1 lb. of pounded sugar, the grated rind of 1 lemon, the strained juice of 2, 6 chopped bitter almonds, 2 tablespoonfuls of brandy.

Mode: Select young carrots; wash and scrape them clean, cut them into round pieces, put them into a saucepan with sufficient water to cover them, and let them simmer until perfectly soft; then beat them through a sieve. Weigh the pulp, and to every lb. allow the above ingredients. Put the pulp into a preserving-pan with the sugar, and let this boil for 5 minutes, stirring and skimming all the time. When cold, add the lemon-rind and juice, almonds and brandy; mix these well with the jam; then put it into pots, which must be well covered and kept in a dry place. The brandy may be omitted, but the preserve will then not keep: with the brandy it will remain good for months.

To Make Cherry Brandy

Ingredients: Morella cherries, good brandy; to every lb. of cherries allow 3 oz. of pounded sugar.

Mode: Have ready some glass bottles, which must be perfectly dry. Ascertain that the cherries are not too ripe and are freshly gathered, and cut off about half of the stalks. Put them into the bottles, with the above proportion of sugar to every lb. of fruit; strew this in between the cherries, and, when the bottles are nearly full, pour in sufficient brandy to reach just below the cork. A few peach or apricot kernels will add much to their flavour, or a few blanched bitter almonds. Put corks or bungs into the bottles, tie over them a piece of bladder, and store away in a dry place. The cherries will be fit to eat in 2 or 3 months, and will remain good for years. They are liable to shrivel and become tough if too much sugar be added to them.

Black-Currant Jelly

Ingredients: Black currants; to every pint of juice allow 1/4 pint of water, 1 lb. of loaf sugar.

Mode: Strip the currants from the stalks, which may be done in an expeditious manner, by holding the bunch in one hand, and passing a small silver fork down the currants: they will then readily fall from the stalks. Put them into a jar, place this jar in a saucepan of boiling water, and simmer them until their juice is extracted; then strain them, and to every pint of juice allow the above proportion of sugar and water; stir these ingredients together cold until the sugar is dissolved; place the preserving-pan on the fire, and boil the jelly for about 1/2 hour, reckoning from the time it commences to boil all over, and carefully remove the scum as it rises.

If the jelly becomes firm when a little is put on a plate, it is done; it should then be put into small pots, and covered the same as the jam in the preceding recipe. If the jelly is wanted very clear, the fruit should not be squeezed dry; but, of course, so much juice will not be obtained. If the fruit is not much squeezed, it may be converted into a jam for immediate eating, by boiling it with a little common sugar: this answers very well for a nursery preserve.

Red-Currant Jam

Ingredients: To every lb. of fruit allow 3/4 lb. of loaf sugar.

Mode: Let the fruit be gathered on a fine day; weigh it, and then strip the currants from the stalks; put them into a preserving-pan with sugar in the above proportion; stir them, and boil them for about 3/4 hour. Carefully remove the scum as it rises. Put the jam into pots, and, when cold, cover with oiled papers; over these put a piece of tissue-paper brushed over on both sides with the white of an egg; press the paper round the top of the pot, and, when dry, the covering will be quite hard and air-tight.

Red-Currant Jelly.

Ingredients: Red currants; to every pint of juice allow 3/4 lb. of loaf sugar.

Mode: Have the fruit gathered in fine weather; pick it from the stalks, put it into a jar, and place this jar in a saucepan of boiling water over the fire, and let it simmer gently until the juice is well drawn from the currants; then strain them through a jelly-bag or fine cloth, and, if the jelly is wished very clear, do not squeeze them too much, as the skin and pulp from the fruit will be pressed through with the juice, and so make the jelly muddy. Measure the juice, and to each pint allow 3/4 lb. of loaf sugar; put these into a preserving-pan, set it over the fire, and keep stirring the jelly until it is done, carefully removing every particle of scum as it rises, using a wooden or silver spoon for the purpose, as metal or iron ones would spoil the colour of the jelly when it has boiled from 20 minutes to 1/2 hour, put a little of the jelly on a plate, and if firm when cool, it is done.

Take it off the fire, pour it into small gallipots, cover each of the pots with an oiled paper, and then with a piece of tissue-paper brushed over on both sides with the white of an egg. Label the pots, adding the year when the jelly was made, and store it away in a dry place. A jam may be made with the currants, if they are not squeezed too dry, by adding a few fresh raspberries, and boiling all together, with sufficient sugar to sweeten it nicely. As this preserve is not worth storing away, but is only for immediate eating, a smaller proportion of sugar than usual will be found enough: it answers very well for children's puddings, or for a nursery preserve.

White-Currant Jelly

Ingredients: White currants; to every pint of juice allow 3/4 lb. of good loaf sugar.

Mode: Pick the currants from the stalks, and put them into a jar; place this jar in a saucepan of boiling water, and simmer until the juice is well drawn from the fruit, which will be in from 3/4 to 1 hour. Then strain the currants through a fine cloth or jelly-bag; do not squeeze them too much, or the jelly will not be clear, and put the juice into a very clean preserving-pan, with the sugar. Let this simmer gently over a clear fire until it is firm, and keep stirring and skimming until it is done; then pour it into small pots, cover them, and store away in a dry place.

Preserve of Damsons

Ingredients: To every quart of damsons allow 1/2 lb. of loaf sugar.

Mode: Put the damsons (which should be picked from the stalks and quite free from blemishes) into a jar, with pounded sugar sprinkled amongst them in the above proportion; tie the jar closely down, set it in a saucepan of cold water; bring it gradually to boil, and simmer gently until the damsons are soft, without being broken. Let them stand till cold; then strain the juice from them, boil it up well, strain it through a jelly-bag, and pour it over the fruit. Let it cool, cover with oiled papers, and the jars with tissue-paper brushed over on both sides with the white of an egg, and store away in a dry cool place.

To Preserve any kind of Plums

Ingredients: Damsons or plums; boiling water.

Mode: Pick the fruit into clean dry stone jars, taking care to leave out all that are broken or blemished. When full, pour boiling water on the plums, until it stands one inch above the fruit; cut a piece of paper to fit the inside of the jar, over which pour melted mutton-suet; cover down with brown paper, and keep the jars in a dry cool place. When used, the suet should be removed, the water poured off, and the jelly at the bottom of the jar used and mixed with the fruit.

To Bottle Fresh Fruit.

Ingredients: Fresh fruits, such as currants, raspberries, cherries, gooseberries, plums of all kinds, damsons, &c.; wide-mouthed glass bottles, new corks to fit them tightly.

Mode: Let the fruit be full grown, but not too ripe, and gathered in dry weather. Pick it off the stalks without bruising or breaking the skin, and reject any that is at all blemished: if gathered in the damp, or if the skins are cut at all, the fruit will mould. Have ready some perfectly dry glass bottles, and some nice new soft corks or bungs; burn a match in each bottle, to exhaust the air, and quickly place the fruit in to be preserved; gently cork the bottles, and put them into a very cool oven, where let them remain until the fruit has shrunk away a fourth part. Then take the bottles out; do not open them, but immediately beat the corks in tight, cut off the tops, and cover them with melted resin. If kept in a dry place, the fruit will remain good for months; and on this principally depends the success of the preparation; for if stored away in a place that is in the least damp, the fruit will soon spoil.

White or Green Gooseberry Jam

Ingredients: Equal weight of fruit and sugar.

Mode: Select the gooseberries not very ripe, either white or green, and top and tail them. Boil the sugar with water (allowing 1/2 pint to every lb.) for about 1/4 hour, carefully removing the scum as it rises; then put in the gooseberries, and simmer gently till clear and firm: try a little of the jam on a plate; if it jellies when cold, it is done, and should then be poured into pots. When cold, cover with oiled paper, and tissue-paper brushed over on both sides with the unbeaten white of an egg, and store away in a dry place.

Greengage Jam

Ingredients: To every lb. of fruit, weighed before being stoned, allow 3/4 lb. of lump sugar.

Mode: Divide the greengages, take out the stones, and put them into a preserving-pan. Bring the fruit to a boil, then add the sugar, and keep stirring it over a gentle fire until it is melted. Remove all the scum as it rises, and, just before the jam is done, boil it rapidly for 5 minutes. To ascertain when it is sufficiently boiled, pour a little on a plate, and if the syrup thickens and appears firm, it is done. Have ready half the kernels blanched; put them into the jam, give them one boil, and pour the preserve into pots. When cold, cover down with oiled papers, and, over these, tissue-paper brushed over on both sides with the white of an egg.

To Preserve and Dry Greengages

Ingredients: To every lb. of sugar allow 1 lb. of fruit, 1/4 pint of water.

Mode.-For this purpose, the fruit must be used before it is quite ripe, and part of the stalk must be left on. Weigh the fruit, rejecting all that is in the least degree blemished, and put it into a lined saucepan with the sugar and water, which should have been previously boiled together to a rich syrup. Boil the fruit in this for 10 minutes, remove it from the fire, and drain the greengages. The next day, boil up the syrup and put in the fruit again, and let it simmer for 3 minutes, and drain the syrup away. Continue this process for 5 or 6 days, and the last time place the greengages, when drained, on a hair sieve, and put them in an oven or warm spot to dry; keep them in a box, with paper between each layer, in a place free from damp.

Preserved Greengages In Syrup

Ingredients: To every lb. of fruit allow 1 lb. of loaf sugar 1/4 pint of water.

Mode: Boil the sugar and water together for about 10 minutes; divide the greengages, take out the stones, put the fruit into the syrup, and let it simmer gently until nearly tender. Take it off the fire, put it into a large pan, and, the next day, boil it up again for about 10 minutes with the kernels from the stones, which should be blanched. Put the fruit carefully into jars, pour over it the syrup, and, when cold, cover down, so that the air is quite excluded. Let the syrup be well skimmed both the first and second day of boiling, otherwise it will not be clear.

Iced Currants

Ingredients: 1/4 pint of water, the whites of 2 eggs, currants, pounded sugar.

Mode: Select very fine bunches of red or white currants, and well beat the whites of the eggs. Mix these with the water; then take the currants, a bunch at a time, and dip them in; let them drain for a minute or two, and roll them in very fine pounded sugar. Lay them to dry on paper, when the sugar will crystallize round each currant, and have a very pretty effect. All fresh fruit may be prepared in the same manner; and a mixture of various fruits iced in this manner, and arranged on one dish, looks very well for a summer dessert.

Preserved Mulberries

Ingredients: To 2 lbs. of fruit and 1 pint of juice allow 2-1/2 lbs. of loaf sugar.

Mode: Put some of the fruit into a preserving-pan, and simmer it gently until the juice is well drawn. Strain it through a bag, measure it, and to every pint allow the above proportion of sugar and fruit. Put the sugar into the preserving-pan, moisten it with the juice, boil it up, skim well, and then add the mulberries, which should be ripe, but not soft enough to break to a pulp. Let them stand in the syrup till warm through, then set them on the fire to boil gently; when half done, turn them carefully into an earthen pan, and let them remain till the next day; then boil them as before, and when the syrup is thick, and becomes firm when cold, put the preserve into pots. In making this, care should be taken not to break the mulberries: this may be avoided by very gentle stirring, and by simmering the fruit very slowly.

Stewed Normandy Pippins

Ingredients: 1 lb. of Normandy pippins, 1 quart of water, 1/2 teaspoonful of powdered cinnamon, 1/2 teaspoonful of ground ginger, 1 lb. of moist sugar, 1 lemon.

Mode.-Well wash the pippins, and put them into 1 quart of water with the above proportion of cinnamon and ginger, and let them stand 12 hours; then put these all together into a stewpan, with the lemon sliced thinly, and half the moist sugar. Let them boil slowly until the pippins are half done; then add the remainder of the sugar, and simmer until they are quite tender. Serve on glass dishes for dessert.

Iced Oranges

Ingredients: Oranges; to every lb. of pounded loaf sugar allow the whites of 2 eggs.

Mode: Whisk the whites of the eggs well, stir in the sugar, and beat this mixture for 1/4 hour. Skin the oranges, remove as much of the white pith as possible without injuring the pulp of the fruit; pass a thread through the centre of each orange, dip them into the sugar, and tie them to a stick. Place this stick across the oven, and let the oranges remain until dry, when they will have the appearance of balls of ice. They make a pretty dessert or supper dish. Care must be taken not to have the oven too fierce, or the oranges would scorch and acquire a brown colour, which would entirely spoil their appearance.

Orange Marmalade

Ingredients: Equal weight of fine loaf sugar and Seville oranges; to 12 oranges allow 1 pint of water.

Mode: Let there be an equal weight of loaf sugar and Seville oranges, and allow the above proportion of water to every dozen oranges. Peel them carefully, remove a little of the white pith, and boil the rinds in water 2 hours, changing the water three times to take off a little of the bitter taste. Break the pulp into small pieces, take out all the pips, and cut the boiled rind into chips. Make a syrup with the sugar and water; boil this well, skim it, and, when clear, put in the pulp and chips. Boil all together from 20 minutes to 1/2 hour; pour it into pots, and, when cold, cover down with bladders or tissue-paper brushed over on both sides with the white of an egg. The juice and grated rind of 2 lemons to every dozen of oranges, added with the pulp and chips to the syrup, are a very great improvement to this marmalade.

Orange Marmalade Made With Honey

Ingredients: To 1 quart of the juice and pulp of Seville oranges allow 2 lbs. of honey, 1 lb. of the rind.

Mode: Peel the oranges and boil the rind in water until tender, and cut it into strips. Take away the pips from the juice and pulp, and put it with the honey and chips into a preserving-pan; boil all together for about 1/2 hour, or until the marmalade is of the proper consistency; put it into pots, and, when cold, cover down with bladders.

Orange Salad

Ingredients: 6 oranges, 1/4 lb. of muscatel raisins, 2 oz. of pounded sugar, 4 tablespoonfuls of brandy.

Mode: Peel 5 of the oranges; divide them into slices without breaking the pulp, and arrange them on a glass dish. Stone the raisins, mix them with the sugar and brandy, and mingle them with the oranges. Squeeze the juice of the other orange over the whole, and the dish is ready for table. A little pounded spice may be put in when the flavour is liked; but this ingredient must be added very sparingly.

Peaches Preserved In Brandy

Ingredients: To every lb. of fruit weighed before being stoned, allow 1/4 lb. of finely-pounded loaf sugar; brandy.

Mode: Let the fruit be gathered in dry weather; wipe and weigh it, and remove the stones as carefully as possible, without injuring the peaches much. Put them into a jar, sprinkle amongst them pounded loaf sugar in the above proportion, and pour brandy over the fruit. Cover the jar down closely, place it in a saucepan of boiling water over the fire, and bring the brandy to the simmering-point, but do not allow it to boil.

Take the fruit out carefully, without breaking it; put it into small jars, pour over it the brandy, and, when cold, exclude the air by covering the jars with bladders, or tissue-paper brushed over on both sides with the white of an egg. Apricots may be done in the same manner, and, if properly prepared, will be found delicious.

Baked Pears.

Ingredients: 12 pears, the rind of 1 lemon, 6 cloves, 10 whole allspice; to every pint of water allow 1/2 lb. of loaf sugar.

Mode: Pare and cut the pears into halves, and, should they be very large, into quarters; leave the stalks on, and carefully remove the cores. Place them in a clean baking-jar, with a closely-fitting lid; add to them the lemon-rind cut in strips, the juice of 1/2 lemon, the cloves, pounded allspice, and sufficient water just to cover the whole, with sugar in the above proportion. Cover the jar down closely, put it into a very cool oven, and bake the pears from 5 to 6 hours, but be very careful that the oven is not too hot. To improve the colour of the fruit, a few drops of prepared cochineal may be added; but this will not be found necessary if the pears are very gently baked.

Preserved Pears

Ingredients: Jargonelle pears; to every lb. of sugar allow 1/2 pint of water.

Mode: Procure some Jargonelle pears, not too ripe; put them into a stewpan with sufficient water to cover them, and simmer them till rather tender, but do not allow them to break; then put them into cold water. Boil the sugar and water together for 5 minutes, skim well, put in the pears, and simmer them gently for 5 minutes. Repeat the simmering for 3 successive days, taking care not to let the fruit break. The last time of boiling, the syrup should be made rather richer, and the fruit boiled for 10 minutes. When the pears are done, drain them from the syrup, and dry them in the sun, or in a cool oven; or they may be kept in the syrup, and dried as they are wanted.

Stewed Pears

Ingredients: 8 large pears, 5 oz. of loaf sugar, 6 cloves, 6 whole allspice, 1/2 pint of water, 1/4 pint of port wine, a few drops of prepared cochineal.

Mode: Pare the pears, halve them, remove the cores, and leave the stalks on; put them into a lined saucepan with the above ingredients, and let them simmer very gently until tender, which will be in from 3 to 4 hours, according to the quality of the pears. They should be watched, and, when done, carefully lifted out on to a glass dish without breaking them. Boil up the syrup quickly for 2 or 3 minutes; allow it to cool a little, pour it over the pears, and let them get perfectly cold. To improve the colour of the fruit, a few drops of prepared cochineal may be added, which rather enhances the beauty of this dish. The fruit must not be boiled fast, but only simmered, and watched that it be not too much done.

Pineapple Chips

Ingredients: Pineapples; sugar to taste.

Mode: Pare and slice the fruit thinly, put it on dishes, and strew over it plenty of pounded sugar. Keep it in a hot closet, or very slow oven, 8 or 10 days, and turn the fruit every day until dry; then put the pieces of pine on tins, and place them in a quick oven for 10 minutes. Let them cool, and store them away in dry boxes, with paper between each layer.

Preserved Pineapple

Ingredients: To every lb. of fruit, weighed after being pared, allow 1 lb. of loaf sugar; 1/4 pint of water.

Mode: The pines for making this preserve should be perfectly sound but ripe. Cut them into rather thick slices, as the fruit shrinks very much in the boiling. Pare off the rind carefully, that none of the pine be wasted; and, in doing so, notch it in and out, as the edge cannot be smoothly cut without great waste. Dissolve a portion of the sugar in a preserving-pan with 1/4 pint of water; when this is melted, gradually add the remainder of the sugar, and boil it until it forms a clear syrup, skimming well. As soon as this is the case, put in the pieces of pine, and boil well for at least 1/2 hour, or until it looks nearly transparent. Put it into pots, cover down when cold, and store away in a dry place.

Plum Jam

Ingredients: To every lb. of plums, weighed before being stoned, allow 3/4 lb. of loaf sugar.

Mode: In making plum jam, the quantity of sugar for each lb. of fruit must be regulated by the quality and size of the fruit, some plums requiring much more sugar than others. Divide the plums, take out the stones, and put them on to large dishes, with roughly-pounded sugar sprinkled over them in the above proportion, and let them remain for one day; then put them into a preserving-pan, stand them by the side of the fire to simmer gently for about 1/2 hour, and then boil them rapidly for another 15 minutes. The scum must be carefully removed as it rises, and the jam must be well stirred all the time, or it will burn at the bottom of the pan, and so spoil the colour and flavour of the preserve. Some of the stones may be cracked, and a few kernels added to the jam just before it is done: these impart a very delicious flavour to the plums. The above proportion of sugar would answer for Orleans plums; the Impératrice Magnum-bonum, and Winesour would not require quite so much.

Preserved Plums

Ingredients: To every lb. of fruit allow 3/4 lb. of loaf sugar; for the thin syrup, 1/4 lb. of sugar to each pint of water.

Mode: Select large ripe plums; slightly prick them, to prevent them from bursting, and simmer them very gently in a syrup made with the above proportion of sugar and water. Put them carefully into a pan, let the syrup cool, pour it over the plums, and allow them to remain for two days. Having previously weighed the other sugar, dip the lumps quickly into water, and put them into a preserving-pan with no more water than hangs about them; and boil the sugar to a syrup, carefully skimming it. Drain the plums from the first syrup; put them into the fresh syrup, and simmer them very gently until they are clear; lift them out singly into pots, pour the syrup over, and when cold, cover down to exclude the air. This preserve will remain good some time, if kept in a dry place, and makes a very nice addition to a dessert. The magnum-bonum plums answer for this preserve better than any other kind of plum. Greengages are also very delicious done in this manner.

Preserved Pumpkin

Ingredients: To each lb. of pumpkin allow 1 lb. of roughly pounded loaf sugar, 1 gill of lemon-juice.

Mode: Obtain a good sweet pumpkin; halve it, take out the seeds, and pare off the rind; cut it into neat slices, or into pieces about the size of a five-shilling piece. Weigh the pumpkin, put the slices in a pan or deep dish in layers, with the sugar sprinkled between them; pour the lemon-juice over the top, and let the whole remain for 2 or 3 days. Boil altogether, adding 1/4 pint of water to every 3 lbs. of sugar used until the pumpkin becomes tender; then turn the whole into a pan, where let it remain for a week; then drain off the syrup, boil it until it is quite thick; skim, and pour it, boiling, over the pumpkin. A little bruised ginger and lemon-rind, thinly pared, may be boiled in the syrup to flavour the pumpkin.

Quince Jelly

Ingredients: To every pint of juice allow 1 lb. of loaf sugar.

Mode: Pare and slice the quinces, and put them into a preserving-pan with sufficient water to float them. Boil them until tender, and the fruit is reduced to a pulp; strain off the clear juice, and to each pint allow the above proportion of loaf sugar. Boil the juice and sugar together for about 3/4 hour; remove all the scum as it rises, and, when the jelly appears firm when a little is poured on a plate, it is done. The residue left on the sieve will answer to make a common marmalade, for immediate use, by boiling it with 1/2 lb. of common sugar to every lb. of pulp.

Raisin Cheese

Ingredients: To every lb. of raisins allow a lb. of loaf sugar; pounded cinnamon and cloves to taste.

Mode: Stone the raisins; put them into a stewpan with the sugar, cinnamon, and cloves, and let them boil for 1-1/2 hour, stirring all the time. Let the preparation cool a little, pour it into a glass dish, and garnish with strips of candied lemon-peel and citron. This will remain good some time, if kept in a dry place.

Raspberry Jam

Ingredients: To every lb. of raspberries allow 1 lb. of sugar, 1/4 pint of red-currant juice.

Mode: Let the fruit for this preserve be gathered in fine weather, and used as soon after it is picked as possible. Take off the stalks, put the raspberries into a preserving-pan, break them well with a wooden spoon, and let them boil for 1/4 hour, keeping them well stirred. Then add the currant-juice and sugar, and boil again for

1/2 hour. Skim the jam well after the sugar is added, or the preserve will not be clear. The addition of the currant juice is a very great improvement to this preserve, as it gives it a piquant taste, which the flavour of the raspberries seems to require.

Raspberry Jelly

Ingredients: To each pint of juice allow 3/4 lb. of loaf sugar.

Mode: Let the raspberries be freshly gathered, quite ripe, and picked from the stalks; put them into a large jar, after breaking the fruit a little with a wooden spoon, and place this jar, covered, in a saucepan of boiling water. When the juice is well drawn, which will be in from 3/4 to 1 hour, strain the fruit through a fine hair sieve or cloth; measure the juice, and to every pint allow the above proportion of loaf sugar. Put the juice and sugar into a preserving-pan, place it over the fire, and boil gently until the jelly thickens when a little is poured on a plate; carefully remove all the scum as it rises, pour the jelly into small pots, cover down, and keep in a dry place. This jelly answers for making raspberry cream, and for flavouring various sweet dishes, when, in winter, the fresh fruit is not obtainable.

Strawberries And Cream

Ingredients: To every pint of picked strawberries allow 1/3 pint of cream, 2 oz. of finely-pounded sugar.

Mode: Pick the stalks from the fruit, place it on a glass dish, sprinkle over it pounded sugar, and slightly stir the strawberries, that they may all be equally sweetened; pour the cream over the top, and serve. Devonshire cream, when it can be obtained, is exceedingly delicious for this dish; and, if very thick indeed, may be diluted with a little thin cream or milk.

Strawberry Jam

Ingredients: To every lb. of fruit allow 1/2 pint of red-currant juice, 1-1/4 lb. of loaf sugar.

Mode: Strip the currants from the stalks, put them into a jar; place this jar in a saucepan of boiling water, and simmer until the juice is well drawn from the fruit; strain the currants, measure the juice, put it into a preserving-pan, and add the sugar. Select well-ripened but sound strawberries; pick them from the stalks, and when the sugar is dissolved in the currant juice, put in the fruit. Simmer the whole over a moderate fire, from 1/2 to 3/4 hour, carefully removing the scum as it rises. Stir the jam only enough to prevent it from burning at the bottom of the pan, as the fruit should be preserved as whole as possible. Put the jam into jars, and when cold, cover down.

Preserved Strawberries in Wine

Ingredients: To every quart bottle allow 1/4 lb. of finely-pounded loaf sugar; sherry or Madeira.

Mode: Let the fruit be gathered in fine weather, and used as soon as picked. Have ready some perfectly dry glass bottles, and some nice soft corks or bungs. Pick the stalks from the strawberries, drop them into the bottles, sprinkling amongst them pounded sugar in the above proportion, and when the fruit reaches to the neck of the bottle, fill up with sherry or Madeira. Cork the bottles down with new corks, and dip them into melted resin.

To Make Everton Toffee

Ingredients: 1 lb. of powdered loaf sugar, 1 teacupful of water, 1/4 lb. of butter, 6 drops of essence of lemon.

Mode: Put the water and sugar into a brass pan, and beat the butter to a cream. When the sugar is dissolved, add the butter, and keep stirring the mixture over the fire until it sets, when a little is poured on to a buttered dish; and just before the toffee is done, add the essence of lemon. Butter a dish or tin, pour on it the mixture, and when cool, it will easily separate from the dish. Butter-Scotch, an excellent thing for coughs, is made with brown, instead of white sugar, omitting the water, and flavoured with 1/2 oz. of powdered ginger. It is made in the same manner as toffee.

9

Production of Creams, Jellies, Souffles, Omelets and Sweet Dishes

The yellowish-white, opaque fluid, smooth and unctuous to the touch, which separates itself from new milk, and forms a layer on its surface, when removed by skimming, is employed in a variety of culinary preparations. The analyses of the contents of cream have been decided to be, in 100 parts — butter, 3.5; curd, or matter of cheese, 3.5; whey, 92.0. That cream contains an oil, is evinced by its staining clothes in the manner of oil; and when boiled for some time, a little oil floats upon the surface. The thick animal oil which it contains, the well-known butter, is separated only by agitation, as in the common process of churning, and the cheesy matter remains blended with the whey in the state of buttermilk.

Of the several kinds of cream, the principal are the Devonshire and Dutch clotted creams, the Costorphin cream, and the Scotch sour cream. The Devonshire cream is produced by nearly boiling the milk in shallow tin vessels over a charcoal fire, and kept in that state until the whole of the cream is thrown up. It is used for eating with fruits and tarts. The Scotch "sour cream" is a misnomer; for it is a material produced without cream. A small tub filled with skimmed milk is put into a larger one, containing hot water, and after remaining there all night, the thin milk (called wigg) is drawn off, and the remainder of the contents of the smaller vessel is "sour cream."

Jellies are not the nourishing food they were at one time considered to be, and many eminent physicians are of opinion that they are less digestible than the flesh, or muscular part of animals; still, when acidulated with lemon-juice and flavoured with wine, they are very suitable for some convalescents. Vegetable jelly is a distinct principle, existing in fruits, which possesses the property of gelatinizing when boiled and cooled; but it is a principle entirely different from the gelatine of animal bodies, although the name of jelly, common to both, sometimes leads to an erroneous idea on that subject.

Animal jelly, or gelatine, is glue, whereas vegetable jelly is rather analogous to gum. Liebig places gelatine very low indeed in the scale of usefulness. He says, "Gelatine, which by itself is tasteless, and when eaten, excites nausea, possesses no nutritive value; that, even when accompanied by the savoury constituents of flesh, it is not capable of supporting the vital process, and when added to the usual diet as a substitute for plastic matter, does not increase, but, on the contrary, diminishes the nutritive value of the food, which it renders insufficient in quantity and inferior in quality." It is this substance which is most frequently employed in the manufacture of the jellies supplied by the confectioner; but those prepared at home from calves' feet do possess some nutrition, and are the only sort that should be given to invalids. Isinglass is the purest variety of gelatine, and is prepared from the sounds or swimming-bladders of certain fish, chiefly the sturgeon. From its whiteness it is mostly used for making blanc-mange and similar dishes.

The White Of Eggs is perhaps the best substance that can be employed in clarifying jelly, as well as some other fluids, for the reason that when albumen (and the white of eggs is nearly pure albumen) is put into a liquid that is muddy, from substances suspended in it, on boiling the liquid, the albumen coagulates in a flocculent manner, and, entangling with it the impurities, rises with them to the surface as a scum, or sinks to the bottom, according to their weight.

Souffles, Omelets, And Sweet Dishes, in which eggs form the principal ingredient, demand, for their successful manufacture, an experienced cook. They are the prettiest, but most difficult of all entremets. The most essential thing to insure success is to secure the best ingredients from an honest tradesman. The entremets coming within the above classification, are healthy, nourishing, and pleasant to the taste, and may be eaten with safety by persons of the most delicate stomachs.

Recipes for Creams and Jellies

Baked Apple Custard

Ingredients: 1 dozen large apples, moist sugar to taste, 1 small teacupful of cold water, the grated rind of one lemon, 1 pint of milk, 4 eggs, 2 oz. of loaf sugar.

Mode: Peel, cut, and core the apples; put them into a lined saucepan with the cold water, and as they heat, bruise them to a pulp; sweeten with moist sugar, and add the grated lemon-rind. When cold, put the fruit at the bottom of a pie-dish, and pour over it a custard, made with the above proportion of milk, eggs, and sugar; grate a little nutmeg over the top, place the dish in a moderate oven, and bake from 25 to 35 minutes. The above proportions will make rather a large dish.

Apple Fritters

Ingredients: For the batter, 1/2 lb. of flour, 1/2 oz. of butter,

1/2 saltspoonful of salt, 2 eggs, milk, apples, hot lard or clarified beef-dripping.

Mode: Break the eggs; separate the whites from the yolks, and beat them separately. Put the flour into a basin, stir in the butter, which should be melted to a cream; add the salt, and moisten with sufficient warm milk to make it of a proper consistency, that is to say, a batter that will drop from the spoon. Stir this well, rub down any lumps that may be seen, and add the whites of the eggs, which have been previously well whisked; beat up the batter for a few minutes, and it is ready for use. Now peel and cut the apples into rather thick whole slices, without dividing them, and stamp out the middle of each slice, where the core is, with a cutter. Throw the slices into the batter; have ready a pan of boiling lard or clarified dripping; take out the pieces of apple one by one, put them into the hot lard, and fry a nice brown, turning them -- when required. When done, lay them on a piece of blotting-paper before the fire, to absorb the greasy moisture; then dish on a white d'oyley, piled one above the other; strew over them some pounded sugar, and serve very hot. The flavour of the fritters would be very much improved by soaking the pieces of apple in a little wine, mixed with sugar and lemon-juice, for 3 or 4 hours before wanted for table; the batter, also, is better for being mixed some hours before the fritters are made.

Clear Apple Jelly

Ingredients: 2 dozen apples, 1-1/2 pint of spring-water; to every pint of juice allow 1/2 lb. of loaf sugar, 1/2 oz. of isinglass, the rind of 1/2 lemon.

Mode: Pare, core, and cut the apples into quarters, and boil them, with the lemon-peel, until tender; then strain off the apples, and run the juice through a jelly-bag; put the strained juice, with the sugar and isinglass, which has been previously boiled in 1/2 pint of water, into a lined saucepan or preserving-pan; boil all together for about 1/4 hour, and put the jelly into moulds. When this jelly is nice and clear, and turned out well, it makes a pretty addition to the supper-table, with a little custard or whipped cream round it: the addition of a little lemon-juice improves the flavour, but it is apt to render the jelly muddy and thick. If required to be kept any length of time, rather a larger proportion of sugar must be used.

Apples in Red Jelly

Ingredients: 6 good-sized apples, 12 cloves, pounded sugar, 1 lemon, 2 teacupfuls of water, 1 tablespoonful of gelatine, a few drops of prepared cochineal.

Mode: Choose rather large apples; peel them and take out the cores, either with a scoop or a small silver knife, and put into each apple 2 cloves and as much sifted sugar as they will hold. Place them, without touching each other, in a large pie-dish; add more white sugar, the juice of 1 lemon, and 2 teacupfuls of water. Bake in the oven, with a dish over them, until they are done. Look at them frequently, and, as each apple is cooked, place it in a glass dish. They must not be left in the oven after they are done, or they will break, and so would spoil the appearance of the dish.

When the apples are neatly arranged in the dish without touching each other, strain the liquor in which they have been stewing, into a lined saucepan; add to it the rind of the lemon, and a tablespoonful of gelatine which has been previously dissolved in cold water, and, if not sweet, a little more sugar, and 6 cloves. Boil till quite clear; colour with a few drops of prepared cochineal, and strain the jelly through a double muslin into a jug; let it cool a little; then pour it into the dish round the apples. When quite cold, garnish the tops of the apples with a bright-coloured marmalade, a jelly, or the white of an egg, beaten to a strong froth, with a little sifted sugar.

Apple Souffle

Ingredients: 6 oz. of rice, 1 quart of milk, the rind of 1/2 lemon, sugar to taste, the yolks of 4 eggs, the whites of 6, 1-1/2 oz. of butter, 4 tablespoonfuls of apple marmalade.

Mode: Boil the milk with the lemon-peel until the former is well flavoured; then strain it, put in the rice, and let it gradually swell over a slow fire, adding sufficient sugar to sweeten it nicely. Then crush the rice to a smooth pulp with the back of a wooden spoon; line the bottom and sides of a round cake-tin with it, and put it into the oven to set; turn it out of the tin carefully, and be careful that the border of rice is firm in every part. Mix with the marmalade the beaten yolks of eggs and the butter, and stir these over the fire until the mixture thickens. Take it off the fire; to this add the whites of the eggs, which should be previously beaten to a strong froth; stir all together, and put it into the rice border. Bake in a moderate oven for about 1/2 hour, or until the soufflé rises very light. It should be watched, and served instantly, or it will immediately fall after it is taken from the oven.

Apple Trifle

Ingredients: 10 good-sized apples, the rind of 1/2 lemon, 6 oz. of pounded sugar, 1/2 pint of milk, 1/2 pint of cream, 2 eggs, whipped cream.

Mode: Peel, core, and cut the apples into thin slices, and put them into a saucepan with 2 tablespoonfuls of water, the sugar, and minced lemon-rind. Boil all together until quite tender, and pulp the apples through a sieve; if they should not be quite sweet enough, add a little more sugar, and put them at the bottom of the dish to form a thick layer. Stir together the milk, cream, and eggs, with a little sugar, over the fire, and let the mixture thicken, but do not allow it to reach the boiling-point. When thick, take it off the fire; let it cool a little, then pour it over the apples. Whip some cream with sugar, lemon-peel, &c., the same as for other trifles; heap it high over the custard, and the dish is ready for table. It may be garnished as fancy dictates, with strips of bright apple jelly, slices of citron, &c.

Apricot Cream

Ingredients: 12 to 16 ripe apricots, 1/4 lb. of sugar, 1-1/2 pint of milk, the yolks of 8 eggs, 1 oz. of isinglass.

Mode: Divide the apricots, take out the stones, and boil them in a syrup made with 1/4 lb. of sugar and 1/4 pint of water, until they form a thin marmalade, which rub through a sieve. Boil the milk with the other 1/4 lb. of sugar, let it cool a little, then mix with it the yolks of eggs which have been previously well beaten; put this mixture into a jug, place this jug in boiling water, and stir it one way over the fire until it thickens; but on no account let it boil. Strain through a sieve, add the isinglass, previously boiled with a small quantity of water, and keep stirring it till nearly cold; then mix the cream with the apricots; stir well, put it into an oiled mould, and, if convenient, set it on ice; at any rate, in a very cool place. It should turn out on the dish without any difficulty.

Arrowroot Blanc-Mange

Ingredients: 4 heaped tablespoonfuls of arrowroot, 1-1/2 pint of milk, 3 laurel-leaves or the rind of 1/2 lemon, sugar to taste.

Mode: Mix to a smooth batter the arrowroot with 1/2 pint of the milk; put the other pint on the fire, with laurel-leaves or lemon-peel, whichever may be preferred, and let the milk steep until it is well flavoured. Then strain the milk, and add it, boiling, to the mixed arrowroot; sweeten it with sifted sugar, and let it boil, stirring it all the time, till it thickens sufficiently to come from the saucepan. Grease a mould with pure salad-oil, pour in the blanc-mange, and when quite set, turn it out on a dish, and pour round it a compôte of any kind of fruit, or garnish it with jam. A tablespoonful of brandy, stirred in just before the blanc-mange is moulded, very much improves the flavour of this sweet dish.

Blanc-Mange

Ingredients: 1 pint of new milk, 1-1/4 oz. of isinglass, the rind of 1/2 lemon, 1/4 lb. of loaf sugar, 10 bitter almonds, 1/2 oz. of sweet almonds, 1 pint of cream.

Mode: Put the milk into a saucepan, with the isinglass, lemon-rind, and sugar, and let these ingredients stand by the side of the fire until the milk is well flavoured; add the almonds, which should be blanched and pounded in a mortar to a paste, and let the milk just boil up; strain it through a fine sieve or muslin into a jug, add the cream, and stir the mixture occasionally until nearly cold. Let it stand for a few minutes, then pour it into the mould, which should be previously oiled with the purest salad-oil, or dipped in cold water. There will be a sediment at the bottom of the jug, which must not be poured into the mould, as, when turned out, it would very much disfigure the appearance of the blanc-mange.

This blanc-mange may be made very much richer by using 1-1/2 pint of cream, and melting the isinglass in 1/2 pint of boiling water. The flavour may also be very much varied by adding bay-leaves, laurel-leaves, or essence of vanilla, instead of the lemon-rind and almonds. Noyeau, Maraschino, Curaçoa, or any favourite liqueur, added in small proportions, very much enhances the flavour of this always favourite dish. In turning it out, just loosen the edges of the blanc-mange from the mould, place a dish on it, and turn it quickly over; it should come out easily, and the blanc-mange have a smooth glossy appearance when the mould is oiled, which it frequently has not when it is only dipped in water. It may be garnished as fancy dictates.

Cheap Blanc-Mange

Ingredients: 1/4 lb. of sugar, 1 quart of milk, 1-1/2 oz. of isinglass, the rind of 1/2 lemon, 4 laurel-leaves.

Mode: Put all the ingredients into a lined saucepan, and boil gently until the isinglass is dissolved; taste it occasionally, to ascertain when it is sufficiently flavoured with the laurel-leaves; then take them out, and keep stirring the mixture over the fire for about 10 minutes. Strain it through a fine sieve into a jug, and, when nearly cold, pour it into a well-oiled mould, omitting the sediment at the bottom. Turn it out carefully on a dish, and garnish with preserves, bright jelly, or a compote of fruit.

Isinglass or Gelatine Jelly

Ingredients: 3 oz. of isinglass or gelatine, 2 quarts of water.

Mode: Put the isinglass or gelatine into a saucepan with the above proportion of cold water; bring it quickly to boil, and let it boil very fast, until the liquor is reduced one-half. Carefully remove the scum as it rises, then strain it through a jelly-bag, and it will be ready for use. If not required very clear, it may be merely strained through a fine sieve, instead of being run through a bag. Rather more than 1/2 oz. of isinglass is about the proper quantity to use for a quart of strong calf's-feet stock, and rather more than 2 oz. for the same quantity of fruit juice. As isinglass varies so much in quality and strength, it is difficult to give the exact proportions. The larger the mould, the stiffer should be the jelly; and where there is no ice, more isinglass must be used than if the mixture were frozen. This forms a stock for all kinds of jellies, which may be flavoured in many ways.

Simple Apple Charlotte.

Ingredients: 9 slices of bread and butter, about 6 good-sized apples, 1 tablespoonful of minced lemon-peel, 2 tablespoonfuls of juice, moist sugar to taste.

Mode: Butter a pie-dish; place a layer of bread and butter, without the crust, at the bottom; then a layer of apples, pared, cored, and cut into thin slices; sprinkle over these a portion of the lemon-peel and juice, and sweeten with moist sugar. Place another layer of bread and butter, and then one of apples, proceeding in this manner until the dish is full; then cover it up with the peel of the apples, to preserve the top from browning or burning; bake in a brisk oven for rather more than 3/4 hour; torn the charlotte on a dish, sprinkle sifted sugar over, and serve.

Charlotte Russe

Ingredients: About 18 Savoy.biscuits, 3/4 pint of cream, flavouring of vanilla, liqueurs, or wine, 1 tablespoonful of pounded sugar, 1/2 oz. of isinglass.

Mode: Procure about 18 Savoy biscuits, or ladies'-fingers, as they are sometimes called; brush the edges of them with the white of an egg, and line the bottom of a plain round mould, placing them like a star or rosette. Stand them upright all round the edge; carefully put them so closely together that the white of the egg connects them firmly, and place this case in the oven for about 5 minutes, just to dry the egg. Whisk the cream to a stiff froth, with the sugar, flavouring, and melted isinglass; fill the charlotte with it, cover with a slice of sponge-cake cut in the shape of the mould; place it in ice, where let it remain till ready for table; then turn it on a dish, remove the mould, and serve.

1 tablespoonful of liqueur of any kind, or 4 tablespoonfuls of wine, would nicely flavour the above proportion of cream. For arranging the biscuits in the mould, cut them to the shape required, so that they fit in nicely, and level them with the mould at the top, that, when turned out, there may be something firm to rest upon. Great care and attention is required in the turning out of this dish, that the cream does not burst the case; and the edges of the biscuits must have the smallest quantity of egg brushed over them, or it would stick to the mould, and so prevent the charlotte from coming away properly.

Cream A La Valois.

Ingredients: 4 sponge-cakes, jam, 3/4 pint of cream, sugar to taste, the juice of 1/2 lemon, 1/4 glass of sherry, 1-1/4 oz. of isinglass.

Mode: Cut the sponge-cakes into thin slices; place two together, with preserve between them, and pour over them a small quantity of sherry mixed with a little brandy. Sweeten and flavour the cream with the lemon-juice and sherry; add the isinglass, which should be dissolved in a little water, and beat up the cream well. Place a little in an oiled mould; arrange the pieces of cake in the cream; then fill the mould with the remainder; let it cool, and turn it out on a dish. By oiling the mould, the cream will have a much smoother appearance, and will turn out more easily than when merely dipped in cold water.

Boiled Custards

Ingredients: 1 pint of milk, 5 eggs, 3 oz. of loaf sugar, 3 laurel-leaves, or the rind of 4 lemon, or a few drops of essence of vanilla, 1 tablespoonful of brandy.

Mode: Put the milk into a lined saucepan, with the sugar, and whichever of the above flavourings may be preferred (the lemon-rind flavours custards most deliciously), and let the milk steep by the side of the fire until it is well flavoured. Bring it to the point of boiling, then strain it into a basin; whisk the eggs well, and, when the milk has cooled a little, stir in the eggs, and strain this mixture into a jug. Place this jug in a saucepan of boiling water over the fire; keep stirring the custard one way until it thickens; but on no account allow it to reach the boiling-point, as it will instantly curdle and be full of lumps.

Take it off the fire, stir in the brandy, and, when this is well mixed with the custard, pour it into glasses, which should be rather more than three-parts full; grate a little nutmeg over the top, and the dish is ready for table. To make custards look and eat better, ducks' eggs should be used, when obtainable; they add very much to the flavour and richness, and so many are not required as of the ordinary eggs, 4 ducks' eggs to the pint of milk making a delicious custard. When desired extremely rich and good, cream should be substituted for the milk, and double the quantity of eggs used, to those mentioned, omitting the whites.

French Pancakes

Ingredients: 2 eggs, 2 oz. of butter, 2 oz. of sifted sugar, 2 oz. of flour, 1/2 pint of new milk.

Mode: Beat the eggs thoroughly, and put them into a basin with the butter, which should be beaten to a cream;

stir in the sugar and flour, and when these ingredients are well mixed, add the milk; keep stirring and beating the mixture for a few minutes; put it on buttered plates, and bake in a quick oven for 20 minutes. Serve with a cut lemon and sifted sugar, or pile the pancakes high on a dish, with a layer of preserve or marmalade between each.

Dutch Flummery

Ingredients: 1-1/2 oz. of isinglass, the rind and juice of 1 lemon, 1 pint of water, 4 eggs, 1 pint of sherry, Madeira, or raisin-wine; sifted sugar to taste.

Mode: Put the water, isinglass, and lemon-rind into a lined saucepan, and simmer gently until the isinglass is dissolved; strain this into a basin, stir in the eggs, which should be well beaten, the lemon-juice, which should be strained, and the wine; sweeten to taste with pounded sugar, mix all well together, pour it into a jug, set this jug in a saucepan of boiling water over the fire, and keep stirring it one way until it thickens; but take care that it does not boil. Strain it into a mould that has been oiled or laid in water for a short time, and put it in a cool place to set. A tablespoonful of brandy stirred in just before it is poured into the mould, improves the flavour of this dish: it is better if made the day before it is required for table.

Chocolate Souffle

Ingredients: 4 eggs, 3 teaspoonfuls of pounded sugar, 1 teaspoonful of flour, 3 oz. of the best chocolate.

Mode: Break the eggs, separating the whites from the yolks, and put them into different basins; add to the yolks the sugar, flour, and chocolate, which should be very finely grated, and stir these ingredients for 5 minutes. Then well whisk the whites of the eggs in the other basin, until they are stiff, and, when firm, mix lightly with the yolks, till the whole forms a smooth and light substance; butter a round cake-tin, put in the mixture, and bake in a moderate oven from 15 to 20 minutes. Pin a white napkin round the tin, strew sifted sugar over the top of the soufflé, and send it immediately to table. The proper appearance of this dish depends entirely on the expedition with which it is served, and some cooks, to preserve its lightness, hold a salamander over the soufflé until it is placed on the table. If allowed to stand after it comes from the oven, it will be entirely spoiled, as it falls almost immediately.

Darioles A La Vanille.

Ingredients: 1/2 pint of milk, 1/2 pint of cream, 2 oz. of flour, 3 oz. of pounded sugar, 6 eggs, 2 oz. of butter, puff-paste, flavouring of essence of vanilla.

Mode: Mix the flour to a smooth batter, with the milk; stir in the cream, sugar, the eggs, which should be well whisked, and the butter, which should be beaten to a cream. Put in some essence of vanilla, drop by drop, until the mixture is well flavoured; line some dariole-moulds with puff-paste, three-parts fill them with the batter, and bake in a good oven from 25 to 35 minutes. Turn them out of the moulds on a dish, without breaking them; strew over sifted sugar, and serve. The flavouring of the darioles may be varied by substituting lemon, cinnamon, or almonds, for the vanilla.

Chocolate Cream.

Ingredients: 3 oz. of grated chocolate, 1/4 lb. of sugar, 1-1/2 pint of cream, 1/2 oz. of clarified isinglass, the yolks of 6 eggs.

Mode: Beat the yolks of the eggs well; put them into a basin with the grated chocolate, the sugar, and 1 pint of the cream; stir these ingredients well together, pour them into a jug, and set this jug in a saucepan of boiling water; stir it one way until the mixture thickens, but do not allow it to boil, or it will curdle. Strain the cream through a sieve into a basin; stir in the isinglass and the other 1/2 pint of cream, which should be well whipped; mix all well together, and pour it into a mould which has been previously oiled with the purest salad-oil, and, if at hand, set it in ice until wanted for table.

Geneva Wafers

Ingredients: 2 eggs, 3 oz. of butter, 3 oz. of flour, 3 oz. of pounded sugar.

Mode: Well whisk the eggs; put them into a basin, and stir to them the butter, which should be beaten to a cream; add the flour and sifted sugar gradually, and then mix all well together. Butter a baking-sheet, and drop on it a teaspoonful of the mixture at a time, leaving a space between each. Bake in a cool oven; watch the pieces of paste, and, when half done, roll them up like wafers, and put in a small wedge of bread or piece of wood, to keep them in shape. Return them to the oven until crisp. Before serving, remove the bread, put a spoonful of preserve in the widest end, and fill up with whipped cream. This is a very pretty and ornamental dish for the supper-table, and is very nice and very easily made.

Ginger Cream

Ingredients: The yolks of 4 eggs, 1 pint of cream, 3 oz. of preserved ginger, 2 dessertspoonfuls of syrup, sifted sugar to taste, 1 oz. of isinglass.

Mode: Slice the ginger finely; put it into a basin with the syrup, the well-beaten yolks of eggs, and the cream; mix these ingredients well together, and stir them over the fire for about 10 minutes, or until the mixture thickens;

then take it off the fire, whisk till nearly cold, sweeten to taste, add the isinglass, which should be melted and strained, and serve the cream in a glass dish. It may be garnished with slices of preserved ginger or candied citron.

Indian Fritters

Ingredients: 3 tablespoonfuls of flour, boiling water, the yolks of 4 eggs, the whites of 2, hot lard or clarified dripping, jam.

Mode: Put the flour into a basin, and pour over it sufficient boiling water to make it into a stiff paste, taking care to stir and beat it well, to prevent it getting lumpy. Leave it a little time to cool, and then break into it (without beating them at first) the yolks of 4 eggs and the whites of 2, and stir and beat all well together. Have ready some boiling lard or butter; drop a dessertspoonful of batter in at a time, and fry the fritters of a light brown. They should rise so much as to be almost like balls. Serve on a dish, with a spoonful of preserve or marmalade dropped in between each fritter. This is an excellent dish for a hasty addition to dinner, if a guest unexpectedly arrives, it being so easily and quickly made, and it is always a great favourite.

Indian Trifle

Ingredients: 1 quart of milk, the rind of 1/2 large lemon, sugar to taste, 5 heaped tablespoonfuls of rice-flour, 1 oz. of sweet almonds, 1/2 pint of custard.

Mode: Boil the milk and lemon-rind together until the former is well flavoured; take out the lemon-rind and stir in the rice-flour, which should first be moistened with cold milk, and add sufficient loaf sugar to sweeten it nicely. Boil gently for about 5 minutes, and keep the mixture stirred; take it off the fire, let it cool a little, and pour it into a glass dish. When cold, cut the rice out in the form of a star, or any other shape that may be preferred; take out the spare rice, and fill the space with boiled custard. Blanch and cut the almonds into strips; stick them over the trifle, and garnish it with pieces of brightly-coloured jelly, or preserved fruits, or candied citron.

Italian Cream

Ingredients: 1 pint of milk, 4 pint of cream, sugar to taste, 1 oz. of isinglass, 1 lemon, the yolks of 4 eggs.

Mode: Put the cream and milk into a saucepan, with sugar to sweeten, and the lemon-rind. Boil until the milk is well flavoured then strain it into a basin, and add the beaten yolks of eggs. Put this mixture into a jug; place the jug in a saucepan of boiling water over the fire, and stir the contents until they thicken, but do not allow them to boil. Take the cream off the fire, stir in the lemon-juice and isinglass, which should be melted, and whip well; fill a mould, place it in ice if at hand, and, when set, turn it out on a dish, and garnish as taste may dictate. The mixture may be whipped and drained, and then put into small glasses, when this mode of serving is preferred.

Jaunemange

Ingredients: 1 oz. of isinglass, 1 pint of water, 1/2 pint of white wine, the rind and juice of 1 large lemon, sugar to taste, the yolks of 6 eggs.

Mode: Put the isinglass, water, and lemon-rind into a saucepan, and boil gently until the former is dissolved; then add the strained lemon-juice, the wine, and sufficient white sugar to sweeten the whole nicely. Boil for 2 or 3 minutes, strain the mixture into a jug, and add the yolks of the eggs, which should be well beaten; place the jug in a saucepan of boiling water; keep stirring the mixture one way until it thickens, but do not allow it to boil; then take it off the fire, and keep stirring until nearly cold. Pour it into a mould, omitting the sediment at the bottom of the jug, and let it remain until quite firm.

Jelly Moulded with Fresh Fruit, or Macedoine De Fruits

Ingredients: Rather more than 1-1/2 pint of jelly, a few nice strawberries, or red or white currants, or raspberries, or any fresh fruit that may be in season.

Mode: Have ready the above proportion of jelly, which must be very clear and rather sweet, the raw fruit requiring an additional quantity of sugar. Select ripe, nice-looking fruit; pick off the stalks, unless currants are used, when they are laid in the jelly as they come from the tree. Begin by putting a little jelly at the bottom of the mould, which must harden; then arrange the fruit round the sides of the mould, recollecting; that it will be reversed when turned out; then pour in some more jelly to make the fruit adhere, and, when that layer is set, put another row of fruit and jelly until the mould is full. If convenient, put it in ice until required for table, then wring a cloth in boiling water, wrap it round the mould for a minute, and turn the jelly carefully out.

Peaches, apricots, plums, apples, &c., are better for being boiled in a little clear syrup before they are laid in the jelly; strawberries, raspberries, grapes, cherries, and currants are put in raw. In winter, when fresh fruits are not obtainable, a very pretty jelly may be made with preserved fruits or brandy cherries: these, in a bright and clear jelly, have a very pretty effect; of course, unless the jelly be very clear, the beauty of the dish will be spoiled. It may be garnished with the same fruit as is laid in the jelly; for instance, an open jelly with strawberries might have, piled in the centre, a few of the same fruit prettily arranged, or a little whipped cream might be substituted for the fruit.

Lemon Blancmange

Ingredients: 1 quart of milk, the yolks of 4 eggs, 3 oz. of ground rice, 6 oz. of pounded sugar, 1-1/2 oz. of fresh butter, the rind of 1 lemon, the juice of 2, 1/2 oz. of gelatine.

Mode: Make a custard with the yolks of the eggs and 1/2 pint of the milk, and, when done, put it into a basin: put half the remainder of the milk into a saucepan with the ground rice, fresh butter, lemon-rind, and 3 oz. of the sugar, and let these ingredients boil until the mixture is stiff, stirring them continually; when done, pour it into the bowl where the custard is, mixing both well together. Put the gelatine with the rest of the milk into a saucepan, and let it stand by the side of the fire to dissolve; boil for a minute or two, stir carefully into the basin, adding 3 oz. more of pounded sugar. When cold, stir in the lemon-juice, which should be carefully strained, and pour the mixture into a well-oiled mould, leaving out the lemon-peel, and set the mould in a pan of cold water until wanted for table. Use eggs that have rich-looking yolks; and, should the weather be very warm, rather a larger proportion of gelatine must be allowed.

Lemon Creams of Custards

Ingredients: 5 oz. of loaf sugar, 2 pints of boiling water, the rind of 1 lemon and the juice of 3, the yolks of 8 eggs.

Mode: Make a quart of lemonade in the following manner:-- Dissolve the sugar in the boiling water, having previously, with part of the sugar, rubbed off the lemon-rind, and add the strained juice. Strain the lemonade into a saucepan, and add the yolks of the eggs, which should be well beaten; stir this one way over the fire until the mixture thickens, but do not allow it to boil, and serve in custard-glasses, or on a glass dish. After the boiling water is poured on the sugar and lemon, it should stand covered for about 1/2 hour before the eggs are added to it, that the flavour of the rind may be extracted.

Lemon Jelly

Ingredients: 6 lemons, 3/4 lb. of lump sugar, 1 pint of water, 1-1/2 oz. of isinglass, 1/4 pint of sherry.

Mode: Peel 3 of the lemons, pour 1/2 pint of boiling water on the rind, and let it infuse for 1/2 hour; put the sugar, isinglass, and 1/2 pint of water into a lined saucepan, and boil these ingredients for 20 minutes; then put in the strained lemon-juice, the strained infusion of the rind, and bring the whole to the point of boiling; skim well, add the wine, and run the jelly through a bag; pour it into a mould that has been wetted or soaked in water; put it in ice, if convenient, where let it remain until required for table. Previously to adding the lemon-juice to the other ingredients, ascertain that it is very nicely strained, as, if this is not properly attended to, it is liable to make the jelly thick and muddy. As this jelly is very pale, and almost colourless, it answers very well for moulding with a jelly of any bright hue; for instance, half a jelly bright red, and the other half made of the above, would have a very good effect. Lemon jelly may also be made with calf's-feet stock, allowing the juice of 3 lemons to every pint of stock.

Lemon Sponge

Ingredients: 2 oz. of isinglass, 1-3/4 pint of water, 3/4 lb. of pounded sugar, the juice of 5 lemons, the rind of 1, the whites of 3 eggs.

Mode: Dissolve the isinglass in the water, strain it into a saucepan, and add the sugar, lemon-rind, and juice. Boil the whole from 10 to 15 minutes; strain it again, and let it stand till it is cold and begins to stiffen. Beat the whites of the eggs, put them to it, and whisk the mixture till it is quite white; put it into a mould which has been previously wetted, and let it remain until perfectly set; then turn it out, and garnish it according to taste.

Liqueur Jelly

Ingredients: 1 lb. of lump sugar, 2 oz. of isinglass, 1-1/2 pint of water, the juice of 2 lemons, 1/4 pint of liqueur.

Mode: Put the sugar, with 1 pint of the water, into a stewpan, and boil them gently by the side of the fire until there is no scum remaining, which must be carefully removed as fast as it rises. Boil the isinglass with the other 1/2 pint of water, and skim it carefully in the same manner. Strain the lemon-juice, and add it, with the clarified isinglass, to the syrup; put in the liqueur, and bring the whole to the boiling-point. Let the saucepan remain covered by the side of the fire for a few minutes; then pour the jelly through a bag, put it into a mould, and set the mould in ice until required for table. Dip the mould in hot water, wipe the outside, loosen the jelly by passing a knife round the edges, and turn it out carefully on a dish. Noyeau, Maraschino, Curaçoa, brandy, or any kind of liqueur, answers for this jelly; and, when made with isinglass, liqueur jellies are usually prepared as directed above.

Meringues

Ingredients: 1/2 lb. of pounded sugar, the whites of 4 eggs.

Mode: Whisk the whites of the eggs to a stiff froth, and, with a wooden spoon, stir in quickly the pounded sugar; and have some boards thick enough to put in the oven to prevent the bottom of the meringues from acquiring too much colour. Cut some strips of paper about 2 inches wide; place this paper on the board, and drop a tablespoonful at a time of the mixture on the paper, taking care to let all the meringues be the same size.

In dropping it from the spoon, give the mixture the form of an egg, and keep the meringues about 2 inches apart from each other on the paper. Strew over them some sifted sugar, and bake in a moderate oven for 1/2 hour. As soon as they begin to colour, remove them from the oven; take each slip of paper by the two ends, and turn it gently on the table, and, with a small spoon, take out the soft part of each meringue.

Spread some clean paper on the board, turn the meringues upside down, and put them into the oven to harden and brown on the other side. When required for table, fill them with whipped cream, flavoured with liqueur or vanilla, and sweetened with pounded sugar. Join two of the meringues together, and pile them high in the dish, as shown in the annexed drawing. To vary their appearance, finely-chopped almonds or currants may be strewn over them before the sugar is sprinkled over; and they may be garnished with any bright-coloured preserve.

Great expedition is necessary in making this sweet dish; as, if the meringues are not put into the oven as soon as the sugar and eggs are mixed, the former melts, and the mixture would run on the paper, instead of keeping its egg-shape. The sweeter the meringues are made, the crisper will they be; but, if there is not sufficient sugar mixed with them, they will most likely be tough. They are sometimes coloured with cochineal; and, if kept well covered in a dry place, will remain good for a month or six weeks.

Noyeau Cream

Ingredients: 1-1/2 oz. of isinglass, the juice of 2 lemons, noyeau and pounded sugar to taste, 1-1/2 pint of cream.

Mode: Dissolve the isinglass in a little boiling water, add the lemon-juice, and strain this to the cream, putting in sufficient noyeau and sugar to flavour and sweeten the mixture nicely; whisk the cream well, put it into an oiled mould, and set the mould in ice or in a cool place; turn it out, and garnish the dish to taste.

Open Jelly with Whipped Cream

Ingredients: 1-1/2 pint of jelly, 1/2 pint of cream, 1 glass of sherry, sugar to taste.

Mode: Make the above proportion of calf's-feet or isinglass jelly, colouring and flavouring it in any way that may be preferred; soak a mould, open in the centre, for about 1/2 hour in cold water; fill it with the jelly, and let it remain in a cool place until perfectly set; then turn it out on a dish; fill the centre with whipped cream, flavoured with sherry and sweetened with pounded sugar; pile this cream high in the centre, and serve. The jelly should be made of rather a dark colour, to contrast nicely with the cream.

Orange Jelly

Ingredients: 1 pint of water, 1-1/2 to 2 oz. of isinglass, 1/2 lb. of loaf sugar, 1 Seville orange, 1 lemon, about 9 China oranges.

Mode: Put the water into a saucepan, with the isinglass, sugar, and the rind of 1 orange, and the same of 1/2 lemon, and stir these over the fire until the isinglass is dissolved, and remove the scum; then add to this the juice of the Seville orange, the juice of the lemon, and sufficient juice of China oranges to make in all 1 pint; from 8 to 10 oranges will yield the desired quantity. Stir all together over the fire until it is just on the point of boiling; skim well; then strain the jelly through a very fine sieve or jelly-bag, and when nearly cold, put it into a mould previously wetted, and, when quite set, turn it out on a dish, and garnish it to taste. To insure this jelly being clear, the orange-and lemon-juice should be well strained, and the isinglass clarified, before they are added to the other ingredients, and, to heighten the colour, a few drops of prepared cochineal may be added.

To Make a Plain Omelet

Ingredients: 6 eggs, 1 saltspoonful of salt, 1/3 saltspoonful of pepper, 1/4 lb. of butter.

Mode: Break the eggs into a basin, omitting the whites of 3, and beat them up with the salt and pepper until extremely light; then add 2 oz. of the butter broken into small pieces, and stir this into the mixture. Put the other 2 oz. of butter into a frying-pan, make it quite hot, and, as soon as it begins to bubble, whisk the eggs, &c. very briskly for a minute or two, and pour them into the pan; stir the omelet with a spoon one way until the mixture thickens and becomes firm, and when the whole is set, fold the edges over, so that the omelet assumes an oval form; and when it is nicely brown on one side, and quite firm, it is done.

To take off the rawness on the upper side, hold the pan before the fire for a minute or two, and brown it with a salamander or hot shovel. Serve very expeditiously on a very hot dish, and never cook it until it is just wanted. The flavour of this omelet may be very much enhanced by adding minced parsley, minced onion or eschalot, or grated cheese, allowing 1 tablespoonful of the former, and half the quantity of the latter, to the above proportion of eggs. Shrimps or oysters may also be added: the latter should be scalded in their liquor, and then bearded and cut into small pieces.

In making an omelet, be particularly careful that it is not too thin, and, to avoid this, do not make it in too large a frying-pan, as the mixture would then spread too much, and taste of the outside. It should also not be greasy, burnt, or too much done, and should be cooked over a gentle fire, that the whole of the substance may be heated without drying up the outside. Omelets are sometimes served with gravy; but this should never be poured over them, but served in a tureen, as the liquid causes the omelet to become heavy and flat, instead of eating light and soft. In making the gravy, the flavour should not overpower that of the omelet, and should be thickened with arrowroot or rice flour.

Ham Omelet

Ingredients: 6 eggs, 4 oz. of butter, 1/2 saltspoonful of pepper, 2 tablespoonfuls of minced ham.

Mode: Mince the ham very finely, without any fat, and fry it for 2 minutes in a little butter; then make the batter for the omelet, stir in the ham, and proceed. Do not add any salt to the batter, as the ham is usually sufficiently salt to impart a flavour to the omelet. Good lean bacon, or tongue, answers equally well for this dish; but they must also be slightly cooked previously to mixing them with the batter. Serve very hot and quickly, without gravy.

To Make a Plain Sweet Omelet

Ingredients: 6 eggs, 4 oz. of butter, 2 oz. of sifted sugar.

Mode: Break the eggs into a basin, omitting the whites of 3; whisk them well, adding the sugar and 2 oz. of the butter, which should be broken into small pieces, and stir all these ingredients well together. Make the remainder of the butter quite hot in a small frying-pan, and when it commences to bubble, pour in the eggs, &c. Keep stirring them until they begin to set; then turn the edges of the omelet over, to make it an oval shape, and finish cooking it. To brown the top, hold the pan before the fire, or use a salamander, and turn it carefully on to a very hot dish: sprinkle sifted sugar over, and serve.

Orange Cream

Ingredients: 1 oz. of isinglass, 6 large oranges, 1 lemon, sugar to taste, water, 1/2 pint of good cream.

Mode: Squeeze the juice from the oranges and lemon; strain it, and put it into a saucepan with the isinglass, and sufficient water to make in all 1-1/2 pint. Rub the sugar on the orange and lemon-rind, add it to the other ingredients, and boil all together for about 10 minutes. Strain through a muslin bag, and, when cold, beat up with it 1/2 pint of thick cream. Wet a mould, or soak it in cold water; pour in the cream, and put it in a cool place to set. If the weather is very cold, 1 oz. of isinglass will be found sufficient for the above proportion of ingredients.

Orange Fritters

Ingredients: For the batter, 1/2 lb. of flour, 1/2 oz. of butter, 1/2 saltspoonful of salt, 2 eggs, milk, oranges, hot lard or clarified dripping.

Mode: Make a nice light batter with the above proportion of flour, butter, salt, eggs, and sufficient milk to make it the proper consistency; peel the oranges, remove as much of the white skin as possible, and divide each orange into eight pieces, without breaking the thin skin, unless it be to remove the pips; dip each piece of orange in the batter. Have ready a pan of boiling lard or clarified dripping; drop in the oranges, and fry them a delicate brown from 8 to 10 minutes. When done, lay them on a piece of blotting-paper before the fire, to drain away the greasy moisture, and dish them on a white d'oyley; sprinkle over them plenty of pounded sugar, and serve quickly.

Richer Pancakes

Ingredients: 6 eggs, 1 pint of cream, 1/4 lb. of loaf sugar, 1 glass of sherry, 1/2 teaspoonful of grated nutmeg, flour.

Mode: Ascertain that the eggs are extremely fresh, beat them well, strain and mix with them the cream, pounded sugar, wine; nutmeg, and as much flour as will make the batter nearly as thick as that for ordinary pancakes. Make the frying-pan hot, wipe it with a clean cloth, pour in sufficient batter to make a thin pancake, and fry it for about 5 minutes. Dish the pancakes piled one above the other, strew sifted sugar between each, and serve.

Plain Fritters

Ingredients: 3 oz. of flour, 3 eggs, 1/3 pint of milk.

Mode: Mix the flour to a smooth batter with a small quantity of the milk; stir in the eggs, which should be well whisked, and then the remainder of the milk; boat the whole to a perfectly smooth batter, and should it be found not quite thin enough, add two or three tablespoonfuls more milk. Have ready a frying-pan, with plenty of boiling lard in it; drop in rather more than a tablespoonful at a time of the batter, and fry the fritters a nice brown, turning them when sufficiently cooked on one side. Drain them well from the greasy moisture by placing them upon a piece of blotting-paper before the fire; dish them on a white d'oyley, sprinkle over them sifted sugar, and send to table with them a cut lemon and plenty of pounded sugar.

Potato Fritters

Ingredients: 2 large potatoes, 4 eggs, 2 tablespoonfuls of cream, 2 ditto of raisin or sweet wine, 1 dessertspoonful of lemon-juice, 4 teaspoonful of grated nutmeg, hot lard.

Mode: Boil the potatoes, and beat them up lightly with a fork, but do not use a spoon, as that would make them heavy. Beat the eggs well, leaving out one of the whites; add the other ingredients, and beat all together for at least 20 minutes, or until the batter is extremely light. Put plenty of good lard into a frying-pan, and drop a tablespoonful of the batter at a time into it, and fry the fritters a nice brown. Serve them with the following sauce:-- A glass of sherry mixed with the strained juice of a lemon, and sufficient white sugar to sweeten the whole nicely. Warm these ingredients, and serve the sauce separately in a tureen. The fritters should be neatly dished on a white d'oyley, and pounded sugar sprinkled over them; and they should be well drained on a piece of blotting-paper before the fire previously to being dished.

Rice Blancmange

Ingredients: 1/4 lb. of ground rice, 3 oz. of loaf sugar, 1 oz. of fresh butter, 1 quart of milk, flavouring of lemon-peel, essence of almonds or vanilla, or laurel-leaves.

Mode: Mix the rice to a smooth batter with about 1/2 pint of the milk, and the remainder put into a saucepan, with the sugar, butter, and whichever of the above flavourings may be preferred; bring the milk to the boiling-point, quickly stir in the rice, and let it boil for about 10 minutes, or until it comes easily away from the saucepan, keeping it well stirred the whole time. Grease a mould with pure salad-oil; pour in the rice, and let it get perfectly set, when it should turn out quite easily; garnish it with jam, or pour round a compote of any kind of fruit, just before it is sent to table. This blancmange is better for being made the day before it is wanted, as it then has time to become firm. If laurel-leaves are used for flavouring, steep 3 of them in the milk, and take them out before the rice is added: about 8 drops of essence of almonds, or from 12 to 16 drops of essence of vanilla, would be required to flavour the above proportion of milk.

Rice Croquettes

Ingredients: 1/2 lb. of rice, 1 quart of milk, 6 oz. of pounded sugar, flavouring of vanilla, lemon-peel, or bitter almonds, egg and bread crumbs, hot lard.

Mode: Put the rice, milk, and sugar into a saucepan, and let the former gradually swell over a gentle fire until all the milk is dried up; and just before the rice is done, stir in a few drops of essence of any of the above flavourings. Let the rice get cold; then form it into small round balls, dip them into yolk of egg, sprinkle them with bread crumbs, and fry them in boiling lard for about 10 minutes, turning them about, that they may get equally browned. Drain the greasy moisture from them, by placing them on a cloth in front of the fire for a minute or two; pile them on a white d'oyley, and send them quickly to table. A small piece of jam is sometimes introduced into the middle of each croquette, which adds very much to the flavour of this favourite dish.

Rice Fritters

Ingredients: 6 oz. of rice, 1 quart of milk, 3 oz. of sugar, 1 oz. of fresh butter 6 oz. of orange marmalade, 4 eggs.

Mode: Swell the rice in the milk, with the sugar and butter, over a slow fire until it is perfectly tender, which will be in about 3/4 hour. When the rice is done, strain away the milk, should there be any left, and mix with it the marmalade and well-beaten eggs; stir the whole over the fire until the eggs are set; then spread the mixture on a dish to the thickness of about 1/2 inch, or rather thicker. When it is perfectly cold, cut it into long strips, dip them in a batter the same as for apple fritters, and fry them a nice brown. Dish them on a white d'oyley, strew sifted sugar over, and serve quickly.

Strawberry Jelly

Ingredients: Strawberries, pounded sugar; to every pint of juice allow 1-1/4 oz. of isinglass.

Mode: Pick the strawberries, put them into a pan, squeeze them well with a wooden spoon, add sufficient pounded sugar to sweeten them nicely, and let them remain for 1 hour, that the juice may be extracted; then add 1/2 pint of water to every pint of juice. Strain the strawberry-juice and water through a bag; measure it, and to every pint allow 1-1/4 oz. of isinglass, melted and clarified in 1/4 pint of water. Mix this with the juice; put the jelly into a mould, and set the mould in ice. A little lemon-juice added to the strawberry-juice improves the flavour of the jelly, if the fruit is very ripe; but it must be well strained before it is put to the other ingredients, or it will make the jelly muddy.

Vanilla Cream

Ingredients: 1 pint of milk, the yolks of 8 eggs, 6 oz. of sugar, 1 oz. of isinglass, flavouring to taste of essence of vanilla.

Mode: Put the milk and sugar into a saucepan, and let it get hot over a slow fire; beat up the yolks of the eggs, to which add gradually the sweetened milk; flavour the whole with essence of vanilla, put the mixture into a jug, and place this jug in a saucepan of boiling water. Stir the contents with a wooden spoon one way until the mixture thickens, but do not allow it to boil, or it will be full of lumps. Take it off the fire; stir in the isinglass, which should be previously dissolved in about 1/4 pint of water, and boiled for 2 or 3 minutes; pour the cream into an oiled mould, put it in a cool place to set, and turn it out carefully on a dish. Instead of using the essence of vanilla, a pod may be boiled in the milk instead, until the flavour is well extracted. A pod, or a pod and a half, will be found sufficient for the above proportion of ingredients.

Victoria Sandwiches

Ingredients: 4 eggs; their weight in pounded sugar, butter, and flour; 1/4 saltspoonful of salt, a layer of any kind of jam or marmalade.

Mode: Beat the butter to a cream; dredge in the flour and pounded sugar; stir these ingredients well together, and add the eggs, which should be previously thoroughly whisked. When the mixture has been well beaten for about 10 minutes, butter a Yorkshire-pudding tin, pour in the batter, and bake it in a moderate oven for 20 minutes. Let it cool, spread one half of the cake with a layer of nice preserve, place over it the other half of the cake, press the pieces slightly together, and then cut it into long finger-pieces; pile them in crossbars on a glass dish, and serve.

10

Production of Puddings and Pastry

Puddings and pastry, familiar as they may be, and unimportant as they may be held in the estimation of some, are yet intimately connected with the development of agricultural resources in reference to the cereal grasses. When they began to be made is uncertain; but we may safely presume, that a simple form of pudding was amongst the first dishes made after discovering a mode of grinding wheat into flour. Traditional history enables us to trace man back to the time of the Deluge.

After that event he seems to have recovered himself in the central parts of Asia, and to have first risen to eminence in the arts of civilization on the banks of the Nile. From this region, Greece, Carthage, and some other parts along the shores of the Mediterranean Sea, were colonized. In process of time, Greece gave to the Romans the arts which she had thus received from Egypt, and these subsequently diffused them over Europe. How these were carried to or developed in India and China, is not so well ascertained; and in America their ancient existence rests only on very indistinct traditions. The traditions of different countries ascribe it to various fabulous personages, whose names it is here unnecessary to introduce.

The habits of a people, to a great extent, are formed by the climate in which they live, and by the native or cultivated productions in which their country abounds. In Greece, the products cultivated in antiquity were the same kinds of grains and legumes as are cultivated at present, with the vine, the fig, the olive, the apple, and other fruits. So with the Romans, and so with other nations. As to the different modes of artificially preparing those to please the taste, it is only necessary to say that they arise from the universal desire of novelty, characteristic of man in the development of his social conditions. Thus has arisen the whole science of cookery, and thus arose the art of making puddings.

The porridge of the Scotch is nothing more than a species of hasty pudding, composed of oatmeal, salt, and water; and the "red pottage" for which Esau sold his birthright, must have been something similar. The barley-gruel of the Lacedaemonians, of the Athenian gladiators and common people, was the same, with the exception of the slight seasoning it had beyond the simplicity of Scottish fare. Here is the ancient recipe for the Athenian national dish:-"Dry near the fire, in the oven, twenty pounds of barley-flour; then parch it; add three pounds of linseed-meal, half a pound of coriander-seed, two ounces of salt, and the quantity of water necessary." To this sometimes a little millet was added, in order to give the paste greater cohesion and delicacy.

Although from puddings to pastry is but a step, it requires a higher degree of art to make the one than to make the other. Indeed, pastry is one of the most important branches of the culinary science. It unceasingly occupies itself with ministering pleasure to the sight as well as to the taste; with erecting graceful monuments, miniature fortresses, and all kinds of architectural imitations, composed of the sweetest and most agreeable products of all climates and countries.

At a very early period, the Orientals were acquainted with the art of manipulating in pastry; but they by no means attained to the taste, variety, and splendour of design, by which it is characterized amongst the moderns. At first it generally consisted of certain mixtures of flour, oil, and honey, to which it was confined for centuries, even among the southern nations of the European continent. At the commencement of the middle ages, a change began to take place in the art of mixing it. Eggs, butter, and salt came into repute in the making of paste, which was forthwith used as an inclosure for meat, seasoned with spices. This advance attained, the next step was to inclose cream, fruit, and marmalades; and the next, to build pyramids and castles; when the summit of the art of the pastry-cook may be supposed to have been achieved.

Making of Puddings and Pastry

A few general remarks respecting the various ingredients of which puddings and pastry are composed as follows.

- Flour should be of the best quality, and perfectly dry, and sifted before being used; if in the least damp, the paste made from it will certainly be heavy.
- Butter, unless fresh is used, should be washed from the salt, and well squeezed and wrung in a cloth, to get out all the water and buttermilk, which, if left in, assists to make the paste heavy.
- Lard should be perfectly sweet, which may be ascertained by cutting the bladder through, and, if the knife smells sweet, the lard is good.
- Suet should be finely chopped, perfectly free from skin, and quite sweet; during the process of chopping, it should be lightly dredged with flour, which prevents the pieces from sticking together. Beef suet is considered the best; but veal suet, or the outside

fat of a loin or neck of mutton, makes good crusts; as also the skimmings in which a joint of mutton has been boiled, but without vegetables.

— Clarified Beef Dripping, directions for which will be found in recipes Nos. 621 and 622, answers very well for kitchen pies, puddings, cakes, or for family use. A very good short crust may be made by mixing with it a small quantity of moist sugar; but care must be taken to use the dripping sparingly, or a very disagreeable flavour will be imparted to the paste.

— Strict cleanliness must be observed in pastry-making; all the utensils used should be perfectly free from dust and dirt, and the things required for pastry, kept entirely for that purpose.

— In mixing paste, add the water very gradually, work the whole together with the knife-blade, and knead it until perfectly smooth. Those who are inexperienced in pastry-making, should work the butter in by breaking it in small pieces and covering the paste rolled out. It should then be dredged with flour, and the ends folded over and rolled out very thin again: this process must be repeated until all the butter is used.

— The art of making paste requires much practice, dexterity, and skill: it should be touched as lightly as possible, made with cool hands and in a cool place (a marble slab is better than a board for the purpose), and the coolest part of the house should be selected for the process during warm weather.

— To insure rich paste being light, great expedition must be used in the making and baking; for if it stand long before it is put in the oven, it becomes flat and heavy.

— Puff-paste requires a brisk oven, but not too hot, or it would blacken the crust; on the other hand, if the oven be too slack, the paste will be soddened, and will not rise, nor will it have any colour. Tart-tins, cake-moulds, dishes for baked puddings, pattypans, &c., should all be buttered before the article intended to be baked is put in them: things to be baked on sheets should be placed on buttered paper. Raised-pie paste should have a soaking heat, and paste glazed must have rather a slack oven, that the icing be not scorched. It is better to ice tarts, &c. when they are three-parts baked.

— To ascertain when the oven is heated to the proper degree for puff-paste, put a small piece of the paste in previous to baking the whole, and then the heat can thus be judged of.

— The freshness of all pudding ingredients is of much importance, as one bad article will taint the whole mixture.

— When the freshness of eggs is doubtful, break each one separately in a cup, before mixing them altogether. Should there be a bad one amongst them, it can be thrown away; whereas, if mixed with the good ones, the entire quantity would be spoiled. The yolks and whites beaten separately make the articles they are put into much lighter.

— Raisins and dried fruits for puddings should be carefully picked, and, in many cases, stoned. Currants should be well washed, pressed in a cloth, and placed on a dish before the fire to get thoroughly dry; they should then be picked carefully over, and every piece of grit or stone removed from amongst them. To plump them, some cooks pour boiling water over them, and then dry them before the fire.

— Batter pudding should be smoothly mixed and free from lumps. To insure this, first mix the flour with a very small proportion of milk, and add the remainder by degrees. Should the pudding be very lumpy, it may be strained through a hair sieve.

- All boiled puddings should be put on in boiling water, which must not be allowed to stop simmering, and the pudding must always be covered with the water; if requisite, the saucepan should be kept filled up.
- To prevent a pudding boiled in a cloth from sticking to the bottom of the saucepan, place a small plate or saucer underneath it, and set the pan on a trivet over the fire. If a mould is used, this precaution is not necessary; but care must be taken to keep the pudding well covered with water.
- For dishing a boiled pudding as soon as it comes out of the pot, dip it into a basin of cold water, and the cloth will then not adhere to it. Great expedition is necessary in sending puddings to table, as, by standing, they quickly become heavy, batter puddings particularly.
- For baked or boiled puddings, the moulds, cups, or basins, should be always buttered before the mixture is put in them, and they should be put into the saucepan directly they are filled.
- Scrupulous attention should be paid to the cleanliness of pudding-cloths, as, from neglect in this particular, the outsides of boiled puddings frequently taste very disagreeably. As soon as possible after it is taken off the pudding, it should be soaked in water, and then well washed, without soap, unless it be very greasy. It should be dried out of doors, then folded up and kept in a dry place. When wanted for use, dip it in boiling water, and dredge it slightly with flour.
- The dry ingredients for puddings are better for being mixed some time before they are wanted; the liquid portion should only be added just before the pudding is put into the saucepan.

— A pinch of salt is an improvement to the generality of puddings; but this ingredient should be added very sparingly, as the flavour should not be detected.

— When baked puddings are sufficiently solid, turn them out of the dish they were baked in, bottom uppermost, and strew over them fine sifted sugar.

— When pastry or baked puddings are not done through, and yet the outside is sufficiently brown, cover them over with a piece of white paper until thoroughly cooked: this prevents them from getting burnt.

PUNDDING AND PASTRY RECIPES

Puff-Paste

Ingredients: To every lb. of flour allow 1 lb. of butter, and not quite 1/2 pint of water.

Mode: Carefully weigh the flour and butter, and have the exact proportion; squeeze the butter well, to extract the water from it, and afterwards wring it in a clean cloth, that no moisture may remain. Sift the flour; see that it is perfectly dry, and proceed in the following manner to make the paste, using a very clean paste-board and rolling-pin:-Supposing the quantity to be 1 lb. of flour, work the whole into a smooth paste, with not quite 1/2 pint of water, using a knife to mix it with: the proportion of this latter ingredient must be regulated by the discretion of the cook; if too much be added, the paste, when baked, will be tough.

Roll it out until it is of an equal thickness of about an inch; break 4 oz. of the butter into small pieces; place these on the paste, sift over it a little flour, fold it over, roll out again, and put another 4 oz. of butter. Repeat the rolling and buttering until the paste has been rolled out 4 times, or equal quantities of flour and butter have been used. Do not omit, every time the paste is rolled out, to dredge a little flour over that and the rolling-pin, to prevent both from sticking. Handle the paste as lightly as possible, and do not press heavily upon it with the rolling-pin.

The next thing to be considered is the oven, as the baking of pastry requires particular attention. Do not put it into the oven until it is sufficiently hot to raise the paste; for the best-prepared paste, if not properly baked, will be good for nothing. Brushing the paste as often as rolled out, and the pieces of butter placed thereon, with the white of an egg, assists it to rise in leaves or flakes. As this is the great beauty of puff-paste, it is as well to try this method.

Medium Puff-Paste

Ingredients: To every lb. of flour allow 8 oz. of butter, 4 oz. of lard, not quite 1/2 pint of water.

Mode: This paste may be made by the directions in the preceding recipe, only using less butter and substituting lard for a portion of it. Mix the flour to a smooth paste with not quite 1/2 pint of water; then roll it out 3 times, the first time covering the paste with butter, the second with lard, and the third with butter. Keep the rolling-pin and paste slightly dredged with flour, to prevent them from sticking, and it will be ready for use.

Common Paste

Ingredients: 1-1/4 lb. of flour, 1/2 lb. of butter, rather more than 1/2 pint of water.

Mode: Rub the butter lightly into the flour, and mix it to a smooth paste with the water; roll it out 2 or 3 times, and it will be ready for use. This paste may be converted into an excellent short crust for sweet tart, by adding to the flour, after the butter is rubbed in, 2 tablespoonfuls of fine-sifted sugar.

French Puff-Paste, or Feuilletage

Ingredients: Equal quantities of flour and butter -- say 1 lb. of each; 1/2 saltspoonful of salt, the yolks of 2 eggs, rather more than 1/4 pint of water.

Mode: Weigh the flour; ascertain that it is perfectly dry, and sift it; squeeze all the water from the butter, and wring it in a clean cloth till there is no moisture remaining. Put the flour on the paste-board, work lightly into it 2 oz. of the butter, and then make a hole in the centre; into this well put the yolks of 2 eggs, the salt, and about 1/4 pint of water (the quantity of this latter ingredient must be regulated by the cook, as it is impossible to give the exact proportion of it); knead up the paste quickly and lightly, and, when quite smooth, roll it out square to the thickness of about 1/2 inch. Presuming that the butter is perfectly free from moisture, and as cool as possible, roll it into a ball, and place this ball of butter on the paste; fold the paste over the butter all round, and secure it by wrapping it well all over.

Flatten the paste by rolling it lightly with the rolling-pin until it is quite thin, but not thin enough to allow the butter to break through, and keep the board and paste dredged lightly with flour during the process of making it. This rolling gives it the first turn. Now fold the paste in three, and roll out again, and, should the weather be very warm, put it in a cold place on the ground to cool between the several turns; for, unless this is particularly attended to, the paste will be spoiled. Roll out the paste again twice, put it by to cool, then roll it out twice more, which will make 6 turnings in all. Now fold the paste in two, and it will be ready for use. If properly baked and well made, this crust will be delicious, and should rise in the oven about 5 or 6 inches.

The paste should be made rather firm in the first instance, as the ball of butter is liable to break through. Great attention must also be paid to keeping the butter very cool, as, if this is in a liquid and soft state, the paste will not answer at all. Should the cook be dexterous enough to succeed in making this, the paste will have a much better appearance than that made by the process of dividing the butter into 4 parts, and placing it over the rolled-out paste; but, until experience has been acquired. The above paste is used for vols-au-vent, small articles of pastry, and, in fact, everything that requires very light crust.

Short Crust

Ingredients:- To every lb. of flour allow 8 oz. of butter, the yolks of 2 eggs, 2 oz. of sifted sugar, about 1/4 pint of milk.

Mode: Rub the butter into the flour, add the sugar, and mix the whole as lightly as possible to a smooth paste, with the yolks of eggs well beaten, and the milk. The proportion of the latter ingredient must be judged of by the size of the eggs: if these are large, so much will not be required, and more if the eggs are smaller.

Common Short Crust

Ingredients:- To every pound of flour allow 2 oz. of sifted sugar, 3 oz. of butter, about 1/2 pint of boiling milk.

Mode: Crumble the butter into the flour as finely as possible, add the sugar, and work the whole up to a smooth paste with the boiling milk. Roll it out thin, and bake in a moderate oven.

Butter Crust

Ingredients: To every lb. of flour allow 6 oz. of butter, 1/2 pint of water.

Mode: With a knife, work the flour to a smooth paste with 1/2 pint of water; roll the crust out rather thin; place the butter over it in small pieces; dredge lightly over it some flour, and fold the paste over; repeat the rolling once more, and the crust will be ready for use. It may be enriched by adding another 2 oz. of butter; but, for ordinary purposes, the above quantity will be found quite sufficient.

Suet Crust

Ingredients: To every lb. of flour allow 5 or 6 oz. of beef suet, 1/2 pint of water.

Mode: Free the suet from skin and shreds; chop it extremely fine, and rub it well into the flour; work the whole to a smooth paste with the above proportion of water; roll it out, and it is ready for use. This crust is quite rich enough for ordinary purposes, but when a better one is desired, use from 1/2 to 3/4 lb. of suet to every lb. of flour. Some cooks, for rich crusts, pound the suet in a mortar, with a small quantity of butter. It should then be laid on the paste in small pieces, the same as for puff-crust, and will be found exceedingly nice for hot tarts. 5 oz. of suet to every lb. of flour will make a very good crust; and even 1/4 lb. will answer very well for children, or where the crust is wanted very plain.

Common Crust for Raised Pies

Ingredients: To every lb. of flour allow 1/2 pint of water, 1-1/2 oz. of butter, 1-1/2 oz. of lard, 1/2 saltspoonful of salt.

Mode: Put into a saucepan the water; when it boils, add the butter and lard; and when these are melted, make a hole in the middle of the flour; pour in the water gradually; beat it well with a wooden spoon, and be particular in not making the paste too soft. When it is well mixed, knead it with the hands until quite stiff, dredging a little flour over the paste and board, to prevent them from sticking. When it is well kneaded, place it before the fire, with a cloth covered over it, for a few minutes; it will then be more easily worked into shape. This paste does not taste so nicely as the preceding one, but is worked with greater facility, and answers just as well for raised pies, for the crust is seldom eaten.

Lard or Flead Crust

Ingredients: To every lb. of flour allow 1/2 lb. of lard or flead, 1/2 pint of water, 1/2 saltspoonful of salt.

Mode: Clear the flead free from skin, and slice it into thin flakes; rub it into the flour, add the salt, and work the whole into a smooth paste, with the above proportion of water; fold the paste over two or three times, beat it well with the rolling-pin, roll it out, and it will be ready for use. The crust made from this will be found extremely light, and may be made into cakes or tarts; it may also be very much enriched by adding more flead to the same proportion of flour.

Almond Cheesecakes

Ingredients: 1/4 lb. of sweet almonds, 4 bitter ones, 3 eggs, 2 oz. of butter, the rind of 1/4 lemon, 1 tablespoonful of lemon-juice, 3 oz. of sugar.

Mode: Blanch and pound the almonds smoothly in a mortar, with a little rose—or spring-water; stir in the eggs, which should be well beaten, and the butter, which should be warmed; add the grated lemon-peel and -- juice, sweeten, and stir well until the whole is thoroughly mixed. Line some pattypans with puff-paste, put in the mixture, and bake for 20 minutes, or rather less in a quick oven.

Almond Paste

Ingredients: 1 lb. of sweet almonds, 6 bitter ones, 1 lb. of very finely sifted sugar, the whites of 2 eggs.

Mode: Blanch the almonds, and dry them thoroughly; put them into a mortar, and pound them well, wetting them gradually with the whites of 2 eggs. When well pounded, put them into a small preserving-pan, add the sugar, and place the pan on a small but clear fire (a hot-plate is better); keep stirring until the paste is dry, then take it out of the pan, put it between two dishes, and, when cold, make it into any shape that fancy may dictate.

Baked Almond Pudding

Ingredients: 1/4 lb. of almonds, 4 bitter ditto, 1 glass of sherry, 4 eggs, the rind and juice of 1/2 lemon, 3 oz. of butter, 1 pint of cream, 2 tablespoonfuls of sugar.

Mode: Blanch and pound the almonds to a smooth paste with the water; mix these with the butter, which should be melted; beat up the eggs, grate the lemon-rind, and strain the juice; add these, with the cream, sugar, and wine, to the other *Ingredients*, and stir them well together. When well mixed, put it into a pie-dish lined with puff-paste, and bake for 1/2 hour.

Small Almond Puddings

Ingredients: 1/2 lb. of sweet almonds, 6 bitter ones, 1/4 lb. of butter, 4 eggs, 2 tablespoonfuls of sifted sugar, 2 tablespoonfuls of cream, 1 tablespoonful of brandy.

Mode: Blanch and pound the almonds to a smooth paste with a spoonful of water; warm the butter, mix the almonds with this, and add the other ingredients, leaving out the whites of 2 eggs, and be particular that these are well beaten. Mix well, butter some cups, half fill them, and bake the puddings from 20 minutes to 1/2 hour. Turn them out on a dish, and serve with sweet sauce.

Almond Puffs

Ingredients: 2 tablespoonfuls of flour, 2 oz. of butter, 2 oz. of pounded sugar, 2 oz. of sweet almonds, 4 bitter almonds.

Mode: Blanch and pound the almonds in a mortar to a smooth paste; melt the butter, dredge in the flour, and add the sugar and pounded almonds. Beat the mixture well, and put it into cups or very tiny jelly-pots, which should be well buttered, and bake in a moderate oven for about 20 minutes, or longer should the puffs be large. Turn them out on a dish, the bottom of the puff upper-most, and serve.

Aunt Nelly's Pudding

Ingredients: 1/2 lb. of flour, 1/2 lb. of treacle, 1/2 lb. of suet, the rind and juice of 1 lemon, a few strips of candied lemon-peel, 3 tablespoonfuls of cream, 2 eggs.

Mode: Chop the suet finely; mix with it the flour, treacle, lemon-peel minced, and candied lemon-peel; add the cream, lemon-juice, and 2 well-beaten eggs; beat the pudding well, put it into a buttered basin, tie it down with a cloth, and boil from 3-1/2 to 4 hours.

Apple Cheesecakes

Ingredients: 1/2 lb. of apple pulp, 1/4 lb. of sifted sugar, 1/4 lb. of butter, 4 eggs, the rind and juice of 1 lemon.

Mode: Pare, core, and boil sufficient apples to make 1/2 lb. when cooked; add to these the sugar, the butter, which should be melted; the eggs, leaving out 2 of the whites, and take grated rind and juice of 1 lemon; stir the mixture well; line some patty-pans with puff-paste, put in the mixture, and bake about 20 minutes.

Rich Baked Apple Pudding

Ingredients: 1/2 lb. of the pulp of apples, 1/2 lb. of loaf sugar, 6 oz. of butter, the rind of 1 lemon, 6 eggs, puff-paste.

Mode: Peel, core, and cut the apples, as for sauce; put them into a stewpan, with only just sufficient water to prevent them from burning, and let them stew until reduced to a pulp. Weigh the pulp, and to every 1/2 lb. add sifted sugar, grated lemon-rind, and 6 well-beaten eggs. Beat these ingredients well together; then melt the butter, stir it to the other things, put a border of puff-paste round the dish, and bake for rather more than 1/2 hour. The butter should not be added until the pudding is ready for the oven.

Rich Sweet Apple Pudding

Ingredients: 1/2 lb. of bread crumbs, 1/2 lb. of suet, 1/2 lb. of currants, 1/2 lb. of apples, 1/2 lb. of moist sugar, 6 eggs, 12 sweet almonds, 1/2 saltspoonful of grated nutmeg, 1 wineglassful of brandy.

Mode: Chop the suet very fine; wash the currants, dry them, and pick away the stalks and pieces of grit; pare, core, and chop the apple, and grate the bread into fine crumbs, and mince the almonds. Mix all these ingredients together, adding the sugar and nutmeg; beat up the eggs, omitting the whites of three; stir these to the pudding, and when all is well mixed, add the brandy, and put the pudding into a buttered mould; tie down with a cloth, put it into boiling water, and let it boil for 3 hours.

Baked Apple Pudding

Ingredients: 5 moderate-sized apples, 2 tablespoonfuls of finely-chopped suet, 3 eggs, 3 tablespoonfuls of flour, 1 pint of milk, a little grated nutmeg.

Mode: Mix the flour to a smooth batter with the milk; add the eggs, which should be well whisked, and put this batter into a well-buttered pie-dish. Wipe the apples clean, but do not pare them; cut them in halves, and take out the cores; lay them in the batter, rind uppermost; shake the suet on the top, over which, also grate a little nutmeg; bake in a moderate oven for an hour, and cover, when served, with sifted loaf sugar. This pudding is also very good with the apples pared, sliced, and mixed with the batter.

Apple Snowballs

Ingredients: 2 teacupfuls of rice, apples, moist sugar, cloves.

Mode: Boil the rice in milk until three-parts done; then strain it off, and pare and core the apples without dividing them. Put a small quantity of sugar and a clove into each apple, put the rice round them, and tie each ball separately in a cloth. Boil until the apples are tender; then take them up, remove the cloths, and serve.

Alma Pudding

Ingredients: 1/2 lb. of fresh butter, 1/2 lb. of powdered sugar, 1/2 lb. of flour, 1/4 lb. of currants, 4 eggs.

Mode: Beat the butter to a thick cream, strew in, by degrees, the sugar, and mix both these well together; then dredge the flour in gradually, add the currants, and moisten with the eggs, which should be well beaten. When all the ingredients are well stirred and mixed, butter a mould that will hold the mixture exactly, tie it down with a cloth, put the pudding into boiling water, and boil for 5 hours; when turned out, strew some powdered sugar over it, and serve.

Baked Apricot Pudding

Ingredients: 12 large apricots, 3/4 pint of bread crumbs, 1 pint of milk, 3 oz. of pounded sugar, the yolks of 4 eggs, 1 glass of sherry.

Mode: Make the milk boiling hot, and pour it on to the bread crumbs; when half cold, add the sugar, the well-whisked yolks of the eggs, and the sherry. Divide the apricots in half, scald them until they are soft, and break them up with a spoon, adding a few of the kernels, which should be well pounded in a mortar; then mix the fruit and other *Ingredients* together, put a border of paste round the dish, fill with the mixture, and bake the pudding from 1/2 to 3/4 hour.

Apricot Tart

Ingredients: 12 or 14 apricots, sugar to taste, puff-paste or short crust.

Mode: Break the apricots in half, take out the stones, and put them into a pie-dish, in the centre of which place a very small cup or jar, bottom uppermost; sweeten with good moist sugar, but add no water. Line the edge of the dish with paste, put on the cover, and ornament the pie in any of the usual modes. Bake from 1/2 to 3/4 hour, according to size; and if puff-paste is used, glaze it about 10 minutes before the pie is done, and put it into the oven again to set the glaze. Short crust merely requires a little sifted sugar sprinkled over it before being sent to table.

Baked or Boiled Arrowroot Pudding

Ingredients: 2 tablespoonfuls of arrowroot, 1-1/2 pint of milk, 1 oz. of butter, the rind of 1/2 lemon, 2 heaped tablespoonfuls of moist sugar, a little grated nutmeg.

Mode: Mix the arrowroot with as much cold milk as will make it into a smooth batter, moderately thick; put the remainder of the milk into a stewpan with the lemon-peel, and let it infuse for about 1/2 hour; when it boils, strain it gently to the batter, stirring it all the time to keep it smooth; then add the butter; beat this well in until thoroughly mixed, and sweeten with moist sugar.

Put the mixture into a pie-dish, round which has been placed a border of paste, grate a little nutmeg over the top, and bake the pudding from 1 to 1-1/4 hour, in a moderate oven, or boil it the same length of time in a well-buttered basin. To enrich this pudding, stir to the other ingredients, just before it is put in the oven, 3 well-whisked eggs, and add a tablespoonful of brandy. For a nursery pudding, the addition of the latter ingredients will be found quite superfluous, as also the paste round the edge of the dish.

Bakewell Pudding

Ingredients: - 1/4 lb. of puff-paste, 5 eggs, 6 oz. of sugar, 1/4 lb. of butter, 1 oz. of almonds, jam.

Mode: Cover a dish with thin paste, and put over this a layer of any kind of jam, 1/2 inch thick; put the yolks of 5 eggs into a basin with the white of 1, and beat these well; add the sifted sugar, the butter, which should be melted, and the almonds, which should be well pounded; beat all together until well mixed, then pour it into the dish over the jam, and bake for an hour in a moderate oven.

Baroness Pudding

Ingredients: 3/4 lb. of suet, 3/4 lb. of raisins weighed after being stoned, 3/4 lb. of flour, 1/2 pint of milk, 1/4 saltspoonful of salt.

Mode: Prepare the suet, by carefully freeing it from skin, and chop it finely; stone the raisins, and cut them in halves, and mix both these ingredients with the salt and flour; moisten the whole with the above proportion of milk, stir the mixture well, and tie the pudding in a floured cloth, which has been previously wrung out in boiling water. Put the pudding into a saucepan of boiling water, and let it boil, without ceasing, 4-1/2 hours. Serve merely with plain sifted sugar, a little of which may be sprinkled over the pudding.

Barberry Tart

Ingredients: To every lb. of barberries allow 3/4 lb. of lump sugar; paste.

Mode: Pick the barberries from the stalks, and put the fruit into a stone jar; place this jar in boiling water, and let it simmer very slowly until the fruit is soft; then put it into a preserving-pan with the sugar, and boil gently for 15 minutes; line a tartlet-pan with paste, bake it, and, when the paste is cold, fill with the barberries, and ornament the tart with a few baked leaves of paste, cut out, as shown in the engraving.

Boiled Batter Pudding

Ingredients: 3 eggs, 1 oz. of butter, 1 pint of milk, 3 tablespoonfuls of flour, a little salt.

Mode: Put the flour into a basin, and add sufficient milk to moisten it; carefully rub down all the lumps with a spoon, then pour in the remainder of the milk, and stir in the butter, which should be previously melted; keep beating the mixture, add the eggs and a pinch of salt, and when the batter is quite smooth, put it into a well-buttered basin, tie it down very tightly, and put it into boiling water; move the basin about for a few minutes after it is put into the water, to prevent the flour settling in any part, and boil for 1-1/4 hour.

This pudding may also be boiled in a floured cloth that has been wetted in hot water; it will then take a few minutes less than when boiled in a basin. Send these puddings very quickly to table, and serve with sweet sauce, wine sauce, stewed fruit, or jam of any kind: when the latter is used, a little of it may be placed round the dish in small quantities, as a garnish.

Orange Batter Pudding

Ingredients: 4 eggs, 1 pint of milk, 1-1/4 oz. of loaf sugar, 3 tablespoonfuls of flour.

Mode: Make the batter with the above ingredients, put it into a well-buttered basin, tie it down with a cloth, and boil for 1 hour. As soon as it is turned out of the basin, put a small jar of orange marmalade all over the top, and send the pudding very quickly to table.

Baked Bread Pudding

Ingredients: 1/2 lb. of grated bread, 1 pint of milk, 4 eggs, 4 oz. of butter, 4 oz. of moist sugar, 2 oz. of candied peel, 6 bitter almonds, 1 tablespoonful of brandy.

Mode: Put the milk into a stewpan, with the bitter almonds; let it infuse for 1/4 hour; bring it to the boiling point; strain it on to the bread crumbs, and let these remain till cold; then add the eggs, which should be well whisked, the butter, sugar, and brandy, and beat the pudding well until all the ingredients are thoroughly mixed; line the bottom of a pie-dish with the candied peel sliced thin, put in the mixture, and bake for nearly 3/4 hour.

Plain Bread Pudding

Ingredients: Odd pieces of crust or crumb of bread; to every quart allow 1/2 teaspoonful of salt, 1 teaspoonful of grated nutmeg, 3 oz. of moist sugar, 1/2 lb. of currants, 1-1/4 oz. of butter.

Mode: Break the bread into small pieces, and pour on them as much boiling water as will soak them well. Let these stand till the water is cool; then press it out, and mash the bread with a fork until it is quite free from lumps. Measure this pulp, and to every quart stir in salt, nutmeg, sugar, and currants in the above proportion; mix all well together, and put it into a well-buttered pie-dish. Smooth the surface with the back of a spoon, and place the butter in small pieces over the top; bake in a moderate oven for 1-1/2 hour, and serve very hot. Boiling milk substituted for the boiling water would very much improve this pudding.

Canary Pudding

Ingredients: The weight of 3 eggs in sugar and butter, the weight of 2 eggs in flour, the rind of 1 small lemon, 3 eggs.

Mode: Melt the butter to a liquid state, but do not allow it to oil; stir to this the sugar and finely-minced lemon-peel, and gradually dredge in the flour, keeping the mixture well stirred; whisk the eggs; add these to the pudding; beat all the ingredients until thoroughly blended, and put them into a buttered mould or basin; boil for 2 hours, and serve with sweet sauce.

Baked or Boiled Carrot Pudding

Ingredients: 1/2 lb. of bread crumbs, 4 oz. of suet, 1/4 lb. of stoned raisins, 3/4 lb. of carrot, 1/4 lb. of currants, 3 oz. of sugar, 3 eggs, milk, 1/4 nutmeg.

Mode: Boil the carrots until tender enough to mash to a pulp; add the remaining ingredients, and moisten with sufficient milk to make the pudding of the consistency of thick batter. If to be boiled, put the mixture into a buttered basin, tie it down with a cloth, and boil for 2-1/2 hours: if to be baked, put it into a pie-dish, and bake for nearly an hour; turn it out of the dish, strew sifted sugar over it, and serve.

Cold Pudding

Ingredients: 4 eggs, 1 pint of milk, sugar to taste, a little grated lemon-rind, 2 oz. of raisins, 4 tablespoonfuls of marmalade, a few slices of sponge cake.

Mode: Sweeten the milk with lump sugar, add a little grated lemon-rind, and stir to this the eggs, which should be well whisked; line a buttered mould with the raisins, stoned and cut in half; spread the slices of cake with the marmalade, and place them in the mould; then pour in the custard, tie the pudding down with paper and a cloth, and boil gently for 1 hour: when cold, turn it out, and serve.

College Puddings

Ingredients: 1 pint of bread crumbs, 6 oz. of finely-chopped suet, 1/4 lb. of currants, a few thin slices of candied peel, 3 oz. of sugar, 1/4 nutmeg, 3 eggs, 4 tablespoonfuls of brandy.

Mode: Put the bread crumbs into a basin; add the suet, currants, candied peel, sugar, and nutmeg, grated, and stir these ingredients until they are thoroughly mixed. Beat up the eggs, moisten the pudding with these, and put in the brandy; beat well for a few minutes, then form the mixture into round balls or egg-shaped pieces; fry these in hot butter or lard, letting them stew in it until thoroughly done, and turn them two or three times, till of a fine light brown; drain them on a piece of blotting-paper before the fire; dish, and serve with wine sauce.

Baked Custard Pudding

Ingredients: 1-1/2 pint of milk, the rind of 1/4 lemon, 1/4 lb. of moist sugar, 4 eggs.

Mode: Put the milk into a saucepan with the sugar and lemon-rind, and let this infuse for about 4 hour, or until the milk is well flavoured; whisk the eggs, yolks and whites; pour the milk to them, stirring all the while; then have ready a pie-dish, lined at the edge with paste ready baked; strain the custard into the dish, grate a little nutmeg over the top, and bake in a very slow oven for about 1/2 hour, or rather longer. The flavour of this pudding may be varied by substituting bitter almonds for the lemon-rind; and it may be very much enriched by using half cream and half milk, and doubling the quantity of eggs.

Damson Tart

Ingredients: 1-1/4 pint of damsons, 1/4 lb. of moist sugar, 1/2 lb. of short or puff crust.

Mode: Put the damsons, with the sugar between them, into a deep pie-dish, in the midst of which, place a small cup or jar turned upside down; pile the fruit high in the middle, line the edges of the dish with short or puff crust, whichever may be preferred; put on the cover, ornament the edges, and bake from 1/2 to 3/4 hour in a good oven. If puff-crust is used, about 10 minutes before the pie is done, take it out of the oven, brush it over with the white of an egg beaten to a froth with the blade of a knife; strew some sifted sugar over, and a few drops of water, and put the tart back to finish baking: with short crust, a little plain sifted sugar, sprinkled over, is all that will be required.

Damson Pudding

Ingredients: 1-1/2 pint of damsons, 1/4 lb. of moist sugar, 3/4 lb. of suet or butter crust.

Mode: Make a suet crust with 3/4 lb. of flour; line a buttered pudding-basin with a portion of it; fill the basin with the damsons, sweeten them, and put on the lid; pinch the edges of the crust together, that the juice does not escape; tie over a floured cloth, put the pudding into boiling water, and boil from 2-1/2 to 3 hours.

Empress Pudding

Ingredients: 1/2 lb. of rice, 2 oz. of butter, 3 eggs, jam, sufficient milk to soften the rice.

Mode: Boil the rice in the milk until very soft; then add the butter boil it for a few minutes after the latter ingredient is put in, and set it by to cool. Well beat the eggs, stir these in, and line a dish with puff-paste; put over this a layer of rice, then a thin layer of any kind of jam, then another layer of rice, and proceed in this manner until the dish is full; and bake in a moderate oven for 3/4 hour. This pudding may be eaten hot or cold; if the latter, it will be much improved by having a boiled custard poured over it.

Fig Pudding

Ingredients: - 2 lbs. of figs, 1 lb. of suet, 1/2 lb. of flour, 1/2 lb. of bread crumbs, 2 eggs, milk.

Mode: Cut the figs into small pieces, grate the bread finely, and chop the suet very small; mix these well together, add the flour, the eggs, which should be well beaten, and sufficient milk to form the whole into a stiff paste; butter a mould or basin, press the pudding into it very closely, tie it down with a cloth, and boil for 3 hours, or rather longer; turn it out of the mould, and serve with melted butter, wine-sauce, or cream.

Folkestone Pudding-Pies

Ingredients: 1 pint of milk, 3 oz. of ground rice, 3 oz. of butter, 1/4 lb. of sugar, flavouring of lemon-peel or bay-leaf, 6 eggs, puff-paste, currants.

Mode: Infuse 2 laurel or bay leaves, or the rind of 1/2 lemon, in the milk, and when it is well flavoured, strain it, and add the rice; boil these for 1/4 hour, stirring all the time; then take them off the fire, stir in the butter, sugar, and eggs, and let these latter be well beaten before they are added to the other ingredients; when nearly cold, line some patty-pans with puff-paste, fill with the custard, strew over each a few currants, and bake from 20 to 25 minutes in a moderate oven.

Ginger Pudding

Ingredients: 1/2 lb. of flour, 1/4 lb. of suet, 1/4 lb. of moist sugar, 2 large teaspoonfuls of grated ginger.

Mode: Shred the suet very fine, mix it with the flour, sugar, and ginger; stir all well together; butter a basin, and put the mixture in dry; tie a cloth over, and boil for 3 hours.

Golden Pudding

Ingredients: 1/4 lb. of bread crumbs, 1/4 lb. of suet, 1/4 lb. of marmalade, 1/4 lb. of sugar, 4 eggs.

Mode: Put the bread crumbs into a basin; mix with them the suet, which should be finely minced, the marmalade, and the sugar; stir all these ingredients well together, beat the eggs to a froth, moisten the pudding with these, and when well mixed, put it into a mould or buttered basin; tie down with a floured cloth, and boil for 2 hours. When turned out, strew a little fine-sifted sugar over the top, and serve.

Herodotus Pudding

Ingredients: 1/2 lb. of bread crumbs, 1/2 lb. of good figs, 6 oz. of suet, 6 oz. of moist sugar, 1/2 saltspoonful of salt, 3 eggs, nutmeg to taste.

Mode: Mince the suet and figs very finely; add the remaining ingredients, taking care that the eggs are well whisked; beat the mixture for a few minutes, put it into a buttered mould, tie it down with a floured cloth, and boil the pudding for 5 hours. Serve with wine sauce.

Hunter's Pudding.

Ingredients: 1 lb. of raisins, 1 lb. of currants, 1 lb. of suet, 1 lb. of bread crumbs, 3 lb. of moist sugar, 8 eggs, 1 tablespoonful of flour, 3 lb. of mixed candied peel, 1 glass of brandy, 10 drops of essence of lemon, 10 drops of essence of almonds, 1/2 nutmeg, 2 blades of mace, 6 cloves.

Mode: Stone and shred the raisins rather small, chop the suet finely, and rub the bread until all lumps are well broken; pound the spice to powder, cut the candied peel into thin shreds, and mix all these ingredients well together, adding the sugar. Beat the eggs to a strong froth, and as they are beaten, drop into them the essence of lemon and essence of almonds; stir these to the dry ingredients, mix well, and add the brandy. Tie the pudding firmly in a cloth, and boil it for 6 hours at the least: 7 or 8 hours would be still better for it. Serve with boiled custard, or red-currant jelly, or brandy sauce.

Iced Pudding

Ingredients: 1/2 lb. of sweet almonds, 2 oz. of bitter ones, 3/4 lb. of sugar, 8 eggs, 1-1/2 pint of milk.

Mode: Blanch and dry the almonds thoroughly in a cloth, then pound them in a mortar until reduced to a smooth paste; add to these the well-beaten eggs, the sugar, and milk; stir these ingredients over the fire until they thicken, but do not allow them to boil; then strain and put the mixture into the freezing-pot; surround it with ice, and freeze it as directed in recipe 1290. When quite frozen, fill an iced-pudding mould, put on the lid, and keep the pudding in ice until required for table; then turn it out on the dish, and garnish it with a compôte of any fruit that may be preferred, pouring a little over the top of the pudding. This pudding may be flavoured with vanilla, Curaçoa, or Maraschino.

Baked Lemon Pudding

Ingredients: The yolks of 4 eggs, 4 oz. of pounded sugar, 1 lemon, 1/4 lb. of butter, puff-crust.

Mode: Beat the eggs to a froth; mix with them the sugar and warmed butter; stir these ingredients well together, putting in the grated rind and strained juice of the lemon-peel. Line a shallow dish with puff-paste; put in the mixture, and bake in a moderate oven for 40 minutes; turn the pudding out of the dish, strew over it sifted sugar, and serve.

Sweet Macaroni Pudding

Ingredients: 2-1/2 oz. of macaroni, 2 pints of milk, the rind of 1/2 lemon, 3 eggs, sugar and grated nutmeg to taste, 2 tablespoonfuls of brandy.

Mode: Put the macaroni, with a pint of the milk, into a saucepan with the lemon-peel, and let it simmer gently until the macaroni is tender; then put it into a pie-dish without the peel; mix the other pint of milk with the eggs; stir these well together, adding the sugar and brandy, and pour the mixture over the macaroni. Grate a little nutmeg over the top, and bake in a moderate oven for 1/2 hour. To make this pudding look nice, a paste should be laid round the edges of the dish, and, for variety, a layer of preserve or marmalade may be placed on the macaroni: in this case omit the brandy.

Marmalade and Vermicelli Pudding

Ingredients: 1 breakfastcupful of vermicelli, 2 tablespoonfuls of marmalade, 1/4 lb. of raisins, sugar to taste, 3 eggs, milk.

Mode: Pour some boiling milk on the vermicelli, and let it remain covered for 10 minutes; then mix with it the marmalade, stoned raisins, sugar, and beaten eggs. Stir all well together, put the mixture into a buttered mould, boil for 1-1/2 hour, and serve with custard sauce.

Nesselrode Pudding

Ingredients: 40 chestnuts, 1 lb. of sugar, flavouring of vanilla, 1 pint of cream, the yolks of 12 eggs, 1 glass of Maraschino, 1 oz. of candied citron, 2 oz. of currants, 2 oz. of stoned raisins, 1/2 pint of whipped cream, 3 eggs.

Mode: Blanch the chestnuts in boiling water, remove the husks, and pound them in a mortar until perfectly smooth, adding a few spoonfuls of syrup. Then rub them through a fine sieve, and mix them in a basin with a pint of syrup made from 1 lb. of sugar, clarified, and flavoured with vanilla, 1 pint of cream, and the yolks of 12 eggs. Set this mixture over a slow fire, stirring it without ceasing, and just as it begins to boil, take it off and pass it through a tammy.

When it is cold, put it into a freezing-pot, adding the Maraschino, and make the mixture set; then add the sliced citron, the currants, and stoned raisins (these two latter should be soaked the day previously in Maraschino and sugar pounded with vanilla); the whole thus mingled, add a plateful of whipped cream mixed with the whites of 3 eggs, beaten to a froth with a little syrup. When the pudding is perfectly frozen, put it into a pineapple-shaped mould; close the lid, place it again in the freezing-pan, covered over with pounded ice and saltpetre, and let it remain until required for table; then turn the pudding out, and serve.

Pastry Sandwiches

Ingredients: Puff-paste, jam of any kind, the white of an egg, sifted sugar.

Mode: Roll the paste out thin; put half of it on a baking-sheet or tin, and spread equally over it apricot, greengage, or any preserve that may be preferred. Lay over this preserve another thin paste; press the edges together all round; and mark the paste in lines with a knife on the surface, to show where to cut it when baked. Bake from 20 minutes to 1/2 hour; and, a short time before being done, take the pastry out of the oven, brush it over with the white of an egg, sift over pounded sugar, and put it back in the oven to colour. When cold, cut it into strips; pile these on a dish pyramidically, and serve. These strips, cut about 2 inches long, piled in circular rows, and a plateful of flavoured whipped cream poured in the middle, make a very pretty dish.

Petites Bouchees

Ingredients: 6 oz. of sweet almonds, 1/4 lb. of sifted sugar, the rind of 1/2 lemon, the white of 1 egg, puff-paste.

Mode: Blanch the almonds, and chop them fine; rub the sugar on the lemon-rind, and pound it in a mortar; mix this with the almonds and the white of the egg. Roll some puff-paste out; cut it in any shape that may be preferred, such as diamonds, rings, ovals, &c., and spread the above mixture over the paste. Bake the bouchées in an oven, not too hot, and serve cold.

Christmas Plum-Pudding

Ingredients: 1-1/2 lb. of raisins, 1/2 lb. of currants, 1/2 lb. of mixed peel, 3/4 lb. of bread crumbs, 3/4 lb. of suet, 8 eggs, 1 wineglassful of brandy.

Mode: Stone and cut the raisins in halves, but do not chop them; wash, pick, and dry the currants, and mince the suet finely; cut the candied peel into thin slices, and grate down the bread into fine crumbs. When all these dry ingredients are prepared, mix them well together; then moisten the mixture with the eggs, which should be well beaten, and the brandy; stir well, that everything may be very thoroughly blended, and press the pudding into a buttered mould; tie it down tightly with a floured cloth, and boil for 5 or 6 hours. It may be boiled in a cloth without a mould, and will require the same time allowed for cooking.

As Christmas puddings are usually made a few days before they are required for table, when the pudding is taken out of the pot, hang it up immediately, and put a plate or saucer underneath to catch the water that may drain from it. The day it is to be eaten, plunge it into boiling water, and keep it boiling for at least 2 hours; then turn it out of the mould, and serve with brandy-sauce. On Christmas-day a sprig of holly is usually placed in the middle of the pudding, and about a wineglassful of brandy poured round it, which, at the moment of serving, is lighted, and the pudding thus brought to table encircled in flame.

A Pound Plum-Pudding

Ingredients: 1 lb. of suet, 1 lb. of currants, 1 lb. of stoned raisins, 8 eggs, 1/2 grated nutmeg, 2 oz. of sliced candied peel, 1 teaspoonful of ground ginger, 1/2 lb. of bread crumbs, 1/2 lb. of flour, 1/2 pint of milk.

Mode: Chop the suet finely; mix with it the dry ingredients; stir these well together, and add the well-beaten eggs and milk to moisten with. Beat up the mixture well, and should the above proportion of milk not be found sufficient to make it of the proper consistency, a little more should be added. Press the pudding into a mould, tie it in a floured cloth, and boil for 5 hours, or rather longer, and serve with brandy-sauce.

Potato Pasty

Ingredients: 1-1/2 lb. of rump-steak or mutton cutlets, pepper and salt to taste, 1/3 pint of weak broth or gravy, 1 oz. of butter, mashed potatoes.

Mode: Place the meat, cut in small pieces, at the bottom of the pan; season it with pepper and salt, and add the gravy and butter broken, into small pieces. Put on the perforated plate, with its valve-pipe screwed on, and fill up the whole space. to the top of the tube with nicely-mashed potatoes mixed with a little milk, and finish the surface of them in any ornamental manner. If carefully baked, the potatoes will be covered with a delicate brown crust, retaining all the savoury steam rising from the meat. Send it to table as it comes from the oven, with a napkin folded round it.

Potato Pudding

Ingredients: 1/2 lb. of mashed potatoes, 2 oz. of butter, 2 eggs, 1/4 pint of milk, 3 tablespoonfuls of sherry, 1/4 saltspoonful of salt, the juice and rind of 1 small lemon, 2 oz. of sugar.

Mode: Boil sufficient potatoes to make 1/2 lb. when mashed; add to these the butter, eggs, milk, sherry, lemon-juice, and sugar; mince the lemon-peel very finely, and beat all the ingredients well together. Put the pudding into a buttered pie-dish, and bake for rather more than 1/2 hour. To enrich it, add a few pounded almonds, and increase the quantity of eggs and butter.

Baked Rice Pudding.

Ingredients: 1 small teacupful of rice, 4 eggs, 1 pint of milk, 2 oz. of fresh butter, 2 oz. of beef marrow, 1/4 lb. of currants, 2 tablespoonfuls of brandy, nutmeg, 1/4 lb. of sugar, the rind of 1/2 lemon.

Mode: Put the lemon-rind and milk into a stewpan, and let it infuse till the milk is well flavoured with the lemon; in the mean time, boil the rice until tender in water, with a very small quantity of salt, and, when done, let it be thoroughly drained. Beat the eggs, stir to them the milk, which should be strained, the butter, marrow, currants, and remaining ingredients; add the rice, and mix all well together. Line the edges of the dish with puff-paste, put in the pudding, and bake for about 3/4 hour in a slow oven. Slices of candied-peel may be added at pleasure, or Sultana raisins may be substituted for the currants.

Miniature Rice Puddings

Ingredients: 1/4 lb. of rice, 1-1/2 pint of milk, 2 oz. of fresh butter, 4 eggs, sugar to taste; flavouring of lemon-peel, bitter almonds, or vanilla; a few strips of candied peel.

Mode: Let the rice swell in 1 pint of the milk over a slow fire, putting with it a strip of lemon-peel; stir to it the butter and the other 1/2 pint of milk, and let the mixture cool. Then add the well-beaten eggs, and a few drops of essence of almonds or essence of vanilla, whichever may be preferred; butter well some small cups or moulds, line them with a few pieces of candied peel sliced very thin, fill them three parts full, and bake for about 40 minutes; turn them out of the cups on to a white d'oyley, and serve with sweet sauce. The flavouring and candied peel might be omitted, and stewed fruit or preserve served instead, with these puddings.

Quickly-Made Puddings

Ingredients: 1/4 lb. of butter, 1/2 lb. of sifted sugar, 1/4 lb. of flour, 1 pint of milk, 5 eggs, a little grated lemon-rind.

Mode: Make the milk hot; stir in the butter, and let it cool before the other ingredients are added to it; then stir in the sugar, flour, and eggs, which should be well whisked, and omit the whites of 2; flavour with a little grated lemon-rind, and beat the mixture well. Butter some small cups, rather more than half fill them; bake from 20 minutes to 1/2 hour, according to the size of the puddings, and serve with fruit, custard, or wine sauce, a little of which may be poured over them.

Tapioca Pudding

Ingredients: 3 oz. of tapioca, 1 quart of milk, 2 oz. of butter, 1/4 lb. of sugar, 4 eggs, flavouring of vanilla, grated lemon-rind, or bitter almonds.

Mode: Wash the tapioca, and let it stew gently in the milk by the side of the fire for 1/4 hour, occasionally stirring it; then let it cool a little; mix with it the butter, sugar, and eggs, which should be well beaten, and flavour with either of the above ingredients, putting in about 12 drops of the essence of almonds or vanilla, whichever is preferred. Butter a pie-dish, and line the edges with puff-paste; put in the pudding, and bake in a moderate oven for an hour. If the pudding is boiled, add a little more tapioca, and boil it in a buttered basin 1-1/2 hour.

Suet Pudding, to serve with Roast Meat

Ingredients: 1 lb. of flour, 6 oz. of finely-chopped suet, 1/2 saltspoonful of salt, 1/2 saltspoonful of pepper, 1/2 pint of milk or water.

Mode: Chop the suet very finely, after freeing it from skin, and mix it well with the flour; add the salt and pepper (this latter ingredient may be omitted if the flavour is not liked), and make the whole into a smooth paste with the above proportion of milk or water. Tie the pudding in a floured cloth, or put it into a buttered basin, and boil from 2-1/2 to 3 hours. To enrich it, substitute 3 beaten eggs for some of the milk or water, and increase the proportion of suet.

Vermicelli Pudding

Ingredients: 4 oz. of vermicelli, 1-1/2 pint of milk, 1/2 pint of cream, 3 oz. of butter, 3 oz. of sugar, 4 eggs.

Mode: Boil the vermicelli in the milk until it is tender; then stir in the remaining ingredients, omitting the cream, if not obtainable. Flavour the mixture with grated lemon-rind, essence of bitter almonds, or vanilla; butter a pie-dish; line the edges with puff-paste, put in the pudding, and bake in a moderate oven for about 3/4 hour.

West-Indian Pudding

Ingredients: 1 pint of cream, 1/2 lb. of loaf-sugar, 1/2 lb. of Savoy or sponge-cakes, 8 eggs, 3 oz. of preserved green ginger.

Mode: Crumble down the cakes, put them into a basin, and pour over them the cream, which should be previously sweetened and brought to the boiling-point; cover the basin, well beat the eggs, and when the cream is soaked up, stir them in. Butter a mould, arrange the ginger round it, pour in the pudding carefully, and tie it down with a cloth; steam or boil it slowly for 1-1/2 hour, and serve with the syrup from the ginger, which should be warmed, and poured over the pudding.

11

General Directions for Making Soups

The basis of all good soups are Lean, Juicy Beef, Mutton, and Veal. It is advisable to procure those pieces which afford the richest succulence, and such as are fresh-killed. Stale meat renders them bad, and fat is not so well adapted for making them.

The principal art in composing good rich soup, is so to proportion the several ingredients that the flavour of one shall not predominate over another, and that all the articles of which it is composed, shall form an agreeable whole. To accomplish this, care must be taken that the roots and herbs are perfectly well cleaned, and that the water is proportioned to the quantity of meat and other ingredients.

Generally a quart of water may be allowed to a pound of meat for soups, and half the quantity for gravies. In making soups or gravies, gentle stewing or simmering is incomparably the best. It may be remarked, however, that a really good soup can never be made but in a well-closed vessel, although, perhaps, greater wholesomeness is obtained by an occasional exposure to the air.

Soups will, in general, take from three to six hours doing, and are much better prepared the day before they are wanted. When the soup is cold, the fat may be much more easily and completely removed; and when it is poured off, care must be taken not to disturb the settlings at the bottom of the vessel, which are so fine that they will escape through a sieve.

A tamis is the best strainer, and if the soup is strained while it is hot, let the tamis or cloth be previously soaked in cold water. Clear soups must be perfectly transparent, and thickened soups about the consistence of cream. To thicken and give body to soups and gravies, potato-mucilage, arrow-root, bread-raspings, isinglass, flour and butter, barley, rice, or oatmeal, in a little water rubbed well together, are used.

A piece of boiled beef pounded to a pulp, with a bit of butter and flour, and rubbed through a sieve, and gradually incorporated with the soup, will be found an excellent addition. When the soup appears to be too thin or too weak, the cover of the boiler should be taken off, and the contents allowed to boil till some of the watery parts have evaporated; or some of the thickening materials, above mentioned, should be added.

When soups and gravies are kept from day to day in hot weather, they should be warmed up every day, and put into fresh scalded pans or tureens, and placed in a cool cellar. In temperate weather, every other day may be sufficient.

Various herbs and vegetables are required for the purpose of making soups and gravies. Of these the principal are, – Scotch barley, pearl barley, wheat flour, oatmeal, bread-raspings, pease, beans, rice, vermicelli, macaroni, isinglass, potato-mucilage, mushroom or mushroom ketchup, champignons, parsnips, carrots, beetroot, turnips, garlic, shalots, and onions.

Sliced onions, fried with butter and flour till they are browned, and then rubbed through a sieve, are excellent to heighten the colour and flavour of brown soups and sauces, and form the basis of many of the fine relishes furnished by the cook. The older and drier the onion, the stronger will be its flavour. Leeks, cucumber, or burnet vinegar; celery or celery-seed pounded.

The latter, though equally strong, does not impart the delicate sweetness of the fresh vegetable; and when used as a substitute, its flavour should be corrected by the addition of a bit of sugar. Cress-seed, parsley, common thyme, lemon thyme, orange thyme, knotted marjoram, sage, mint, winter savoury, and basil. As fresh green basil is seldom to be procured, and its fine flavour is soon lost, the best way of preserving the extract is by pouring wine on the fresh leaves.

For the seasoning of soups, bay-leaves, tomato, tarragon, chervil, burnet, allspice, cinnamon, ginger, nutmeg, clove, mace, black and white pepper, essence of anchovy, lemon-peel, and juice, and Seville orange-juice, are all taken. The latter imparts a finer flavour than the lemon, and the acid is much milder. These materials, with wine, mushroom ketchup, Harvey's sauce, tomato sauce, combined in various proportions, are, with other ingredients, manipulated into an almost endless variety of excellent soups and gravies. Soups, which are intended to constitute the principal part of a meal, certainly ought not to be flavoured like sauces, which are only designed to give a relish to some particular dish.

Soup, Broth and Bouillon

It has been asserted, that English cookery is, nationally speaking, far from being the best in the world. More than this, we have been frequently told by brilliant foreign writers, half philosophers, half chefs, that we are the worst cooks on the face of the earth, and that the proverb which alludes to the divine origin of food, and the precisely opposite origin of its preparers, is peculiarly applicable to us islanders.

Not, however, to the inhabitants of the whole island; for, it is stated in a work which treats of culinary operations, north of the Tweed, that the "broth" of Scotland claims, for excellence and wholesomeness, a very close second place to the bouillon, or common soup of France. "Three hot meals of broth and meat, for about the price of one roasting joint," our Scottish brothers and sisters get, they say; and we hasten to assent to what we think is now a very well-ascertained fact.

We are glad to note, however, that soups of vegetables, fish, meat, and game, are now very frequently found in the homes of the English middle classes, as well as in the mansions of the wealthier and more aristocratic; and we take this to be one evidence, that we are on the right road to an improvement in our system of cookery. One great cause of many of the spoilt dishes and badly-cooked meats which are brought to our tables, arises, we think, and most will agree with us, from a non-acquaintance with "common, every-day things."

Accordingly, this is the proper place to treat of the quality of the flesh of animals, and describe some of the circumstances which influence it for good or bad. We will, therefore, commence with the circumstance of age, and examine how far this affects the quality of meat. During the period between the birth and maturity of animals, their flesh undergoes very considerable changes.

For instance, when the animal is young, the fluids which the tissues of the muscles contain, possess a large proportion of what is called albumen. This albumen, which is also the chief component of the white of eggs, possesses the peculiarity of coagulating or hardening at a certain temperature, like the white of a boiled egg, into a soft, white fluid, no longer soluble, or capable of being dissolved in water.

As animals grow older, this peculiar animal matter gradually decreases, in proportion to the other constituents of the juice of the flesh. Thus, the reason why veal, lamb, and young pork are white, and without gravy when cooked, is, that the large quantity of albumen they contain hardens, or becomes coagulated. On the other hand, the reason why beef and mutton are brown, and have gravy, is, that the proportion of albumen they contain, is small, in comparison with their greater quantity of fluid which is soluble, and not coagulable.

The quality of the flesh of an animal is considerably influenced by the nature of the food on which it has been fed; for the food supplies the material which produces the flesh. If the food be not suitable and good, the meat cannot be good either; just as the paper on which these words are printed, could not be good, if the rags from which it is made, were not of a fine quality.

To the experienced in this matter, it is well known that the flesh of animals fed on farinaceous produce, such as corn, pulse, &c., is firm, well-flavoured, and also economical in the cooking; that the flesh of those fed on succulent and pulpy substances, such as roots, possesses these qualities in a somewhat less degree; whilst the flesh of those whose food contains fixed oil, as linseed, is greasy, high coloured, and gross in the fat, and if the food has been used in large quantities, possessed of a rank flavour.

It is indispensable to the good quality of meat, that the animal should be perfectly healthy at the time of its slaughter. However slight the disease in an animal may be, inferiority in the quality of its flesh, as food, is certain to be produced. In most cases, indeed, as the flesh of diseased animals has a tendency to very rapid putrefaction, it becomes not only unwholesome, but absolutely poisonous, on account of the absorption of the virus of the unsound meat into the systems of those who partake of it.

The external indications of good and bad meat will be described under its own particular head, but we may here premise that the layer of all wholesome meat, when freshly killed, adheres firmly to the bone. Another circumstance greatly affecting the quality of meat, is the animal's treatment before it is slaughtered. This influences its value and wholesomeness in no inconsiderable degree. It will be easy to understand this, when we reflect on those leading principles by which the life of an animal is supported and maintained.

These are, the digestion of its food, and the assimilation of that food into its substance. Nature, in effecting this process, first reduces the food in the stomach to a state of pulp, under the name of chyme, which passes into the intestines, and is there divided into two principles, each distinct from the other. One, a milk-white fluid, – the nutritive portion, – is absorbed by innumerable vessels which open upon the mucous membrane, or inner coat of the intestines.

These vessels, or absorbents, discharge the fluid into a common duct, or road, along which it is conveyed to the large veins in the neighbourhood of the heart. Here it is mixed with the venous blood returning from every part of the body, and then it supplies the waste which is occasioned in the circulating stream by the arterial (or pure) blood having furnished matter for the substance of the animal.

The blood of the animal having completed its course through all parts, and having had its waste recruited by the digested food, is now received into the heart, and by the action of that organ it is urged through the lungs, there to receive its purification from the air which the animal inhales. Again returning to the heart, it is forced through the arteries, and thence distributed, by innumerable ramifications, called capillaries, bestowing to every part of the animal, life and nutriment.

The other principle – the innutritive portion – passes from the intestines, and is thus got rid of. It will now be readily understood how flesh is affected for bad, if an animal is slaughtered when the circulation of its blood has been increased by over-driving, ill-usage, or other causes of excitement, to such a degree of rapidity as to be too great for the capillaries to perform their functions, and causing the blood to be congealed in its minuter vessels.

Where this has been the case, the meat will be dark-coloured, and become rapidly putrid; so that self-interest and humanity alike dictate kind and gentle treatment of all animals destined to serve as food for man.

Chemical and Economic Methods of Soup Making

Stock being the basis of all meat soups, and, also, of all the principal sauces, it is essential to the success of these culinary operations, to know the most complete and economical method of extracting, from a certain quantity of meat, the best possible stock or broth. The theory and philosophy of this process we will, therefore, explain, and then proceed to show the practical course to be adopted.

As all meat is principally composed of fibres, fat, gelatine, osmazome, and albumen, it is requisite to know that the fibres are inseparable, constituting almost all that remains of the meat after it has undergone a long boiling. Fat is dissolved by boiling; but as it is contained in cells covered by a very fine membrane, which never dissolves, a portion of it always adheres to the fibres. The other portion rises to the surface of the stock, and is that which has escaped from the cells which were not whole, or which have burst by boiling.

Gelatine is soluble: it is the basis and the nutritious portion of the stock. When there is an abundance of it, it causes the stock, when cold, to become a jelly.

Osmazome: Osmazome is soluble even when cold, and is that part of the meat which gives flavour and perfume to the stock. The flesh of old animals contains more osmazome than that of young ones. Brown meats contain more than white, and the former make the stock more fragrant. By roasting meat, the osmazome appears to acquire higher properties; so, by putting the remains of roast meats into your stock-pot, you obtain a better flavour.

Albumen: Albumen is of the nature of the white of eggs; it can be dissolved in cold or tepid water, but coagulates when it is put into water not quite at the boiling-point. From this property in albumen, it is evident that if the meat is put into the stock-pot when the water boils, or after this is made to boil up quickly, the albumen, in both cases, hardens.

In the first it rises to the surface, in the second it remains in the meat, but in both it prevents the gelatine and osmazome from dissolving; and hence a thin and tasteless stock will be obtained. It ought to be known, too, that the coagulation of the albumen in the meat, always takes place, more or less, according to the size of the piece, as the parts farthest from the surface always acquire that degree of heat which congeals it before entirely dissolving it.

Bones: *Bones* ought always to form a component part of the stock-pot. They are composed of an earthy substance, – to which they owe their solidity, – of gelatine, and a fatty fluid, something like marrow. Two ounces of them contain as much gelatine as one pound of meat; but in them, this is so incased in the earthy substance, that boiling water can dissolve only the surface of whole bones. By breaking them, however, you can dissolve more, because you multiply their surfaces; and by reducing them to powder or paste, you can dissolve them entirely; but you must not grind them dry.

We have said that gelatine forms the basis of stock; but this, though very nourishing, is entirely without taste; and to make the stock savoury, it must contain osmazome. Of this, bones do not contain a particle; and that is the reason why stock made entirely of them, is not liked; but when you add meat to the broken or pulverized bones, the osmazome contained in it makes the stock sufficiently savoury.

The following condensed hints and directions should be attended to in the economy of soup-making:

I. *Beef makes the best stock*; veal stock has less colour and taste; whilst mutton sometimes gives it a tallowy smell, far from agreeable, unless the meat has been previously roasted or broiled. Fowls add very little to the flavour of stock, unless they be old and fat. Pigeons, when they are old, add the most flavour to it; and a rabbit or partridge is also a great improvement. From the freshest meat the best stock is obtained.

II. *If the meat be boiled solely to make stock*, it must be cut up into the smallest possible pieces; but, generally speaking, if it is desired to have good stock and a piece of savoury meat as well, it is necessary to put a rather large piece into the stock-pot, say sufficient for two or three days, during which time the stock will keep well in all weathers. Choose the freshest meat, and have it cut as thick as possible; for if it is a thin, flat piece, it will not look well, and will be very soon spoiled by the boiling.

III. *Never wash meat*, as it deprives its surface of all its juices; separate it from the bones, and tie it round with tape, so that its shape may be preserved, then put it into the stock-pot, and for each pound of meat, let there be one pint of water; press it down with the hand, to allow the air, which it contains, to escape, and which often raises it to the top of the water.

IV. *Put the stock-pot on a gentle fire,* so that it may heat gradually. The albumen will first dissolve, afterwards coagulate; and as it is in this state lighter than the liquid, it will rise to the surface; bringing with it all its impurities. It is this which makes the scum. The rising of the hardened albumen has the same effect in clarifying stock as the white of eggs; and, as a rule, it may be said that the more scum there is, the clearer will be the stock. Always take care that the fire is very regular.

V. *Remove the scum* when it rises thickly, and do not let the stock boil, because then one portion of the scum will be dissolved, and the other go to the bottom of the pot; thus rendering it very difficult to obtain a clear broth. If the fire is regular, it will not be necessary to add cold water in order to make the scum rise; but if the fire is too large at first, it will then be necessary to do so.

VI. *When the stock is well skimmed,* and begins to boil, put in salt and vegetables, which may be two or three carrots, two turnips, one parsnip, a bunch of leeks and celery tied together. You can add, according to taste, a piece of cabbage, two or three cloves stuck in an onion, and a tomato. The latter gives a very agreeable flavour to the stock. If fried onion be added, it ought, according to the advice of a famous French chef, to be tied in a little bag: without this precaution, the colour of the stock is liable to be clouded.

VII. *By this time* we will now suppose that you have chopped the bones which were separated from the meat, and those which were left from the roast meat of the day before. Remember, as was before pointed out, that the more these are broken, the more gelatine you will have. The best way to break them up is to pound them roughly in an iron mortar, adding, from time to time, a little water, to prevent them getting heated.

It is a great saving thus to make use of the bones of meat, which, in too many English families, we fear, are entirely wasted; for it is certain, as previously stated, that two ounces of bone contain as much gelatine as one pound of meat. In their broken state tie them up in a bag, and put them in the stock-pot; adding the gristly parts of cold meat, and trimmings, which can be used for no other purpose. If, to make up the weight, you have received from the butcher a piece of mutton or veal, broil it slightly over a clear fire before putting it in the stock-pot, and be very careful that it does not contract the least taste of being smoked or burnt.

VIII. *Add now the vegetables*, which, to a certain extent, will stop the boiling of the stock. Wait, therefore, till it simmers well up again, then draw it to the side of the fire, and keep it gently simmering till it is served, preserving, as before said, your fire always the same. Cover the stock-pot well, to prevent evaporation; do not fill it up, even if you take out a little stock, unless the meat is exposed; in which case a little boiling water may be added, but only enough to cover it. After six hours' slow and gentle simmering, the stock is done; and it should not be continued on the fire, longer than is necessary, or it will tend to insipidity.

It is on a good stock, or first good broth and sauce, that excellence in cookery depends. If the preparation of this basis of the culinary art is intrusted to negligent or ignorant persons, and the stock is not well skimmed, but indifferent results will be obtained.

The stock will never be clear; and when it is obliged to be clarified, it is deteriorated both in quality and flavour. In the proper management of the stock-pot an immense deal of trouble is saved, inasmuch as one stock, in a small dinner, serves for all purposes. Above all things, the greatest economy, consistent with excellence, should be practised, and the price of everything which enters the kitchen correctly ascertained. The theory of this part of Household Management may appear trifling; but its practice is extensive, and therefore it requires the best attention.

Bibliography

Baker, Walter. *Cocoa and Chocolate: A Short History of their Production and Use* . Boston: Walter Baker & Co., 1886.

Beckett, S.T. ed. *Industrial Chocolate Manufacture and Use* . New York: AVI, 1988.

Graziano, Martha Makra. "Food of the Gods as Mortals' Medicine: The Uses of Chocolate and Cacao Products." *Pharmacy in History* 40/4 (1998): 132-146.

Hartel, R.W. and L.A. Espinel, *Freeze Concentration of Skim Milk, J. Food Engineering* 20 pp.101-120, 1993.

Knapp, A. W. *The Cocoa and Chocolate Industry: The Tree, The Bean, The Beverage* . London: Sir Isaac Pitman and Sons, 1923.

Minifie, Bernard W. *Chocolate, Cocoa and Confectionary: Science and Technology* . Second Edition. Westport: AVI Publishing, Inc., 1980.

Rosen, J., "Freeze concentration beats the heat", *Mechanical Engineering* December 1990, pp.46-50, 1990.

Szogyi, Alex, ed. *Chocolate: Food of the Gods* . Westport: Greenwood Press, 1997.

Thijssen, H.A.C., "Current developments in the freeze concentration of liquid foods", in: S.A. Goldblith, L. Rey and W.W. Rothmayr (eds.) *Freeze drying and advanced food technology,* Academic Press, London, UK., 1975

Van Mil, P.J.J.M and S. Bouman, "Freeze concentration of dairy products", *Netherlands Milk Dairy Journal* 44 pp.21-31, 1990.

Whorton, James. "The Phenolphthalein Follies: Purgation and the Pleasure Principle in the Early Twentieth Century." *Pharmacy in History* 35/1 (1993) 3-24.

Young, Allen M. *The Chocolate Tree: A Natural History of Cacao* Washington: The Smithsonian Institution Press, 1994.

Zhang, Z. and R.W. Hartel, "A Multilayer Freezer for Freeze Concentration of Liquid Milk", *Journal of Food Engineering* 29 pp.23-38, 1996.

Index

FOOD SCIENCE AND NUTRITION

FOOD AND BEVERAGE MANAGEMENT

(In 3 Volumes)

FOOD SCIENCE AND NUTRITION

(Volume-3)

Editor
Anupama Mukherjee

ISHA

ISHA BOOKS

DELHI-110033

Food Science and Nutrition

Rs. 2000 (Set)

ISBN: 81-8205-334-X (Set)
ISBN : 81-8205-337-4 (Vol. 3)

© Anupama Mukherjee

All rights reserved. No part of this book may be reproduced in any manner without written permission.

Published in 2006 in India by
Isha Books
D-43, Prithviraj Road,
Adarsh Nagar, Delhi-110033
e-mail : ishabooks@hotmail.com

Laser Typesetting at : Shiva Infosystem, Delhi
Printed at : Mehra Offset Press, Delhi

Preface

All living things need food and water to live. Beyond that, one needs good food, meaning food with the proper nutrients, to live well. Nutrition is the science of how the body uses food. Its primary task is figuring out which foods and beverages provide the energy and building material you need to construct and maintain every organ and system. To do this, it concentrates on food's two basic attributes: energy and nutrients. Energy is the ability to do work. Virtually every bite of food gives you energy, even when it doesn't give you nutrients. Without enough food, you don't have enough energy. Nutrients are chemical substances your body uses to build, maintain, and repair tissues. They also empower cells to send messages back and forth so as to conduct essential chemical reactions such as the ones that make it possible for you to breathe, see, move, hear, eliminate, waste, smell, think, taste and do everything else natural to a living body.

Written as an introductory text, this book is an essential reading for students, heath scientists and food industry professionals to understand the fundamental aspects of food and nutrition. It deals with foods and food systems and their utilisation to satisfy human nutritional needs. It also includes wide range of topics such as food poisoning, food preservation, food additives, food adulteration, digestion and metabolism of food etc.

Editor

Contents

1

Food Poisoning

Food poisoning is a general term for health problems arising from eating contaminated food. Food may be contaminated by bacteria, viruses, environmental toxins, or toxins present within the food itself, such as the poisons in some mushrooms. Symptoms of food poisoning usually involve the prompt onset of vomiting and diarrhea. Some toxins also affect the nervous system.

Classical food poisoning, sometimes incorrectly called ptomaine poisoning, is caused by a variety of different bacteria. The most common are Salmonella, Staphylococcus aureus, Escherichia coli O157:H7, Shigella, and Clostridium botulinum. Each has a slightly different incubation period and duration, but all except C. botulinum cause inflammation of the intestines and diarrhea. Sometimes food poisoning is called bacterial gastroenteritis or infectious diarrhea. Food and water can also be contaminated by viruses (cholera), environmental toxins (heavy metals), and poisons produced within the food itself (mushroom poisoning or fish and shellfish poisoning). Careless food handling creates conditions for the growth of bacteria that make people sick.

Food can become contaminated at many different points during its trip from farm to table. Vegetables that are eaten raw, such as lettuce, may be contaminated by bacteria in soil, water, and dust during washing and packing. Home canned and commercially canned food may be improperly processed at too low a temperature or for too short a time to kill the bacteria.

Raw meats carry many foodborne bacterial diseases. The United States Food and Drug Administration (FDA) estimates that 60% or more of raw poultry sold at retail carry some disease-causing bacteria. Other raw meat products and eggs are contaminated to a lesser degree. Thorough cooking kills the bacteria and makes the food harmless.

However, properly cooked food can become re-contaminated if it comes in contact with plates, cutting boards, counter tops, or utensils that were used with raw meat and not cleaned and sanitized. Cooked foods can also be contaminated after cooking by bacteria carried by food handlers or from bacteria in the environment. It is estimated that 50% of healthy people have the bacteria Staphylococcus aureus in their nasal passages and throat, and on their skin and hair.

Rubbing a runny nose, then touching food can introduce the bacteria into cooked food. Bacteria flourish at room temperature, and will rapidly grow into quantities capable of making people sick. To prevent this growth, food must be kept hot or cold, but never just warm. Although the food supply in the United States is probably the safest in the world, anyone can get food poisoning. Serious outbreaks are rare. When they occur, the very young, the very old, and those with immune system weaknesses have the most severe and life-threatening cases.

For example, this group is 20 times more likely to become infected with the Salmonella bacteria than the general population. Travel outside the United States to countries where less attention is paid to sanitation, water purification, and good food handling practices increases the chances that a person will get food poisoning. People living in institutions such as nursing homes are also more likely to get food poisoning.

Types of Food Poisoning

Types of Food poisoning mentioned in various sources includes:

— *Typhoid fever*: A gastrointestinal condition mainly in the developing world. It is caused by a bacterial infection, usually as a form of food poisoning. Typhoid fever is unrelated to the similarly named typhus (a tick-borne infection). Typhoid fever is a life-threatening illness caused by the bacterium Salmonella Typhi.

— *Botulism food poisoning*: Extremely dangerous food poisoning requiring medical attention, but not always recognized because of its non-abdominal symptoms. Botulism is a rare but serious paralytic illness caused by a nerve toxin that is produced by the bacterium Clostridium botulinum. There are three main kinds of botulism. Foodborne botulism is caused by eating foods that contain the botulism toxin.

Wound botulism is caused by toxin produced from a wound infected with Clostridium botulinum. Infant botulism is caused by consuming the spores of the botulinum bacteria, which then grow in the intestines and release toxin. All forms of botulism can be fatal and are considered medical emergencies. Foodborne botulism can be especially dangerous because many people can be poisoned by eating a contaminated food

— *Ptomaine food poisoning*: General term just meaning any type of food poisoning caused by bacteria

— *E-coli food poisoning*: Type of bacterial food poisoning

— *E. coli O157:H7*: E. coli O157:H7 is one of hundreds of strains of the bacterium Escherichia coli. Although most strains are harmless and live in the intestines of healthy humans and animals, this strain produces a powerful toxin and can cause severe illness. E. coli O157:H7 was first recognized as a cause of illness in 1982 during an outbreak of severe bloody diarrhea; the outbreak was traced to contaminated hamburgers. Since then, most infections have come from eating undercooked ground beef. The combination of letters and numbers in the name of the bacterium refers to the specific markers found on its surface and distinguishes it from other types of E. coli.

— *Salmonella food poisoning*: Salmonellosis is an infection with a bacteria called Salmonella. Most persons infected with Salmonella develop diarrhea, fever, and abdominal cramps 12 to 72 hours after infection. The illness usually lasts 4 to 7 days, and most persons recover without treatment. However, in some persons the diarrhea may be so severe that the patient needs to be hospitalized. In these patients, the Salmonella infection may spread from the intestines to the blood stream, and then to other body sites and can cause death unless the person is treated promptly with antibiotics. The elderly, infants, and those with impaired immune systems are more likely to have a severe illness.

— *Campylobacter food poisoning*: Campylobacteriosis is an infectious disease caused by bacteria of the genus Campylobacter. Most people who become ill with campylobacteriosis get diarrhea, cramping, abdominal pain, and fever within 2 to 5 days after exposure to the organism. The diarrhea may be bloody and can be accompanied by nausea and vomiting. The illness typically lasts 1 week. Some persons who are infected with Campylobacter don't have any symptoms at all. In persons with compromised immune systems, Campylobacter occasionally spreads to the bloodstream and causes a serious life-threatening infection.

— *Shigella food poisoning*: Shigellosis is an infectious disease caused by a group of bacteria called Shigella. Most who are infected with Shigella develop diarrhea, fever, and stomach cramps starting a day or two after they are exposed to the bacterium. The diarrhea is often bloody. Shigellosis usually resolves in 5 to 7 days. In some persons, especially young children and the elderly, the diarrhea can be so severe that the patient needs to be hospitalized. A severe infection with high fever may also be associated with seizures in children less than 2 years old. Some persons who are infected may have no symptoms at all, but may still pass the Shigella bacteria to others.

— *Vibrio vulnificus*: Vibrio vulnificus is a bacterium in the same family as those that cause cholera. It normally lives in warm seawater and is part of a group of vibrios that are called "halophilic" because they require salt

— *Vibrio parahaemolyticus*: Vibrio parahaemolyticus is a bacterium in the same family as those that cause cholera. It lives in brackish saltwater and causes gastrointestinal illness in humans. V. parahaemolyticus naturally inhabits coastal waters in the United States and Canada and is present in higher concentrations during summer; it is a halophilic, or salt-requiring organism.

— *Yersinia enterocolitica*: Yersiniosis is an infectious disease caused by a bacterium of the genus Yersinia. In the United States, most human illness is caused by one species, Y. enterocolitica. Infection with Y.

enterocolitica can cause a variety of symptoms depending on the age of the person infected. Infection with Y. enterocolitica occurs most often in young children.

— *Norwalk-like viruses*: Calicivirus, or Norwalk-like virus is an extremely common cause of foodborne illness, though it is rarely diagnosed, because the laboratory test is not widely available. It causes an acute gastrointestinal illness, usually with more vomiting than diarrhea, that resolves within two days.

— Hepatitis A - occasionally foodborne.

— Giardia lamblia - occasionally foodborne.

— Cryptosporidia - occasionally foodborne.

— Mushroom poisoning

— Toadstool poisoning

— Pesticide poisoning

— Staphylococcus aureus food poisoning

— Clostridium perfringens food poisoning

— Marine toxins

Cause of Poisoning

Harmful bacteria are the most common causes of foodborne illnesses. Some bacteria may be present on foods when you purchase them. Raw foods are not sterile. Raw meat and poultry may become contaminated during slaughter. Seafood may become contaminated during harvest or through processing. One in 20,000 eggs may be contaminated with Salmonella inside the egg shell.

Produce such as lettuce, tomatoes, sprouts, and melons can become contaminated with Salmonella, Shigella, or Escherichia coli (E. coli) O157:H7.

Contamination can occur during growing, harvesting, processing, storing, shipping, or final preparation. Sources of contamination are varied; however, these items are grown in the soil and therefore may become contaminated during growth or through processing and distribution. Contamination may also occur during food preparation in the restaurant or in the person's kitchen.

When food is cooked and left out for more than 2 hours at room temperature, bacteria can multiply quickly. Most bacteria grow undetected because they do not produce an "off" odor or change the color or texture of the food. Freezing food slows or stops bacteria's growth but does not destroy the bacteria. The microbes can become reactivated when the food is thawed. Refrigeration may slow the growth of some bacteria, but thorough cooking is needed to destroy the bacteria.

Salmonella

According to the Centers for Disease Control and Prevention (CDC), Salmonella caused almost 50,000 documented cases of food poison in the United States in 1995. Between two and four million more are believed to have gone unreported. Salmonella is found in egg yolks from infected chickens, in raw and undercooked poultry and in other meats, dairy products, fish, shrimp, and many more foods.

The CDC estimates that one out of every 50 consumers is exposed to a contaminated egg yolk each year. However, thorough cooking kills the bacteria and makes the food harmless. Salmonella is also found in the feces of pet reptiles such as turtles, lizards, and snakes. About one out of every 1,000 people get food poisoning from Salmonella. Of these, two-thirds are under age 20, with the majority under age nine. Most cases occur in the warm months between July and October.

Symptoms of food poisoning begin 12-72 hours after eating food contaminated with Salmonella. These include traditional food poisoning symptoms of abdominal pain, diarrhea, vomiting, and fever. The symptoms generally last two to five days. Dehydration can be a complication in severe cases. People generally recover without antibiotic treatment, although they may feel tired for a week after the active symptoms subside.

Staphylococcus Aureus

Staphylococcus aureus is found in the environment in dust, air, and sewage. The bacteria is spread primarily by food handlers using poor sanitary practices. Almost any food can be contaminated, but salad dressings, milk products, cream pastries, and any food kept at room temperature, rather than hot or cold are likely candidates. It is difficult to estimate the number of cases of food poisoning from Staphylococcus aureus that occur each year, because its symptoms are so similar to those caused by other foodborne bacteria.

Many cases are mild and the victim never sees a doctor. Symptoms appear rapidly, usually two to eight hours after the contaminated food is eaten. The acute symptoms of vomiting, diarrhea, and severe abdominal cramps usually last only three to six hours and rarely more than 24 hours. Most people recover without medical assistance. Deaths are rare.

Escherichia Coli (E. coli)

There are many strains of E. coli, and not all of them are harmful. The strain that causes most severe food poisoning is E. coli O157:H7. Food poisoning by E. coli occurs in three out of every 10,000 people. Foodborne E. coli is found mainly in food derived from cows such as dairy products and beef, especially ground beef. Symptoms of food poisoning from E. coli are slower to appear than those caused by some of the other foodborne bacteria. E. coli produces toxins in the large intestine rather than higher up in the digestive system. This accounts for the delay in symptoms and the fact that vomiting rarely occurs in E. coli food poisoning.

One to three days after eating contaminated food, the victim with E. coli O157:H7 begins to have severe abdominal cramps and watery diarrhea that usually becomes bloody within 24 hours. There is little or no fever, and rarely does the victim vomit. The bloody, watery diarrhea lasts from one to eight days in uncomplicated cases.

Campylobacter Jejuni (C. jejuni)

According to the FDA, C. jejuni is the leading cause of bacterial diarrhea in the United States. It is responsible for more cases of bacterial diarrhea than Shigella and Salmonella combined. Anyone can get food poisoning from C. jejuni, but children under five and young adults between the ages of 15-29 are more frequently infected.

C. jejuni is carried by healthy cattle, chickens, birds, and flies. It is not carried by healthy people in the United States or Europe. The bacteria is also found ponds and stream water. The ingestion of only a few hundred C. jejuni bacteria can make a person sick. Symptoms of food poisoning begin two to five days after eating food contaminated with C. jejuni. These symptoms include fever, abdominal pain, nausea, headache, muscle pain, and diarrhea.

The diarrhea can be watery or sticky and may contain blood. Symptoms last from 7-10 days, and relapses occur in about one quarter of people who are infected. Dehydration is a common complication. Other complications such as arthritis-like joint pain and hemolytic-uremic syndrome (HUS) are rare.

Shigella

Shigella is a common cause of diarrhea in travelers to developing countries. It is associated with contaminated food and water, crowded living conditions, and poor sanitation. The bacterial toxins affect the small intestine. Symptoms of food poisoning by Shigella appear 36-72 hours after eating contaminated food. These symptoms are slightly different from those associated with most foodborne bacteria.

In addition to the familiar watery diarrhea, nausea, vomiting, abdominal cramps, and fever, up to 40% of children with severe infections show neurological symptoms. These include seizures caused by fever, confusion, headache, lethargy, and a stiff neck that resembles meningitis. The disease runs its course in two to three days. Dehydration is a common complication. Most people recover on their own, although they may feel exhausted, but children who are malnourished or have weakened immune systems may die.

Clostridium Botulinum (C. botulinum)

C. botulinum, which causes both adult botulism and infant botulism, is unlike any of the other foodborne bacteria. First, C. botulinum is an anaerobic bacterium that can only live in the absence of oxygen. Second, the toxins from C. botulinum are neurotoxins. They poison the nervous system, causing paralysis without the vomiting and diarrhea associated with other foodborne illnesses. Third, toxins that cause adult botulism are released when the bacteria grows in an airless environment outside the body. They can be broken down and made harmless by heat.

Finally, botulism is much more likely to be fatal even in tiny quantities.

Adult botulism outbreaks are usually associated with home canned food, although occasionally commercially canned or vacuum packed foods are responsible for the disease. C. botulinum grows well in non-acidic, oxygen-free environments. If food is canned at too low heat or for too brief a time, the bacteria is not killed. It reproduces inside the can or jar, releasing its deadly neurotoxin. The toxin can be made harmless by heating the contaminated food to boiling for ten minutes.

However, even a very small amount of the C. botulinum toxin can cause serious illness or death. Symptoms of adult botulism appear about 18-36 hours after the contaminated food is eaten, although there are documented times of onset ranging from four hours to eight days. Initially a person suffering from botulism feels weakness and dizziness followed by double vision. Symptoms progress to difficulty speaking and swallowing. Paralysis moves down the body, and when the respiratory muscles are paralyzed, death results from asphyxiation. People who show any signs of botulism poisoning must receive immediate emergency medical care to increase their chance of survival.

Infant botulism is a form of botulism first recognized in 1976. It differs from foodborne botulism in its causes and symptoms. Infant botulism occurs when a child under the age of one year ingests the spores of C. botulinum. These spores are found in soil, but a more common source of spores is honey.

The C. botulinum spores lodge in the baby's intestinal tract and begin to grow, producing their neurotoxin. Onset of symptoms is gradual. Initially the baby is constipated. This is followed by poor feeding, lethargy, weakness, drooling, and a distinctive wailing cry. Eventually the baby loses the ability to control its head muscles. From there the paralysis progresses to the rest of the body.

Symptoms of Food Poisoning

General information about symptoms of Food poisoning: The symptom information attempts to provide a list of some possible symptoms of Food poisoning. This symptom information has been gathered from various sources, may not be fully accurate, and may not be the full list of symptoms of Food poisoning.

Furthermore, symptoms of Food poisoning may vary on an individual basis for each patient. Only your doctor can provide adequate diagnosis of symptoms and whether they are indeed symptoms of Food poisoning. List of symptoms of Food poisoning: The list of symptoms mentioned in various sources for Food poisoning includes:

— Symptoms depend on the type of food poisoning

— Gastrointestinal symptoms

— Nausea

— Vomiting

— Abdominal cramps

— Diarrhea

— Dehydration

— Bloody stool

— Retching

— Weakness

— Fatigue

— Fever

— Headache

— Flu-like symptoms
— Cold-like symptoms

After they are swallowed, there is a delay, called the incubation period, before the symptoms of illness begin. This delay may range from hours to days, depending on the organism, and on how many of them were swallowed. During the incubation period, the microbes pass through the stomach into the intestine, attach to the cells lining the intestinal walls, and begin to multiply there. Some types of microbes stay in the intestine, some produce a toxin that is absorbed into the bloodstream, and some can directly invade the deeper body tissues.

The symptoms produced depend greatly on the type of microbe. Numerous organisms cause similar symptoms, especially diarrhea, abdominal cramps, and nausea. There is so much overlap that it is rarely possible to say which microbe is likely to be causing a given illness unless laboratory tests are done to identify the microbe, or unless the illness is part of a recognized outbreak. Symptoms vary widely depending on etiologic agent. Diarrhea and vomiting are the most common.

In addition to the above information, to get a full picture of the possible symptoms of this condition and its related conditions, it may be necessary to examine symptoms that may be caused by complications of Food poisoning, underlying causes of Food poisoning, associated conditions for Food poisoning, risk factors for Food poisoning, or other related conditions.

Food Poisoning and Risk Factors

Risk factors for Food poisoning are factors that do not seem to be a direct cause of the disease, but seem to be associated in some way. Having a risk factor for Food poisoning makes the chances of getting a condition higher but does not always lead to Food poisoning. Also, the absence of any risk factors or having a protective factor does not necessarily guard you against getting Food poisoningThe list of risk factors mentioned for Food poisoning in various sources includes:

— Immunocompromise

— Elderly

— Infants

— Young children

— Pregnant women

— Risks factors for listeria:

— Undercooked animal products

— Soft French style cheeses

— Pates

— Uncooked hot dogs

— Sliced deli meats

— Alfalfa sprouts

— Unpasteurized juices

— Bottle-fed infants - risk of Salmonella in milk bottles

— Risk factors for Vibrio vulnifi:

— Raw oysters

— Liver disease

— Hepatitis Risk factors discussion:

Some people are at greater risk for bacterial infections because of their age or immune status. Young children, pregnant women and their fetuses, the elderly, and people with lowered immunity are at greatest risk. Some persons at particularly high risk should take more precautions.

— Pregnant women, the elderly, and those weakened immune systems are at higher risk for severe infections such as Listeria and should be particularly careful not to consume undercooked animal products. They should avoid soft French style cheeses, pates, uncooked hot dogs and sliced deli meats, which have been sources of Listeria infections. Persons at high risk should also avoid alfalfa sprouts and unpasteurized juices.

— A bottle-fed infant is at higher risk for severe infections with Salmonella or other bacteria that can grow in a bottle of warm formula if it is left at room temperature for many hours. Particular care is needed to be sure the baby's bottle is cleaned and disinfected and that leftover milk formula or juice is not held in the bottle for many hours.

— Persons with liver disease are susceptible to infections with a rare but dangerous microbe called Vibrio vulnificus, found in oysters. They should avoid eating raw oysters. All persons. Infants, elderly, and the immunocompromised at greatest risk of serious illness and death.

Food Poisoning Complications

Complications of Food poisoning are secondary conditions, symptoms, or other disorders that are caused by Food poisoning. In many cases the distinction between symptoms of Food poisoning and complications of Food poisoning is unclear or arbitrary. The list of complications that have been mentioned in various sources for Food poisoning includes:

— Complications depend on the type of food poisoning

— Spontaneous abortion - mainly from listeria or botulism

— Death - mainly from listeria or botulism

— Hemolytic uremic syndrome - from E. coli O157:H7

— Septicemia

— Abortion (see Pregnancy symptoms)

— Localized infections

— Arthritis

— Guillain-Barré syndrome

Some micro-organisms, such as Listeria monocytogenes and Clostridium botulinum, cause far more serious illness than vomiting or diarrhea. They can cause spontaneous abortion or death. In some people, especially children, hemolytic uremic syndrome (HUS) can result from infection by a particular strain of bacteria, E. coli O157:H7, and can lead to kidney failure and death. HUS is a rare disorder that affects primarily young children between the ages of 1 and 10 years and is the leading cause of acute renal failure in previously healthy children.

The child may become infected after consuming a contaminated food, such as meat (especially undercooked ground beef), unpasteurized apple cider or apple juice, or raw sprouts. The most common symptoms of infection are vomiting, abdominal pain, and diarrhea, which may be bloody. In 5 to 10 percent of cases, HUS develops about 2 to 6 days after the onset of illness. This disease may last from 1 to 15 days and is fatal in 3 to 5 percent of cases. Symptoms of HUS include fever, lethargy, irritability, and pallor.

In about half the cases, the disease progresses until the kidneys are unable to remove waste products from the blood and excrete them into the urine (acute renal failure). A decrease in circulating red blood cells and blood platelets and reduced blood flow to organs may lead to multiple organ failure. Seizures, heart failure, inflammation of the pancreas, and diabetes can also result. However, most children recover completely.

You need to see a doctor right away if you have any of the following symptoms, with or without gastrointestinal symptoms:

— Signs of shock, such as weak or rapid pulse; shallow breathing; cold, clammy, pale skin; shaking or chills; or chest pain.

— Signs of severe dehydration, such as dry mouth, sticky saliva, decreased urine output, dizziness, fatigue, sunken eyes, low blood pressure, or increased heart rate and breathing.

— Confusion or difficulty reasoning.

Associated Conditions of Food Poisoning

Associated conditions are those which appear statistically related, but do not have a clear cause or effect relationship. Whereas the complications are caused by Food poisoning, and underlying causes may be causes of Food poisoning, the following list shows associated conditions that simply appear with higher frequency in people who have Food poisoning.

In some cases, there may be overlap between this list and risk factors for Food poisoning. People with Food poisoning may be more likely to get a condition on the list of associated conditions, or the reverse may be true, or both. Whether they are causes of, caused by, or simply coincidentally related to Food poisoning is not always clear.

Associated medical conditions: Scientists suspect that foodborne pathogens are linked to chronic disorders and can even cause permanent tissue or organ destruction. Research suggests that when some people are infected by foodborne pathogens, the activation of their immune system can trigger an inappropriate autoimmune response, which means the immune system attacks the body's own cells. In some people, an autoimmune response leads to a chronic health condition. Chronic disorders that may be triggered by foodborne pathogens are

— Arthritis
— Inflammatory bowel disease
— Kidney failure
— Guillain-Barré syndrome
— Autoimmune disorders

Tests and Diagnosis for Food Poisoning

One important aspect of diagnosing food poisoning is for doctors to determine if a number of people have eaten the same food and show the same symptoms of illness. When this happens, food poisoning is strongly suspected. The diagnosis is confirmed when the suspected bacteria is found in a stool culture or a fecal smear from the person. Other laboratory tests are used to isolate bacteria from a sample of the contaminated food. Botulism is usually diagnosed from its distinctive neurological symptoms, since rapid treatment is essential.

Many cases of food poisoning go undiagnosed, since a definite diagnosis is not necessary to effectively treat the symptoms. Because it takes time for symptoms to develop, it is not necessarily the most recent food one has eaten that is the cause of the symptoms. Your doctor may be able to diagnose foodborne illness from a list of what you've recently eaten and results from the proper laboratory tests. Diagnostic tests for foodborne illness should include examination of the feces.

A sample of the suspected food, if available, can also be tested for bacteria and their toxins as well as for viruses and parasites. The infection is usually diagnosed by specific laboratory tests that identify the causative organism. Bacteria such as Campylobacter, Salmonella, E. coli O157 are found by culturing stool samples in the laboratory and identifying the bacteria that grow on the agar or other culture medium. Parasites can be identified by examining stools under the microscope.

Viruses are more difficult to identify, as they are too small to see under a light microscope and are difficult to culture. Viruses are usually identified by testing stool samples for genetic markers that indicate a specific virus is present. Many foodborne infections are not identified by routine laboratory procedures and require specialized, experimental, and/or expensive tests that are not generally available.

If the diagnosis is to be made, the patient has to seek medical attention, the physician must decide to order diagnostic tests, and the laboratory must use the appropriate procedures. Because many ill persons to not seek attention, and of those that do, many are not tested, many cases of foodborne illness go undiagnosed. For example, CDC estimates that 38 cases of salmonellosis actually occur for every case that is actually diagnosed and reported to public health authorities.

Treatment

Treatment of food poisoning, except that caused by C. botulinum, focuses on preventing dehydration by replacing fluids and electrolytes lost through vomiting and diarrhea. Electrolytes are salts and minerals that form electrically charges particles (ions) in body fluids. Electrolytes are important because they control body fluid balance and are important for all major body reactions. Pharmacists can recommend effective, pleasant-tasting, electrolytically balanced replacement fluids that are available without a prescription.

When more fluids are being lost than can be consumed, dehydration may occur. Dehydration more likely to happen in the very young, the elderly, and people who are taking diuretics. To prevent dehydration, a doctor may give fluids intravenously. In very serious cases of food poisoning, medications may be given to stop abdominal cramping and vomiting. Anti-diarrheal medications are not usually given. Stopping the diarrhea keeps the toxins in the body longer and may prolong the infection.

People with food poisoning should modify their diet. During period of active vomiting and diarrhea they should not try to eat and should drink only clear liquids frequently but in small quantities. Once active symptoms stop, they should eat bland, soft, easy to digest foods for two to three days. One example is the BRAT diet of bananas, rice, applesauce, and toast, all of which are easy to digest.

Milk products, spicy food, alcohol and fresh fruit should be avoided for a few days, although babies should continue to breastfeed. These modifications are often all the treatment that is necessary. Severe bacterial food poisonings are sometimes treated with antibiotics. Trimethoprim and sulfamethoxazole (Septra, Bactrim), ampicillin (Amcill, Polycill) or ciprofloxacin (Ciloxan, Cipro) are most frequently used.

Botulism is treated in a different way from other bacterial food poisonings. Botulism antitoxin is given to adults, but not infants, if it can be administered within 72 hours after symptoms are first observed. If given later, it provides no benefit. Both infants and adults require hospitalization, often in the intensive care unit. If the ability to breathe is impaired, patients are put on a mechanical ventilator to assist their breathing and are fed intravenously until the paralysis passes.

Alternative practitioners offer the same advice as traditional practitioners concerning diet modification. In addition they recommend taking charcoal tablets, Lactobacillus acidophilus, Lactobacillus bulgaricus, and citrus seed extract. An electrolyte replacement fluid can be made at home by adding one teaspoon of salt and four teaspoons of sugar to one quart of water. For food poisoning other than botulism, two homeopathic remedies, either Arsenicum album or Nux vômica, are strongly recommended.

Prognosis

Most cases of food poisoning (except botulism) clear up on their own within one week without medical assistance. The ill person may continue feel tired for a few days after active symptoms stop. So long as the ill person does not become dehydrated, there are few complications. Deaths are rare and usually occur in the very young, the very old and people whose immune systems are already weakened.

Complications of Salmonella food poisoning include arthritis-like symptoms that occur three to four weeks after infection. Although deaths from Salmonella are rare, they do occur. Most deaths caused by Salmonella food poisoning have occurred in elderly people in nursing homes. Adults usually recover without medical intervention, but many children need to be hospitalized as the result of E. coli food poisoning. E. coli toxins may be absorbed into the blood stream where they destroy red blood cells and platelets.

Platelets are important in blood clotting. About 5% of victims develop hemolytic-uremic syndrome which results in sudden kidney failure and makes dialysis necessary. (Dialysis is a medical procedure used to filter the body's waste product when the kidneys have failed). Botulism is the deadliest of the bacterial foodborne illnesses. With prompt medical care, the death rate is less than 10%.

Prevention

Methods of prevention of Food poisoning mentioned in various sources includes those listed below. This prevention information is gathered from various sources, and may be inaccurate or incomplete. None of these methods guarantee prevention of Food poisoning.

— Keep hot foods hot and cold foods cold.

— Cook meat to the recommended internal temperature. Use a meat thermometer to check. Cook eggs until they are no longer runny.

— Refrigerate leftovers promptly. Do not let food stand at room temperature.

— Avoid contaminating surfaces and other foods with the juices of uncooked meats.

— Wash fruits and vegetables before using.

— Purchase pasteurized dairy products and fruit juices.

— Throw away bulging or leaking cans or any food that smells spoiled.

— Wash hands well before and during food preparation and after using the bathroom.

— Sanitize food preparation surfaces regularly.

Most cases of foodborne illness can be prevented through proper cooking or processing of food, which kills bacteria. In addition, because bacteria multiply rapidly between 40°F and 140°F, food must be kept out of this "danger zone." To prevent harmful bacteria from growing in food, always

— Refrigerate foods promptly. If you let prepared food stand at room temperature for more than 2 hours, it may not be safe to eat. Set your refrigerator at 40°F or lower and your freezer at 0°F.

— Cook food to the appropriate temperature (145°F for roasts, steaks, and chops of beef, veal, and lamb; 160°F for pork, ground veal, and ground beef; 165°F for ground poultry; and 180°F for whole poultry). Use a thermometer to be sure! Foods are properly cooked only when they are heated long enough and at a high enough temperature to kill the harmful bacteria that cause illness.

— Prevent cross-contamination. Bacteria can spread from one food product to another throughout the kitchen and can get onto cutting boards, knives, sponges, and countertops. So keep raw meat, poultry, seafood, and their juices away from other foods that are ready to eat.

— Handle food properly. Always wash your hands before touching food and after using the bathroom, changing diapers, or handling pets, as well as after handling raw meat, poultry, fish, shellfish, or eggs. Clean surfaces well before preparing food on them.

— Keep cold food cold and hot food hot.

— Maintain hot cooked food at 140°F or higher.

— Reheat cooked food to at least 165°F.

— Refrigerate or freeze perishables, prepared food, and leftovers within 2 hours.

— Never defrost food on the kitchen counter. Use the refrigerator, cold running water, or the microwave oven.

— Never let food marinate at room temperature; refrigerate it.

— Divide large amounts of leftovers into small, shallow containers for quick cooling in the refrigerator.

— Remove the stuffing immediately from poultry and other meats and refrigerate it in a separate container.

— Do not pack the refrigerator. Cool air must circulate to keep food safe.

A few simple precautions can reduce the risk of foodborne diseases:

— COOK meat, poultry and eggs thoroughly. Using a thermometer to measure the internal temperature of meat is a good way to be sure that it is cooked sufficiently to kill bacteria. For example, ground beef should be cooked to an internal temperature of 160o F. Eggs should be cooked until the yolk is firm.

— SEPERATE: Don't cross-contaminate one food with another. Avoid cross-contaminating foods by washing hands, utensils, and cutting boards after they have been in contact with raw meat or poultry and before they touch another food. Put cooked meat on a clean platter, rather back on one that held the raw meat.

— CHILL: Refrigerate leftovers promptly. Bacteria can grow quickly at room temperature, so refrigerate leftover foods if they are not going to be eaten within 4 hours. Large volumes of food will cool more quickly if they are divided into several shallow containers for refrigeration.

— CLEAN: Wash produce. Rinse fresh fruits and vegetables in running tap water to remove visible dirt and grime. Remove and discard the outermost leaves of a head of lettuce or cabbage. Because bacteria can grow well on the cut surface of fruit or vegetable, be careful not to contaminate these foods while slicing them up on the cutting board, and avoid leaving cut produce at room temperature for many hours. Don't be a source of foodborne illness yourself.

Wash your hands with soap and water before preparing food. Avoid preparing food for others if you yourself have a diarrheal illness. Changing a baby's diaper while preparing food is a bad idea that can easily spread illness.

— REPORT: Report suspected foodborne illnesses to your local health department. The local public health department is an important part of the food safety system. Often calls from concerned citizens are how outbreaks are first detected. If a public health official contacts you to find our more about an illness you had, your cooperation is important. In public health investigations, it can be as important to talk to healthy people as to ill people. Your cooperation may be needed even if you are not ill.

Treating raw meat and poultry with irradiation at the slaughter plant could eliminate bacteria commonly found on raw meat and raw poultry, such as E. coli O157:H7, Salmonella, and Campylobacter. These organisms currently cause millions of infections and thousands of hospitalizations in the United States every year. Irradiating prepared ready-to-eat meats like hot dogs and deli meats, could eliminate the risk of Listeria from such foods.

Irradiation could also eliminate parasites like Cyclospora and bacteria like Shigella and Salmonella from fresh produce. The potential benefit is also great for those dry foods that might be stored for long times and transported over great distances, such as spices and grains. Animal feeds are often contaminated with bacteria like Salmonella. Irradiation of animal feeds could prevent the spread of Salmonella and other pathogens to livestock through feeds.

2

Disinfection and Sterilisation

Disinfection is the destruction of pathogenic and other kinds of microorganisms by physical or chemical means. Disinfectants are chemical substances used to destroy viruses and microbes (germs), such as bacteria and fungi. The ideal disinfectant would offer complete sterilisation, without harming other forms of life, be inexpensive, and non-corrosive.

Unfortunately ideal disinfectants do not exist. Many disinfectants are only able to partially sterilize. The most resistant pathogens are bacteria spores but some viruses and bacteria are also highly resistant to many disinfectants. All disinfectants are also, by their very nature, potentially harmful (even toxic) to humans or animals. They should be treated with appropriate care. Most come with safety instructions printed on the packaging, which should be read in full before using the disinfectant.

Most modern household disinfectants contain Bitrex, an exceptionally bitter substance designed to discourage ingestion, as an added safety measure. Those that are used in people's homes should never be mixed with other cleaning products as chemical reactions can occur. They are frequently used in hospitals, dental surgeries, kitchens and bathrooms to kill infectious organisms. The choice of the disinfectant to be used depends on the particular situation. Some disinfectants have a wide spectrum (kill nearly all microorganisms). Others kill a smaller range of disease-causing organisms but are preferred for other properties.

Disinfectants sterilize surfaces, medical equipment and other man-made objects. Antiseptics disinfect skin. Antibiotics either kill or interfere with the life cycle of bacteria inside the body. Substances which kill bacteria are said to have a bactericidal effect, while those which interfere with cell growth and reproduction are said to be bacteriostatic. Disinfectants and antiseptics are bactericidal (some disinfectants are becteriostatic at low concentrations): antibiotics can be either bactericidal or bacteriostatic. Sanitation refers to killing 99+ % of germs in applicable situations. Sanitizers are compounds that sanitize.

Types of Disinfectants

- *Chlorine:* Used to disinfect swimming pools, and is added in small quantities to drinking water to reduce waterborne diseases.
- *Chlorine dioxide:* Used as an advanced disinfectant for drinking water to reduce waterborne diseases. In certain parts of the world, it has largely replaced chlorine because it forms fewer byproducts.
- *Sodium chlorite, sodium chlorate, and potassium chlorate* have little disinfection effect but are used as precursors for generating chlorine dioxide
- *Alcohol:* Usually ethanol or isopropanol - Wiped over benches and skin and allowed to evaporate for quick disinfection. Alcohols are more effective combined with water, 70% alcohol is more active than 95% alcohol. Alcohol is not effective against bacterial spores.

— *Hydrogen peroxide:* Used in hospitals to disinfect surfaces. It is sometimes mixed with colloidal silver. It is often preferred because it causes far fewer allergic reactions than alternative disinfectants. Also used in the food packaging industry to disinfect foil containers.A 3% solution is also used as an antiseptic. When hydrogen peroxide come into contact with the catalase enzyme in cells it is broken down into water and oxygen. It is the oxygen that kills bacteria. However, as recent studies have show hydrogen peroxide to be toxic to growing cells as well as bacteria, its use as an antiseptic is not longer recommended.

— *Iodine:* Usually dissolved in an organic solvent or as Lugol's iodine solution. It is used in the poultry industry. It is added to the birds' drinking water. Iodine is rapidly neutralised by the presence of organic material, so surfaces must be cleaned prior to disinfection. Tincture of iodine has also been used as an antiseptic for skin cuts and scrapes.

— *Ozone:* a gas that can be added to water for sanitation.

— *Phenol and other phenolics:* The active ingredient in most bottles of "household disinfectant". It is also to found in some mouthwashes and in disinfectant soap and handwashes. Phenol is probably the oldest disinfectant and was called carbolic acid in the early days of antiseptics. Phenol is rather corrosive to the skin and sometimes toxic to sensitive people, so the somewhat less corrosive substitute phenolic. o-phenylphenol is often used as part of a disinfectant formula. Hexachlorophene is a phenolic which was once used as an germicidal additive to some household products but was banned due to suspected harmful effects.

— *Potassium permanganate*—used to disinfect aquariums.

- *Quaternary ammonium salts* (quats) are a large group of related compounds. Some have been used as a low level disinfectant. They are effective against bacteria, but not against spores or viruses. Quats are biocides which also kill algae and are used as an additive in large-scale industrial water systems to minimize undesired biological growth.
- *Hypochlorites:* Sodium hypochlorite, often in the form of common household bleach, is used in the home to disinfect drains, and toilets. A dilute form is used under the brand name milton to disinfect baby bottles. Other hypochlorites such as calcium hypochlorite are also used, especially as a swimming pool additive. Hypochlorite gives off free chlorine and it is the chlorine that is the true disinfectant. Hypobromite solutions are also sometimes used.
- *Parvo-Virucide:* a total biocidal agent used mainly in animal contact areas such as kennels, catteries, veterinary surgeries etc. It can be used in clean and dirty areas contaminated with high levels of organic matter such as urine and faeces without loss of biocidal activity, whereas most disinfectants are severely challenged by organic matter and their effectiveness much reduced.

Parvo-Virucide was originally manufactured to specifically inactivate the Canine parvovirus (CPV), which is a relatively new usually fatal disease affecting puppies. Parvo-virucide was evaluated by the Central Veterinary Laboratory of the U.K. Ministry of Agriculture (now DEFRA) who tested the disinfectant under severe conditions and discovered that "Parvo-Virucide disinfectant inactivated canine parvovirus at a dilution of 1:200 using the UK yeast method".

- *Toluene*

— *Virkon:* A wide-spectrum disinfectant used in labs. It kills bacteria, viruses, and fungi. It is used as a 1% solution in water, and keeps for 1 week once it is made up. It is expensive, but very effective, its pink colour fades as it is used up so it is possible to see at a glance if it is still fresh.

In addition to these methods ultraviolet light can be used for disinfecting water. One way to compare disinfectants is to compare how well they do against a known disinfectant and rate them accordingly. Phenol is the standard, and the corresponding rating system is called the "Phenol coefficient". The disinfectant to be tested is compared with phenol on a standard microbe (usually Salmonella typhi or Staphylococcus aureus). Disinfectants that are more effective than phenol have a coefficient > 1. Those that are less effective have a coefficient < 1.

Floor Disinfection

Many environmental surfaces, including floors in a medical facility, can harbor disease-causing germs. Although not directly involved in disease transmission, environmental surfaces may indirectly contribute to secondary cross-contamination by the hands of healthcare workers or by contact with medical instruments that will subsequently come into contact with patients/residents.

Housekeeping surfaces include floors, walls, counters, and furniture and are considered non-critical items that require low-level disinfection. Cleanliness and infection control of these surfaces can be ensured by removal of soil on a routine basis. The primary function of the housekeeping department in a healthcare facility is to create a clean, safe, and healthy environment for patients or residents, staff, and visitors.

Included in this function is the disinfection of all environmental surfaces, which comprises floors, walls, counters, furniture, etc. Establishing and adhering to a sound program is the key to effective cleaning and disinfecting of environmental surfaces throughout a healthcare facility.

Martin Favero and Walter Bond expanded Dr. E.H. Spaulding's original classification of medically related surfaces to define more clearly the relative risks of disease transmission. This expansion included dividing the classification of environmental surfaces into two sub-groups: medical equipment surfaces and housekeeping surfaces. Housekeeping surfaces, of course, include floors, walls, counters, and furniture and are considered non-critical items that require low-level disinfection.

Cleanliness and infection control of these surfaces can be ensured by removal of soil on a routine basis. This can be accomplished using water and a detergent or a low-level, EPA-registered, nontuberculocidal, hospital-grade disinfectant designed for general housekeeping procedures.

A good floor care disinfection program comprises three key elements: use of effective disinfectants--detergents, tools, and procedures. All three elements must be present to be successful in physically and chemically removing soil and microorganisms. Extraordinary attempts to disinfect floors are usually unnecessary. The actual physical removal of soil and microorganisms is probably at least as important as the germicidal activity of the disinfectant used.

Effective disinfectant detergents

Low-level, hospital-grade disinfectants are the recommended products for floor care disinfection in healthcare settings. The Environmental Protection Agency (EPA) regulates and registers all low-level disinfectants. To be considered a hospital grade disinfectant, manufacturers must test their germicidal products against three microorganisms: Staphylococcus aureus, Salmonella choleraesuis, and Pseudomonas aeruginosa. Usually products are tested against a variety of other microorganisms, especially in today's age of antibiotic resistance (MRSA and VRE) and concern with bloodborne viruses.

To obtain a one-step cleaner disinfectant claim, testing of these products is usually done in the presence of organic serum (at least five percent) and hard water (at least 400 ppm). This testing is always done at the manufacturer's recommended dilution rate; therefore, it is important for the user to mix a disinfectant according to the manufacturer's label.

The "cleaner" part of the product acts as a penetrating agent through soil loads and allows the disinfectant part of the product to penetrate the cell wall of the microorganism so that the killing action can take place. A one-step claim is very important in today's cost-conscious healthcare environment because it reduces labor and product costs. In laboratory testing, microorganisms must come into contact with the disinfectant for 10 minutes; however, actual kill time might be less than 10 minutes.

In real world applications, floors usually do not stay wet from damp mopping procedures for 10 minutes. A few minutes can be expected, which should give most disinfectants adequate time to kill. Physical removal with a mop or autoscrubber in itself will remove a significant share of microorganisms present. If a mop is used, it will be immersed in a solution of disinfectant upon completion of the mopping procedure.

If an autoscrubber is used, any solution applied to the floor will be picked up by the machine and will be held in a recovery tank until emptied. A related corollary to contact time is residual activity. Disinfectants in a dry state do not have a residual activity. Disinfectant action can only take place when moisture is present.

Selecting a disinfectant

When selecting a disinfectant, first review technical research bulletins provided by vendors. These bulletins will identify the different microorganisms that the disinfectant has been tested against. Then match the tested microorganisms against those most prevalent in your particular environment. In addition to the microorganisms most prevalent, a disinfectant should have a broad range of kill; it should be capable of killing Gram positive and Gram negative bacteria, fungi, and viruses. Second, compute the parts per million (PPM) of active disinfectant. This computation simply translates the percentage of active ingredients into parts per million. This computation is:

$$\frac{\text{\% of active ingredients X 10,000}}{\text{Dilution Rate}}$$

The resulting number can be used to determine how effective a disinfectant will be as you introduce soil load. As the employee mops a floor and immerses the mop into the bucket of disinfectant solution, the solution will degrade. At a certain point, approximately 300 to 350 ppm, a disinfectant will be rendered ineffective. Therefore, it is recommended to change the soiled disinfectant solution on a routine basis, usually every three to four rooms.

Exceptions to this rule would include isolation cases, discharges, cleaning in surgery or delivery, and cleaning of blood spills. A disinfectant should be noncorrosive, nonirritating, effective in hard water, able to dilute in hot or cold water (preferably cold water), and as close to neutral pH as possible so as not to affect floor finishes. Neutralization of the product due to soil load should not occur.

Finally, a disinfectant should be economical to use. To determine how economical it is, focus on the end use cost not the price per gallon. To calculate and use cost, simply divide the cost per gallon by the dilution rate per gallon.

Tools and procedures

As important as the disinfectant-detergent is in the floor care disinfection program, the tools and procedures used are as equally as important. Appropriate selection, use, and care of dust mops, wet/dry vacuums, and wet mops are critical to the success of the program.

Proper dust removal is critical. Bertha and Warren Litsky demonstrated in 1968 that effective dust removal before wet mopping or scrubbing of floors proved to be an important part of the cleaning and disinfecting process. Dust removal prior to scrubbing or mopping will collect a large portion of debris, dirt, and dust that, if uncollected will affect the disinfecting capability of the disinfectant-detergent. Litsky recommends the following order for dust removal effectiveness:

— A wet/dry vacuum or vacuum with a filtration system is a superior dust-removal tool. This tool is recommended for areas like the operating room, delivery room, and nursery.

— A chemically treated disposable dust mop head.

— A freshly machine laundered dry dust mop head.

Sweeping floors with a broom is not recommended because particles become airborne and can be transferred throughout the facility. Since microorganisms are attracted to dust and dirt for a food source, any chance of creating an airborne situation is not advised. To eliminate this concern in areas like the operating or delivery room and where a wet/dry vacuum is not available, a broom dipped into disinfectant can be used.

Dipping the broom into the disinfectant will eliminate any dust particles from becoming airborne, thus negating a potentially hazardous situation. Proper care of all dust removal tools should be taken to maintain the life of the equipment as well as to eliminate cross contamination. Wet/dry vacuums should be cleaned internally and externally daily with a disinfectant and after each use when contaminated with blood or body fluids that visibly contain blood.

Disposable dust mops should be discarded when thoroughly soiled. Laundered dust mops should be laundered daily. With proper dust removal, the wet mopping or scrubbing process is much more effective. Litsky recommends the use of sterile wet mops or freshly machine laundered wet mops for the wet mopping process. Mops should be replaced after each isolation room cleaning, discharge cleaning, clean up of blood spills, and cleaning in surgery and delivery suites.

A routine of changing mops after a certain number of rooms should also be adopted. It is not unusual for wet mops to become contaminated even after dust removal, so it is important to adopt a routine of changing disinfectant solutions and mops frequently. Dirty mops immersed in a bucket of disinfectant, can become a medium for growth of live microorganisms. Solutions should be changed after every 3-4 rooms if using a single bucket method or 6-8 rooms if using a two-bucket (both buckets contain disinfectant solution), two mop system.

In large open areas like hallways or lobbies, wet mopping of floors is not necessarily the most productive and cost effective process. In these instances, use of an automatic scrubber is appropriate. An automatic scrubber applies the disinfectant-detergent to the floor, scrubs the floor with pads or brushes, and then vacuums the floor dry. It is a very productive tool for large areas and very effective in the soil removal process. When using an automatic scrubber to clean and disinfect a floor, double scrubbing is recommended.

Double scrubbing is the process of applying the disinfectant-detergent on the floor and scrubbing twice prior to vacuuming the solution. Double scrubbing will allow the disinfectant more contact time with a microorganism, thus creating a better killing situation. Automatic scrubbers should be cleaned daily by running a solution of disinfectant through the machine. Pads or brushes should also be cleaned in disinfectant for 10 minutes and allowed to air dry.

STERILISATION

Sterilisation (or sterilisation) is the elimination of all transmissible agents (such as bacteria, prions and viruses) from a surface or piece of equipment. This is different from disinfection, where only organisms that can cause disease are removed by a disinfectant. In general, any instrument that enters an already sterile part of the body (such as the blood, or beneath the skin) should be sterilized. This includes equipment like scalpels, hypodermic needles and artificial pacemakers.

Heat Sterilisation

Probably the most widely used method for heat sterilisation is the autoclave. Autoclaves commonly use steam heated to 121°C, at 103 kPa (15 psi), for 15 minutes. The steam and pressure allow sufficient heat is transferred into the organism to kill them. Proper autoclave treatment will inactivate all fungi, bacteria, viruses and also bacterial spores, which can be quite resistant. It will not however necessarily eliminate all prions.

To ensure the autoclaving process was able to cause sterilisation, most autoclaves haves meters and charts that record or display pertinent information such as temperature and pressure as a function of times. Indicator tape is often taped onto packages of products to be autoclaved. The tape contains a chemical that will change color if the appropriate conditions have been met.

Some types of packaging have built-in indicators on them. Biological indicators, (such as the Attests), can also be used. These contain Bacillus sterothermophilus spores, which are amongst the toughest organisms an autoclave will have to destroy. After a run in an autoclave, the internal glass in the Attest vial is shattered, allowing the spores into a differential liquid medium. If the autoclave destroyed the spores, the medium will remain a blue color. If autoclaving was unsuccessful the B. sterothermophilus will metabolize, causing a yellow color change after two days of incubation at 56°C.

For effective autoclaving, the steam needs to be able to penetrate everywhere. For this reason, an autoclave must not be overcrowded, and the lids of bottles and containers must be ajar. Indicators should be placed in the most difficult place sterilisation is wanted, for instance if you are sterilizing the contents of universals (a universal is a type of small glass jar), the Attest vial should be placed in a universal, to ensure that steam actually penetrates these areas. For autoclaving, as for all disinfection of sterilisation methods, the cleaning off of any biological material is also critical.

Biological matter or any grime may shield organisms from the property intended to kill them, whether it physical or chemical. Cleaning can also remove a large number of organisms at once. Proper cleaning can be achieved by physical scrubbing to remove dirt; this should be done with detergent and warm water to get the best results. Where it is not feasible, ultrasound or pulsed air can be used to remove debris. Other heat methods include using dry heat, boiling, flaming and incineration.

Flaming is done to loops and straight-wires in microbiology labs. Leaving the loop in a Bunsen burner until it glows red, ensures that any infectious agent gets oxidized completely into small molecules. Heating small metal or glass objects is really the extent to which this method is used. Incineration will also burn any organism to ash. It obviously is only used to sanitize unwanted medical and other waste before its ash goes to the tip.

Boiling in water for 15 minutes is unsuitable for sterilisation. It's a simple and familiar enough process for anyone to do, though is hazardous and cumbersome. Boiling will kill bacteria and viruses, but it is ineffective against many bacterial spores and prions. Dry heat can be used to sterilize items, but as the heat takes much longer to be transferred to the organism, both the time, and the temperature required, must be increased. The standard setting for a hot air oven is at least two hours at 160°C. A rapid method heats air to 190°C for 6-12 hours.

Dry heat has the advantage that it can be used on powders and other heat-stable items that are adversely affected by steam. In terms of prion elimination there is no agreed ideal time and temperature. The prion that causes the disease scrapie (strain 263K) is inactivated relatively quickly by standard sterilisation procedures. Other strains of scrapie, as well as strains of CJD and BSE have shown much more resistance.

Using mice as a test animal, one experiment showed that heating BSE positive brain tissue at 134-138°C for 18 minutes resulted in only a 2.5 log decrease in prion infectivity. (The initial BSE concentration in the tissue was relatively low). To have a significant margin of safety, cleaning should reduce infectively 4 logs, and the sterilisation method reduce it a further 5 logs. The recommendations state 121-132°C for 60 minutes, and 134°C for at least 18 minutes. By combining immersion in sodium hydroxide (NaOH 0.09N) for two hours, with one hour autoclaving (121°C) several investigators have shown complete (>7.4 logs) inactivation. (Sodium hydroxide may, though, be deleterious to surgical instruments.)

Chemical Sterilisation

Chemicals also have a place in sterilisation. Heating provides the most effective ways to rid and object of all transmissible agents, though it is not always appropriate, because of the material an object is made of. (Such as plastics, fiber optics, and electronics.) Ethylene oxide (EO) gas is a commonly used sterilisation procedure for objects that cannot survive temperatures greater than 60°C. Ethylene oxide treatment is generally carried out at 54-60°C in 60-75% humidity for at least 12 hours. Ethylene oxide penetrates very well, moving through paper, cloth, and same plastic films.

It is however highly flammable and requires a much longer time than any heat treatment. It also needs time to aerate completely, as it is a potential carcinogen. There is a new rapid biological indicator for use in EO sterilizers. These indicators contain Bacillus subtilis, which is a very resistant organism. If sterilisation fails, incubation at 37°C will cause a fluorescent change within four hours, which is read by an auto-reader. After 96 hours, a visible color change will have occurred.

The fluorescence is emitted when a particular (EO resistant) enzyme is present, which means spores are still active. The color change is brought on by a pH shift due to bacterial metabolism. The test is suitable for most types of ethylene oxide cycles. The rapid results mean that if a cycle was found to be ineffective, the objects treated can be quarantined and physicians quickly advised of possible contamination.

Glutaraldehyde is an accepted liquid antiseptic, provided the immersion time is long enough - it can take up to 12 hours to kill all spores. It is not a particularly nice chemical to deal with, it is toxic and skin contact should be avoided. It has quite a short shelf-left (<2 weeks), and is expensive.

A new chemical comparable to gluteraldehyde is ortho-phthalaldehyde (OPA), which got FDA clearance in late 1999. Typically used in a 0.55% solution, OPA shows better myco-bactericidal activity than gluteraldehyde. It also is effective against gluteraldehyde-resistant spores. OPA has superior stability, has less odor and does not irritate skin or eyes, and it acts more quickly than gluteraldehyde. It is more expensive though, and will stain proteins (including skin) gray in color.

Another chemical antiseptic used is hydrogen peroxide. Hydrogen peroxide is made of two atoms of hydrogen and two of oxygen, because of this it is non-toxic and leaves no residue. The Sterrad 50 as well as other Sterrad sterilisation chambers use hydrogen peroxide vapor to sterilize heat-sensitive equipment such an endoscapes. The Sterrad 50 sterilizes in 45 minutes, and it sterilizes as effectively as ethylene oxide treatment, also penetrating small lumened devices.

Endoclens is also a device to sterilize endoscopes. It mixes two chemicals (hydrogen peroxide and formic acid) together to make its antiseptic as needed. The machine has two independent asynchronous bays, and cleans (in warm detergent with pulsed air), sterilizes and dries the endoscopes automatically. All air and water inlets are filtered, and the machine handles temperature, timing and chemical concentration.

The total time for the whole process is 30 minutes, and a hard-copy report of the cycle is printed as well as being stored electronically. Studies with synthetic soil containing bacterial sports showed this machine achieved sterilisation effectively. Another chemical used to sterilize instruments is peracetic acid (0.2%), which is used in the Steris system.

Prions show a great deal of resistance to these sterilisation chemicals. Hydrogen peroxide (3%) for one hour was shown to be ineffective in that it had a less than 3 log reduction. Iodine, formaldehyde, gluteraldehyde and peracetic acid also fail this test. Only chlorine, a phenolic, guanidine thiocyanate and sodium hydroxide (NaOH) reduce the titre by more than 4 logs.

Chlorine and NaOH are the most consistent of these. Chlorine though is sometimes too corrosive to use on certain objects. Sodium hydroxide has had many studies showing its effectiveness. In all, the chemical antiseptics do not work well against prions. An interesting note is that treatment with aldehydes (e.g. formaldehyde) have been shown to increase prion resistance. It must be remembered that prion elimination is not important in most cases, as CJD and BSE are not common.

Radiation Sterilisation

Methods exist to sterilize using radiation such as X-rays or gamma rays. Devices to do so are used, for example, by the United States Postal Service to sterilize mail in the DC area. Also, some foods are irradiated for sterilisation. Irradiation does not make things radioactive.

Antiseptic

An antiseptic is a substance that kills or prevents the growth and reproduction of various microorganisms, including bacteria, fungi, protozoa, and viruses on the external surfaces of the body. The objective of antiseptics is to reduce the possibility of sepsis, infection or putrefaction by germs.

Antibacterials have the same objective but only act against bacteria. antibiotics perform a similar function, preventing the growth or reproduction of bacteria within the body. disinfectants operate on nonliving objects such as medical instruments. Some common antiseptics are as follows:

— *Alcohol*: Used to disinfect the skin before injections are given.

— *Quaternary ammonium compounds* (such as benzalkonium chloride): Used as a pre-operative skin disinfectant. Antiseptic towels are often impregnated with this chemical.

— *Boric acid*: Used in suppositories to treat yeast infections of the vagina, in eyewashes, and as an antiviral to shorten the duration of cold sore attacks. Put into creams for burns. Also common in trace amounts in eye contact solution.

— *Chlorhexidine Gluconate*: Used as a skin antiseptic and to treat inflammation of the gums (gingivitis)

— *Hydrogen peroxide*: Used as a 6% (20Vols) solution to clean and deodorise wounds and ulcers.

— *Iodine*: Usually used in an alcoholic solution or as Lugol's iodine solution to disinfect minor wounds and as a pre- and post-operative antiseptic.

— *Mercurochrome*: Not recognized as safe and effective by the U.S. FDA due to concerns about its mercury content.

— *Phenol compounds*: Used as a "scrub" for pre-operative hand cleansing. Used in the form of a powder as an antiseptic baby powder, where it is dusted onto the belly button as it heals. Also used in mouthwashes and throat lozenges, where it has a painkilling effect as well as an antiseptic one.

— *Sodium chloride*: Used as a general cleanser. Also used as an antiseptic mouthwash.

3

Hand Dishwashing

Dishwashing is probably subject to more variables than any other household clean-up job. In theory at least, any detergent or soap can be used for hand dishwashing, except an automatic dishwasher detergent. However, soap has become almost extinct as a dishwashing product and many laundry detergents are not very acceptable. Laundry detergents, may leave spots and streaks, the powders may not completely dissolve, or may discolour certain metals with soaking.

Liquid Hand Dishwashing Detergent

A light-duty liquid hand dishwashing detergent is the best choice. Regardless of brand, certain characteristics are important in a hand dishwashing liquid: lasting suds, effective cleaning performance, mildness to hands, safety for dishes and other washables, storage stability, pleasant fragrance and appearance, convenient packaging and dispensing.

In formulating a product to meet these criteria, manufacturers, in general, use certain basic ingredients. Surfactants or surface active agents are the primary ingredients in a liquid hand dishwashing detergent. Often a combination of surfactants is used to produce good grease cutting capability and soil suspension, mildness in water of varying degrees of hardness, and a high, stable suds level. All surfactants in these detergents are biodegradable. Stability and Dispensing Aids are added to keep the product homogeneous under varying storage conditions, and to provide desirable dispensing characteristics.

Alcohols, hydrotropes, and salts are often used. Fragrance and Colour Additives are what give a product its "personality," and are important, though present in extremely small amounts. Mildness Additives may include moisturizing agents, certain oils and emollients, certain protein compounds, or other neutralizing or beneficial ingredients. Preservatives are added, if needed, in small quantities to help prevent any microbiological growth in the product which could cause colour or odour change, poor performance and separation of the ingredients.

Antibacterial Agents are sometimes added to provide antibacterial protection for the hands. Hand dishwashing liquids are relatively easy for consumers to compare. Users can experiment by trying various brands and deciding which product features are important to them: performance, price, sudsing, fragrance and "feel," or perhaps the packaging. Usage is often based on the amount it takes to produce a rich, thick layer of suds.

Though detergents are not as affected by water hardness as soap is, some additional product may be necessary in very hard water. An important difference in the quantity of liquid hand dishwashing detergent required is the concentration of the surfactants vs. water in a product. More concentrated products are more efficient and may be more economical to use than the more dilute ones. Grease removal is more effective in warm water than in cold water.

Automatic Dishwashing Procedures

An automatic dishwasher produces clean dishes, keeps the kitchen free of clutter before and after meals, generally uses less water than hand dishwashing, reduces breakage, helps control germs and frees time for other activities. Automatic dishwashers vary from brand to brand, model to model, but all clean by the action of hot detergent solution that is circulated by spray arms and towers. Water temperature, detergent concentration, and proper loading of the racks are all important to good results.

Water Temperature

For the best cleaning results, be sure water temperature in the dishwasher is hot. Most new dishwashers heat the water right in the tub to compensate for low temperature hot water supplies. If the dishwasher does not have a heat booster, run the hot water at the kitchen sink for a few minutes to clear the line of cool water before turning on the dishwasher.

Scraping and Prerinsing

Prerinsing dishes and glassware should not be necessary. An automatic dishwasher detergent and a properly installed and operating dishwasher of reasonably current vintage will do a thorough job with just a scraping off of large food particles. If dishes are loaded into the dishwasher and washed later, the "rinse-hold" cycle can be used; but experience may show that even this is not necessary. Extra heavily soiled cookware may need a rinse, soak or a prewash.

Loading the Dishwasher

Variations in dishwashers make it important to study directions and diagrams in the user's manual. The most important factor is the positioning of the dishes and utensils in relation to the wash action.

— Be sure to place the heavily soiled side of each item facing the source of the water spray at the center of the tub. Don't let large items shield small ones. Place cups, bowls and glasses upside down. Flatware should be loaded according to the manufacturer's instructions.

— Avoid crowding or nesting spoons together so water can reach the soiled areas.

— Place sharp items with points down for safety reasons.

— Be sure more delicate items are firmly supported by the rack so they won't topple and possibly break or chip. Experience and results will show how closely together dishes can be placed and how fully the racks can be loaded for satisfactory results.

— Do not put stainless steel and silver flatware in the same silverware basket compartment. Direct contact between these metals can cause permanent damage to the silver. If possible, avoid placing the basket compartment directly in front of the dtergent dsipenser cups.

Adding Detergent

Use only a product made specifically for automatic dishwashers. Any other type will cause oversudsing and possible damage to the dishwasher. Use the amount recommended on the detergent container and in the user's manual, adjusting it to the amount of soil, water hardness and load size. Some detergent dispensers have lines to indicate the amount of detergent to add.

In hard water, it is particularly important to use detergent as recommended by the dishwasher manufacturer. In general, the harder the water, the more detergent is required. In soft water, less detergent can be used. Add the detergent to the dispenser cup(s) after the dishwasher is loaded and is ready to be operated. Be sure the dispenser is dry and clean before adding detergent to maintain optimum performance. This also helps prevent powder detergents from becoming caked in the dispenser. Also, be sure to close the dispenser cup lid. Don't sprinkle or pour detergent on flatware or other metals; spotting and pitting may occur.

Setting the Controls

Depending on the model, various cycles are available to the user. They may vary by the number of washes and rinses, type of load, degree of soil, and type of drying (air or heated). For most full loads, the regular or "normal" cycle will do the job well, but consider all the options and use any of the features the dishwasher offers. Special "energy-saving" cycles may be offered. Don't shorten the normal wash time just to save energy; the washing action itself takes very little power. A too-short cycle may be a waste of hot water and detergent if results are poor.

Unloading Dishes

When dry and cool, a load of dishes can be left in the dishwasher until needed. Most users agree that unloading should be done before starting to prepare the next meal. To avoid the doubt about "clean or dirty," leave the door latched until all clean dishes are put away. Some newer models have a signal device to indicate the dishwasher has been run.

The forceful action, hot water and alkaline detergent in a dishwasher can be harmful to some items. Always check the dishwasher manufacturer's instructions about washing. Here are some items to be considered with caution:

Aluminum utensils: Aluminum, with a colored or metallic copper or gold look usually on the lids of pans and molds, has a thin anodized coat that is not dishwasher safe. The harder gray or charcoal-colored anodic finish applied inside and out to some of the professional type cookware can also be permanently damaged. Plain aluminum will darken when exposed to water, some foods, detergents, and alkaline cleaners such as ammonia or a heated solution of baking soda and water.

The degree of discoloration depends partly on the length of contact and metal (some alloys are more resistant). Aluminum can be washed in the dishwasher if the discoloration or the necessity of additional cleaning with steel wool or an acid cleaner is not objectionable.

Retail Food Operations and Hand Wash Program

Food Employees shall clean their hands and exposed portions of their arms with a cleaning compound in a lavatory that is equipped as specified ----by vigorously rubbing together the surfaces of their lathered hands and arms for at least 20 seconds and thoroughly rinsing with clean water. Employees shall pay particular attention to the areas underneath the fingernaills and between the fingers.

The only standard hand washing procedure for food workers to use that assures removal of pathogenic microorganisms (such as those from fecal sources) from fingertips, is that developed and described by the Hospitality Institute of Technology and Management. The emphasis of this hand washing procedure is the use of a fingernail brush and a large volume of flowing water. In most food production and foodservice operations, food workers receive little or no training concerning hand and fingertip washing.

Regulatory authorities only check to see if there is a hand wash sink in the food preparation / production / service area, if this hand washing area is supplied with soap, and if the sink functions properly. Checking operational hand washing facilities provides no verification that employees are washing their hands sufficiently to reduce fecal pathogens on their hands and fingertips to a safe level.

As more American consumers become aware of the danger of pathogen transmission in food, they become concerned that food workers are not washing their hands after using the toilet or touching contaminated items. Since consumers have no way of knowing if food workers have washed their hands, they are demanding that foodservice personnel wear plastic gloves. People assume that if food workers wear plastic gloves when handling food, food products are safe to consume. This logic is based on the presumption that gloves prevent transmission of microorganisms on hands and fingertips to food.

However, this is not the case, because microorganisms found on hands and fingertips contaminate both exterior and interior glove surfaces when gloves are put on, unless hands and fingertips have been washed thoroughly. Plastic gloves used in foodservice operations may also have pinholes or other defects that allow microorganisms from hands and fingertips to escape through the glove surfaces.

Skin Physiology

In order to understand the principles of safe hand washing, one must understand the physiology of the skin. The skin is the largest and most accessible organ of the human body. The skin provides protection by serving as an impenetrable barrier between bacteria-free tissues of the body and an environment that is contaminated with all types of microorganisms. When a cross section of human skin is examined under the microscope, it can be seen that it is basically composed of two layers, the epidermis and dermis, which lie atop the subcutaneous layer of tissue. The dermis and subcutaneous tissue are free of microbial flora.

However, bacterial flora are on and within the epidermis and can become established in the hair follicles and in the sweat and sebaceous glands. Although skin appears smooth, the epidermis actually contains many cracks, crevices, and hollows, which can trap and provide favorable growth areas for bacteria. The outer surface (stratum corneum) of the skin is also covered with a protective, waxy cuticle or sebum that can help microbes adhere.

The average human has a skin area of about 1 to 75m^2 that is composed of a mosaic of about 109 flat, pavement-like cells known as skin scales or squames. The cells are about 25m m square and 3 to 5m m thick. These cells that are lost in the process of desquamation, a complete layer being lost every 1 to 4 days. These dead cells are microscopic and are lost in a shower or bath, deposited in clothing, and scattered into the air. The loss of this outer layer is important in the distribution of both transient and resident microflora.

The greater the body movement, the more cells will be dispersed in the air. Routine bathing and hand washing have a direct influence on the microflora of the stratum corneum and determine the kinds and amount of microorganisms that remain or are dispersed with the dead cell fragments.

Microflora of the skin

Microorganisms carried on the skin of the human body have been divided into two distinct populations: resident and transient. Resident microorganisms are considered as permanent inhabitants of the skin of most people and are found on the superficial skin surface.

However, 10 to 20% of this total resident flora are found within the epidermal layer of skin and in skin crevices, where skin oils and hardened skin make their removal difficult and complete sterilisation of skin impossible. It is impossible to completely remove all microflora from the skin, even with a surgical scrub. This is one reason surgeons wear gloves. The other reason is to protect themselves from pathogens of patients.

Resident microorganisms include the coagulase-negative staphylococci; members of the Corynebacterium, Propionibacterium, and Acinetobacter species; and certain members of the Enterobacteriaceae family. Corynebacteria and oxygen-requiring coagulase-negative staphylococci comprise the majority of the resident microflora. The anaerobic bacterium, P. acnes, that causes acne, particularly in oily parts of the skin, is also a member of the resident flora.

The population of Staphylococcus epidermidis far out numbers S. aureus on healthy skin. Staphylococcus aureus (cause of staphylococcal food poisoning) is the only true pathogenic organism included in the resident microflora group of skin. About 35% of normal adults carry S. aureus in the anterior nostrils of the nose and are particularly susceptible to infection when the normal protective skin barrier is broken. It is generally considered safe to consume 1,000 S. aureus per gram of food, because foodborne illness due to the growth of this pathogen requires a population of 106 S. aureus per gram of food to produce a sufficient amount of illness-producing toxin.

The presence of resident microorganisms on the skin aids in preventing pathogenic microorganisms from becoming attached and causing their specific illnesses or diseases. Transient microorganisms. As the name implies, these are organisms that are found on and within the epidermal layer of skin, as well as other areas of the body, where they do not normally reside. Almost all disease-producing microorganisms belong to this category. They are organisms that may take advantage of some disturbance in the normal resident microflora to gain a foothold and cause infections and symptoms of disease or illness.

Transient microorganisms are deposited on the skin through direct contact or by aerosol. The Association for Professionals in Infection Control Guidelines for Infection Control Practice (APIC) defines transient flora as microorganisms isolated from the skin but not demonstrated to be consistently present in the majority of persons. Transient microflora are of concern in health care settings and food operations because of the likely transmission of this type of microflora by hands.

Unless transient microorganisms are removed from hands by washing with soap and water using mechanical friction, or reduced by the application of some antiseptic hand rub, spread of pathogenic microorganisms and food spoilage microorganisms, such as Pseudomonas spp., can occur. Transient microorganisms (bacteria, yeast, molds, viruses, and parasites) can be of any type, from any source with which the body has had contact, and are found on the palms of hands, fingertips, and under fingernails.

Pathogens that may be present on the skin as transient types include: Escherichia coli, Salmonella spp., Shigella spp., Clostridium perfringens, Giardia lamblia, Norwalk virus, and Hepatitis A virus. High levels of transient microorganisms attach to hand, fingertip, and fingernail surfaces when:

— Fecal contamination remains on hands and fingertips after using the toilet, changing diapers, or cleaning up after pets at home.

— Contaminated raw products (e.g. raw meat, poultry, fish, unwashed fruits and vegetables) are touched.

— Infected cuts and boils are touched or picked, or if a person has an infected fingernail.

The areas around and under the fingernails provide a microenvironment that is quite conducive to microbial growth. It is this area of the hand that often harbors the highest microbial population that is most difficult to remove. Resident microorganisms will always be present and survive on skin. Transient microorganisms remain or are destroyed by the skin's environment at a rate determined by the skin characteristics of each individual.

Pether and Gilbert reported that salmonellas and E. coli can survive on the fingertips for a few hours. Casewell and Phillips reported that Klebsiella spp. survived on artificially inoculated hands for 150 minutes. Coates et al. reported that survival time for campylobacters (suspended in 0.1% peptone solution) on hands ranged from less than a minute to slightly more than 4 minutes. However, when the campylobacters were suspended in chicken liquor or blood, these pathogenic bacteria survived on the hands for longer periods of time.

Filho et al. reported a study of the survival of applied cultures of Pseudomonas aeruginosa, Klebsiella pneumoniae, Serratia marcescens, E. coli, and S. aureus on the fingertips and hands of four volunteers. Over 99% of the bacteria died within 2 minutes after application, but about 105 cells (0.01%) remained on the fingers for up to 90 minutes.

When suspended in saline, L. monocytogenes survived up to 60 minutes on fingertips, but survival times were greatly extended (up to 5 hours) when the inoculum was suspended in milk. Survival time was apparently affected by skin lipids, the skin's normal flora, or the fat content of the milk. Different serotypes displayed similar results for the percentage persistence over a 2-hour period when suspended in milk, except for an isolate of L. monocytogenes serotype 7, which had a greater percentage survival than other organisms tested.

In contrast, Escherichia coli failed to survive for 1 hour under the same conditions. Hand washing with either soap or a water-based chlorhexidine hand cleanser usually failed to completely decontaminate fingertips to which an inoculum of 104 / CFU per fingertip suspended in milk was applied, but a solution of chlorhexidine gluconate in methanol was found to be effective.

Personal Hygiene: Management must train employees to know the importance of good personal hygiene and use this knowledge in preparation for work. This includes bathing daily, using deodorants, and keeping fingernails clean and clipped short (to 1/16 inch).

Many people use a deodorant soap for bathing or showering. A study reported by Bibel indicated that there was no significant difference in the number of skin microflora of individuals using deodorant soap compared to those using plain soap. However, it was noted that the resident bacterial population of the skin was changed when deodorant soaps were used. More S. epidermidis was seen when plain soap (Ivory®) was used, while washing with deodorant soap seemed to favor Acinetobacter calcoaceticus and Micrococcus luteus.

Importance of Hand Washing

Food production workers and foodservice personnel must be taught to use correct hand and fingertip washing, by management, in preparation for work. Regulatory authorities do not require the use of a fingernail brush. However, correct use of a fingernail brush to wash hands and fingertips is the best way to assure removal of transient microorganisms.

Not only is hand washing critical in foodservice and food production operations, it is also important in homes and day care operations. Black et al. reported a study that demonstrated a decline in diarrheal illnesses (due to Shigella, Giardia and rotavirus) in day care centers when employees were taught to use good hand washing procedures. The incidence of diarrhea in 2 day care centers with a hand-washing program was half that of 2 control centers for an entire 35 week study period.

Employees in the hand washing program washed their hands before handling food and after arriving at the day care center, helping a child use the toilet, or using the toilet themselves. When children entered the day care center, used the toilet, were diapered, or prepared to eat, employees washed their hands using bar soap and paper towels. However, the authors did not specify what constitutes a good hand-wash procedure. Shigella is associated with poor hygiene. The effectiveness of the simple intervention of hand washing with soap and water in preventing the spread of shigellosis was investigated.

Several pieces of soap and earthenware pitchers for storing water were provided to the study families and they were advised to wash their hands with soap and water after defecation and before meals. Compliance was monitored daily by observing the size of the soap and residual water. Rectal swabs of contact of both of the groups were obtained daily for culture. The secondary infection rate was 10.1% in the study group and 32.4% in the control group.

Khan demonstrated that secondary infection rates within families in Bangladesh due to transfer of pathogenic bacteria decreased, when people were taught to wash their hands after defecation and before eating. The study population was comprised of confirmed cases of shigellosis. These and matched controls were followed up for 10 days.

Lack of Effective Fingertip and Hand Washing

In 1996, a national survey was conducted to assess hand washing behavior of adults in the United States. More than 7,000 people participated in the two-part survey that was conducted by an international research firm. Participants were most likely to say they washed their hands after changing a diaper (78%) and before handling or eating food (81%). However, most people said they did not wash up after petting an animal (48%), coughing or sneezing (33%), or handling money (22%).

While hand washing is a simple and easy task, studies have indicated that personnel in both health care and foodservice industries have incorrect hand washing habits. Sixty percent of foodservice personnel in one study were reported not to wash their hands as required by these types of positions. "The food handler is one link in the complex multiphase process of contaminated food - infection - enteric disease."

Of greatest concern is contamination of hands and forearms by transient microorganisms from feces. Clothing can become contaminated from pieces of fecal matter collected on the hairs around the anal region. When people use the toilet, their hands or forearms may become contaminated with intestinal microorganisms which include C. perfringens, shigellae, salmonellae, hepatitis A virus, and other enteric bacteria. Thus, these contaminated hands / forearms can transfer intestinal microbes to foods, equipment, and other workers in the food storage and preparation areas unless correct personal hygiene and adequate hand washing procedures are followed.

A study that monitored restroom hand washing compliance by foodservice workers at a managed care facility and two commercial foodservice operations was conducted. The workers at the managed care facility had the best compliance. This was thought to be due to the emphasis on hand washing by management personnel as well as the training and continued in-service instruction of employees.

Monitoring hand washing was beneficial for increasing and maintaining employee compliance with hand washing. Horwood and Minch reported the results of numbers and types of bacteria obtained from 34 hand washing samples obtained in 22 foodservice establishments in the Cambridge and Boston, Massachusetts areas (cafeterias, lunch rooms, drug stores, and restaurants). The range in total plate count was 6,200 to 16,000,000,000 per ml. E. coli was found in 13 of the 34 samples.

Twenty-nine of the 30 samples showed hemolytic staphylococci, 19 showed hemolytic streptococci, and 19 showed a mixture of both hemolytic streptococci and staphylococci. The number of aerobic spore-forming bacilli ranged from 4 to 400 per ml. When this research was done over 45 years ago, the authors at that time concluded that the hands of food handlers must be kept clean. They stressed that food handlers must be given instruction and that management must assume the responsibility for daily education and enforcement of hand washing.

Test for Fingertip Washing: By reviewing the results of the study by Horwood and Minch, it can be assumed that E. coli can be used as an indicator of effective fingertip washing. It is a simple matter to assess employee hand washing compliance by using E. coli Petrifilm™. To accomplish this, foodservice and food production personnel can be asked to rinse their fingers in a small plastic bag containing 10 ml. letheen broth. A 1 ml. sample of this "fingertip rinse" can then be plated and incubated on E. coli Petrifilm™. While there may be a small background count of E. coli from handling food, an E. coli count of more than 20 per milliliter indicates that fingertip washing procedures were inadequate.

Effectiveness of Toilet Paper

In under developed nations of the world, toilet paper is considered to be extremely expensive, and hence, is not used by a large portion of the world's population of people. These people use one hand to wipe themselves after defecating and then wipe their hands on some leaves or rinse their hands in water from a pitcher. When they eat or cook, they use the other hand.

When these people immigrate to countries that routinely have toilet paper available, they must learn to use toilet paper, and be taught the importance of washing their hands with soap and flowing water after defecating. The use of toilet paper was not common in the United States until after the early 1900's. The problem today is that there is a total reliance on toilet paper to keep feces off the fingertips, however there are no performance standards for toilet paper.

Consumer Reports reviewed toilet paper performance and found a wide variation among samples tested in wet strength, tear resistance, and absorbency. As long as there are no performance standards, or standards for use, no one should assume that toilet paper provides an effective barrier to keep fingertips free of fecal pathogens.

Unmedicated Hand Soaps, Detergents and Hand Disinfectants

Most research studies for hand washing and hand disinfectants have been done for personnel (surgeons, nurses, and other health care workers) in health care settings where patients are immune compromised or are at high risk of wound, surgical, or burn infection.

The effectiveness of hand washing agents in removing infant-acquired organisms from the hands of personnel working in a hospital nursery. The following preparations were used: 3% hexachlorophene (Phiso-Hex) in liquid saponified coconut oil; 7.5% providone-iodine, 0.75% iodine (Betadine); a 70% ethyl alcohol emulsion; and Ivory® soap bars and tap water. The results of this study indicated that all agents were equally effective when followed by drying with a paper towel.

Results of a research study by Bannan and Judge indicated that hand washing with bar soap (Ivory®) reduced a population of 2 x 109 Serratia to 6.2 x 105 (a 99.97% reduction in bacteria). The hand washing method used in this study did not use a nail brush or a double wash, but did use a lot of flowing water. Mahl found that many commercial hand wash products containing antimicrobial agents do not rapidly reduce numbers of inoculated bacteria in fingernail regions to any greater extent than non-antimicrobial hand washes.

In another study of acceptable methods for washing hands for hospital procedures, Ayliffe et al., described research in which fingertips were inoculated with cultures of S. aureus, Staphylococcus saprophyticus, E. coli, and Pseudomonas aeruginosa. Bacterial counts from the fingertips were made after disinfection with various antiseptic detergents, alcoholic solutions, or unmedicated soap. There was less than a 100 to 1 reduction in all cases.

A preparation containing 70% alcohol with chlorhexadine was the most effective preparation. Antiseptic detergents were only slightly more effective against gram negative bacteria than was plain soap. Ayliffe et al. suggested that soap and water was adequate for general hand washing procedures and that germicidal agents should only be required for aseptic procedures.

Alcohols, usually 60 to 90% ethyl or isopropyl, inactivate both the resident and transient microorganisms on the skin surface, but have no persistent effect and do not remove fecal microorganisms completely. Alcohol removes surface oils from the skin and has a drying effect. Newer emollient-containing formulations are more acceptable to users but still have a skin-drying tendency. Isopropyl alcohol is a toxic chemical, and if used in any food production area, must be carefully monitored and stored so that it cannot get into food.

The 1997 FDA Food Code does not consider the replacement of hand washing with soap and water by the use of alcohol, alcohol formulations, or alcohol wipes to be an effective method for cleaning hands in food production and food preparation areas. Even when alcohol is used as a hand antiseptic, hands must be washed with soap and water before the alcohol is applied. Studies by the author have shown that soap and water give as much or more reduction in hand microorganisms as alcohol. Since even alcohol preparations with emollients dry the skin and cause dermatitis, there is no reason to use alcohol for hand disinfection if there is an adequate supply of water for hand washing.

A discussion of the use of antibacterial agents in hand soaps and detergents for use by food workers is presented by Paulson. Chlorhexidine gluconate (CHG) is a common antimicrobial ingredient in antibacterial soaps and will reduce resident bacteria when it is used repeatedly over a long period of time. CHG does not act as rapidly as do alcohols, and it takes several applications of CHG to reduce flora comparable to alcohol application. However, CHG is milder than alcohols (an important factor in frequent washings) and has some residual chemical activity on the skin (an advantage when gloves are worn).

Quantity of soap necessary for hospital personnel to use for effective hand washing. Subjects using 3-ml amounts of antiseptic soap in a single wash with no fingernail brush on uninoculated hands had slightly greater reductions in bacterial counts than those using 1 to 3 ml of plain liquid soap and 1-ml amounts of antiseptic soap, as would be expected. It was concluded that personnel should use 3 to 5 ml of soap to remove both transient and superficial resident microorganisms from hand surfaces.

Employees must use enough soap on the fingernail brush and then on their hands to produce a good lather. The standard for how long to wash hands is then governed by removal of the soapy lather. When the lather is gone and the fingertips are "squeaky clean" (less than 20 seconds), the population of transient microorganisms has been effectively reduced.

Detergency or Lathering Ability: There are no performance standards for the detergency (lathering ability) of soaps or hand detergents. This is another important factor in removing transient microorganisms from hands, and is influenced by type and amount of soil and mineral content of the water. A soap product or liquid detergent with high detergency is necessary to remove a large amount of fat, protein, or other types of organic soil that bind transient microflora. Water with high amounts of calcium, magnesium, or iron is "hard" and requires high-detergency products for lathering and emulsification ability.

Hand soaps or detergents must be user tested in specific food operation facilities with local water in order to determine which products lather sufficiently to clean hands in the easiest, most acceptable manner. This means that a national foodservice company should not dictate the use of one hand soap for all locations throughout the U.S. Hand soaps or detergents must be matched to type of water at the location of use.

"In healthy skin, a thin film of water repellent substance is secreted by sebaceous glands within the skin. This keeps the skin supple and helps prevent the ingress of water and dirt. The removal of this layer by irritating chemical compounds quickly leads to intense inflammation of the skin". For example, some antibacterial soaps, alcohol and alcohol preparations, and chlorine and iodine solutions or soaps may irritate the skin of some individuals and cause it to become excessively dry, rough, and red.

When the epidermal layer of hands becomes irritated, people do not wash their hands as often or as well. Hence, it is recommended that employees involved in routine food handling and food production be provided with regular bar or liquid soap (not an antibacterial product) for routine hand washing. "An acceptable hand soap motivates hand washing by making hand washing pleasant."

Many regulatory agencies forbid the use of bar soaps for employee hand washing and have mandated the use of liquid hand soaps or detergents for hand washing. This is not necessary. The use of liquid soap has not been demonstrated to be better for removing transient microorganisms than the use of plain bar soap for washing hands and fingertips.

Liquid soap products are frequently available in dispenser containers or bottles. Hospital studies have shown that dispensers must be replaced and not refilled. Pseudomonas spp., a pathogen present in many health care facilities, has been shown to grow and multiply in some liquid hand soap and detergent products. This is another reason many manufacturers add disinfectants to their liquid soaps.

The data collected from hand washing research studies indicate that regular hand soap or detergents (bar or liquid) are effective for hand washing for personnel in most food production or foodservice facilities. In aseptic food production facilities where food with a very low pathogen / total plate count must be prepared (e.g., infant formula, tube feedings), sterile gloves should probably be used after the hands are properly washed.

Fingernail Brushes

Fingernail brushes are necessary to dislodge the accumulation of debris from under and around fingernails. It is this subungual area that contains the highest number of microorganisms on hand surfaces. However, too frequent use of the fingernail brush or use of a nail brush that is too stiff will loosen too much of the epidermal layer on the tips of the fingers, causing the fingers to crack and bleed. The tips of the fingernail brush are used to produce lather on hand surfaces, particularly around the fingertips and fingernails during the first part of the double wash method of hand washing.

In order to ensure removal of fecal pathogens the double hand wash method [though no longer a recommendation of the 1997 FDA Food Code, should be required when employees begin a shift and after they use the toilet. The single hand wash method that does not require the use of a nail brush is adequate during normal food handling operations for removal of most transient pathogenic bacteria acquired by routine hand contact with food.

The Hospitality Institute of Technology and Management recently conducted an inoculated finger washing experiment to evaluate the effectiveness of ordinary hand washing compared with the double hand wash. In this study, high levels of Serratia marcescens were placed on the thumb and first and second fingers of the hands of 3 people. One tenth milliliter (0.1 ml) of a solution containing 20,000,000 to 100,000,000 S. marcescens per ml. were placed on the fingers and thumb.

The subjects then washed their hands using selected experimental procedures in order to evaluate the reduction of the indicator organism, S. marcescens. The population of S. marcescens was measured at each step by rinsing the thumb and first 2 fingers in 10 ml of phosphate buffer.

The first hand wash procedure tested was a simple 13-second hand wash, whereby the hands were soaped, lathered, and, during the lathering, rinsed underneath a faucet of flowing water. There was a reduction of 325 to 1 (a 99.7% reduction). The volume of water used for rinsing the hands, not the time of the wash, was the critical reduction factor. When the hands were washed according to the double hand wash procedure using a fingernail brush and soap, the total time was about 20 seconds for the entire washing process, including the time necessary for soap removal.

The first wash with the nail brush reduced the S. marcescens indicator organism by a factor of 62,000 to 1 (a 99.998% reduction), or 200 times more than the simple, single hand wash without a nail brush. The second hand wash, without the nail brush, which took approximately 13 seconds, reduced the indicator organism from 120, 000 to 1 (a 99.999% reduction), or 320 times more than a simple hand wash.

In order to determine the residual population of S. marcescens remaining on the fingernail brush, the brush was rinsed in 10 ml of phosphate buffer. Compared with the population reduction on the fingers, there was a reduction of 418,000 to 1 (a 99.9998% reduction) on the brush. This points out that the nail brush will have fewer residual microorganisms than the fingertips. Those residual microorganisms remaining on the brush could be transferred to the next person using the nailbrush.

However, there will be another 99.98% reduction when that person uses the nail brush for hand and fingertip washing. Therefore, the potential for transfer of microorganisms by the nail brush is minimal. Door knobs, soap dispenser levers and paper towel dispenser levers probably have a greater potential for cross-contamination than the common use of a nail brush for hand washing.

The normal resident microflora (skin bacteria) of the hands were also measured every time the fingers were rinsed in the phosphate buffer. No matter how many times the hands were washed, a population of skin bacteria ranging from 10,000 to 1,000,000 per ml. were recovered from the subjects' fingers and thumbs. This confirms findings of previous hand wash studies of the past 50 years that it is virtually impossible to remove all microorganisms from the skin.

Whenever people touch food, they must realize that skin cells and skin bacteria are added to the food. This has been taking place for thousands of years, and is obviously not a food safety issue. In fact, this "sharing" may be important for developing and maintaining immunity.

After hands are washed and rinsed, they must be thoroughly dried. Blow dryers should not be used because they accumulate microorganisms from toilet aerosols, and can cause contamination of hands as they are dried by the drier. It is also apparent that many individuals do not dry their hands thoroughly when using a blow drier; hence, moisture, which is conducive to microbial growth, remains on hands, or people dry their hands on their clothing.

In a hand drying study reported by Redway et al., standard techniques were used to identify and count the bacteria associated with hand washing and drying under natural conditions. Average bacterial counts were reduced when towels (either cloth or paper) were used to dry hands, the most significant decrease being with paper towels. Hot air dryers produced a highly significant increase in all bacteria on hands.

In a further study, Redway et al. reported that bacteria were isolated from swabs taken from the air flow nozzle and air inlet of 35 hot air dryers in 9 types of locations (including hospitals, eating places, railway stations, public houses, colleges, shops, and sports clubs.) Bacteria were relatively numerous in the air flows and on the inlets of 100% of dryers sampled, and in 97% of the nozzles. Staphylococci and micrococci (probably from skin and hair) were blown out of all of the dryers sampled for these type of bacteria, and 95% showed evidence of the potential pathogen S. aureus.

At least 6 species of enterobacteria were isolated from the air flows of 63% of the dryers, indicating fecal contamination. The authors concluded that hot air dryers have the potential for depositing pathogenic bacteria onto the hands and body and that bacteria could also be inhaled as they are distributed into the general environment whenever dryers are running. It was suggested that the use of hot air dryers should be carefully considered on health grounds, especially in sensitive locations.

Cloth roller towels are not recommended because they become common-use towels at the end of the roll, and can be a source of pathogen transfer to clean hands. Brodie demonstrated that staphylococci can be transmitted by use of a communal towel for drying hands after washing and recommended that paper towels be used for drying hands. The use of roller towels for drying hands in food production facilities is banned by most regulatory agencies.

Hand Lotions

Hands may become dry and irritated with frequent hand washing, and therefore there is a tendency for personnel to want to use hand lotions. However, the use of hand lotions in food production and food service units is discouraged, as it is in health care units, because of possible contamination of these products. If the use of hand lotions is allowed, only small packets or small bottles of lotion should be allowed on the premises so that they are replaced frequently. The use of hand lotion products should be monitored.

The following is a list of situations that may lead to hazardous contamination of foods.

1. Touching the body, human contact
   — Anywhere on the head (ears, nose, eyes, mouth, pimples)
   — Shaking hands with people
   — Using a nose tissue, handkerchief
2. Touching selected raw food (particularly raw meat, fish, and poultry products)
3. Touching bottoms of boxes that could be contaminated by meat and poultry juices on the floor of the delivery truck

Situations that do not lead to a hazard, but where hand washing visible to customer's is recommended, because consumers will feel threatened, include:

1. Touching other items
   — Money
   — Soiled apron, soiled uniform / clothes
   — Shoes
   — Items that have fallen on the floor
   — Floor
   — Soiled cleaning tools (mops, brooms)
   — Hair, skin
   — Items such as used tableware before handling ready-to-eat food, particularly wet, ready-to-eat food such as lettuce

Situations that do not lead to a hazard and where hands do not need to be washed after touching the item because consumers will not feel threatened, include:

1. Touching equipment
   — Cash register / scale keys
   — Clean wipe rags, wash water, rinse water
   — Clean slicer / knife handles, serving utensil handles
2. Touching facilities
   — Door handles on refrigerators holding ready-to-eat food
   — Door knobs, faucet handles, fixtures, furniture
3. Touching supplies
   — Sterilized, pasteurized, washed food

However, foodservice and food production personnel should be trained and encouraged to wash their hands at any time if there is any possibility of cross-contamination. Hand washing facilities in food preparation, food production and food service facilities must be accessible and maintained. Whenever possible, foodservice personnel should indicate to customers that they have washed their hands by asking the customer to pardon them for a moment while they wash and dry their hands.

Food service personnel should always minimize bare hand and arm contact with ready-to-eat food by preparing and mixing food with clean, sanitized equipment and utensils and by serving food with deli tissues, spatulas, tongs, or other dispensing equipment.

Uses of Gloves

Some states, such as New York, and local or city ordinances have made glove wearing by food workers mandatory, in spite of the fact that there is no documented evidence that food prepared and served by people wearing gloves is safer than food prepared by people who use effective hand washing procedures. No regulatory agency has been able to force the food industry through regulation and inspection to ensure that all food workers wash their hands because they have no way to measure if hands have been washed.

Therefore, some regulatory agencies have chosen to enforce glove use by food workers to contain fecal pathogens on the fingers. When retail food personnel use gloves to prepare and serve food, they must be trained to realize that microorganisms adhere to the surfaces of gloves and thus gloves can be sources of cross-contamination just as much as unwashed hands. Disposable gloves must be changed frequently. However, at this time, there are no data or government rules on how long gloves should be worn. The 1997 FDA Food Code recommends the following:

§3-304.15 Gloves, Use Limitation: If used, single-use gloves shall be used for only one task such as working with ready-to-eat foods or with raw animal food, used for no other purpose, and discarded when damaged or soiled or when interruptions occur in the operation.

However, considerations for length of time that gloves are worn in addition to type(s) of food being handled, also include material and thickness of gloves, fit, type of work being done, and chemicals coming in contact with gloves. Establishing guidelines for the frequency of changing gloves thus becomes very difficult. The environment created on the hand covered by a glove is very conducive to the multiplication of pathogenic microorganisms such as S. aureus and E. coli. This is due to the fact that the skin surface on the gloved hand is moist, warm, and protected.

Any hole, tear, slit, or puncture of a glove allows the entrance and exit of pathogenic microorganisms. Many inexpensive plastic gloves are porous. If individuals do not wash their hands before putting on gloves, both the interior and exterior of the gloves become contaminated with surface microorganisms on the hand. This condition has also been recognized by health care professionals. It can also be observed that many employees wearing gloves in a foodservice facility have not been trained and do not know when to change gloves, or even wash their gloved hands after touching contaminated objects.

Hands must be washed and dried as soon as gloves are removed, as well as before gloves are put on, to eliminate high levels of microorganisms on the hand surfaces. This means that if employees are to use gloves correctly, the government must require that specific procedures be taught by management so that enforcement can be objective. There have been many inquiries concerning the advisability and feasibility of washing gloved hands. However, at the present time, regulations concerning washing of gloved hands and reuse of gloves by workers in food production and foodservice has not been defined.

Pathogenic microorganisms are not as likely to multiply on the skin surface of clean, dry, ungloved hands if the hands are dry, because millions of competitive resident microorganisms inhibit their growth, and the pH of the skin is not optimal for growth. Wearing gloves to prepare and serve food does not prevent cross-contamination of food and foodborne illness. The reasons for this statement are listed as follows:

— Glove wearers continue to touch their faces, eyes, environmental surfaces, and contaminated raw food, inoculating the glove surfaces with microorganisms. In many instances, because of inadequate training, personnel wearing gloves assume that because they are wearing gloves, it is unnecessary to wash their gloved hands, or even change gloves.

— Oils adhere to gloves and promote the subsequent adherence of microorganisms.

— If people do not wash their hands and fingertips at all or adequately after using the toilet or touching highly contaminated items such as raw meat and poultry products, before putting gloves on, pathogenic microorganisms can contaminate both the inside and outer surface of gloves.

— Makulowich reported that gloves are porous and can allow the entrance of viruses. Hence, it can be concluded that the porosity of gloves will also allow the exit of viruses carried on hands within gloves (e.g., hepatitis viruses, Norwalk and others).

— When a total of 480 examination gloves were stressed at the highest stress level, 63% of 60 vinyl gloves leaked a selected bacteriophage, compared with 7% of 60 latex gloves. At lower-use level, there was no statistical difference in leakage. Gloves may become punctured during use, and the inside may become wet with perspiration, encouraging an increase in bacteria on the skin surface. When gloves are removed, hands must be washed thoroughly to reduce high populations of microorganisms in the moist environment on hands inside of gloves.

— It must be emphasized that gloved hands touch as many contaminated objects and surfaces as ungloved hands, and must be changed or washed frequently. However, at this time, there are no reliable data on how long gloves should be worn. No government agency has done any studies on glove contamination.

— Some people develop contact dermatitis when wearing gloves. The causes have been traced to allergic reactions to powders within the gloves and the chemical composition of both latex and synthetic gloves themselves.

The sensitivity of some people to latex is recognized by the medical profession. Latex allergy is a type I reaction to natural rubber latex proteins with clinical manifestations ranging from contact dermatitis to fatal anaplylaxis. People with a latex sensitivity cannot wear latex gloves without causing extreme skin irritation to both the hands and adjacent skin areas. A recent report has also traced adverse allergic reactions in sensitized individuals to consumption of sandwiches and salads prepared by food handlers wearing latex gloves.

— Persons with infections on their hands should be discouraged from handling ready-to eat food. However, if they continue to work in the retail food industry in the preparation, production, or service of food to the public, an antiseptic should be used on the infected area, which should then be covered with a bandage. A glove should be worn over bandaged area, and only the bandaged hand should be gloved. The gloved hand, in turn, must be washed along with the ungloved hand to keep it clean, or changed each time the ungloved hand is washed. Another reason for wearing a glove over bandaged hand areas is to keep the bandage(s) from falling into food.

Hospitality Institute of Technology (HITM)

Since the government has not provided any effective program for hand washing, HITM has developed a program. It has been in use for over 15 years by thousands of employees in many food establishments without any indication of a foodborne illness because of unwashed fingertips. Management is responsible for training employees to understand the importance of hand washing, as well as the use of correct hand washing methods, in order to prevent outbreaks of foodborne illness. The following guidelines and tools can be used in the development of a Safe Hands program.

Item	Description
I	Manager's Information on Safe Hand Washing
II	Employee Safe Hand Washing Policies, Procedures, and Standards. (To be written by the owner / manager(s).
III	Video tape: Safe Hand Washing
IV	Employee Safe Hand Washing Test and Record and answers
V	Safe Hand Washing HACCP Flow Chart.
VI	Safe Hand Washing Checklist
VIl	Safe hand washing poster for above the hand sink
VIII	Anchor surgeon's brush: Super Scrub #2000B.
IX	Glo-Germ kit: Orange fluorescent powder in mineral oil for hand washing training; white tracking powder to show what people touch and how they transfer germs; fluorescent light to cause the powder to "glow" in a darkened room.

4

Food Additives

A food additive is any substance added to food or improve its flavour and appearance. Legally, the term refers to "any substance the intended use which results or may reasonably be expected to result-directly or indirectly-in its becoming a component or otherwise affecting the characteristics of any food." This definition includes any substance used in the production, processing, treatment, packaging, transportation or storage of food.

If a substance is added to a food for a specific purpose in that food, it is referred to as a direct additive. For example, the low-calorie sweetener aspartame, which is used in beverages, puddings, yogurt, chewing gum and other foods, is considered a direct additive. Many direct additives are identified on the ingredient label of foods.

Indirect food additives are those that become part of the food in trace amounts due to its packaging, storage or other handling. For instance, minute amounts of packaging substances may find their way into foods during storage. Food packaging manufacturers must prove to the U.S. Food and Drug Administration (FDA) that all materials coming in contact with food are safe, before they are permitted for use in such a manner.

USE OF ADDITIVES

Additives perform a variety of useful functions in foods that are often taken for granted. Since most people no longer live on farms, additives help keep food wholesome and appealing while en route to markets sometimes thousands of miles away from where it is grown or manufactured.

Additives also improve the nutritional value of certain foods and can make them more appealing by improving their taste, texture, consistency or color. Some additives could be eliminated if we were willing to grow our own food, harvest and grind it, spend many hours cooking and canning, or accept increased risks of food spoilage. But most people today have come to rely on the many technological, aesthetic and convenience benefits that additives provide in food. Additives are used in foods for five main reasons:

— To Maintain product consistency. Emulsifiers give products a consistent texture and prevent them from separating. Stabilizers and thickeners give smooth uniform texture. Anti-caking agents help substances such as salt to flow freely.

— To improve or maintain nutritional value. Vitamins and minerals are added to many common foods such as milk, flour, cereal and margarine to make up for those likely to be lacking in a person's diet or lost in processing. Such fortification and enrichment has helped reduce malnutrition among the U.S. population. All products containing added nutrients must be appropriately labeled.

— To maintain palatability and wholesomeness. Preservatives retard product spoilage caused by mold, air, bacteria, fungi or yeast. Bacterial contamination can cause foodborne illness, including life-threatening botulism. Antioxidants are preservatives that prevent fats and oils in baked goods and other foods from becoming rancid or developing an off-flavor. They also prevent cut fresh fruits such as apples from turning brown when exposed to air.

— To provide leavening or control acidity/alkalinity. Leavening agents that release acids when heated can react with baking soda to help cakes, biscuits and other baked goods to rise during baking. Other additives help modify the acidity and alkalinity of foods for proper flavor, taste and color.

— To enhance flavor or impart desired color. Many spices and natural and synthetic flavors enhance the taste of foods. Colors, likewise, enhance the appearance of certain foods to meet consumer expectations. Examples of substances that perform each of these functions are provided in the chart "Common Uses of Additives."

Many substances added to food may seem foreign when listed on the ingredient label, but are actually quite familiar. For example, ascorbic acid is another name for Vitamin C; alphatocopherol is another name for Vitamin E; and beta-carotene is a source of Vitamin A. Although there are no easy synonyms for all additives, it is helpful to remember that all food is made up of chemicals. Carbon, hydrogen and other chemical elements provide the basic building blocks for everything in life.

Color Additive

A color additive is any dye, pigment or substance that can impart color when added or applied to a food, drug, or cosmetic, or to the human body. Color additives may be used in foods, drugs, cosmetics, and certain medical devices such as contact lenses. Color additives are used in foods for many reasons, including to offset color loss due to storage or processing of foods and to correct natural variations in food color. Colors permitted for use in foods are classified as certified or exempt from certification. Certified colors are man-made, with each batch being tested by the manufacturer and FDA to ensure that they meet strict specifications for purity.

There are nine certified colors approved for use in the United States. One example is FD&C Yellow No.6, which is used in cereals, bakery goods, snack foods and other foods. Color additives that are exempt from certification include pigments derived from natural sources such as vegetables, minerals or animals. For example, caramel color is produced commercially by heating sugar and other carbohydrates under strictly controlled conditions for use in sauces, gravies, soft drinks, baked goods and other foods. Most colors exempt from certification also must meet certain legal criteria for specifications and purity.

Food colours are added to a variety of foods. They have no nutritional value and are only present to improve the appearance of the food. Foods that contain food colours include:

— Soft drinks

— Confectionery (e.g. sweets)

— Fish fingers (breadcrumbs)

— Cheese

— Margarine

Food colours separation

A mixture of food colours can be separated by paper chromatography. Special paper that looks like filter paper is used. A small spot of the food colour is placed on the filter paper as Figure 4 shows. The chromatography paper is then dipped into a solvent such as water or ethanol (alcohol). As the solvent soaks up the paper it carries with it the different food colours. Some of the food colours are attracted strongly to the paper and do not travel very far, other food colours are less strongly attracted to the paper and travel much further. Once the solvent has soaked almost to the top of the chromatography paper, the paper is removed from the solvent and dried. This produces a chromatogram.

Emulsifiers

Emulsifiers are found in foods that contain oil and water - such as salad cream and mayonnaise. Normally, oil and water do not mix. Instead, they form two separate layers, with the oil normally floating on top of the water. This would make foods that contain oil and water look rather unappealing. It would also make them difficult to use - each time you wanted salad cream you would have to shake the bottle up thoroughly to get the layers to mix. Emulsifiers are added to foods to stop the oil and water separating. Emulsifiers have molecules that have:

— a water-loving (hydrophilic) end that is attracted towards water molecules,

— a water-hating (hydrophobic) end that is not attracted to water molecules but is attracted to fat or oil molecules.

Emulsifiers work because their molecules can attract both water and oil molecules at the same time. This ensures that water and oil molecules are close to one another and do not separate easily.

Food Additives Categories

Food additives can be divided into several groups, although there is some overlap between them.

— *Acids*: Food acids are added to make flavours "sharper", and also act as preservatives and antioxidants. Common food acids include vinegar, citric acid, tartaric acid, malic acid, fumaric acid, lactic acid.

— *Acidity regulators*: Acidity regulators are used to change or otherwise control the acidity and alkalinity of foods.

— *Anticaking agents*: Anticaking agents keep powders such as milk powder flowing freely.

— *Antifoaming agents*: Antifoaming agents reduce or prevent foaming in foods.

— *Antioxidants*: Antioxidants such as vitamin C act as preservatives by inhibiting the effects of oxygen on food, and are generally beneficial to health.

— *Bulking agents*: Bulking agents such as starch are additives that increase to bulk of a food without affecting its nutritional value.

— *Food coloring*: Colorings are added to food to replace colours lost during preparation, or to make food look more attractive.

— *Colour retention agents*: In contrast to colourings, colour retention agents are used to preserve a food's existing colour.

— *Emulsifiers*: Emulsifiers allow water and oils to remain mixed together in an emulsion, as in mayonnaise, ice cream, and homogenised milk.

— *Flavours*: Flavours are additives that give food a particular taste or smell, and may be derived from natural ingredients or created articially.

— *Flavour enhancers*: Flavour enhancers enhance a food's existing flavours.

— *Flour treatment agents*: Flour treatment agents are added to flour to improve its colour or its use in baking.
— *Humectants*: Humectants prevent foods from drying out.
— *Preservatives*: Preservatives prevent or inhibit spoilage of food due to fungi, bacteria and other microorganisms.
— *Propellants*: Propellants are pressurised gases used to expel food from its container.
— *Stabilizers*: Stabilizers, thickeners and gelling agents work with emulsifiers to give foods a firmer texture, like agar, or the pectin used in jam.
— *Sweeteners*: Sweeteners are added to foods for flavoring. Sweeteners other than sugar are added to keep the food energy (calories) low, or because they have beneficial effects for diabetes mellitus and tooth decay.

Most food additives are tested in isolation rather than in combination with other additives. The long term effects of consuming a combination of different additives are currently unknown. Some people are sensitive to particular food additives and may have reactions like hives or diarrhoea. This doesn't mean that all foods containing additives need to be automatically treated with suspicion. Many of the food additives used occur naturally within foods that are regularly consumed.

All foods are made up of chemicals, many of which are not always 'safer' than those found in food additives. For instance, people with food allergies and intolerances are also often sensitive to chemicals found naturally in certain foods, such as nuts or shellfish.

Many people view food additives as a major food threat; however, in terms of health risk, food additives would come in at the end of the line, after food-borne microorganisms (like salmonella), inappropriate hygiene and eating habits, environmental contaminants and naturally occurring toxins.

Types of Food Additives

The different types of food additive and their uses include:

— *Anti-caking agents* - stop ingredients from becoming lumpy.

— *Antioxidants* - prevent foods from oxidising, or going rancid.

— *Artificial sweeteners* - increase the sweetness.

— *Emulsifiers* - stop fats from clotting together.

— *Food acids* - maintain the right acid level.

— *Colours* - enhance or add colour.

— *Humectants* - keep foods moist.

— *Flavours* - add flavour.

— *Flavour enhancers* - increase the power of a flavour.

— *Mineral salts* - enhance texture.

— *Preservatives* - stop microbes from multiplying and spoiling the food.

— *Thickeners* - enhance texture.

— *Stabilisers* - maintains uniformity of food dispersion.

— *Flour treatment* - improves baking quality.

— *Glazing agent* - improves appearance and can protect food.

— *Propellants* - help propel food from a container.

Food Additives and Processed Foods: There is a common misconception that processed foods automatically contain food additives. Foods like long-life milk, canned foods and frozen foods are all processed, yet none of them need extra chemicals. If you are unsure whether or not a product contains an additive, check the label. However, some listed ingredients may contain food additives without mentioning them on the label. For instance, 'margarine' might be a listed ingredient, and margarine contains food additives.

For most people, additives are not a problem. However, 50 of the 400 currently approved additives in Australia have been associated with adverse reactions in some people. Some food additives are more likely than others to cause reactions in sensitive people. It is often the additives that are used to give a food a marketable quality, such as colour, that most commonly cause allergic reactions. Some of these hypersensitive reactions include:

— *Digestive disorders* - diarrhoea and colicky pains.

— *Nervous disorders* - hyperactivity, insomnia and irritability.

— *Respiratory problems* - asthma, rhinitis and sinusitis.

— *Skin problems* - hives, itching, rashes and swelling.

It is important to realise that many of the symptoms experienced as a result of food sensitivities can be caused by other disorders. Medical diagnosis is important. If you try to diagnose yourself, you may restrict your diet unnecessarily and neglect an illness. Some food additives that may cause problems for some people and their code numbers include:

— *Flavour enhancers* - monosodium glutamate (MSG) 621.

— *Food colourings* - tartrazine 102; yellow 2G107; sunset yellow FCF110; cochineal 120.

— *Preservatives* - benzoates 210, 211, 212, 213; nitrates 249, 250, 251, 252; sulphites 220, 221, 222, 223, 224, 225 and 228.

In the case of a sensitivity being identified, the usual practice is to eliminate all suspect foods from the diet and then reintroduce them one by one, to see which additive (or additives) causes the reaction. This should only be done under medical supervision, since some of the reactions - such as asthma - can be serious.

- Food additives are chemicals that keep foods fresh or enhance their colour, flavour or texture.
- A small percentage of people are sensitive to some food additives.
- Diagnosing sensitivity to food additives needs professional help, since all of the symptoms of sensitivity can also be caused by other disorders.

Food Adulteration

Food Adulteration is the act of adding or mixing something inferior, harmful, useless and unnecessary substance to food. In other words, any food item may be considered as adulterated if its nature and quality are not up to the standard. Unscrupulous traders normally adulterate food.

In the process of adulteration, extraneous matters are directly added to food grains. Sands and crushed rock are added to increase weight. Mixing infested and damaged grains to good quality grains is a common practice. Sometimes grain polishing and husks are added to increase the weight. Nowadays, plastic beads that have the shape of food grains are often mixed with cereal grains. Coloured beads are added to the pulses. Sometimes water is sprayed over the grain stock to increase the weight.

Adulteration of fats and oils is easy and cannot be easily detected. Ghee (butter oil) is adulterated with hydrogenated oil and animal fats. Recently, because of the discovery of synthetic colours and flavours, any fat can be made to look like ghee and customers may easily be cheated. Til oil and coconut oil are often mixed with groundnut or cottonseed oil as the latter are cheaper. Mustard seeds are often mixed with argemone seeds and extracted together.

Argemone oil contains an alkaloid-sanguinarine which is highly toxic and results in dropsy and paralysis. Adding allylisothiocyanate to soybean oil or palm oil gives the characteristic pungent smell of mustard oil. Mixing of palm oil with soybean oil is a common practice among dishonest traders for more profits. The adulteration of milk is normally done with the addition of water and removal of fat. Sometimes extraneous substances like soybean and groundnut milk, wheat flour, etc are mixed. Selling diluted buffalo milk as cow milk is a common practice in rural areas. Addition of wheat flour, semolina, etc to milk powder is also common.

TEA leaves may be adulterated with the addition of used tea leaves, sawdust, and dried and ground leaves other than tea leaves. Spices like chillies and turmeric powder are adulterated with the addition of lead pigment to impart brightness in colour and good appearance. Metanil yellow, a carcinogenic agent, is used for colouring turmeric powder.

CHILLI powder is normally adulterated by adding brick powder. Excessive use of wheat flour in place of milk protein (chhana) in the preparation of sweetmeat is an example of adulteration. Use of carboxy methyl cellulose (CMC) in lieu of liquid glucose or sugar syrup in the preparation of soft drinks is an example of extortion. In the name of various fruit juices, imitation products are prepared by using artificial and prohibited ingredients instead of using original fruit juice. Recently, a special drink named mineral water is being prepared and marketed with little or no assurance of quality.

Disadvantages of Additives

The major disadvantages of using food additives are their possible side effects. In most cases the side effects have not been proven but there is enough evidence to make people concerned about the number and the amount of food additives they eat. The following additives have been linked with possible side effects. The list of side effects and the number of food additives involved are increasing with more research.

— *E100 Curcumin*: This is a natural colour obtained from the root of the curcuma (turmeric) plant. Curcumin is a potential hazard for anyone with a salicylate sensitivity.

— *E102 Tartrazine*: This is a synthetic food colour. Tartrazine has been linked with hyperactivity, itching, blurred vision, sleep problems, and migraines.

— *E120 Cochineal*: This is a natural colour extracted from the scales of dried insects. It has been linked with hyperactivity, skin rashes and anaphylaxis.

— *E249-E252 Nitrates and nitrites*: These have been linked with certain cancers. Most processed meat contains added nitrates.

Vitamins

Vitamins are organic compounds that are required in the diet only in small amounts. Vitamins are needed for normal growth, digestion, mental alertness, resistance to infections and reproduction. There are two types of vitamin:

— Fat-soluble vitamins

— Water-soluble vitamins

The body tries to maintain an optimal level of each vitamin and keep the amount circulating in the bloodstream constant. The water-soluble vitamins are not stored in the body very easily so they need to be taken in every day in food and drink. Excess water-soluble vitamins are excreted in the urine. The fat-soluble vitamins can be stored in body fat. Because they are stored, excess fat-soluble vitamins can accumulate in the body and become toxic. The human body is especially sensitive to too much vitamin A and D. Taking in more of these vitamins than recommended is therefore not necessarily better for you - it can even be harmful.

Vitamin C

Vitamin C is also known as ascorbic acid. The body needs it to make collagen, the major component of connecting tissue such as tendons, ligaments and the connective tissue that helps hold skin together.

Good sources of vitamin C are red and green peppers, broccoli, citrus fruit, spinach, tomatoes and potatoes. Most people today get enough vitamin C, but in the past sailors who went on long sea voyages with no fresh fruit used to become vitamin C deficient. They developed scurvy - their skin and gums developed weakness because they couldn't make enough collagen and they sometimes died.

5
Nutrition

In fact, nutrition is life and it is the science of how the body uses food. Nutrition's primary task is figuring out which foods and beverages provide the energy and building material you need to construct and maintain every organ and system. To do this, it concentrates on food's two basic attributes: energy and nutrients.

PRINCIPLES OF NUTRITION

Energy from Food

Energy is the ability to do work. Virtually every bite of food gives you energy, even when it doesn't give you nutrients. The amount of energy in food is measured in calories, the amount of heat produced when food is burned (metabolized) in your body cells. Food is the fuel on which your body runs. Without enough food, you don't have enough energy.

Nutrients in Food

Nutrients are chemical substances your body uses to build, maintain, and repair tissues. They also empower cells to send messages back and forth so as to conduct essential chemical reactions such as the ones that make it possible for you to breathe, think, see, hear, move, smell, taste, eliminate waste, . . and do everything else natural to a living body.

Nutrients groups

There are two different and distinct gruops of nutrients groups

— Macronutrients (macro = big): protein, fat, carbohydrates, and water

— Micronutrients (micro = small): vitamins and minerals

The amount you need each day. Your daily requirements for macronutrients generally exceed one gram. (For comparison's sake, 28 grams are in an ounce.) For example, a man needs about 63 grams of protein a day (slightly more than two ounces), and a woman needs 50 grams (slightly less than two ounces). Your daily requirements for micronutrients are much smaller. For example, the Recommended Dietary Allowance (RDA) for vitamin C is measured in milligrams (1.1,000 of a gram), while the RDAs for vitamin D, vitamin B_{12}, and folate are even smaller and are measured in micrograms (1.1,000,000 of a gram). You can find out much more about the RDAs, including how they vary for people of different ages.

Essential Nutrient

In nutritionspeak, an essential nutrient is a very special thing:

— An essential nutrient cannot be manufactured in the body. You have to get essential nutrients from food or from a nutritional supplement.

— An essential nutrient is linked to a specific deficiency disease.

For example, people who go without protein for extended periods of time develop the protein-deficiency disease kwashiorkor. People who do not get enough vitamin C develop the vitamin C-deficiency disease scurvy. A diet rich in the essential nutrient cures the deficiency disease, but you need the proper nutrient. In other words, you can't cure a protein deficiency with extra amounts of vitamin C.

Essential nutrients for human beings include many well-known vitamins and minerals, several amino acids (the so-called building blocks of proteins), and at least two fatty acids. Not all nutrients are essential for all species of animals. For example, vitamin C is an essential nutrient for human beings, but not for dogs. A dog's body makes the vitamin C it needs. Check out the list of nutrients on a can or bag of dog food.

The latest flash in the nutrition sky is caused by phytochemicals. Phyto is the Greek word for plants, so phytochemicals are simply - yes, you've got it -chemicals from plants. Although the 13-letter group name may be new to you, you're already familiar with some phytochemicals. Vitamins are phytochemicals. Colors such as beta carotene, a deep yellow pigment in fruits and vegetables that your body can convert to a form of vitamin A, are phytochemicals.

And then there are phytoestrogens, hormonelike chemicals that grabbed the spotlight when it was suggested that a diet high in phytoestrogens, such as the isoflavones found in soybeans, may lower the risk of heart disease and reduce the incidence of reproductive cancers. More recent studies suggest that phytoestrogens may have some problems of their own, so to find out more about phytochemicals, including phytoestrogens.

Nutritional Status

Nutritional status is a phrase used to describe the state of your health related to your diet. For example, people who are starving do not get the nutrients or calories they need for optimum health. These people are said to be malnourished, which means their nutritional status is, to put it gently, definitely not good. Malnutrition may arise from

— A diet that does not provide enough food. This situation may occur in times of famine or through voluntary starvation because of an eating disorder or because something in your life disturbs your appetite. For example, older people may be at risk of malnutrition because of tooth loss or age-related loss of appetite or because many live alone and sometimes just forget to eat.

— A diet that, while otherwise adequate, is deficient in a specific nutrient, such as vitamin C.

— A metabolic disorder that prevents your body from absorbing specific nutrients, such as protein or carbohydrates.

— A medical condition that prevents your body from using nutrients.

For example, people who abuse alcohol are often malnourished because alcohol depresses appetite and interferes with the body's ability to metabolize the nutrients it does get.

NUTRITION FACTS

Getting reliable information about nutrition can be a daunting challenge. For the most part, your nutrition information is likely to come from TV and radio talk shows or news, your daily newspaper, your favorite magazine, a variety of nutrition-oriented books, and the Internet.

Nutritional People

The people who make nutrition news may be scientists,

reporters, or simply someone who wandered in with a new theory, the more bizarre the better. But several groups of people are most likely to give you news you can use with confidence. For example:

— *Nutrition scientists* are the people with graduate degrees (usually in chemistry, biology, biochemistry, or physics) engaged in research dealing primarily with the effects of food on animals and human beings.

— *Nutrition researchers*: These may be either nutrition scientists or professionals in another field such as medicine or sociology whose research (study or studies) concentrates on the effects of food.

— *Nutritionists*: These are people who concentrate on the study of nutrition. In some states, a person who uses the title "nutritionist" must have a graduate degree in basic science courses related to nutrition.

— *Dietitians*: These people have undergraduate degrees in food and nutrition science or the management of food programs. A person with the letters RD after his or her name has completed a dietetic internship and passed an American Dietetic Association licensing exam.

— *Nutrition reporters and writers*: These are people who specialize in giving you information about the medical and/or scientific aspects of food. Like reporters who concentrate on politics or sports, nutrition reporters gain their expertise through years of covering their beat.

Most have the science background required to make it possible for them to translate technical information into language nonscientists can understand; some have been trained as dietitians, nutritionists, or nutrition scientists. Consumer alert: Regardless of the source, nutrition news should always pass what you may call The Reasonableness Test.

In other words, if a story, or report, or study sounds ridiculous, it probably is. Fatty foods increase your risk of cancer or heart disease. So you throw out the offending food or drink or rearrange your daily routine to avoid the once-acceptable, now-dangerous food, beverage, or additive. And then what happens? Two weeks, two months, or two years down the road, a second, equally prestigious group of scientists publishes a second study conclusively proving that the first group got it wrong: In fact, coffee has no effect on the risk of heart disease - and may even improve athletic performance. Salt does not cause hypertension except in certain sensitive individuals. Only some fatty foods are risky.

Animal studies can alert researchers to potential problems, but working with animals alone cannot give you conclusive proof. Different species react differently to various chemicals and diseases. Although outright poisons such as cyanide clearly traumatize any living body, many foods or drugs that harm a laboratory rat won't harm you. And vice versa. For example, mouse and rat embryos suffer no ill effects when their mothers are given thalidomide, the sedative that's known to cause deformed fetal limbs when given to pregnant monkeys - and human beings at the point in pregnancy when limbs are developing.

Functional Foods

Underlying the development of functional foods is the concept of "food as medicine," a philosophy that dates back to Hippocrates. Powerful market forces are fueling the interest in functional foods:

— rapid advances in scientific knowledge supporting the vital role of diet in health and disease prevention

— consumer demand and the change in perspective of food, which is no longer viewed as merely a means of providing sustenance

— skyrocketing health care costs

— an aging population

— technical advances in the food industry that are allowing the development of health-promoting foods that can be marketed to health-conscious consumers at a premium

— the changing regulatory environment

Contrary to dietitians' expectations, consumers are extremely receptive to the idea of health-enhancing foods and interested to learn more about such foods and how they might provide long-term health benefits. Focus group studies conducted by The International Food Information Council (IFIC) in June 1996 found that consumers view functional foods as a natural evolution of the traditional foods they have always eaten.

Dietitians and other health care professionals expected consumers to be looking for the "easy way out" and more interested in pills that could give health benefits than in learning about foods that could provide these benefits. Instead consumers were quite positive about the prospect of enhancing familiar foods with health-promoting components.

Global Perspective

There is clearly a difference between the Western perspective on functional foods and the Eastern perspective. In the West, functional foods are viewed as a revolution and represent a fast growing segment of the food industry. Food companies, drug companies, chemical companies and boutique companies arising from grass-roots research and development efforts are all racing to bring functional foods to market. In the Orient, in contrast, functional foods have been a part of the culture for centuries.

In Traditional Chinese Medicine, foods that have medicinal effects have been documented since at least 1000 BC From ancient times, the Chinese have understood that foods have both preventive and therapeutic effects and are an integral part of health, a view that is now being increasingly recognized around the world.

The number of functional foods is potentially very large and encompasses natural foods, isolated components from these foods that are added to other foods or packaged as dietary supplements, and food components synthesized in the laboratory. Examples of just a few of the functional foods or food components that already exist include: fruits and vegetables of enormous variety, black and green tea, cranberry juice, garlic and onions, edible mushrooms, probiotic-enhanced dairy foods, allyl sulfides, antioxidants, capsaicin, chitosan, ellagic acid, flavonoids, fructo- and other oligosaccharides, genistein, glucosamine, glycyrrhizin, indoles, lutein, lycopene, maitake mushroom fraction D, polyphenols, resveratrol, and sulforaphane.

Most researchers in the area of functional foods agree that any food designated as "functional" and ascribed specific health benefits should receive scientific scrutiny before specific health claims are permitted. In countries with a rich cultural tradition of belief in the health-enhancing properties of various foods and food components, many foods are associated with specific health claims but may not have scientific documentation to parallel the long-standing experience with these foods.

In the US. the 1990 Nutrition Labeling and Education Act allows, for the first time, health or disease prevention claims on a food label. Food and Drug Administration (FDA) requires that health claims be supported by solid research and that the claims be approved by the FDA.

To date only a limited number of claims have been approved, and we're probably several years away from having the necessary research that will support or disprove suspected health benefits of functional foods.In the meantime, the results of the many studies underway will be published not only in scientific journals but likely on the front page of the nation's newspapers.

Consumers are eager to act on these findings. Dietetics professionals should continue to recommend a varied, plant-based, balanced diet and follow the studies of specific foods and food components as both treatment and preventative therapy against particular diseases.

Safety Issues

In addition to the normal expectation that any food item or ingredient be safe for consumption, functional foods have the additional safety requirements related to the novelty of the raw materials used, of the processes used to produce the food, or of the potential use in the diet. For example, it is very likely that many food components already present in foods will be found to have positive health benefits and will be used in a novel way in the diet, which could increase the amount of these foods consumed each day or might increase the use of these foods by at-risk groups that currently do not use much of these foods or their components.

The safety evaluation must then take into account the effect of increased consumption on various age groups and the infirm and ask whether increased use might lead to increased exposure to potentially harmful components, such as natural toxins or pesticides.When a functional food contains novel ingredients or is produced by a novel process, it becomes particularly important that safety as well as acceptability be considered. With traditional foods, safety assurance comes from a long history of safe use by large populations over a number of generations. Such history is lacking for novel ingredients and novel processes, and a safety assessment is required before such foods are released into the food supply.

Regulatory Issues

Functional foods exist at the interface between food and drugs. There is no provision in our existing food regulations for foods intended to be consumed to prevent disease. As things stand, dietary supplements will be marketed under the Dietary Supplement Health and Education Act, and foods will be marketed under the Nutrition Labeling and Education Act. The concept of "substantial equivalence" was developed as a practical approach for evaluating the safety of foods that contained or were produced from genetically modified organisms. This approach asks whether the novel food is substantially equivalent or sufficiently similar to its traditional counterpart.

This concept was not intended to be applied to other types of novel foods but appears to be increasingly used by various regulatory agencies. The idea is that, by focusing on what is different between a novel food and a traditional food, the safety assessment can zero in on the differences and thereby minimize the expense and time required for the assessment. An International Life Sciences Institute-Europe technical committee established three different classes of equivalence and set up guidelines for safety assessments of novel foods:

— Class I foods or food ingredients are those substantially equivalent to a traditional reference food or ingredient

— Class II are those that are sufficiently similar to a traditional reference food

— Class III are those that are neither substantially equivalent nor sufficiently similar to a traditional reference food or ingredient. In order to establish the appropriate equivalency class, extensive background information about the food is required, which ranges from the raw material source and its origins to methods of production and expected use of the novel food.

Class I foods would not be subject to safety assessment, Class II foods would be but the testing would focus on the differences between it and the traditional food or ingredient, and Class III foods would be subjected to rigorous safety assessment on a case-by-case basis.

Assuming the food or ingredient passes the rigorous safety considerations, each health claim will need to be subjected to scientific evaluation as well, which could take years to carry out. In the meantime, consumers will become increasingly interested in using functional foods, and we need to stay on top of developments in this area.

As consumers worldwide become more health conscious, the demand for health-promoting foods and food components is expected to grow. The market for such foods is predicted to be quite large. Before the full market potential can be realized, however, consumers will need to be assured of the safety and efficacy of functional foods. Current and future scientific studies are expected to provide this assurance and to inspire confidence in functional foods in the minds of consumers worldwide.

Designer foods: Coined in 1989 by the National Cancer Institute to describe foods that naturally contain or are enriched with cancer-preventing substances such as phytochemicals.

Functional foods: Defined by the Institute of Medicine of the US National Academy of Sciences as foods that encompass potentially healthful products, including any modified food or food ingredient that may provide a health benefit beyond the nutrients it contains.

Medical foods: Special dietary food intended for use solely under medical supervision to meet nutritional requirements in specific medical conditions. Although a legal classification of foods under the jurisdiction of the FDA and technically confined to enteral formulas used to feed hospitalized patients and people with rare diseases, more recently spin-offs of these formulas have begun to be marketed to the public, especially to the elderly, as a source of supplemental nutrition.

Novel foods: Food or food ingredients that have not been used for human consumption to a significant degree or have been produced by processes that result in a significant change in their composition or nutritional value or intended use.

Nutraceuticals: A term popularized by the Foundation for Innovation in Medicine that refers to "any substance that may be considered a food or part of a food and provides medical or health benefits, including the prevention and treatment of disease.

Phytochemical/Phytonutrient: Plant components that have health-promoting properties; originally this term was limited to substances found in edible fruits and vegetables that appeared to be protective against cancer.

Nutrition is about why you eat what you eat and how the food you get affects your body and your health.

6

Malnutrition and Deficiency Diseases

Malnutrition is a general term for the medical condition in a person or animal caused by an unbalanced diet-either too little or too much food, or a diet missing one or more important nutrients. Most commonly, malnourished people or animals either do not have enough calories in their diet, or are eating a diet that lacks protein, vitamins, or trace minerals. Medical problems arising from malnutrition are commonly referred to as deficiency diseases. Scurvy is a well-known and now rare form of malnutrition, in which the victim lacks vitamin C.

Common forms of malnutrition include protein-energy malnutrition (PEM) and micronutrient malnutrition. PEM refers to inadequate availability or absorption of energy and proteins in the body. Micronutrient malnutrition refers to inadequate availability of some essential nutrients such as vitamins and trace elements that are required by the body in small quantities. Micronutrient deficiencies lead to a variety of diseases and impair normal functioning of the body.

Deficiency in micronutrients such as Vitamin A reduces the capacity of the body to resist diseases. Deficiency in iron, iodine and vitamin A is widely prevalent and represent major a public health challenge. The record of World War II is notable for the virtual absence of nutritional disease among troops. The Army operated under a high standard of nutritional adequacy in the soldier's diet (as set up by the Food Nutrition Board, National Research Council, together with a set of minimal allowances for short periods for use in emergencies), and an assumption that adequate nutrition is necessary for maximum efficiency and health.

Concern was felt with regard to deviations from these standards-during the time the soldier drew upon his body reserves when there was a shortage of food, either because of logistic problems, or personal reactions to the food available as issued, prepared, and served. Under such circumstances frank nutritional disease, except for loss of weight, seldom occurred. This is in great contrast to what might have been expected and would probably have occurred only a few years earlier. The magnificent development and use of new knowledge of all matters concerned with nutrition made possible, and successful, operations of great magnitude, conducted under serious logistic difficulties occasioned by extremes of environment and distance, such as the tropical heat and humidity of the jungles of the South Sea islands and the frigid climate of Iceland.

It is safe to say that many operations of World War II would not have been possible or could have been carried out only partially had it not been possible to prevent nutritional disease. Only under extreme conditions, mostly in prisoners of war subjected to the neglect and cruelties of their captors, and in sporadic instances of individuals conditioned by injury, disease, or some personal peculiarity, did those terrible spectres of other wars-scurvy, dropsy, pellagra, beriberi, and xerophthalmia-return. Such was the achievement of preventive medicine.

To refer, as will be done below, to the occurrence of an appreciable amount of nutritional deficiency is not the contradiction that it seems. It is to be explained by the changing concept of nutritional deficiency states, the recognition of the fact that there are degrees of deficiency, insufficient to warrant such diagnoses as scurvy, pellagra, or beriberi which require a considerable period for development even under controlled conditions. Partial deficiency may exist to an extent sufficient to prevent the fullest state of health, physical strength, and fitness, without causing overt or gross disability.

Such conditions existed in the general population before the war and their presence was reflected in a similar occurrence in the troops under average conditions, although as their service lengthened it was decreased by the highly efficient control of food and nutrition in the Army. It is in this respect that preventive medicine finds its greatest opportunity in the field of nutritional deficiency disease and the opportunity to ensure optimal health and physical fitness as far as nutrition can secure them, by preventing even slight deficiencies.

It is impossible to state accurately the prevalence of nutritional deficiency in the Army as a whole or in any considerable portion of it. Fully developed clinical forms of the deficiencies such as scurvy and beriberi are reportable in rates, as hospital admissions, per annum, but these give but little indication of the actual prevalence of deficiencies. The prevalence of nutritional deficiencies below the level of the classical expressions of disease is uncertain because individuals with deficiencies of these grades alone are not usually patients, nor are they considered ill; the opportunity and special needs for diagnosis are lacking and the conditions exist unknown and often unsuspected.

Some idea of the prevalence of nutritional deficiency disease can be secured, however, from special research studies and from a search of hospital records. The special research studies were made on groups of presumably healthy troops under field conditions, giving information on the prevalence of the mild or slight forms of the deficiency, and on special groups such as prisoners of war and patients in hospitals with advanced deficiency disease. The latter will give only the incidence of advanced stages as they are recorded in hospital practice under the standard forms of diagnosis.

Minor Nutritional Deficiency Diseases

It has been known for some time that a number of apparently well persons have minor grades of nutritional deficiencies, sufficient to present recognizable evidence on physical or laboratory examination. It was this group which was of particular concern from the point of view of preventive medicine because of the subtle effect of such disease on efficiency and morale. Also, a potential result could be a large number of troops who were "under par" and would be quick to succumb to severe disabling nutritional disease during periods of stress arising from injury and disease or temporary severe dietary restriction.

It was clearly recognized that under some unavoidable circumstances severe undernutrition might develop despite all efforts to prevent it. It was known, however, that by proper care and attention good nutritional state and good reserve could be maintained in all but rare instances. Such action would lessen and prevent the frequency and severity of advanced deficiency states when circumstances tended unavoidably to produce them. Thus injury and disease may produce nutritional disturbances which in turn diminish the resistance to and recovery from illness and injury.

Good nutrition prior to injury or illness offers some protection against the effects of such nutritional disease.

Similarly, periods of severe restriction of food are less serious if nutrition is good before the starvation begins. Evidence of the prevalence of those milder forms of deficiency was found in the ration trials at Camp Carson, Colorado, May to August 1944.1 In this experiment, incident to the study of the effect of a variety of special rations, the test subjects were examined for evidence of nutritional deficiency disease by physical and laboratory examinations before the start of the experimental period. These troops consisted of a battalion, approximately 1,000 strong, undergoing rigid advanced infantry training, and may be considered fairly representative of a considerable number of similar troops training at that time in the western part of the Zone of Interior.

Mild caloric deficiency, due simply to an insufficiency of food, was fairly common in the Army under combat conditions. This was usually the result of a combination of causes-difficulties of supply, the necessity of using packaged rations calorically inadequate for the energy expended, and decreased consumption of food because of emotional strain, fatigue, and exigencies of the situation. Except among prisoners of war, however, such caloric deficiencies rarely were great enough over long enough periods to cause protein deficiency and physical disability.

For example, the nutritional survey of troops in the Pacific theater showed that although troops fresh from combat had some caloric deficiency, as evidenced by loss of weight, their physical fitness was equal to that of troops in the Zone of Interior and in at least one instance, superior. Neither were these mild caloric deficiencies often accompanied by vitamin or mineral deficiencies. The reduced caloric intake lessened the need for vitamins and minerals, and the rations, even when only partly consumed, supplied a considerable amount. This circumstance, together with the fact that existing body stores under the system of Army feeding and practice were nearly always high at the outset of a campaign, was sufficient to prevent significant deficiencies except in occasional individuals in whom it could usually be classed as conditioned.

Beriberi: Beriberi (Vitamin B1, Thiamine), as a primary, idiopathic disease in noncaptured American troops was almost nonexistent. For example, in Cutts' report of over 125 cases of beriberi,7 none occurred among American troops. All cases were observed in Chinese troops. Although 5 cases in the entire Army were reported in admissions to hospitals in 1942, most of these must have been "conditioned cases." Occasional reports, mostly rumors, of mild cases of B1 deficiency were received, especially from the China-Burma-India theater, but in most instances the diagnosis was not sufficiently established and the evidence consisted of nonspecific signs and symptoms such as nervousness and fatigability. Such diagnoses were strongly controverted by evidence of a liberal intake of thiamine in the food.

Riboflavin: No outspoken cases of idiopathic riboflavin deficiency disease were reported and the only possible instances of this deficiency were mild cases detected on special surveys and examination, in which careful examination and laboratory tests were made. Even some of these may be considered doubtful in view of changing ideas of the specificity of certain signs such as cheilosis and vascularization of the cornea, previously thought to be due to this deficiency; also, because of a lowering of values formerly believed to represent intake requirements.

Niacin: A few cases of pellagra in otherwise well individuals occurred from time to time in all theaters of operations. For the most part, these were caused by a deficient intake of proper food due to habit, food dislikes and prejudices, irregularities of eating related to duty assignments, and similar causes, such as could be ascertained by questioning the patients. These cases exhibited no differences from those observed in civilian practice.

Vitamin C: A number of reports of scurvy and vitamin C deficiency as well as special studies of vitamin C nutrition were made.9 Some reason for concern and a suspicion of the existence of this deficiency were justified because in certain of the rations, particularly in the C, K, and ten-in-one, the source of most of the vitamin C was the synthetic fruit juice powders, which, on the whole, were not well consumed by the soldiers. It was often forgotten, however, that the standard of daily requirements for this nutrient was set at a very high level, 75 mg. per day, an amount three times as great as that actually needed to protect against a state of true physiologic deficiency. It is, therefore, not surprising that in many instances, reported cases and outbreaks of scurvy and vitamin C deficiency could not be substantiated when subjected to careful analysis. There was also some tendency on the part of medical officers to attach too much significance to such signs and symptoms as gingivitis and bleeding gums, which, while suggestive, are not very specific or reliable, especially in mild or early deficiencies.

Vitamin A: Vitamin A deficiency, too, was very seldom seen, though it was often suspected, or diagnosed when it was not present. Considerable anxiety was expressed concerning it, especially in relation to visual acuity in dim light or the dark (night blindness), particularly in the Air Forces. Again, it was forgotten that it takes months, probably over a year, to deplete a normal adult's stores of vitamin A and that the diet of all troops before being subjected to any dietary shortages was high in vitamin A. It was also commonly forgotten, or not known, that much of the vitamin A is ingested in the form of carotene, obtained from such foods as green and yellow vegetables and that vitamin A is quite stable.

It is not necessary to have all or even most of the vitamin A as such, as in animal foods. Finally, it is probable that the standard of requirements, 5,000 international units daily, which was in general well supplied and consumed even under conditions of difficult supply and feeding, was so high as to provide a large margin of safety. It is not surprising then that there was little or no primary vitamin A deficiency of a significant grade in American troops. This does not exclude the probability, however, of a slight dietary deficiency for long periods prior to Army service, and the existence of a chronic low-grade deficiency yet insufficient to produce such classical disease as xerophthalmia.

Some evidence of such a mild deficiency could be found in any body of troops if one was willing to take as evidence the presence of mild perifollicular hyperkeratosis of either the dry, horny, or the acneform type, which though not highly specific is suggestive. Such evidence can be found in any group of the population in this country.

Vitamin D and Calcium Deficiency: Much concern also was expressed concerning vitamin D and calcium deficiency. Such deficiency was not infrequently reported in Essential Technical Medical Data (ETMD) reports. For the most part these reports came from the more distant or remote overseas theaters, especially the China-Burma-India, the Pacific, and some of the Arctic stations. This concern and such diagnoses were based largely on two circumstances: the lack of milk and the presence of subjective symptoms, the latter usually highly unreliable and susceptible of numerous other explanations.

In the Arctic, lack of sunshine was sometimes considered a factor. Again, the rations, even under restricted conditions, usually provided calcium in amounts equal or close to standard requirements which are probably very liberal. There were shortages as the result of difficulties in supply and failure of mess personnel to incorporate the milk and milk products in the prepared foods. So far as it is known, no instances of idiopathic calcium or vitamin D deficiency, established by blood calcium studies, demonstration of significant demineralization of bone, or the occurrence of tetany were observed. It should be remembered that the normal adult possesses a large reserve store of calcium in his skeleton and deficiency must be severe and long continued to produce an actual pathologic state of calcium deficiency in otherwise normal persons. Vitamin D requirements are, of course, very small in adults and deficiency of this vitamin is uncommon.

Iron: Iron deficiency anemia is likewise very unusual in the normal adult male and in the nonchildbearing female because of the extreme conservation of iron by the body. Such iron deficiency anemia as might occur would most likely have existed before entry into the service and would have constituted a probable cause for rejection. Recent studies, however, particularly those on "folic" acid, have shown that an anemia of the macrocytic type might occur with a restriction of foods generally considered to furnish much of the B complex vitamins.

The presence of troops in areas where tropical anemia (probably a macrocytic type) existed suggested such a possibility. Reports of anemia among Army nurses in the Pacific area led to the inclusion of an inquiry into this disease in a general survey of nutrition during March-May 1945 in the Pacific theater. However, a significant degree of anemia was found to be relatively uncommon, and its dependence on dietary factors was not established. As has been indicated, frank nutritional disease was extremely rare among the troops. It must be realized that these cases include only those of primary nutritional disease admitted with the diagnosis.

Undoubtedly, additional cases of severe nutritional deficiency occurred as complications of other injury and disease and, even though recognized, failed to be included in the diagnosis because of the tendency to omit the diagnosis of complications. This is particularly true of the less well-known and established deficiencies such as the protein, iron, and riboflavin deficiencies. Even sodium chloride deficiency is apt to be omitted. Therefore, even the hospital records will fail to give all of such cases.

The greatest incidence of evident nutritional deficiency disease occurred in recovered Allied prisoners of war and in civilians of liberated and conquered countries. In the Asiatic and Pacific theaters the number of instances of these diseases was much greater than in Europe. No reliable data are available as to the actual prevalence because of lack of records. The best sources of information in this field are the reports of the examination of prisoners of war made during the period of incarceration and following their release and return to this country. These cases of deficiency diseases, while conforming in general to the pattern traditionally established, revealed certain characteristics of unusual interest, particularly in the cases of starvation edema and in cases of thiamine deficiency.

In these subjects, both those in Europe and in the Pacific, loss of body tissues (emaciation) caused by inadequate caloric intakes was the most pronounced and most frequent deficiency state accompanying this starvation. There was, in many cases, an edema characteristic of starvation or famine edema. Such edema has ordinarily been considered in recent years to be a manifestation of protein deficiency dependent for its immediate production on hypoproteinemia.

In April and May 1945 a considerable number of Japanese prisoners of war suffering from nutritional deficiency disease were seen by the writer in Leyte. Among some 20 or 30 such patients the principal disease seemed to be starvation and protein deficiency. Though many had been diagnosed as beriberi, the persistence of the tendon reflexes, the absence of significant sensory changes, and atrophy and muscle weakness, indicated that the edema present was more probably a result of caloric and protein deficiency.

In attempting to discover the explanation for these observations, in apparent variance to previous concepts, the following facts must be kept in mind. In many instances the observations consisted of a single determination of the serum protein concentration which was interpreted in its relation to edema without consideration of such factors as salt and water intake, diarrhea, dehydration, physical activity, and other factors known to affect the relationship between serum protein concentration levels and the occurrence of edema. Nevertheless the observations were made so frequently and under so many independent circumstances that they strongly suggest another important factor in the production of edema in these persons.

With the severe emaciation (caloric and protein deficiency) there were seen a percentage of other nutritional deficiency diseases. These were for the most part beriberi and pellagra.

There was, however, a great difference in the two major theaters, European and Pacific, in this respect. The vitamin deficiencies in florid form appear to have been uncommon in the European theater but were fairly frequent in the Pacific. How much this was concerned with the factor of length of incarceration is not clear. There appears to be no data available indicating the relation between the occurrence of these other diseases and the period of captivity. It might be suspected, however, that such a relationship was at least a partial explanation for the difference in the two theaters. In general, the feeding of prisoners of the Germans was more nearly adequate until the last few weeks before release. In general, the prisoners in the Pacific were badly fed during the entire period.

Experimental studies as well as clinical observations suggest that the characteristics of deficiency disease resulting from relatively acute and chronic deficiency states vary considerably. This difference may be illustrated by some unusual features of the cases of thiamine deficiency from the Pacific. Among these, there occurred an unusual and unexpected number with evidence of involvement of the second (optic) and eighth (acoustic) cranial nerves. Involvement of the optic nerve in thiamine deficiency had only rarely been observed and reported previously. The writer has seen two cases, apparently of this kind, with atrophy of the nerve head and at certain stages an optic neuritis characterizing the findings.

While some doubt has existed as to the etiology, and a suspicion of a toxic optic neuritis from methanol poisoning existed in some, this does not seem to be an entirely adequate explanation. There is, furthermore, the theoretical possibility that a primary thiamine deficiency may have predisposed and conditioned to an effect of methanol which would otherwise not have occurred. The cases in civilian life observed by the writer occurred in chronic alcoholics. So far the condition has remained stationary in most of these subjects with little or no evidence of improvement in function and no change in the morphologic appearance. Unfortunately, a variety of treatment and modification of the nutritional condition before studies were begun to determine the nutritional status and possible etiology made later studies essentially valueless.

Much the same situation occurred in those subjects with involvement of the eighth nerve. Deafness, partial or nearly complete, of a "nerve" type, with little tendency to improve was the principal finding. Other findings of unusual interest in recovered prisoners from the Pacific suffering from nutritional deficiencies (thiamine) was a loss of libido, testicular atrophy, loss of hair (body hair in particular), and certain manifestations of feminization, particularly enlargement of the breast. These changes are of particular interest in view of recent work suggesting a relation between the sex hormones, liver function, and the B complex group of vitamins. Similar observations were made in the experimental studies already mentioned.

Although much of the research in nutrition dealt with such aspects of preventive medicine as the requirements of the various nutrients, considerable new knowledge of actual nutritional disease was added by studies conducted by the Office of The Surgeon General or under its auspices. Of these the most extensive was that conducted at the University of Minnesota by Keys and his associates,13 supported in part by the Office of The Surgeon General. These studies consisted in the controlled production of starvation (caloric deficiency) in a group of young men.

By careful adjustment, the caloric intake was maintained at a level sufficiently less than a planned energy output to cause a steady, progressive loss of weight. The energy output was maintained at a moderately high level (3,100 calories). Protein intake was minimum (40 gm.), but animal protein was very low, possibly inadequate in amino acids. Other nutrients, vitamins, and minerals were at levels judged to be minimally adequate. After an initial period of adjustment the subjects were maintained on this regime for some 3 to 4 months. By this time all had been reduced to a severe stage of starvation, and restoration was accomplished by successive increments of food in a manner designed to simulate relief dietaries.

The results of these experiments, in addition to providing much new data on the physiology of such starvation, are of particular interest in comparison with the starvation observed in Allied and enemy prisoners of war, civilian inmates of prison and detention camps, and the general civilian populations. As in most of these latter examples, the outstanding deficiency disease was starvation (loss of weight) and loss of muscle tissue, presumably reflecting at least a relative protein deficiency. Evidence of other deficiencies were uncommon and minor in degree. Among the outstanding changes in both groups were the pigmentation, the loss of body hair, edema, bradycardia, hypotension, and muscular weakness, particularly that related to sustained or rapidly repeated acts.

Changes in the emotions and psyche with a trend to the so-called psychoneuroses were observed. Rehabilitation was slower than might have been expected if all effects are included, and the most rapid and desirable rate of recovery required large feedings. There was some tendency to overweight with recovery. These studies have added much to the knowledge of the effects of starvation.

Crisis of Malnutrition in India

India spends far less than necessary to address its high levels of malnutrition, according to a new World Bank report, Wasting Away: The Crisis of Malnutrition in India. Despite substantial improvement in health and well-being since the country's independence in 1947, malnutrition remains a silent emergency in India, where more than half of all children under the age of four are malnourished, 30 percent of newborns are significantly underweight, and 60 percent of women are anemic. According to the report, malnutrition costs India at least $10 billion annually in terms of lost productivity, illness, and death and is seriously retarding improvements in human development and further reduction of childhood mortality.

The report describes not only the physical wasting wrought by malnutrition, but the wasting of vast financial resources being made available to address the problem. While India has taken the problem of malnutrition seriously and has developed appropriate policies and mounted large-scale programs to address it, says the report, these efforts are having relatively limited impact on nutrition among the poor. "While mortality has declined by half and fertility by two-fifths, malnutrition has only come down by about one-fifth in the last 40 years. The inescapable conclusion is that further progress in human development in India will be difficult to achieve unless malnutrition is tackled with greater vigor and more rapid improvement in the future than in the past," says report co-author Anthony Measham with SASHP.

Malnutrition rates in some parts of the country are highest among children and women, due primarily to inadequate food intake, illness, and such harmful child care practices as delayed complementary feeding. Underlying these are household food insecurity, inadequate preventative and curative health services, and insufficient knowledge of proper care. Widespread malnutrition is a major barrier to further reduction of maternal mortality rates. Malnourishment can also significantly lower cognitive development and learning achievement during the preschool and school years, and subsequently result in lower productivity. Nutritional anemia is implicated in low physical and mental performance.

"Malnutrition not only blights the lives of individuals and families, but also reduces the returns on investment in education and acts as a major barrier to social and economic progress," says Meera Chatterjee, a World Bank senior social development specialist and report co-author. In recent decades, India has established a framework of programs with the potential to combat malnutrition, including a Public Distribution System (PDS), an Integrated Child Development Services (ICDS) program, a National Mid-day Meals Program (NMMP), and several employment schemes providing food for work. But these programs have failed to meet the needs of the poorest because of ineffective targeting, implementation, and coverage.

While the PDS, for example, absorbs 0.5 percent of GDP, it fails to reach the segments of the population that need it most. Furthermore, spending on direct nutritional programs, mainly the ICDS, the NMMP, and the micronutrients programs now amounts to only 0.19 percent of GNP. Sri Lanka, which successfully dealt with malnutrition in the 1980s, spent about 1 percent of GNP on direct nutritional programs while simultaneously improving health services, education for females, and antipoverty measures.

Lacking, argue the report's authors, is sustained political commitment to the problem of malnutrition, as well as a comprehensive policy implementation structure. India also needs to better target nutritional programs and substantially increase their quality and impact. Decentralization of program implementation and major involvement of local government bodies will be crucial. Households below the poverty line must be reached by all of the nutritional programs in order to achieve a major impact.

The Crisis of Malnutrition in India identifies priority actions within the existing nutrition, food delivery, and health programs. Compared to the economic and social toll malnutrition exacts each year, the cost of the actions proposed would be relatively small, say the authors, about $80 million per year for 10 years. According to the report, nothing less than these measures will deal with the crisis of malnutrition in India.

World Bank collaboration with the government of India in its nutrition efforts began in 1980, with the Tamil Nadu Integrated Nutrition Project (TINP). Since then, the Bank has financed a second phase of TINP that has become a model for nutrition programs worldwide. It has also provided support to the ICDS program in nine states. The ongoing Bank-supported Woman and Child Development Project is working to strengthen and improve the quality of the ICDS program nationwide. Bank assistance to India over the last 18 years has totaled $753 million, equivalent to more than one-quarter of Bank assistance for nutrition projects worldwide.

7

Protein Requirements of Adults and Children

ADULTS

Energy requirements

Basal metabolic rate (BMR): Since the BMR depends upon both age and body weight, adults of both sexes have been divided into three age ranges-18-30, 30-60, 60+. Within each age range, values for BMR have been obtained from the body weight by the equations shown in Table 1. The BMR may be determined either from the actual weight, if this is known, or from the median weight, according to age, sex, and height. The choice of method will depend upon the circumstances and objectives of the user. It will be seen that at a given height the BMRs of subjects at the extremes of the acceptable range of weight differ from those at the median weight by less than 10%.

The converse situation is when subjects of the same weight vary in height and hence in body mass index (BMI). Except in the elderly, such variations, within the acceptable range of weight for height, have no importance in men and relatively little importance in women.

Baseline energy need: Since the BMR is measured in the postabsorptive state and at complete rest, for an

Table 1. Equations for predicting basal metabolic rate from body weight (W)

Agerange(years)	kcalth/day	Correlationcoefficient	SD	MJ/day	Correlation coefficient	SDa
Males						
0-3	60.9 W- 54	0.97	53	0.255 W-0.226	0.97	0.222
3-10	22.7 W+495	0.86	62	0.0949 W+2.07	0.86	0.259
10-18	17.5 W+651	0.90	100	0.0732 W+2.72	0.90	0.418
18-30	15.3 W+679	0.65	151	0.0640 W+2.84	0.65	0.632
30-60	11.6 W+879	0.60	164	0.0485 W+3.67	0.60	0.686
> 60	13.5 W+487	0.79	148	0.0565 W+2.04	0.79	0.619
Females						
0-3	61.0 W- 51	0.97	61	0.255 W-0.214	0.97	0.255
3-10	22.5 W+499	0.85	63	0.0941 W+2.09	0.85	0.264
10-18	12.2 W+746	0.75	117	0.0510 W+3.12	0.75	0.489
18-30	14.7 W+496	0.72	121	0.0615 W+2.08	0.72	0.506
30-60	8.7 W+829	0.70	108	0.0364 W+3.47	0.70	0.452
> 60	10.5 W+596	0.74	108	0.0439 W+2.49	0.74	0.452

individual to survive an addition has to be made to cover the metabolic response to food and the energy cost of increased muscle tone and minor movement. A value of 1.4 times the BMR during waking hours, for the energy cost of activities such as washing, dressing, and short periods of standing, can be derived from published figures. If 8 hours a day are spent in bed at the basal rate of energy expenditure, then the requirement over a period of 24 hours amounts to 1.27 times the BMR. It should be emphasized that this requirement allows for minimal movement; it is not compatible with long-term health and makes no allowance for the energy needed to earn a living or prepare food. It could be called the survival requirement and is of practical value in conditions of crisis only, for estimating the short-term needs of totally inactive dependent people.

Energy needs for occupational activities: The energy need will vary with the type of occupation, the time spent in doing the task, and the size of the individuals concerned. Traditionally the occupations of men and women have been classified into those which involve light, moderate, and heavy physical activity. This has facilitated the broad assessment of the energy requirements of populations and has been helpful when the energy needs of a particular occupational group have not been specifically studied.

Table 2 shows how approximate values for the energy costs of occupations involving the three degrees of activity have been obtained. On this basis one can estimate the gross energy expenditure on occupational work at light, moderate, and heavy levels of activity as 1.7, 2.7, and 3.8 times the basal metabolic rate in young men, and 1.7, 2.2, and 2.8 times the BMR in young women. Clearly, care is needed to ensure an accurate description of the activity and the time spent on it. Thus the energy demand on workers undertaking specific jobs, such as farming, mining, shipbuilding, or tree felling, may vary enormously, depending on the degree of mechanization.

For estimating the requirement per day, weekly working hours have to be averaged over 7 days. Thus for those who work for 8 hours per day for 5 days a week, the average would be 5 hours 43 minutes daily over the entire week. For other groups with different work patterns the calculation of time will have to be adjusted.

Discretionary activities: Some activities will be short-lived but require considerable rates of energy expenditure, whereas others have only modest costs but are undertaken for longer periods. In sedentary people the allowance for discretionary activity includes provision for short periods of vigorous exercise to maintain physical fitness and promote cardiovascular health. Five times the BMR represents a steady state of exercise at about 60% of maximal work-load. The energy requirements of the elderly differ from those of the young not only because they often reduce their occupational activities, but also because their basal energy requirements decline. An additional allowance has been made for an extra hour of socially desirable activity at this age.

Once the separate components of energy expenditure have been identified and evaluated, the total requirement can be calculated. As far as possible, these have been calculated from observed patterns of activity described in the literature. On the basis of such patterns, approximate estimates of the total daily energy expenditure corresponding to light, moderate, and heavy work can be derived as multiples of the BMR. It must be emphasized that these figures are intended to be general guidelines. As far as possible, users should make their own calculations, according to the characteristics of the population concerned. This could be done in two stages.

The first step is to develop the appropriate BMR factor. Adjustments can readily be made to accommodate differences in the time spent at work and in discretionary activity. Most occupations involve static activity which develops muscle strength but not cardiorespiratory efficiency. In general, therefore, discretionary activity of a dynamic nature is beneficial. However, this type of exercise may not be possible for those whose work involves heavy labour and physical fatigue. All additional times when individuals are not engaged in occupational or discretionary activities are considered to require a minimum energy expenditure at 1.4 times the BMR, except for the 8 hours assigned to sleeping at a rate equal to the BMR. The second step is to use the equations in Table 1 to obtain the value for the BMR appropriate for the body weight.

Table 2. Derivation of average values of the energy cost of three grades of physical activity at work, for women and men

	Women				Men			
	Cost/ min		Average cost ×BMR		Cost/ min		Average cost ×BMR	
	(kcalth)	(kJ)	(gross)	(net)	(kcalth)	(kJ)	(gross)	(net)
Light work								
75% of time sitting or standing	1.51	6.3			1.79	7.5		
25% of time standing and moving	1.70	7.1			2.51	10.5		
Average	1.56	6.5	1.7	0.7	1.99	8.3	1.7	0.7
Moderate work								
25% of time sitting or standing	1.51	6.3			1.79	7.5		
75% of time spent on specific occupational activity	2.20	9.2			3.61	15.1		

Average	2.03	8.5	2.2	1.2	3.16	13.2	2.7	1.7
Heavy work								
40% of time sitting or standing	1.51	6.3			1.79	7.5		
60% of time spent on specific occupational activity	3.21	13.4			6.22	26.0		
Average	2.54	10.6	2.8	1.8	4.45	18.6	3.8	2.8

Table 3. Energy requirement for a male engaged in heavy work

Age 35 years, weight 65 kg, height 1.72 m, BMI 22Estimated basal metabolic rate: 68 kcalth (284 kJ) per hour			
	hours	kcalth	kJ
In bed at 1.0 × BMR	8	545	2280
Occupational activities at 3.8 × BMR	8	2070	8660
Discretionary activities at 3.0 × BMR	1	205	860
For residual time, maintenance energy needs at 1.4 × BMR	7	670	2800
Total		3490	14580
= 2.14 × BMR			

Adult Protein Requirements

Young men: To derive the protein requirement of young male adults, the Consultation reviewed evidence from both short- and longer-term nitrogen balance studies. In all these studies protein was fed at several levels below and above an amount expected to promote N equilibrium (zero balance). The aggregated data provide an estimated mean requirement of 0.63 g/kg of highly digestible, good-quality protein.

Unpublished studies of men fed 0.73-0.80 g/kg show that N balance was adequately maintained in all subjects at that level. These results suggest that 0.36 g/kg may be regarded as approximating to 2 SD below the mean requirement or less and 0.73-0.80 g/kg as 2 SD above the mean or more. The average amount fed, 0.58 g/kg, is a reasonable estimate of the mean requirement of healthy young men whose habitual intake is well above this level. In a long-term study carried out for another purpose, 21 men received a good mixed diet supplying 6.5 g of N/ day or about 0.64 g of protein/kg.

Only urinary N was measured, but at 109 days the average excretion was 5.2 g, indicating that on the average the men were in N equilibrium. Four men continued on the diet for much longer; average urinary N was 5.19, 5.08, and 5.07 g at 319, 410, and 525 days, respectively. Body weight was 63 kg initially and 62 kg at day 250. These findings suggest that the average figure proposed at least meets and may exceed the average requirement of adapted individuals.

In the absence of better estimates of the average requirement, the Consultation decided to accept the mean of the values derived from the two sets of balance data. The mean values of 0.63 g/kg derived from the short-term balance studies and 0.58 g/kg from the longterm balance studies give a figure of 0.605 which could for most purposes be rounded to 0.6 g/kg per day, representing the average requirement for proteins of high quality, such as those from meat, milk, egg, and fish. The Consultation recognized that this value may be higher than the requirement of fully adapted persons but there was not enough information to improve this estimate.

In order to translate this estimate of average requirement into a level sufficient to cover individual variations within a population group, the coefficient of variation of the requirements must first be estimated. To obtain the coefficient of variation in the absence of data on variability from long-term studies at various levels of protein intake, the Consultation used the available information from short-term N-balance studies performed at different levels of protein intake around zero N balance. These data show that the coefficient of variation in estimates of requirements averaged 16.2%.

Assuming that this variation is approximately equally partitioned between and within subjects (where the within-subject variability includes measurement error as well as biological variability), the Consultation estimated that the true coefficient of variation of the protein requirements of adults was 12.5%. Consequently, a value of 25% (2 SD) above the average physiological requirement would be expected to meet the needs of all but 2.5% of individuals within the population. This level of good-quality protein (0.75 g/kg per day) is, therefore, thought to correspond to the lower end of the safe range of protein intakes. Nitrogen balance data are also available from short-term studies in which men were fed several levels of protein from ordinary mixed diets. These studies predict the mean daily dietary requirement to be 0.54-0.99 g of protein per kg of body weight.

The diets required in larger amounts are mainly those that are poorly digested and the requirement for net absorbed protein does not appear to differ between the high-quality proteins and practical adult diets.

Young women: There are less extensive data available for adult women. On the basis of short-term N-balance studies performed on young women receiving proteins from different sources, there is no evidence to suggest that the efficiency of utilization of dietary protein for meeting their physiological requirements is substantially different from that of young adult men when expressed per unit of body weight.

In industrialized countries young women generally have a higher proportion of body fat than young men and therefore a lower metabolic mass per kg. This has not been found in some less privileged communities. However, it would be unwise to suppose that it is always the case. Therefore, the Consultation concluded that there is no justification for making a distinction between adult males and females when setting the safe intake of protein. Accordingly, the safe intake of good-quality, highly digestible protein was set at 0.75 g/kg per day for both sexes.

Older adults and the elderly: Since many age-related body changes appear to occur continuously throughout adult life, protein allowances for adults should ideally be those that best preserve bodily functions from early adulthood to old age. Protein needs might be expected to change progressively during aging, since body composition, physiological functional capacity, physical activity, total food intake, and frequency of disease alter with age. However, there is not, at present, sufficient information to establish firm recommendations based on such a continuum. Nevertheless, the elderly make up an important section of the population for whom estimates of protein requirements must be developed as a public health measure.

Some recent observations on age-related changes in body composition and protein metabolism, especially relating to muscle, suggest that utilization of dietary protein and essential amino acids may differ between the young and old adult. Direct studies of the amount of dietary protein needed to bring older adults and the elderly into N equilibrium and maintain protein nutritional status are limited. Unfortunately, four recent studies do not provide a consistent picture of the protein needs of the elderly.

In one case, 0.8 g/kg per day of egg protein was not enough to maintain N balance in the majority of elderly men and women over a 30-day period. However, another study, on a group of slightly less elderly subjects, found this level of protein to be adequate. In both these studies body weight was maintained but energy intake was less in the former than in the latter, suggesting that activity patterns may have been different in the two groups. It is improbable that high intakes of protein can prevent the aging process in adults, since measurements showing loss of lean body mass and tissue function with age have been made in Western countries in which the daily consumption of protein by adults is customarily about twice the estimated lower limit of the safe protein intake of 0.75 g/kg

It is not known whether populations living at the level of 0.75 g/kg of dietary protein or less show different losses of lean body mass and tissue function. In view of these considerations, the Consultation concluded that the safe intake of protein should not be lower than 0.75 g/kg per day for older adults and the elderly. This figure is higher than that for younger adults in relation to lean body mass, because it is an accepted fact that protein utilization is less efficient in the elderly.

Pregnancy and Lactation

Requirements during pregnancy

Energy: During pregnancy extra energy is needed for the growth of the fetus, placenta, and associated maternal tissues. Basal metabolism rises, partly due to the increased mass of active tissue (fetal, placental, and maternal), the cost of increased maternal effort (e.g., cardiovascular and respiratory work), and the cost of tissue synthesis. In well nourished populations in the developed countries, the weight gain during pregnancy is about 12.5 kg and the median infant birth weight is 3.3 kg, with a coefficient of variation of 15%. The average extra energy cost of this typical pregnancy has been calculated to be about 335 MJ

(80 000 kcalth) over the 9-month period, distributed as an extra 630 kJ (150 kcalth) day during the first trimester and 1465 kJ (350 kcalth)/day during the second and third trimesters.

It is difficult to calculate accurately the energy needs during pregnancy. Women of small stature tend to have small babies and would logically fall in the lower range of normal weight gains and hence need less additional energy than the average. Obese women need to gain less fat than slimmer women, and women who are underweight for their height should need to gain more than the average. The extra dietary energy requirement in pregnancy also depends on the extent to which mothers can and do reduce their physical activity. It is clearly desirable to increase dietary intake to spare maternal tissue, allow for satisfactory growth of the fetus, adnexa, and breast tissue, and to sustain a desirable pattern of physical activity.

The need for generous fat reserves is arguable, but deposition of some fat is associated with a more satisfactory infant birth weight. Many recent studies of food intakes of well nourished pregnant women indicate that these extra energy requirements for tissue deposition are not always accompanied by commensurate increases in intake. Nevertheless, women receiving less than these extra energy intakes seem to deposit enough extra body fat to provide the reserve needed for subsequent lactation, and the fetal and maternal tissues grow satisfactorily.

Although the evidence is only tentative, it appears that the physical activity of such women is reduced. It is also possible that metabolic changes occur in pregnancy that result in a greater economy of energy utilization. Some but not all studies of well nourished pregnant women indicate that the slowing of self-paced work, e.g., climbing stairs, is usual, so that the energy expended per unit time is maintained at approximately the same level as in the non-pregnant state. However, the energy cost of fixed-pace work is increased, as would be expected from the increases in BMR and body mass, and shows no evidence of improved efficiency under conditions of unrestricted food intake.

If women begin pregnancy with marginal nutritional reserves (e.g., some teenagers in developed countries and many women in developing countries), and if they cannot reduce their previous level of activity, it was the Consultation's view that every effort should be made to provide the full energy allowance. Because some fat should be deposited early in pregnancy, and because appetite and periodic work requirements vary greatly, there is little evidence to suggest that the extra energy requirement differs between the three trimesters. The Consultation advised an average addition of 1200 kJ (285 kcalth) daily throughout pregnancy. Where healthy women reduce their activity, it is considered reasonable to reduce the average additional allowance to 840 kJ (200 kcalth) daily.

Protein: The total protein requirement of a woman gaining 12.5 kg during pregnancy and delivering a 3.3-kg infant has been estimated to be 925 g, or 3.3 g per day throughout pregnancy. The rate of storage is not constant; estimates provided for the first, second, third, and fourth quarters are, respectively, 0.64, 1.84, 4.76, and 6.10 g of protein per day. A second approach has been to study protein needs during pregnancy by N balance. In the second half of pregnancy, there are retentions about 50% greater than can be accounted for by the tissues included in the sum given above (fetus, placenta, maternal tissues, and blood).

The difference between the two estimates is about 330 g of protein, or approximately 1.6 kg of lean body mass. If the higher figure predicted from N balance is correct, then the amount of fat storage during the second half of pregnancy must be far lower than is currently supposed. Analysis of the regression of N balance on weight gain measured in a recent study shows the composition of the gain in the second half of pregnancy to be 12% protein, a figure which is compatible with the body composition of the newborn. There are not sufficient data for the first half of pregnancy to enable a judgement to be made on the quality of the available information.

Clearly, these discrepancies merit further investigation, but for the time being the Consultation felt that protein needs should continue to be assessed on the calculated increment of 925 g protein, the average gain, plus 30% (2 SD of birth weight), which should cover the protein gains during pregnancy of nearly all normal women. These figures for gain must be adjusted for the efficiency with which dietary protein is converted to fetal, placental, and maternal tissues. There is no direct evidence on this subject. Two studies in which graded N levels, all presumed to be above requirement, were fed to pregnant women indicate the efficiency of utilization to be low (25-35%) and quite variable.

At intakes nearer the requirement, the efficiency is unlikely to be so low, and therefore an efficiency factor of 0.70, derived from growth data in children is accepted as applying also to pregnant women. The safe levels of additional protein computed in this manner are 1.2 g, 6.1 g, and 10.7 g per day in the 1st, 2nd, and 3rd trimesters, respectively (Table 4). However, there is evidence from animals that more protein may be deposited early and somewhat less very late in pregnancy so that the distribution of deposition by trimesters may be arbitrary. Thus it is estimated that the protein requirement should be increased by an average of 6 g/day throughout pregnancy. These amounts should be added to the non-pregnant allowance and the sum corrected for digestibility.

Table 4. Safe level of additional protein during pregnancy

Trimester	N gain (g/day)		Efficiency	Additional protein required
	(Average)	(+ 30%)	(0.70)	(g/day)
1	0.104	0.14	0.20	1.2
2	0.525	0.68	0.98	6.1
3	0.922	1.20	1.71	10.7

Requirements during lactation

Energy: The energy cost of lactation is the energy content of the milk secreted plus the energy required to produce it. The average milk production was assumed to demand 3.1 MJ (750 kcalth)/day. Since then, WHO has sponsored a collaborative study of breast-milk volume and composition that suggests a slight revision of the figures. In the five populations examined (Guatemala, Hungary, Philippines, Sweden, Zaire), the volume of milk ingested by infants increased between the second and third months and then remained relatively stable until 6 months.

Very few data are available from Western countries after 6 months of age. In the studies in the developing countries, milk consumption fell between the sixth and twelfth months and the level was even further reduced in the second year. Among these five populations, breast-milk consumption in the first few months was lower for infants whose birth weights had been lower. The present analysis of the energy requirements for lactation is based on the median milk consumption of breast-fed Swedish infants for the first 6 months and on more limited data from all populations for the later periods.

Median milk volume is close to the mean value and the coefficient of variation is about 12.5%. Consumption data have been adjusted upwards by 6% to compensate for an observed underestimation of milk secreted versus milk consumed. The WHO study found the average energy content of breast milk to be 2.9 kJ (0.70 kcalth)/ml, which agrees with earlier estimates. Since there is no new information, the efficiency of conversion of food energy to milk is taken to be 80%.

The pattern of activity of lactating women may be changed, depending upon the circumstances of life. A woman may spend 2-2 ½ hours a day breast-feeding; this is described as "active seated work". There is no evidence yet available to support the suggestion that the BMR may also be altered during lactation. It has been postulated that an enhanced efficiency of energy metabolism might continue from pregnancy into lactation; studies on energy metabolism during lactation, as well as in pregnancy, are clearly a priority for future research.

If the recommendations for pregnancy have been met, the average woman will start lactation with some 150 MJ (36000 kcalth) of fat reserves. A normal body composition should be re-established within 6 months by utilizing this reserve, which would thus provide about 835 kJ (200 kcalth) per day. Allowances during this and subsequent periods will need to be adjusted according to maternal fat stores and patterns of activity. During the later stages of lactation the full allowance of about 2090 kJ (500 kcalth)/ day should be provided. This requirement must be increased if more than one child is being breast-fed.

The average protein content of breast milk (N × 6.25) has been taken as 1.15 g per 100 ml, except during the first month, when the value is approximately 1.3 g per 100 ml. It is accepted that, as for growth in children, an efficiency factor of 70% is necessary to adjust for the conversion of dietary protein to milk protein. While there may be a small amount of tissue protein available from accretion during pregnancy, e.g., from involution of the uterus, this is not a significant factor in providing the extra requirement for lactation. The safe level of provision for the mother should allow for those who are producing, or are capable of producing, more than average amounts of milk. Upward adjustment of the median milk volume, and hence the amount of protein secreted, by 2 SD allows for this.

Infants, Children, and Adolescents

Although, in principle, it would be desirable to determine the requirements of children, in the same way as for adults from measurements of energy expenditure, this approach involves many difficulties in practice. Information is indeed available on the BMRs of children of all ages for which prediction equations are given in Table 1. However, in young infants, in whom the requirement for growth is a substantial component of the total requirement for energy, there are large variations within the normal range, in the rate of growth, and probably also in the composition of the tissue laid down. Moreover, for both infants and children, it is not possible to specify with any confidence the allowance that should be made for a desirable level of physical activity.

Children 1-10 years: In order to calculate the energy requirements of children over 1 year of age from measurements of energy expenditure, both the time and cost of all types of physical activity need to be known. Unfortunately, this information is not available for children in this age group, and it is therefore necessary, as for infants, to evaluate their energy requirements from data on dietary intake.

Physical activity, and thus the energy requirement of children, has declined in recent times, reflecting increasingly sedentary life-styles in the large cities of industrialized countries. There is some evidence of this in older children. If true, such a reduction may well be considered undesirable from the point of view of optimal health and function, as maintenance of adequate levels of physical activity is thought to be necessary in the formative years of the growing child. Therefore the Consultation considered that recommendations for this age group should be based on observed intakes, but that they should be increased by 5% to allow for a desirable level of physical activity.

Little information is available in the literature on the energy intakes of children in the developing countries, who may be expected to lead a more active life, having to walk long distances, undertaking hard physical work, sometimes being less tied to sedentary activities by strict school schedules, etc. Their energy intakes are smaller than those of their counterparts of the same age in developed countries, but the difference largely disappears when the intakes are recalculated on a body-weight basis. One might postulate that in this case, externally imposed limitations may restrict both energy intakes and energy expenditure. The extra 5% added to observed intakes may be considered a realistic estimate of the requirement if enough energy is to be available for a desirable level of physical activity.

Children 10-17 years: After 10 years of age it becomes feasible to base requirements on estimates of energy expenditure built up by the factorial method. The approach is basically the same as for adults.

As in adults, the BMR in children is generally the largest component of the requirement. Because of differences in the timing of the pubertal growth spurt, both weights and heights at any given age are rather variable. For example, in 12-year-old boys, weight may vary from 28 kg (3rd centile) to 59 kg (97th centile), and height from 1.36 to 1.64 m. The best predictor of the BMR is weight and, as in adults, the BMR per kg varies with body weight. At any given weight, variations in height make no difference in boys and only a small difference in girls. The BMR may be estimated either from the actual weight or from the median weight for height and age, as shown in Baldwin's table.

For growth, an addition of 5 kcalth (21 kJ) per g is allowed for the average daily cost of weight gain. It is recognized that growth does not occur at a regular rate from day to day. However, even during the pubertal spurt the requirement for growth is so small compared with the total energy requirement that no extra allowance in the energy intake need be made for this variability. In order to illustrate quantitatively the energy requirements for different patterns of activity, an attempt was made to identify the time that might be spent by each sex and age group sleeping, going to school (including homework), and undertaking light, moderate, and heavy physical activity.

There is little information in the literature on the amount of time children and adolescents spend on different types of activity, but these are bound to be highly variable. The time allocations were estimated as the daily means throughout the year, assuming that the average child still goes to school at the age of 10. It was also assumed that the child begins secondary school at the age of 13. In societies where children begin work rather than go to secondary school, patterns of activity should be calculated accordingly. The gross energy costs were assessed as follows in terms of BMR units:

	Boys	Girls
Going to school and light activity	1.6 BMR	1.5 BMR
Moderate activity	2.5 BMR	2.2 BMR
High activity	6.0 BMR	6.0 BMR

The somewhat lower values given for girls assume that their intensity of activity would decline to the level found in adult women.The BMR factor varies over a rather narrow range, from about 1.6 to 1.75 in boys and from 1.5 to 1.65 in girls. Between 10 and 18 years the new estimates of energy requirements of boys exceed the actual figures of observed energy intakes by an amount that corresponds almost exactly with the amount of energy thought desirable for children to spend in high activity (½ hour at 6.0 × BMR). In girls the discrepancy is greater, presumably reflecting a low level of physical activity in the sample whose intakes were measured. The Consultation considered that the estimated requirements for this age group should not be decreased to match the observed intakes in affluent countries. Fulfilment of the requirements as proposed is likely to be beneficial if physical activity is increased, and in developing countries will provide a margin of safety.

Protein requirements

Infants from birth to 6 months: The average protein content of human milk, calculated as total N × 6.25, has been taken as 1.15 g per 100 ml after the first month of lactation1. It is recognized that human milk contains about 40 mg of non-amino nitrogen per 100 ml (approximately 20% of total N) but, following the usual convention, we have assumed that this nitrogen fraction is utilized. If the average energy content is taken as 70 kcalth (290 kJ) per 100 ml, the protein content is 1.64 g per 100 kcalth (6.85 g per MJ).

Although the amount of milk consumed by infant girls is less than that by boys, on a body-weight basis the intakes are virtually the same. Estimates of the protein intake of breast-fed infants are not shown after the age of 4 months, because from this age there is insufficient information on the intakes of exclusively breast-fed infants who are growing satisfactorily.

Children from 6 months onwards: The period from 6 to 12 months is clearly the most critical, because of rapid growth during this time and because the child increasingly relies on supplementary foods. The first priority must therefore be to establish as reliable an estimate as possible of the safe level of protein intake for children of this age.

One can then with some confidence interpolate the safe level for older children from this estimate.

The protein requirements of children have been calculated in the first instance by a modified factorial method. As with adults, and with the same limitations, the maintenance requirements can in principle be estimated from measurements of nitrogen balance at several levels of intake. There is the additional problem of determining an appropriate value for the N retained during growth and the requirement for achieving this retention.

(a) *Maintenance requirement*: Several short-term N-balance studies have been carried out in older infants and young children to determine the protein requirement by the slope-ratio method. These have been healthy children, usually recovered from malnutrition, short in stature but in the normal range of weight for height. The usual design follows that of adult studies: energy intake is kept constant at a level assumed to be adequate and protein is given at different levels, each for a period of several days. From these studies it is possible to calculate a maintenance requirement (no growth, N equilibrium) from the regression of N balance on N intake, allowing 10 mg of N per kg per day for sweat and miscellaneous N losses. In theory it is also possible from these studies to determine the amount of protein needed in the diet to meet any chosen value for N retention.

Studies of a different design, in which N balance was measured only once or twice in each child over a range of intakes, gave a maintenance requirement of 110 mg of N per kg per day. The results of the balance studies in the older age groups are somewhat variable. The estimated maintenance requirement, corrected to the digestibility of cow's milk, ranged from 80 to 118 mg of N per kg per day. Since the average maintenance requirement in young adults studied in short-term balances was estimated at 98 mg of N per kg per day, it seems reasonable, for intermediate age groups, to interpolate between two well-established values. These, rounded off, would be 120 mg of N per kg per day at 1 year, falling to 100 mg of N per kg per day at 20 years.

In the balance measurements on children the range of inter-individual variation in the estimate of the maintenance requirement was similar to that found in the much more numerous short-term balances in adults, and the Consultation has therefore accepted the same value of 12.5% for the coefficient of variation of the maintenance requirement. It is assumed that this represents variability in the efficiency of utilization-an assumption that is important when the requirement for growth is being considered.

(b) *The requirement for growth*: The mean rate of N accretion during growth can be estimated from the expected daily rate of weight gain (NCHS 50th centile) and the N concentration in the body. This is low at birth, and increases to the adult value by 5 years of age or earlier. The extent of the increase is important between 6 and 12 months, when growth is rapid. At some ages the values were not in good agreement. More recent estimates of N accretion during growth have been provided by Fomon et al..

However it should not be assumed that growth always proceeds at exactly the same rate from day to day, even in apparently healthy children. The cause, extent, and significance of these fluctuations in growth rate are difficult to assess. The variability of gain is much greater than the variability of intake, so that presumably it results to a large extent from variation in the efficiency of utilization of food for growth. Longitudinal studies in Jamaica on reasonably healthy and well nourished children showed that over successive months a period of faltering would usually be followed by a period of weight gain at

2-3 times the normal rate. Very little is known about variations over shorter periods.

Daily measurements of children's weights even under standardized conditions in a metabolic ward show fluctuations, which no doubt resulted partly from differences in the amounts of urine and stool retained at the moment of weighing. They may also represent differences from day to day in the proportions of fat and lean tissue laid down. It is known that individual children, at least when recovering from malnutrition, may differ widely in the composition of weight gain. If it is accepted that different amounts of protein may be laid down from day to day, as part of the normal process of growth, the question then arises, what is the effect of this on the child's daily protein requirement?

In order to maintain a satisfactory overall rate of growth, any failure to lay down protein on one day must be compensated for on a subsequent day. Body has a very limited capacity for storing amino acids or for drawing on the free amino acid pool for protein synthesis. Even during short periods such as 12 hours without food, nitrogen balance becomes negative. Therefore, in accordance with classical teaching, it seems very unlikely that amino acids provided on a day when there was no growth could be held "in stock" to be utilized for growth later on. It follows that since it is impossible to foretell on which days the growth rate will be low or high, it is necessary to provide enough every day for a possible extra demand.

There is no evidence available on which to base a realistic estimate of the extra requirement for protein that might arise in this way. In this situation a judgement has to be made. A reasonable judgement must lead to estimates that are similar to values established independently, such as the intakes of healthy breast-fed children. It was found that if, in the factorial calculation the growth component of the protein requirement is set at 50% above that based on the theoretical daily amount of N laid down, the calculated average requirement at 4 months comes close to the average intake of breast-fed infants. To provide a physiological margin of safety, it was therefore decided to increase the theoretical growth requirement by a factor of 50%.

The amount of dietary nitrogen needed to allow for a given amount of N deposited can be derived from the same slope as the requirement for maintenance. It is assumed that dietary protein is used with the same efficiency for growth as it is for maintenance, and on theoretical grounds there is no reason to suppose that this assumption is not valid. The appropriate slope for diets based on milk or egg has been taken as 0.7 at all ages.

Although the factorial method is not, in fact, used for infants below the age of 6 months, the calculations have been made in order to compare the results with the estimated protein intakes from breast milk. This comparison suggests that the proposed addition of 50% to the nitrogen increment does not unrealistically increase the estimate, and it may even be too small. This is a subject on which more research is urgently needed. Finally, a correction has to be made for the inter-individual variability of growth, in order to arrive at a safe level of protein intake for virtually all healthy children.

In younger children there is little difference from the earlier figures, although the ways in which the values have been derived are different. From 6 years onwards the present estimates are somewhat higher than the earlier ones. This reflects the higher current estimate for adults, since the maintenance requirement has been calculated by linear interpolation between infants and adults. Much of the difference disappears when revised corrections are made for protein score and digestibility.

8

Food Preservation

Preservation usually involves preventing the growth of bacteria, fungi and other micro-organisms, as well as retarding the oxidation of fats which causes rancidity. It also includes processes to inhibit natural ageing and discolouration that can occur during food preparation such as the polyphenoloxidase reaction in apples which causes browning when apples are cut. Some preservation methods require the food to be sealed after treatment to prevent re-contamination with microbes; others, such as drying, allow food to be stored without any special containment for long periods. Preservation Processes include:-

— heating to kill or denature organisms (e. g. boiling),

— oxidation (e. g use of sulphur dioxide)

— toxic inhibition (e. g. smoking, use of carbon dioxide, vinegar, alcohol etc)

— dehydration (drying)

— osmotic inhibition (e. g use of syrups)

— low temperature inactivation (e. g. freezing)

— many combinations of these methods.

Food Preservation Methods

Common methods of applying these processes include

drying, freeze drying, freezing, vacuum-packing, canning, preserving in syrup, sugar crystalisation, food irradiation, adding preservatives or inert gases such as Carbon dioxide. Other methods that not only help to preserve food, but also add flavor, include pickling, salting, smoking, preserving in syrup or alcohol, sugar crystalisation and curing.

Main food preservation methods

Method	Effect on microbial growth or survival
Refrigeration or chilling	Low temperature to retard growth
Freezing	Low temperature and reduction of water activity to prevent growth
Drying, curing and conserving	Reduction in water activity sufficient to delay or prevent growth
Vacuum and oxygen free modified atmosphere packaging	Low oxygen tension in inhibit strict aerobes and delay growth of facultative anaerobes
Carbon dioxide enriched modified atmosphere packaging	Specific inhibition of some micro-organisms by carbon dioxide
Addition of acids	Reduction of pH value and sometimes additional inhibition by the particular acid
Lactic fermentation	Reduction of pH value in situ by microbial action and sometimes additional inhibition by the lactic and acetic acids formed and by other microbial products. (e. g. ethanol, bacteriocins)
Sugar preservation	Cooking in high sucrose concentration creating too high osmotic pressure for most microbial survival.
Ethanol preservation	Steeping or cooking in Ethanol produces toxic inhibition of microbes. Can be combined with sugar preservation
Emulsification	Compartmentalisation and nutrient limitation within the aqueous droplets in water-in-oil emulsion foods

Addition of preservatives such as nitrite or sulphite ions	Inhibition of specific groups of micro-organisms
Pasteurization and appertization	Delivery of heat sufficient to inactivate target micro-organisms to the desired extent
Food irradiation (Radurization, radicidation and radappertization)	Delivery of ionising radiation
Application of high hydrostatic pressure (Pascalization)	Pressure-inactivation of vegetative bacteria, yeasts and moulds

Drying

One of the oldest method of food preservation is by drying, which reduces water activity sufficient to delay or prevent bacterial growth. Most types of meat can be dried and this is especially valuable in the case of pig meat since this is difficult to keep without preservation. Many fruits can also be dried and the process is often applied to apples, pears, bananas, mangos, papaya, coconut etc. Currants, Sultanas and Raisins are all form of dried Grapes. Drying is also the normal means of preservation for cereal grains such as wheat, maize, oats, barley, rice, millet and rye.

Drying removes enough moisture from the food so bacteria, yeasts and molds can't grow. Drying also slows down the action of enzymes because it removes moisture, the food shrinks, and it becomes lighter in weight. When food is ready for use, add water. Dry foods in the oven or a food dehydrator by using the right combination of warmth, low humidity and air currents. Sun drying is not recommended in Minnesota due to high humidity and cool night temperatures. In drying, a warm temperature allows the moisture to evaporate. Air currents speed up drying. Low humidity allows moisture to move from the food to the air.

Preparing food to dry

— Select fresh, good quality fruits and vegetables.

— Peel and trim away seeds, core or damaged portions.

— Cut into halves, strips, or slices about 1/8-inch to 1/4-inch thick that dry readily.

— Blanch vegetables by heating them enough to neutralize enzymes. If you omit this step, or inadequately blanch vegetables, they will have poor flavor and color. Blanch in steam or in hot water. Water blanching is quicker, but may leach out color and nutrients compared to steam blanching. Follow the same times as used when freezing vegetables. It is not necessary to chill blanched vegetables. Drain them well and spread onto drying rack in oven or food dehydrator.

— Pretreat most fruits by dipping them to slow down browning. Use one-half teaspoon Vitamin C (ascorbic acid) per quart of cold water. Dip fruit for one minute, then drain and put on rack to begin drying.

Drying food is a slow process. In a dehydrator, it takes six or more hours to dry foods. In the oven, it takes eight or more hours. Drying time depends on the type of food, the thickness of the cut, the moisture content of the food and the drying method. Don't speed up the drying time by turning up the oven. You will cook the food on the outside before it dries on the inside. This is called "case hardening. "

The food may appear dry on the outside but is wet on the inside. It will mold later on in storage. Vegetables are dry when they are brittle, fruits when they feel like leather. After foods are dried, allow 30 minutes to one hour cooling time. Too long a cooling period allows moisture from the air to re-enter the food. Proper storage prevents insects and rodents from eating the food. It also keeps moisture out and saves nutrients. Use glass jars, metal cans or boxes with tight-fitting lids or vapor-proof freezer cartons. Heavy-duty plastic bags with press-together seals are acceptable, but are not insect- or rodent-proof.

Screw lids or covers on glass jars to prevent insect contamination, but it is not necessary to heat-process the jars. Dried foods keep four months to one year depending on storage conditions. Store in cool, dry, dark areas. For best quality, store under 60 degrees Fahrenheit. Although it is not necessary to store dried food in a refrigerator or freezer, except for meat jerky, low temperatures extend the shelf life. Check containers within seven to 10 days to see if moisture is present. If you see moisture, remove food and redry at 140 to 160 degrees Fahrenheit. If food is moldy, discard it, throw away the plastic freezer bag or sterilize the jar.

Dried fruits can be eaten as nutritious snacks, or can be soaked in water or juice for one to two hours and used in favorite recipes. Sliced vegetables can be eaten dried as tasty vegetable chips for dips. Most vegetables are refreshed with water before use. The water can be added back to vegetables by soaking in tap water for one to two hours. Use two cups of water for each cup of dried food. Using boiling water speeds up the soaking period. Dried vegetables can be added directly to soups or stews without pre-soaking, drawing on the liquid in the soup or stew for rehydration during cooking.

Basic principles of drying

Drying preserves food by lowering the amount of water or moisture in the food material. This is necessary to prevent microbial growth and chemical reactions which can only occur when enough water is present in the food. Equilibrium Relative Humidity (ERH) is a term used to describe the availability of the water to the chemical environment and microorganisms present in foods. The equilibrium relative humidity or percent ERH scale varies from zero to 100. Figure 1 illustrates the meaning of percent ERH.

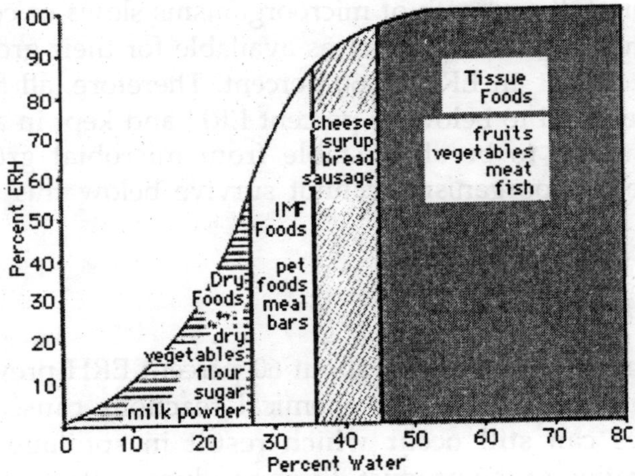

Figure 1. Percent Water

If a food of a certain moisture content is put in a closed chamber which is set to some relative humidity, the food will change its moisture content in an attempt to equal the ERH of the chamber. If a dry food such as a cracker which has an ERH equal to 11 percent is placed in a chamber with a high ERH, for example 60 percent, the cracker will gain water from the air until it reaches the ERH of the air, in this case the cracker will lose its crispness. If a fresh tissue food such as lettuce which has an ERH equal to 98 percent is placed in a chamber set at 60 percent ERH, the lettuce will lose moisture to the air and become wilted. These two foods will have different moistures at 60 percent ERH, but they will both have the same availability of water to chemical reactions and microorganisms present in the food.

Fresh tissue foods, such as meat, vegetables, and fruit products, have an ERH close to 100 percent. An ERH level this high means that the water present in these foods is available for rapid growth of microorganisms leading to deterioration and spoilage of the food. By drying foods it is possible to lower the percent ERH. As the percent ERH is lowered, the growth of microorganisms slows or ceases since the water is no longer as available for their growth. This occurs at an ERH of 60 percent. Therefore, all foods must be dried to below 60 percent ERH and kept in a dry environment to be shelf stable from microbial growth because microorganisms cannot survive below this ERH level.

Chemical changes

Although drying foods to about 60 percent ERH prevents microbial growth, certain chemical reactions caused by enzymes can still occur which result in spoilage and deterioration of the product. Fresh produce contains many different enzymes which cause loss of color, loss of nutrients, and flavor changes in dried vegetables and fruits. These enzymes must be inactivated to prevent such reactions from taking place. Enzymes in vegetables are inactivated by the blanching process.

Blanching is the exposure of the vegetables to boiling water or steam for a brief period of time. Blanched vegetables when dried will have better color and flavor than unblanched. For blanching times consult the tables. The major problem associated with enzymes in fruits is the development of brown colors and loss of vitamins A and C. Fruits are not blanched like vegetables because the blanching process gives fruits a cooked flavor. Instead, the enzymes in fruits are inactivated by using chemical compounds which interfere with deteriorative chemical reactions.

The most common control chemicals used are sodium bisulfite and ascorbic acid (Vitamin C). Ascorbic acid may be used in its pure form or in chemical mixtures of ascorbic acid and other compounds such as "Fruit Fresh." Food grade sodium bisulfite, sodium sulfite or sodium metabisulfite may also be used for pretreatment of fruit. Individuals sensitive to sulfites, particularly some asthmatics, should use ascorbic acid.

Dehydration Processes

Sun-drying

Sun-drying requires constant exposure to direct sunlight during the day and a relative humidity of less than 20 percent. These conditions are usually found in only a few regions of the United States, such as in the Sacramento Valley of California or in Arizona. Foods dried in the sun can take from 3-4 days to dry and if the humidity is high, as is generally the case in Minnesota, the food will mold before it dries. The sun-drying process is inefficient because it requires much more space and drying time than drying in conventional home driers. In addition, food dried in the sun is exposed to dirt, insects, rodents, and bird wastes. The practice of sun-drying is not recommended for home food preservation because complete drying cannot be assured and the quality of the food is questionable.

Dehydrators

Purchased home food dehydrators and portable convection ovens fitted with drying trays, provide better control over climatic conditions and food quality than sun-drying. Drying foods in a conventional oven gives much less satisfactory results. Home dehydrators and convection ovens are equipped with a heating element and fan which blows hot, dry air at moderate speeds around the food. The air serves two purposes. It supplies the heat needed to evaporate the water. As the air heats up its relative humidity decreases allowing the food to dry at a faster rate and reach a low equilibrium relative humidity.

The dry air blown across the food also serves to carry away the water vapor. The air must be kept in motion by the fan because stagnant air takes on as much moisture as it can hold, and if it is not removed, drying no longer takes place. Both counter top dehydrators and portable convection ovens can be used on a 110/120 volt general purpose circuit (15 AMP). The food dehydrators draw 525-800 watts; the convection ovens draw about 1500 watts and should not be used on the same general household circuit with other heating appliances such as a coffee maker or toaster. This may be an important consideration in view of the fact that convection ovens used for drying may be running for many hours.

Food dehydrators and convection ovens differ in their range of temperature settings and available square feet of drying space. The range of temperature settings for dehydrators as a low of 85° to 110° F up to a high of 140° to 145° F. The range for convection ovens has a low of 140° to 175° F up to a high of 500° F. Food dehydrators are usually made to handle more racks and, therefore, have more square feet of drying space than portable convection ovens.

The appliances require 18-24 inches of counter space and vary in height from 10-16 inches. The height is a consideration if it is to fit on a counter with cabinets above. Food dehydrators range in cost from $100 to $250; convection ovens that recommend drying range from $150 to $200; drying racks for convection ovens would be $25 to $50 extra.

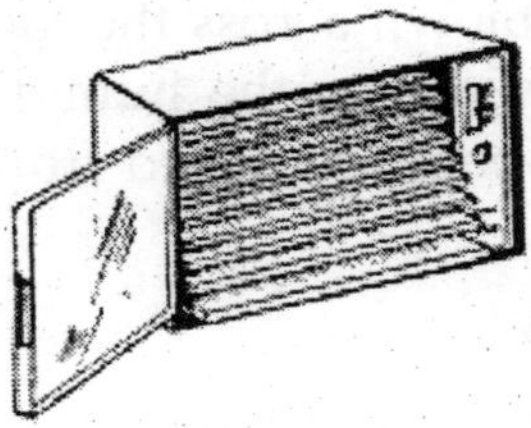

Food Dehydrator

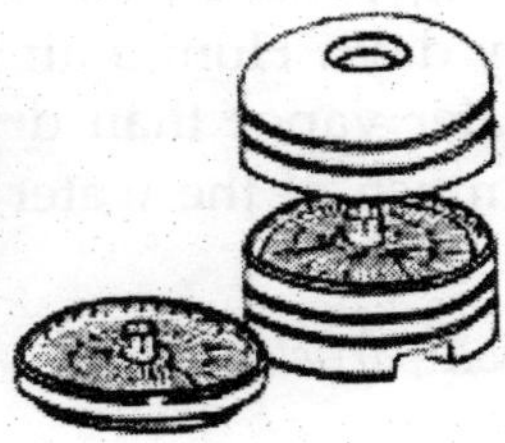

Food Dehydrator

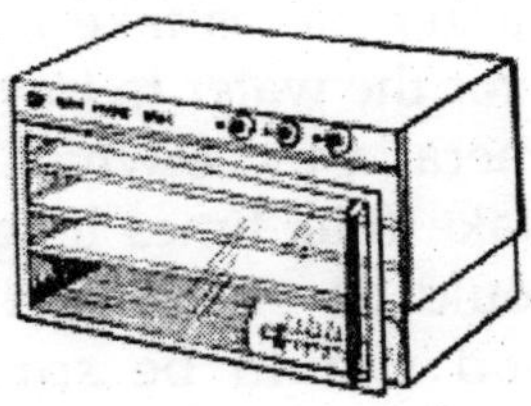

Convection Oven

Factors Affecting Drying Time

Temperature

In general, safe drying temperatures for most vegetables and fruits are between 140° to 145° F. Even on rainy days when the relative humidity is 85 to 95 percent, it is better to dry in this temperature range than to raise the temperature. It is important that very high temperatures are not used to speed the drying process. Higher temperatures only serve to dry the outermost portion of the food while the interior remains moist resulting in what is called case hardening. Such foods will spoil due to microbial growth when the moisture from the interior migrates to the exterior of the product.

In addition, higher temperatures speed up chemical reactions which deteriorate foods. Do not attempt to dry food on rainy days when the relative humidity is high.

The drying process will take much longer than on low humidity days. Humid air blown across the food contains more water vapor than dry air, so the humid air cannot hold as much of the water being removed from the food.

Size of food particles

The size of the pieces of food is another important factor influencing the rate of drying. Food should be cut into halves, strips, or slices and should not be more than 1/8- to ¼-inch thick. Larger pieces take longer to dry because it is more difficult for the water to travel through the pores in the food. In general a piece which is twice as thick as another one will take four times longer to dry. Thus, all pieces of food should be of uniform size and thickness. The pieces of food should be spread evenly on the dehydrator trays in thin layers and stirred occasionally. The trays should be rotated if top trays dry at different rates than the bottom trays.

Capacity of the drier

The amount of food that should be dried at one time depends on the dehydrator. The manufacturer's direction book usually contains specifications about the amount of food that can be dried at one time. Some large dehydrators can hold up to 8 pounds of prepared produce. Portable convection ovens may hold only 2 to 3 pounds of prepared produce. Do not keep adding fresh produce to the dehydrator as the food is drying. This common practice increases the time required to reach an acceptable degree of dryness and will produce a poor quality product.

Determining dryness

A major problem in drying foods at home is determining if and when the food item is dry. In general, vegetables must be dried to about 5 percent water content and fruits to 15 to 20 percent water content. Dried fruits are stable at a higher moisture content than dried vegetables because the concentrated natural sugars and acids in the dried fruit function as preservatives. To determine if vegetables are dry, remove some pieces near the end of the drying process. This time will usually be after a minimum of 6 to 8 hours. Cool the pieces to room temperature. The vegetable is dry if it is brittle or crisp when bitten, and if it will shatter when hit with a hammer. Remove a piece of fruit during the end of the drying period. Cool to room temperature. It should feel pliable, leathery, and have no pockets of moisture.

Time and energy considerations

Preliminary studies conducted at the University of Minnesota give some indication of the time and energy requirements for food dehydration. Drying time per load of fully loaded dryer ranged from 5 to 23 hours. An average of 1 kWh of electricity was needed for drying each pound of fresh prepared produce. This energy cost is similar to the cost to freeze and store food in a freezer for 6 months. Freezer costs were based on 0. 1 kWh per pound to freeze and 0. 7 to 1. 5 kWh to store food for 6 months and assumes a full freezer.

The kWhs required to blanch and dry tomatoes were 1. 324 kWh per pound. Zimmerman reported the energy used in home canning tomatoes in a water bath canner to be 3. 093 kWh for seven quarts which is 0. 173 kWh per pound. A comparison of these figures indicates that home drying tomatoes used considerably more energy than processing them in a water bath canner.

Storage Problems

Dried foods must be stored properly to maintain the low

moisture content and to prevent microbial deterioration. Before packing foods, the dried pieces should be allowed to cool for a short amount of time. Immediately after the product has cooled the food should be stored. To store dried foods, place the dried food in plastic bags, press out air, seal or close, and then place in glass jars which are tightly sealed.

Plastic containers or metal cans with plastic lids are not recommended because moisture can enter through the container. To be sure that the food remains dry, add dessicant or silica gel which you can purchase in the notions or housewares section of a department store or at hobby shops. Place the substance in the glass jar to cover the bottom of the container to a depth of ¼-inch thick.

The dessicant absorbs any moisture from the surroundings and prevents the food from absorbing moisture. Place the dried food wrapped in a sealed plastic bag over the dessicant and tightly seal the jar. Packaged dried food should be stored in a dry, cool, 60° F place. Dried food should also be kept out of the sun to prevent discoloration and nutrient loss. Dried foods in sealed plastic bags may also be stored in the refrigerator or freezer.

In general, the shelf life of home dried vegetables and fruits stored at 60° F is 4 to 6 months. If the product is stored at 70° F, shelf life will be shortened. The shelf life of food dried in the home is not as long as the shelf life of commercially freeze-dried products. This is because freeze-dried foods are first frozen at -40° F and then placed in a chamber connected to a vacuum pump. Heat is applied to the frozen food after the air is evacuated from the chamber and the ice sublimes or evaporates directly into vapor. Because the food is frozen and is at a low temperature during drying, there is little nutrient loss and textural damage. Freeze-drying is not practical for home use because elaborate and expensive equipment is necessary.

Instructions for Drying

All foods should be prepared by properly sorting, washing, and peeling. If possible, gather vegetables or fruits early in the morning and start the drying process as soon as possible to prevent browning or wilting.

Vegetables

Vegetables must be blanched to inactivate enzymes. The blanching time is counted as soon as the vegetable is immersed in vigorously boiling water. Do not add so much food that the water stops boiling. The quality of water used to blanch the vegetables can have an effect on the texture of certain vegetables. Very hard water can cause the toughening of vegetables, such as green beans. If you have problems with excessively tough green beans, check into the level of hardness in your water supply.

1. *To Blanch in Boiling Water*
   - Use 1 gallon water for each pound of vegetable.
   - Bring water to rolling boil.
   - Immerse wire basket or mesh bag containing vegetable.
   - Cover kettle and boil at top heat the required length of time.
   - Begin counting time as you place the vegetable in water. You may use the same blanching water 2 or 3 times. Keep it at required level. Change the water if it becomes cloudy.
   - Drain the vegetables thoroughly.
2. *To Blanch in Steam*

— Put 1 inch of water in kettle, bring to a rolling boil.

— Suspend a thin layer of vegetables in steaming basket or loose cheese cloth bag over rapidly boiling water.

— Cover and steam blanch vegetables required amount of time as listed on table.

— Remove from steamer.

Fruits

Sodium Bisulfite: Pretreating fruit with sodium bisulfite will reduce vitamin loss, flavor loss, browning, and deterioration during storage. Sodium sulfite and sodium metabisulfite, available at wine-making shops, may also be used. However, sulfite-sensitive individuals should not use this method. Prepare a solution of 1 tablespoon sodium bisulfite, or 2 tablespoons sodium sulfite, or 4 tablespoons of sodium metabisulfite to a gallon of water. Soak slices of fruit for 5 minutes and halves of fruit for 15 minutes. When soaking is complete, remove fruit and rinse lightly under cold tap water. Then place the fruit on the drying trays.

Ascorbic Acid: Ascorbic acid (vitamin C) mixed with water is a safe way to prevent fruit browning. However, its protection does not last as long as sulfiting. Ascorbic acid is available in the powdered or tablet form, from drugstores or grocery stores. One teaspoon of powdered ascorbic acid is equal to 3000 mg of ascorbic acid in tablet form.

Directions for Use: Mix 1 teaspoon of powdered ascorbic acid (or 3000 mg of ascorbic acid tablets, crushed) in 2 cups water. Place the fruit in the solution for 3 to 5 minutes. Remove fruit, drain well and place on dryer trays. After this solution is used twice, add more acid.

Fruit Juice Dip: A fruit juice that is high in vitamin C can also be used as a pretreatment, though it is not as effective as pure ascorbic acid. Juices high in vitamin C include orange, lemon, pineapple, grape and cranberry. Each juice adds its own color and flavor to the fruit.

Directions for Use: Place enough juice to cover fruit in a bowl. Add cut fruit. Soak 3 to 5 minutes, remove fruit, drain well and place on dryer trays. This solution may be used twice, before being replaced.

Fruit Leathers: These are chewy candy-like products which are made by pureeing fresh fruits in a blender or food processor. The thick pureed fruit is poured onto a dehydrator tray lined with 4 mil food grade plastic and dried. The puree layer should not be more than ¼-inch thick. Leave a 1 inch border around the puree to allow for spreading during drying. It usually takes 6 to 8 hours to dry fruit leathers.

Dried vegetables need about 2 hours soaking time before cooking. When you soak or rehydrate the vegetables they should plump to nearly the same size they were when fresh. Start with 1½ to 2 cups of water for each cup of dried vegetables. If necessary, add more water during the soaking process. Cook the vegetables in the same water in which they have soaked to save nutrients. Boil or simmer dried vegetables in soups, stews, or other dishes cooked in liquid. Most dried fruit can be eaten or used in recipes as it is. If you wish to plump or soften the fruit slightly to make it more chewable, you can use one of these methods:

— Cover the dried fruit with boiling water. Let it stand for 5 minutes then drain.

— Place the dried fruit in the top of a steamer over boiling water and steam 3 to 5 minutes until the fruit is plump.

Eggs, fish, poultry, and meat (except beef jerky) are not recommended for home drying. Salmonella and Staphylococcus bacteria, which thrive on these foods, can survive and grow at low temperatures used to dry meat and dairy products. These bacteria grow very rapidly in meat and poultry products because all the nutrient needs of these pathogenic or disease producing bacteria are supplied by meats, eggs, and dairy products.

The growth of the pathogenic bacteria will stop when 60 percent ERH is reached, but when water is added to the product, the bacteria will grow again. The poisonous toxin produced by Staphylococcus is not destroyed by cooking the food. Salmonella and Staphylococcus have caused food poisoning outbreaks in home-dried foods.

Freezing

Probably as old as drying, many Arctic communities would preserve food in holes or larders dug into the ice. There is a tradition in Scandinavia of preserving fish and especially herrings in this way. The addition of urine at the time of packing the fish into the ice is said to assist in preservation and to improve the flavour of the food when eaten. Freezing is also one of the most commonly used processes commercially and domestically for preserving a very wide range of food stuffs including prepared footstuffs which would not have required freezing in their unprepared state. I. e. Potato waffles are stores in the freezer but potatoes themselves require only a cool dark place to ensure many months' storage. Cold stores provide large volume, long term storage for strategic food stocks held in case of national emergency in many countries.

Foods in the freezer — are they safe? Every year, thousands of callers to the USDA Meat and Poultry Hotline aren't sure about the safety of items stored in their own home freezers. The confusion seems to be based on the fact that few people understand how freezing protects food. Here is some information on how to freeze food safely and how long to keep it. What Can You Freeze?You can freeze almost any food. Some exceptions are canned food or eggs in shells. However, once the food (such as a ham) is out of the can, you may freeze it. Being able to freeze food and being pleased with the quality after defrosting are two different things.

Some foods simply don't freeze well. Examples are mayonnaise, cream sauce and lettuce. Raw meat and poultry maintain their quality longer than their cooked counterparts because moisture is lost during cooking. Is Frozen Food Safe?Food stored constantly at 0 °F will always be safe. Only the quality suffers with lengthy freezer storage. Freezing keeps food safe by slowing the movement of molecules, causing microbes to enter a dormant stage. Freezing preserves food for extended periods because it prevents the growth of microorganisms that cause both food spoilage and foodborne illness. Does Freezing Destroy Bacteria & Parasites?Freezing to 0 °F inactivates any microbes — bacteria, yeasts and molds — present in food.

Once thawed, however, these microbes can again become active, multiplying under the right conditions to levels that can lead to foodborne illness. Since they will then grow at about the same rate as microorganisms on fresh food, you must handle thawed items as you would any perishable food. Trichina and other parasites can be destroyed by sub-zero freezing temperatures. However, very strict government-supervised conditions must be met. It is not recommended to rely on home freezing to destroy trichina. Thorough cooking will destroy all parasites. Freshness & QualityFreshness and quality at the time of freezing affect the condition of frozen foods. If frozen at peak quality, foods emerge tasting better than foods frozen near the end of their useful life.

So freeze items you won't use quickly sooner rather than later. Store all foods at 0° F or lower to retain vitamin content, color, flavor and texture. Nutrient RetentionThe freezing process itself does not destroy nutrients. In meat and poultry products, there is little change in nutrient value during freezer storage. EnzymesEnzyme activity can lead to the deterioration of food quality. Enzymes present in animals, vegetables and fruit promote chemical reactions, such as ripening. Freezing only slows the enzyme activity that takes place in foods. It does not halt these reactions which continue after harvesting.

Enzyme activity does not harm frozen meats or fish and is neutralized by the acids in frozen fruits. But most vegetables that freeze well are low acid and require a brief, partial cooking to prevent deterioration. This is called "blanching. " For successful freezing, blanch or partially cook vegetables in boiling water or in a microwave oven. Then rapidly chill the vegetables prior to freezing and storage. Consult a cookbook for timing. PackagingProper packaging helps maintain quality and prevent "freezer burn. " It is safe to freeze meat or poultry directly in its supermarket wrapping but this type of wrap is permeable to air. Unless you will be using the food in a month or two, overwrap these packages as you would any food for long-term storage using airtight heavy-duty foil, (freezer) plastic wrap or freezer paper, or place the package inside a (freezer) plastic bag.

Use these materials or airtight freezer containers to repackage family packs into smaller amounts. It is not necessary to rinse meat and poultry before freezing. Freeze unopened vacuum packages as is. If you notice that a package has accidentally been torn or has opened while food is in the freezer, the food is still safe to use; merely overwrap or rewrap it. Freezer BurnFreezer burn does not make food unsafe, merely dry in spots. It appears as grayish-brown leathery spots and is caused by air reaching the surface of the food. Cut freezer-burned portions away either before or after cooking the food. Heavily freezer-burned foods may have to be discarded for quality reasons. Color ChangesColor changes can occur in frozen foods.

The bright red color of meat as purchased usually turns dark or pale brown depending on its variety. This may be due to lack of oxygen, freezer burn or abnormally long storage. Freezing doesn't usually cause color changes in poultry. However, the bones and the meat near them can become dark. Bone darkening results when pigment seeps through the porous bones of young poultry into the surrounding tissues when the poultry meat is frozen and thawed. The dulling of color in frozen vegetables and cooked foods is usually the result of excessive drying due to improper packaging or over-lengthy storage.

Freeze food as fast as possible to maintain its quality. Rapid freezing prevents undesirable large ice crystals from forming throughout the product because the molecules don't have time to take their positions in the characteristic six-sided snowflake. Slow freezing creates large, disruptive ice crystals. During thawing, they damage the cells and dissolve emulsions. This causes meat to "drip"—lose juiciness. Emulsions such as mayonnaise or cream will separate and appear curdled. Ideally, a food 2-inches thick should freeze completely in about 2 hours. If your home freezer has a "quick-freeze" shelf, use it. Never stack packages to be frozen.

Instead, spread them out in one layer on various shelves, stacking them only after frozen solid. Refrigerator - FreezersIf a refrigerator freezing compartment can't maintain zero degrees or if the door is opened frequently, use it for short-term food storage. Eat those foods as soon as possible for best quality. Use a free-standing freezer set at 0° F or below for long-term storage of frozen foods. Keep a thermometer in your freezing compartment or freezer to check the temperature. This is important if you experience power-out or mechanical problems.

Because freezing keeps food safe almost indefinitely, recommended storage times are for quality only. Never defrost foods in a garage, basement, car, dishwasher or plastic garbage bag; out on the kitchen counter, outdoors or on the porch. These methods can leave your foods unsafe to eat. There are three safe ways to defrost food: in the refrigerator, in cold water, or in the microwave. It's best to plan ahead for slow, safe thawing in the refrigerator. Small items may defrost overnight; most foods require a day or two. And large items like turkeys may take longer, approximately one day for each 5 pounds of weight. For faster defrosting, place food in a leak proof plastic bag and immerse it in cold water. (If the bag leaks, bacteria from the air or surrounding environment could be introduced into the food. Tissues can also absorb water like a sponge, resulting in a watery product.)

Check the water frequently to be sure it stays cold. Change the water every 30 minutes. After thawing, cook immediately. When microwave-defrosting food, plan to cook it immediately after thawing because some areas of the food may become warm and begin to cook during microwaving. RefreezingOnce food is thawed in the refrigerator, it is safe to refreeze it without cooking, although there may be a loss of quality due to the moisture lost through defrosting. After cooking raw foods which were previously frozen, it is safe to freeze the cooked foods. If previously cooked foods are thawed in the refrigerator, you may refreeze the unused portion. If you purchase previously frozen meat, poultry or fish at a retail store, you can refreeze if it has been handled properly.

Raw or cooked meat, poultry or casseroles can be cooked or reheated from the frozen state. However, it will take approximately one and a half times the usual cooking time for food which has been thawed. Remember to discard any wrapping or absorbent paper from meat or poultry. When cooking whole poultry, remove the giblet pack from the cavity as soon as you can loosen it. Cook the giblets separately. Read the label on USDA-inspected frozen meat and poultry products. Some, such as pre-stuffed whole birds, must be cooked from the frozen state to ensure a safely cooked product.

The inspection mark on the packaging tells you the product was prepared in a USDA or State-inspected plant under controlled conditions. Follow the package directions for thawing, reheating, and storing. Power Outage in FreezerIf there is a power outage, the freezer fails, or if the freezer door has been left ajar by mistake, the food may still be safe to use. As long as a freezer with its door ajar is continuing to cool, the foods should stay safe overnight. If a repairman is on the way or it appears the power will be on soon, just don't open the freezer door. A freezer full of food will usually keep about 2 days if the door is kept shut; a half-full freezer will last about a day.

The freezing compartment in a refrigerator may not keep foods frozen as long. If the freezer is not full, quickly group packages together so they will retain the cold more effectively. Separate meat and poultry items from other foods so if they begin to thaw, their juices won't drip onto other foods. When the power is off, you may want to put dry ice, block ice, or bags of ice in the freezer or transfer foods to a friend's freezer until power is restored. Use an appliance thermometer to monitor the temperature. When it is freezing outside and there is snow on the ground, it seems like a good place to keep food until the power comes on; however, frozen food can thaw if it is exposed to the sun's rays even when the temperature is very cold.

Refrigerated food may become too warm and foodborne bacteria could grow. The outside temperature could vary hour by hour and the temperature outside will not protect refrigerated and frozen food. Additionally, perishable items could be exposed to unsanitary conditions or to animals. Animals may harbor bacteria or disease; never consume food that has come in contact with an animal. To determine the safety of foods when the power goes on, check their condition and temperature. If food is partly frozen, still has ice crystals, or is as cold as if it were in a refrigerator (40 °F), it is safe to refreeze or use. It's not necessary to cook raw foods before refreezing. Discard foods that have been warmer than 40 °F for more than 2 hours. Discard any foods that have been contaminated by raw meat juices.

Dispose of soft or melted ice cream for quality's sake. Frozen CansAccidentally frozen cans, such as those left in a car or basement in sub-zero temperatures, can present health problems. If the cans are merely swollen — and you are sure the swelling was caused by freezing — the cans may still be usable. Let the can thaw in the refrigerator before opening. If the product doesn't look and/or smell normal, throw it out.

If the seams have rusted or burst, throw the cans out immediately, wrapping the burst can in plastic and disposing the food where no one, including animals can get it. Frozen EggsShell eggs should not be frozen. If an egg accidentally freezes and the shell cracked during freezing, discard the egg. Keep an uncracked egg frozen until needed; then thaw in the refrigerator. It can be hard cooked successfully but other uses may be limited. That's because freezing causes the yolk to become thick and syrupy so it will not flow like an unfrozen yolk or blend very well with the egg white or other ingredients.

Freezer Storage Chart (0 °F)

Item	Months
Bacon and Sausage	1 to 2
Casseroles	2 to 3

Egg whites or egg substitutes	12
Gravy, meat or poultry	2 to 3
Ham, Hotdogs and Lunchmeats	1 to 2
Meat, uncooked roasts	4 to 12
Meat, uncooked steaks or chops	4 to 12
Meat, uncooked ground	3 to 4
Meat, cooked	2 to 3
Poultry, uncooked whole	12
Poultry, uncooked parts	9
Poultry, uncooked giblets	3 to 4
Poultry, cooked	4
Soups and Stews	2 to 3
Wild game, uncooked	8 to 12

Preparing food ahead of time and freezing it can save time, energy and money. Frozen cooked foods also add variety to your menu, offer quick meals for unexpected company and provide nutritious choices for busy days. When you are preparing a main dish, it takes only a little more effort and time to make enough for several meals. You can freeze all of the prepared food in meal size packages, or serve part of the food immediately and freeze the rest. It is more economical to make your own supply of prepared dishes than to purchase commercially prepared foods. Consider freezing:

— Leftovers that cannot be used immediately.

— Foods that ordinarily take a long time to prepare.

— Seasonal fruits and vegetables.

— Foods you can prepare in quantity.

— Foods that still taste good after a reasonable storage time.

Hints for freezing

— Select only fresh, high quality ingredients because freezing does not improve the quality of food.

— Slightly undercook prepared foods. They will finish cooking when reheated.

— Cool foods quickly before packaging. Place the pan of food in a large pan of ice water, crushed ice or cubes. Stirring will help cool the food faster. Use a fan to cool foods that cannot be stirred.

— Freeze food promptly as soon as it is cooled to room temperature.

— Put no more unfrozen food in the freezer than will freeze within 24 hours. Usually this is 2 or 3 pounds per cubic foot of freezer capacity. Stack the food after it is frozen.

— Plan to use frozen prepared foods within a short time. Keep using foods from the freezer and replenish with fresh stock. This makes greater use of freezer space, lowers the cost per pound of food stores, and keeps your store of food fresh.

— The temperature of the freezer should not go above 0°F. Fluctuating temperatures and temperatures that are not low enough cause loss of quality.

— Foods that do not freeze well include mayonnaise, cream puddings and fillings, custard, gelatin salads, cheese, the whites of hard cooked eggs and uncooked egg yolks.

Hints for Packaging

— Use freezer containers or wrappings of moisture/vapor-resistant material.

— Pack food compactly into the container to reduce the amount of air in the package. Allow head room for expansion as food freezes.

— In quart containers, the food may be separated into two or three layers by a double thickness of water resistant wrapping material.

— Quart containers hold four to six servings; pints, two to three.

— Choose containers by the number of servings you will want to serve.

— Use only containers with wide top openings. Food can then be removed without thawing.

— Freeze the prepared foods in your favorite casserole dish. The food can be removed after freezing, wrapped and returned to the freezer for storage.

— For microwave reheating, use plastic wrap for wrapping small amounts of quick breads or breads. Casseroles should be approved for microwave use.

— Label and date all packages, and keep an inventory of all frozen food.

Freeze Drying

Frozen food is subjected to very low air pressures which cause the water content to evaporate without passing through the water stage. This produces a very low water content food without addition of cooking flavours or presence of de-natured proteins. Freeze drying is commonly used to preserve small vegetables such as peas and beans and also a wide range of ready-made foods, such as soups and other convenience foods which only require the addition of hot water prior to consumption. Many foods intended for campers and hikers are freeze dried because of the considerable weight advantage over non freeze dried items. Freeze drying is also widely used for preparation of dried milk and whey products.

Smoking

Smoking is sometimes done in conjunction with drying. Although not sufficient by itself to permit long term storage of food, smoking adds chemicals, particularly poly aromatic hydrocarbons (PAHs) that help inhibit the growth of micro-organisms.

Vacuum Packing

Vacuum-packing stores food in a vacuum environment, usually in an air-tight bag or bottle. The vacuum environment strips bacteria of oxygen needed for survival, hence preventing the food from spoiling. Vacuum-packing is commonly used for storing nuts.

Curing

Curing draws moisture from the meat through a process of osmosis. Meat is cured with salt or sugar, or a combination of the two. Nitrates and nitrites are also often used to cure meat.

Sugar

Sugar is used to preserve fruits, either in syrup with fruit such as apples, pears, peaches, apricots, plums or in crystalised form where the preserved material is cooked in sugar to the point of crystralisation and the resultant product is then stored dry. This method is used for the skins of citrus fruit (candied peel)), angelica and ginger. A modification of this process produces glacé fruit such as glacé cherries where the fruit is preserved in sugar but is then extracted from the syrup and sold, the preservation being maintained by the sugar content of the fruit and the superficial coating of syrup. The use of sugar is often combined with alcohol for preservation of luxury products such as fruit in Brandy or other sprits. These should not be confused with fruit flavoured spirits such as Cherry Brandy or Sloe gin

Pickling

Pickling is a method of preserving food by placing it or cooking it in a substance that inhibits or kills bacteria and other micro-organisms, This material must also be fit for human consumption. Typical pickling agents include brine (high in salt), vinegar, ethanol and vegetable oil especially olive oil but also many other oils. Most pickling processes also involve heating or boiling so that the food being preserved becomes saturated with the pickling agent. A less-common form of pickling uses sodium hydroxide (lye) to make the food too alkaline for bacterial growth. Lye will saponify fats in the food, which will change its flavor and texture. Lutefisk uses lye in its preparation, as do some olive recipes.

Canning and Bottling

Canning involves cooking fruits or vegetables, sealing them in sterile cans or jars, and boiling the containers to kill or weaken any remaining bacteria. Various foods have varying degrees of natural protection against spoilage and may require that the final step occur in a pressure cooker. High-acid fruits like strawberries require no preservatives to can and only a short boiling cycle, whereas marginal fruits such as tomatoes require longer boiling and addition of other acidic elements. Many vegetables require pressure canning. Food preserved by canning or bottling is at immediate risk of spoilage once the can or bottle has been opened.

Canning fruits and vegetables

To can means to heat process food in a glass jar with a lid in place. Heat processing kills microorganisms -- bacteria, yeast, and mold — that contaminate food and cause food spoilage and/or foodborne illness. Processing can be done in a water bath canner or a pressure canner, depending on the food's acidity. High-acid foods (all fruits except figs that are not acidified) can be safely processed in a water bath canner. Acidified figs and tomatoes can also be safely processed in a water bath canner. Microorganisms in or on high-acid foods are easily killed at 212F (the temperature of boiling water).

Low-acid foods (vegetables and tomatoes that are not acidified) must be processed in a pressure canner. The bacteria that produces botulinum toxin cannot grow in high-acid foods but can grow in low-acid foods. The bacteria, Clostridium botulinum, have spores that survive for hours in boiling water. However, these spores are destroyed within a reasonable amount of time at 240F (the temperature reached inside a weighted gauge pressure canner at 10 pounds pressure and at 11 pounds pressure inside a dial-gauge canner).

If low-acid food is processed in a water bath canner, botulinum spores on the food will survive. In the absence of air, a condition found inside a jar after processing, the spores become living bacteria. As the bacteria grow, they form toxins. Eating even a drop of this potent toxin can be fatal to humans and animals. Many cases of botulism have been associated with eating low-acid foods that were improperly canned at home.

To make sure your home canned foods are safe, carefully follow the canning instructions in this fact sheet. Process high-acid foods in a water bath canner and low-acid foods in a pressure canner. Never process any foods in a conventional oven, microwave oven, steamer or dishwasher, as these methods do not kill microorganisms that cause food spoilage and/or foodborne illness.

Before each canning season, assemble and evaluate all of your canning equipment.

Canning jars: Use only standard canning jars (also called Mason jars) with the manufacturer's name printed on the side. These jars can withstand the temperature extremes of canning. And, the sealing edge is smooth and flat so lids will seal properly. Never use commercial jars, such as mayonnaise and pickle jars, for home canning.

These jars are not very resistant to temperature extremes; they break easily. Also, lids may not seal on these jars because their sealing edge may be rounded rather than flat. Finally, the neck of the jar may be so short that the screw band will not hold the lid firmly in place during processing. Canning jars must be in perfect condition. Check all jars, new and used, for hairline cracks, chips or nicks on the sealing edge. Such defects can result in breakage or failure to seal.

Canning lids: The only safe way to seal a canning jar is with a two-piece canning lid. The set consists of a flat metal lid and a screw band. The lid has a sealing compound around the edge and is enameled on the under side to prevent food from reacting with the metal. The screw band holds the lid in place during processing. A vacuum seal forms during cooling, after the jar is removed from the canner. Screw bands that are in good condition may be reused, but always use new lids. Do not use screw bands that are bent or badly rusted.

Two types of canners: Use a water bath canner to process high-acid foods. A water bath canner is a large deep kettle that has a cover and a rack to hold jars. You can also use a big, covered pot that is deep enough to allow water to extend 1 to 2 inches over the tops of the jars with enough room for the water to boil briskly. Also add a rack to keep the jars off the bottom of the pot.

Use a pressure canner to process low-acid foods: A pressure canner is a deep, heavy kettle that has a rack on the bottom for jars to stand on, a tight-fitting lid with a gasket, and a pressure gauge. The gasket keeps steam from leaking out around the cover. If the gasket is worn, stretched, or hardened, replace it. There are two types of pressure measuring gauges, a dial gauge and a weighted gauge.

A dial gauge has a needle that moves along a numbered scale to indicate the pressure inside the canner. Each year check the dial gauge, old or new, for accuracy and during the canning season if heavily used. Call your county extension agent who has food safety responsibilities to find out where testing can be done.

A weighted gauge fits over the air vent tube. It permits pressure in the canner to rise to the desired point and then releases excess steam by "jiggling" or "rocking" to keep the pressure from going higher. Weighted gauges do not need testing for accuracy, but they do need to be kept clean. Check the vent tube to be sure it hasn't been bent or damaged during use.

Wash canning jars in a dishwasher or in hot soapy water and rinse well. Keep jars hot by leaving them in the dishwasher or in hot water until you are ready to fill them. Jars do not need to be sterilized, as this will be accomplished during processing. Jars must be sterilized if they are used for jellied products. Wash and rinse screw bands. Follow the manufacturer's directions for preparing lids. They may need to be boiled in water for a few minutes before use.

Preparing fruits and vegetables for processing

Select high quality, unblemished fruits and vegetables for

canning. Canning will not improve quality. Can them as soon as possible after harvesting. If you must store fruits and vegetables before canning, keep them in the refrigerator. If you buy fruits or vegetables to can, get them fresh from a local farmer's market, a roadside stand or a pick- your-own farm. Thoroughly wash fruits and vegetables before canning even if they will be peeled. Garden soil contains bacteria.

Wash by scrubbing with a vegetable brush and rinsing thoroughly. Or, if more practical, soak in water for several minutes. Lift out of the water so the soil that has been washed off won't settle back on the food. Peel, pit, and/or slice only as much food as you can process at one time. Some fruits and vegetables (apples, apricots, nectarines, peaches, pears and potatoes) darken when cut. To prevent darkening, keep raw, prepared produce in a solution of one teaspoon ascorbic acid to one gallon of cold water. Check among the canners' supplies in the supermarket to get this product.

Sugar and salt

Sugar helps retain the color, shape, and texture of canned fruits. Sugar is usually added as a syrup. To make syrup, pour 4 cups of water into a saucepan and add: 2 cups of sugar to make 5 cups of light syrup or 3 cups of sugar to make 5 1/2 cups of medium syrup or 4 1/4 cups of sugar to make 6 1/2 cups of heavy syrup. Heat until the sugar dissolves. Make 1 to 1-1/2 cups of syrup for each quart of fruit.

Up to half the sugar used in making syrup can be replaced with light corn syrup or mild-flavored honey. Fruits also can be safely canned without sugar. Pack the fruit in extracted juice, in juice from another fruit (such as bottled apple juice, pineapple juice, or white grape juice) or in water. Salt may be added to vegetables and tomatoes before canning. Because its only function is flavor, it can safely be omitted. Canning fruits and vegetables without adding sugar or salt does not affect processing times or microbiological safety.

Packing methods

The two methods of packing food into canning jars are raw pack and hot pack. Raw pack is packing raw, prepared food into clean, hot jars and then adding hot liquid. Fruits and most vegetables need to be packed tightly because they will shrink during processing. However, raw corn, lima beans, and peas should be packed loosely, as they will expand. For a hot pack, heat prepared food to boiling, or partially cook it. It should be loosely packed into clean, hot jars while it is still boiling hot. A hot pack takes more time but has been found to result in higher quality canned foods.

For either packing method, pack high-acid foods, including tomatoes and acidified figs, to within 1/2-inch of the top of the jar. Pack low-acid foods to within 1 inch of the top of the jar. After food is packed into jars, wipe the jar rims clean. Put on the lid with the sealing compound next to the jar rim. Screw the band down firmly so that it is hand-tight. Do not use a jar wrench to tighten screw bands. There must be enough "give" for air to escape from the jars during processing. Process food promptly after packing into jars and adjusting lids. Processing times in recommended resources are given for pints and quarts. If you are using half-pint jars, use processing times for pints. For 1-1/2 pint jars, use processing times for quarts. Fruit juice is the only product that may be canned in a half-gallon jar.

If you live at an altitude of more than 1,000 feet, you will need to modify the processing time for high-acid foods and the pounds pressure you use to process low-acid foods. The processing instructions presented in most recommended resources are for altitudes of 0-1000 feet. To determine your altitude, contact the North Carolina Geological Survey Office. Their address is: 512 North Salisbury Street, Raleigh, NC 27604. Their telephone number is 919-733-2423. After determining your altitude, your local extension center can help you to determine changes you need to make to your canning instructions.

Use a water bath canner to process acidified tomatoes, acidified figs, and all other fruits. There are no instructions for processing tomato products that are not acidified. A pressure canner can be used to process high-acid foods but the quality will not be as good.

1. Fill the canner half full with water; then cover and heat. For raw packed food, have the water hot but not boiling. For hot packed food, have the water boiling.
2. Using a jlar lifter, place jars filled with food on the rack in the canner. If necessary, add boiling water to bring water 1 to 2 inches over the tops of the jars. Do not pour boiling water directly on jars. Cover.
3. When water comes to a rolling boil, start counting the processing time. Keep water at a boil for the entire processing time. Add more boiling water to keep water 1 to 2 inches above jars.
4. As soon as the processing time is up, use a jar lifter to remove jars from canner. If liquid boiled out of the jars during processing, do not open them to add more. Do not retighten screw bands, even if they are noticeably loose.

If you live at an altitude of 0-1000 feet and are using a weighted gauge pressure canner, process at 10 pounds pressure. If you live at altitudes above 1,000 feet, process at 15 pounds pressure. If you live at an altitude of 0-2,000 feet and are using a dial gauge pressure canner, use 11 pounds pressure. If you live at an altitude more than 2,000 feet, you need to increase the pounds pressure at which you process foods. Contact your county extension center to get this information. If tomato products are acidified, they can be safely processed in a water bath canner or a pressure canner. Not instructions are available for processing tomatoes that are not acidified. Here are some pointers for using a pressure canner:

5. Pour 2 or 3 inches of water in the bottom of the canner and heat to boiling.
6. Set jars on the rack in the canner. If you have two layers of jars in the canner, use a rack between them and stagger the second layer.
7. Fasten the canner cover securely so steam cannot escape except through the vent.
8. Once steam pours steadily from vent, let it escape for 10 minutes to drive all air from the canner. During processing, the canner must be filled with steam, not air, since it is steam that reaches the desired temperature of 240F.
9. Processing time:
    a. If the canner has a weighted gauge, start counting the processing time when it jiggles or rocks. The target pressure for this type of canner is 10 pounds pressure. Adjust heat so that gauge jiggles 2 or 3 times a minute or maintains a slow, steady, rocking motion.
    b. If the canner has a dial gauge, bring pressure up quickly to 8 pounds, then adjust the heat to maintain 11 pounds pressure. Start counting the processing times when the gauge registers 11 pounds pressure.

10. When the processing time is up, turn off the burner. (If you are using a coal or wood stove, remove the canner from heat.) Let the pressure in the canner drop to zero by itself. This may take 45 minutes in a 16-quart canner filled with jars and almost an hour in a 22-quart canner. If the vent is opened before the pressure drops to zero or if the cooling is rushed by cold running water over the canner, liquid will be lost from the jars.
11. When the pressure has dropped to zero, open the vent or remove the weighted gauge. (With a weighted gauge canner, pressure is completely reduced if no steam escapes when the gauge is nudged or tilted. If steam spurts out, pressure is not yet down.)
12. Remove the canner cover carefully, tilting it away from your face so that the rising steam cannot burn your face or hands.
13. Remove jars from the canner. If liquid boiled out of jars during processing, do not open jars to add more liquid. Do not retighten screw bands, even if they are noticeably loose.
14. Place hot jars upright to cool on a towel or rack. Leave space between them so air can circulate. Keep jars our of drafts.

Boiling water canners

Most boiling water canners are made of aluminum or porcelain-covered steel. They have fitted lids and removable racks that are either perforated or shaped wire racks. The canner must be deep enough so that at least one inch of briskly boiling water will be over the tops of jars during processing. Some boiling water canners do not have completely flat bottoms. A flat bottom must be used on an electric range. Either a flat or ridged bottom may be used on a gas burner. To ensure uniform processing of all jars with an electric range, the canner should be no more than 4 inches wider in diameter than the element on which it is heated. Follow these steps for successful boiling water canning:

1. Before you start preparing your food, fill the canner half full with clean warm water.
2. Center the canner over the burner and preheat the water to 140 degrees F. for raw-packed foods and to 180 degrees F. for hot-packed foods. You can begin preparing food for your jars while this water is preheating.
3. Load filled jars, fitted with lids, into the canner one at a time, using a jar lifter. When moving jars with a jar lifter, make sure the jar lifter is securely positioned below the neck of the jar (below the screw band of the lid). Keep the jar upright at all times. Tilting the jar could cause food to spill into the sealing area of the lid. If you have a shaped wire rack that has handles to hold it on the canner sides, above the water in the canner, you can load jars onto the rack in the raised position and then use the handles to lower the rack with jars into the water.
4. Add more boiling water, if needed, so the water level is at least one inch above the jar tops. For process times over 30 minutes, the water level should be 2 inches above the jars.
5. Turn the heat setting to its highest position, cover the canner with its lid and heat until the water boils vigorously.
6. Set a timer (after the water is boiling) for the total minutes required for processing the food.
7. Keep the canner covered for the process time. The heat setting may be lowered as long as a gentle but complete boil is maintained for the entire process time.

8. Add more boiling water during the process, if needed, to keep the water level above the jar tops.
9. If the water stops boiling at any time during the process, turn the heat on its highest setting, bring the water back to a vigorous boil, and begin the timing of the process over, from the beginning (using the total original process time).
10. When the jars have been processed in boiling water for the recommended time, turn off the heat and remove the canner lid.
11. Using a jar lifter, remove the jars one at a time, being careful not to tilt the jars. Carefully place them directly onto a towel or cake cooling rack, leaving at least one inch of space between the jars during cooling. Avoid placing the jars on a cold surface or in a cold draft.
12. Let the jars sit undisturbed while they cool, from 12 to 24 hours. Do not tighten ring bands on the lids or push down on the center of the flat metal lid until the jar is completely cooled.
13. Remove ring bands from sealed jars. Put any unsealed jars in the refrigerator and use first.
14. Wash jars and lids to remove all residues.
15. Label jars and store in a cool, dry place out of direct light.

Pressure canners

Pressure canners for use in the home were extensively redesigned beginning in the 1970's. Models made before the 1970's were heavy-walled kettles with clamp-on or turn-on lids. They were fitted with a dial gauge, a vent port in the form of a petcock or covered with a counterweight, and a safety fuse. Modern pressure canners are lightweight, thin-walled kettles; most have turn-on lids fitted with gaskets. They all have removable racks, an automatic vent/cover lock, a vent port (steam vent), and a safety fuse.

Today's pressure canner may have a dial gauge for indicating the pressure or a weighted gauge, for indicating and regulating the pressure. Pressure canners come deep enough for one layer of quart or smaller size jars, or deep enough for two layers of pint or smaller size jars. Serious errors in processes obtained in pressure canners can occur if any of the following conditions exist:

— The altitude at which the canner is operated is above sea level. Internal canner pressures (and therefore temperatures) are lower at higher altitudes. Canners must be operated at increased pressures as the altitude increases. Check canning instructions for altitude adjustments.

— Air is trapped in the closed canner during the process. Air trapped in a pressure canner lowers the temperature obtained for a given pressure (for example, 10 or 15 pounds pressure) and results in underprocessing. To be safe, all pressure canners must be vented 10 minutes before they are pressurized.

To vent a canner, leave the vent port (steam vent) uncovered (or manually open the petcock on some older models) after you fill the canner and lock the canner lid in place. Heat the canner on high until the water boils and generates steam that can be seen escaping through the open vent port or petcock. When a visible funnel-shape of steam is continuously escaping the canner, set a timer for 10 minutes. After 10 minutes of continuous steam, you can close the petcock or place the counterweight or weighted gauge over the vent port to begin pressurizing the canner.

— An inaccurate dial gauge is used. Dial gauges should be checked for accuracy each year before use. If the gauge reads high or low by more than one pound at 5, 10 or 15 pounds pressure, replace it. If the gauge reads low by 1 pound or less, add that amount to the recommended pressure.

Clean lid gaskets and other parts according to the manufacturer's directions. Use only canners that have the Underwriter's Laboratory (UL) approval to ensure their safety. Follow these steps for successful pressure canning:

1. Center the canner over the burner. When you have your jars of food ready for canning, put the rack and 2 to 3 inches of hot water into the canner. For hot packed foods, you can bring the water to 180 degrees F. ahead of time, but be careful not to boil the water or heat it long enough for the depth to decrease.

2. Place filled jars, fitted with lids, on the jar rack in the canner, using a jar lifter. When moving jars with a jar lifter, make sure the jar lifter is securely positioned below the neck of the jar (below the screw band of the lid). Keep the jar upright at all times. Tilting the jar could cause food to spill into the sealing area of the lid.

3. Fasten the canner lid securely. Leave the weight off the vent port or open the petcock.

4. Turn the heat setting to its highest position. Heat until the water boils and steam flows freely in a funnel-shape from the open vent port or petcock. While maintaining the high heat setting, let the steam flow (exhaust) continuously for 10 minutes.

5. After this venting, or exhausting, of the canner, place the counterweight or weighted gauge on the ventport, or close the petcock. The canner will pressurize during the next 3 to 5 minutes.

6. Start timing the process when the pressure reading on the dial gauge indicates that the recommended

pressure has been reached, or, for canners without dial gauges, when the weighted gauge begins to jiggle or rock as the manufacturer describes.

7. Regulate the heat under the canner to maintain a steady pressure at, or slightly above, the correct gauge pressure. One type of weighted gauge should jiggle 2 or 3 times per minute, while another type should rock slowly throughout the process - check the manufacturer's directions.

   — Loss of pressure at any time can result in underprocessing, or unsafe food.

   — Quick and large pressure variations during processing may cause unnecessary liquid losses from jars.

If at any time pressure goes below the recommended amount, bring the canner back to pressure and begin the timing of the process over, from the beginning (using the total original process time). This is important for the safety of the food.

8. When the timed process is completed, turn off the heat, remove the canner from the heat (electric burner) if possible, and let the canner cool down naturally. While it is cooling, it is also de-pressurizing. Do not force cool the canner. Forced cooling may result in food spoilage. Cooling the canner with cold running water or opening the vent port before the canner is fully depressurized are types of forced cooling. They will also cause loss of liquid from jars and seal failures. Force cooling may also warp the canner lid.

Depressurization of older canner models without dial gauges should be timed. Standard size heavy-walled canners require about 30 minutes when loaded with pints and 45 minutes when loaded with quarts. Newer thin-walled canners cool more rapidly and are equipped with vent locks that are designed to open when the pressure is gone. These canners are depressurized when the piston in the vent lock drops to a normal position. Some of these locks are hidden in handles and cannot be seen; however, the lid will not turn open until the lock is released.

9. After the canner is depressurized, remove the weight from the vent port or open the petcock. Wait 2 minutes (as a safety precaution), unfasten the lid and remove it carefully. Lift the lid with the underside away from you so that the steam coming out of the canner does not burn your face.

10. Using a jar lifter, remove the jars one at a time, being careful not to tilt the jars. Carefully place them directly onto a towel or cake cooling rack, leaving at least one inch of space between the jars during cooling. Avoid placing the jars on a cold surface or in a cold draft.

11. Let the jars sit undisturbed while they cool, from 12 to 24 hours. Do not tighten ring bands on the lids or push down on the center of the flat metal lid until the jar is completely cooled.

12. Remove ring bands from sealed jars. Put any unsealed jars in the refrigerator and use first.

13. Wash jars and lids to remove all residues.

14. Label jars and store in a cool, dry place out of direct light.

Dry the canner, lid and gasket. Take off removable petcocks and safety valves; wash and dry thoroughly.

Jellying

Food may be preserved by cooking in a material that solidifies to form a gel. Such materials include gelatine, agar, maize flour and arrowroot flour. Some foods naturally form a protein gel when cooked such as Eels and elvers, and Sipunculid worms which are a delicacy in the town of Xiamen in Fujian province of China. Jellied eels are a delicacy in the East End of London where they are eaten with mashed potatoes. Potted meats in aspic, (the gel made from arrowroot flour) were a common way of serving meat off-cuts in the UK until the 1950s

Irradiation

A 1950s issue of Popular Mechanics details the impending arrival of "food irradiation". However, at the present time, the implications surrounding the irradiation of food are still not fully understood, and the technology is therefore still not in widespread use. However, irradiation of potatoes, strawberries, and meat is common in many countries where refrigerated facilities and trucks are not common. In 2002, the FDA permitted irradiation of meat and poultry to reduce the spread of E. coli and salmonella. In the US and most of Europe irradiation of spices is common, as the only alternative (treatment with gas) has been shown to be potentially carcinogenic. The process is called "cold pasteurization" to avoid the reduced sales from negative implications of the term "irradiation".

Modified Atmosphere

Modified atmosphere is a way to preserve food operating on the atmosphere around it. Salad crops which are notoriously difficult to preserve are now being packaged in sealed bags with an atmosphere modified to reduce the oxygen concentration and increase the carbon dioxide concentration. There is concern that although salad vegetables retain their appearance and texture in such conditions, this method of preservation may not retain nutrient content, especially vitamins.

Grains may be preserved using carbon dioxide. A block of dry ice is placed in the bottom and the can is filled with grain. The can is then "burped" of excess gas. The carbon dioxide from the sublimation of the dry ice prevents insects, mold, and oxidation from damaging the grain. Grain stored in this way can survive five years in a moist garage.

Clamps

Many root vegetables are very resistant to spoilage and require no other preservation other than storage in cool dark conditions, usually in field clamps.

Biological Processes

Some foods, such as many traditional cheeses, will keep for a long time without use of any special procedures. The preservation occurs because of the presence in very high numbers of beneficial bacteria or fungi which use their own biological defences to prevent other organisms gaining a foot-hold.

9

Food Irradiation

Food irradiation is the treatment of food by a certain type of energy. The process involves exposing the food, either packaged or in bulk, to carefully controlled amounts of ionizing radiation for a specific time to achieve certain desirable objectives as will be detailed later in the text. The process cannot increase the normal radioactivity level of the food, regardless of how long the food is exposed to the radiation, or how much of an energy "dose" is absorbed. It can prevent the division of microorganisms which cause food spoilage, such as bacteria and moulds, by changing their molecular structure. It can also slow down ripening or maturation of certain fruits and vegetables by modifying/altering the physiological processes of the plant tissues.

Alongside traditional methods of processing and preserving food, the technology of food irradiation is gaining more and more attention around the world. Although regarded as a new technology by some individuals, research on food irradiation dates back to the turn of the century with the first USA and British patents being issued in 1905 for the use of ionizing radiation to kill bacteria in food.

Today, health and safety authorities in over 40 countries have approved irradiation of over 60 different foods, ranging from spices to grains to deboned chicken meat, to beef, to fruits and vegetables. As of August 1999, over 30 countries are irradiating food for commercial purposes. There are approximately 60 irradiation facilities being used for this purpose with more under construction or at the planning stage.

Interest in the irradiation process is increasing because of persistently high food losses from infestation, contamination, and spoilage; mounting concerns over food-borne diseases; and growing international trade in food products that must meet strict import standards of quality and quarantine, all areas in which food irradiation has demonstrated practical benefits when integrated within an established system for the safe handling and distribution of food.

In addition, with increasingly restricted regulations or complete prohibition on the use of a number of chemical fumigants for insect and microbial control in food, irradiation is an effective alternative to protect food against insect damage and as a quarantine treatment of fresh produce. The FAO has estimated that worldwide about 25% of all food production is lost to insects, bacteria and rodents after harvesting. The use of irradiation alone as a preservation technique will not solve all the problems of post-harvest food losses, but it can play an important role in cutting losses and reducing the dependence on chemical pesticides. Many countries lose vast amounts of grain because of insect infestation and moulds.

For roots and tubers, sprouting is the major cause of losses. Several countries, including Bangladesh, Chile, China, Hungary, Japan, Republic of Korea and Thailand are irradiating one or more food products grains, potatoes, spices, dried fish, onions, garlic, etc.) to control food losses on a commercial basis. Foodborne diseases pose a widespread threat to human health and they are an important cause of reduced economic productivity even in advanced countries which have modern food processing and distribution systems.

In developing countries, diseases caused by parasites such as Taenia solium and Trichinella spiralis constitute a major problem, and together with bacterial foodborne diseases, account for hundreds of millions of cases per year. The relatively low doses of radiation needed to destroy certain bacteria in food can be useful in controlling foodborne disease.

Electron beam irradiation of blocks of frozen mechanically deboned, poultry meat is carried out industrially in France. Spices are being irradiated (instead of being fumigated) in many countries. Trade in food products is a major factor in regional and international commerce, and markets are growing. The inability of countries to satisfy each other's quarantine and public health regulations is a major barrier to trade. For example, not all countries allow importation of chemicallytreated fruit. Moreover, major importing countries, including the USA and Japan, have banned the use of and the import of produce treated with certain fumigants identified as health hazards.

Each year a few hundred thousand tonnes of food products and ingredients are irradiated worldwide. This amount is small in comparison to the total volumes of processed foods and not many of these irradiated food products enter international commerce. One factor influencing the speed with which food irradiation is being adopted is public understanding and acceptance of the process. Contrary to earlier estimates it has been demonstrated that when irradiated foods are available, consumers have purchased them because of their satisfaction with product quality and safety. It is normal to seek reassurance as to the safety and effectiveness of any new process or technology. Therefore, it is hoped that this revised publication will help address concerns and correct myths about food irradiation.

SCIENTIFIC AND TECHNICAL TERMS

The type of radiation used in processing materials is limited to radiations from high energy gamma rays, X-rays and accelerated electrons. These radiations are also referred to as ionizing radiations because their energy is high enough to dislodge electrons from atoms and molecules and to convert them to electrically-charged particles called ions.

Gamma rays and X-rays, like radiowaves, microwaves, ultraviolet and visible light rays, form part of the electromagnetic spectrum and occur in the short-wavelength, high-energy region of the spectrum and have the greatest penetrating power. They have the same properties and effects on materials, their origin being the main difference between them. X-rays with varying energies are generated by machines. Gamma rays with specific energies come from the spontaneous disintegration of radionuclides.

Naturally occurring and man-made radionuclides, also called radioactive isotopes or radioisotopes, emit radiation as they spontaneously revert to a stable state. The time taken by a radionuclide to decay to half the level of radioactivity originally present is known as its half-life, and is specific for each radionuclide of a particular element. The becquerel (Bq) is the unit of radioactivity and equals one disintegration per second.

Only certain radiation sources can be used in food irradiation. These are the radionuclides cobalt-60 or cesium-137; X-ray machines having a maximum energy of five million electron volts (MeV) (an electron volt is the amount of energy gained by an electron when it is accelerated by a potential of one volt in a vacuum); or electron accelerators having a maximum energy of 10 MeV. Energies from these radiation sources are too low to induce radioactivity in any material, including food.

The radionuclide used almost exclusively for the irradiation of food by gamma rays is cobalt-60. It is produced by neutron bombardment in a nuclear reactor of the metal cobalt-59, then doubly encapsulated in stainless steel "pencils" to prevent any leakage during its use in an irradiator. Cobalt-60 has a half-life of 5.3 years, the gamma rays produced are highly penetrating and can be used to treat full boxes of fresh or frozen food. Cesium-137 is the only other gamma-emitting radionuclide suitable for industrial processing of materials. It can be obtained by reprocessing spent, or used, nuclear fuel elements and has a half-life of 30 years.

However, there is no supply of commercial quantities of cesium-137. Cobalt-60 has therefore become the choice for gamma radiation source; over 80% of the cobalt-60 available in the world market is produced in Canada. Other producers are the Russian Federation, the People's Republic of China, India and South Africa.

High energy electron beams can be produced from machines capable of accelerating electrons to near the speed of light by means of a linear accelerator. Since electrons cannot penetrate very far into food, compared with gamma radiation or X-rays, they can be used only for treatment of thin packages of food and free flowing or falling grains. X-rays of various energies are produced when a beam of accelerated electrons bombards a metallic target.

Although X-rays have good penetrability into food, the efficiency of conversion from electrons to X-rays is generally less than 10%, and this has hindered the use of this type of radiation source so far. Radiation dose is the quantity of radiation energy absorbed by the food as it passes through the radiation field during processing. It is measured using a unit called the Gray (Gy).

In early work the unit was the rad (1 Gy = 100 rads; 1 kGy = 1000 Gy). International health and safety authorities have endorsed the safety of irradiation for all foods up to a dose level of 10,000 Gy (10 kGy). Recent evaluation of an international expert study group appointed by FAO, IAEA and WHO showed that food treated according to good manufacturing practices (GMPs) at any dose above 10 kGy is also safe for consumption, making irradiation parallel to heat treatment of food.

In terms of energy relationships, one gray equals one joule of energy absorbed per kilogram of food being irradiated. The maximum dose of 10 kGy recommended by the Codex General Standard for Irradiated Foods is equivalent to the heat energy required to increase the temperature of water by 2.4°C. Irradiation is often referred to as a "cold pasteurization" process as it can accomplish the same objective as thermal pasteurization of liquid foods, for example milk, without any substantial increase in product temperature.

Benefits of Food Irradiation

Finding ways to prevent the deterioration of food and control infection by microorganisms has been a major preoccupation of man over the centuries. Controls such as refrigeration or pasteurization are now commonplace, and it is expected that one day the technique of food irradiation will also be widely used. Food irradiation can offer a wide range of benefits to food industry and the consumer. From a practical point of view, there are three general application and dose categories that are referred to when foods are treated with ionizing radiation:

— *Low-dose irradiation - up to »1 kGy* (sprout inhibition; delay of ripening; insect disinfestation; parasite inactivation).

— *Medium-dose irradiation - 1 to 10 kGy* (reduction in numbers of spoilage microorganisms; reduction in numbers or elimination of non-spore-forming pathogens, i.e. disease causing microorganisms).

— *High-dose irradiation - above 10 kGy* (reduction in numbers of microorganisms to the point of sterility).

Perhaps the most important application of this method of food preservation is to ensure the hygienic quality of solid or semi-solid foods, especially those of animal origin, through inactivation of foodborne pathogens. This application is comparable to thermal pasteurization of liquid foods, for example milk, which is effective and widely applied but is unsuitable for foods such as poultry, meat and seafood that are to be marketed in raw form.

Pathogenic Microorganisms' Reduction

The incidence of foodborne disease arising from the consumption of food contaminated with pathogenic microorganisms is increasing, and there is a heightened public awareness of the health threat posed by pathogens in or on food. Among these, Escherichia coli O157:H7, Salmonella, Campylobacter jejuni, Listeria monocytogenes, and Vibrio are of primary concern from a public health standpoint because of the severity of the illnesses and/or because of the higher number of outbreaks and individual cases of foodborne illness associated with these pathogens.

Of these food poisoning bacteria, Salmonella and C. jejuni are usually associated with poultry. E. coli O157:H7 has also been linked to major foodborne disease outbreaks through many sources including meat and dairy products in the United Kingdom, hamburger meat, apple juice and water in the USA, and vegetables in Japan. Listeria monocytogenes has been associated with dairy products, processed meats and other foods having a relatively long shelf-life under refrigeration. Vibriospp. in turn have been the causitive agents in world cholera pandemics and of many outbreaks of disease caused by consumption of raw mollusks.

Adherence to good manufacturing practice (GMP) is obviously essential but this alone may not be sufficient to reduce the number of food poisoning outbreaks. Pathogens such as those mentioned previously are sensitive to low levels of ionising radiation. As the irradiation dose increases more microorganisms are affected but a higher dose, although not creating any harmful products, may simultaneously introduce changes in sensory qualities and therefore a balance must be attained between the optimum dose required to achieve a desired objective and that which will minimise any sensory changes.

With fresh poultry carcasses, irradiation up to a dose of 2.5 kGy will virtually eliminate Salmonella and Campylobacter under proper production conditions. The same dose of irradiation destroys E. coli O157:H7, a highly virulent bacteria which can lead to illness and death, and which is estimated to cause 20,000 infections and 250 deaths in the USA annually. Irradiation is currently the only known method to inactivate these pathogens in raw and frozen food. Frog legs can be heavily contaminated by Salmonella and other pathogens, and irradiation provides an effective means of decontamination.

Seafood, especially shellfish, is often contaminated with pathogenic organisms such as Salmonella, Vibrio parahaemolyticus, and Shigella. Consumption of raw and inadequately cooked shellfish is considered to present unacceptable risk factors. Nevertheless, many people do eat raw shellfish such as oysters and clams. In frozen shrimp, reduction of pathogens to a safe level requires a dose of about 3 kGy for inactivating Vibrio spp., Salmonella spp. and Aeromonas hydrophila. It is well known in some countries that fresh pork meat must be cooked thoroughly because it may contain Trichinella spiralis, a parasite which may cause illness and death. The larvae of this parasite can be rendered non-infective by irradiation with a minimum dose of 0.3 kGy. Pork treated in this manner is known as "trichina-safe". Another pork parasite Toxoplasma gondii can also be inactivated with a minimum dose of 0.5 kGy.

Decontamination

Spices, herbs and vegetable seasonings are valued for their distinctive flavours, colours and aromas. However, they are often heavily contaminated with microorganisms because of the environmental and processing conditions under which they are produced. Therefore, before they can be safely incorporated into other food products, the microbial load should be reduced. Because heat treatment can cause significant loss of flavour and aroma, a "cold process", such as irradiation, is ideal.

Until recently, most spices and herbs were fumigated, usually with sterilizing gases such as ethylene oxide to destroy contaminating microorganisms. Irradiation has since emerged as a viable alternative and its use results in cleaner, better quality herbs and spices compared to those fumigated with ethylene oxide. Irradiation of spices on a commercial scale is practised in over 20 countries and global production has increased significantly from about 5,000 tonnes in 1990 to over 60,000 tonnes in 1997.

Shelf-life Extension

The shelf-life of many fruits and vegetables, meat, poultry, fish and seafood can be considerably prolonged by treatment with combinations of low-dose irradiation and refrigeration that do not alter flavour or texture. Many spoilage microorganisms, such as Pseudomonas spp., are relatively sensitive to irradiation.

For example, a dose of 2.5 kGy applied to fresh poultry carcasses processed according to good manufacturing practices (GMPs) will be enough to eliminate Salmonella, and will also kill many, but not all, spoilage bacteria. This will double meat shelf-life, provided it is kept below 5°C. Extension of the very short shelf-life of many commercially important plant commodities is highly desirable, and in some cases, critical. Exposure to a low dose of radiation can slow down the ripening of some fruits, control fungal rot in some others and maturation in certain vegetables, thereby extending their shelf-life.

Shelf-life extension can be increased at least two-fold by irradiation and subsequent storage at 10°C, and even longer when stored at a lower temperature compared with non-irradiated mushrooms. Not all fruits and vegetables are suitable for irradiation because undesirable changes in colour or texture, or both, limit their acceptability. Also, different varieties of the same fruit or vegetable may respond differently to irradiation. The time of harvest and the physiological state also affects the response of fruits and vegetables to irradiation. For example, if strawberries are irradiated before they are ripe, the red colour does not develop satisfactorily. For delaying ripening in fruits it is important to irradiate them before ripening starts.

At high doses of irradiation (>25 kGy), foods which are preheated to inactivate enzymes can be commercially sterilized such as occurs in canning. The sterilized products can be stored at room temperature almost indefinitely. Radiationsterilized foods are given to hospital patients who have immune system deficiencies and must therefore have a sterile diet. Irradiation sterilized products are also eaten by astronauts in the NASA space shuttle programme because of their superior quality, safety and variety, in preference to foods treated by other preservation techniques.

Limited commercial-scale sterilization of various ready-to-eat foods by high dose irradiation has been carried out in South Africa during the past 10 years to serve military personnel and outdoor enthusiasts such as campers, yachters and hikers. In total, more than two million light weight food packs (weighing 150 g each) have been produced during this period.

Disinfestation

The chief problem encountered in preservation of grains and grain products is insect infestation. Most of the pests of concern, e.g. beetles, moths, weevils and others, are not quarantine insects, but they cause extensive damage to stored products. Irradiation has been shown to be an effective pest control method for these commodities and a good alternative to methyl bromide, the most widely used fumigant for insect control, which is being phased out globally because of its ozone depleting properties.

Unlike methyl bromide, irradiation is not an ozone depleting substance and unlike phosphine, the other major fumigant used to control grain pests, irradiation is a fast treatment and its efficacy is not temperature dependent. Irradiation can kill or control phosphine-resistant pests. The dosage required for insect control is reasonably low, in the order of 1 kGy or less. Disinfestation is aimed at preventing losses caused by insects in stored grains, pulses, flour, cereals, coffee beans, dried fruits, dried nuts, and other dried food products including dried fish. Proper packaging is required, however, for irradiated products to prevent insect reinfestation.

Radiation disinfestation can facilitate trade in fresh fruits, such as citrus, mangoes, and papayas which often harbour insect pests of quarantine importance. Insects are easily distributed by international trade in such fruits and also by tourism. To prevent or minimize this risk, many countries prohibit importation of such fruits or require quarantine treatment of imported fruits. These measures can create significant barriers to international trade and the free flow of plants and plant products, but they are fully justified from the receiving country's point of view.

The occurrence of fruit flies, such as the Mediterranean, Oriental, Mexican or Caribbean fruit flies, has repeatedly disrupted trade among countries and between states within large countries, for example Australia and the USA. A number of quarantine treatments permitted in the past have recently been banned, fumigation with ethylene dibromide being the most prominent example. It has been demonstrated that low dosages of ionizing radiation, between 0.15 and 0.3 kGy, will very effectively control fruit fly and other insect problems. This makes the use of irradiation for quarantine treatment a very practical possibility.

Sprouting Inhibition

In order to provide consumers with a year-round supply of potato tubers, onion bulbs, yams and other sprouting plant foods, storage over many months is necessary unless shipments from other climatic zones, usually at a much higher price, can replace local production during off-season. Such long-term storage is possible with the aid of refrigeration, which is costly, particularly in subtropical and tropical regions. For many of these crops, the desired inhibitory effects can also be obtained using chemical sprout inhibitors such as maleic hydrazide, propham, or chloropropham.

These chemicals, however, are either not effective under tropical conditions or leave residues in the produce, and for health reasons they are considered by some to be harmful. Thus many countries have prohibited their use. A very low radiation dose of 0.15 kGy or less, inhibits sprouting of products such as potatoes, yams, onions, garlic, ginger, and chestnuts. It leaves no residues and allows storage at higher temperatures. Irradiation of potatoes, stored at higher temperatures (10°-15°C), have better processing quality. Commercial processing of irradiated potatoes has been carried out in Japan since 1973.

Neither irradiation nor any other food treatment can reverse the spoilage process and make bad food good. If food already looks, tastes or smells bad - signs of spoilage before irradiation, it cannot be "saved" by any treatment including irradiation. While irradiation can reduce or eliminate spoilage bacteria or pathogenic microorganisms which may be present in a spoiled food, it cannot improve its sensory properties - the bad appearance, taste or smell will remain.

Treatments such as heat pasteurization, chemical fumigation, and irradiation, however, are effective in destroying or suppressing microbial contamination of food. Heat pasteurization and fumigation have been effectively used in this way for decades to "clean up" foods, specifically to destroy pathogenic microorganisms in milk and other liquid products, and to destroy spoilage microflora or microorganisms and insects in spices and dry foods. These treatments are done intentionally for public health reasons; for example, to destroy microorganisms such as Salmonella, Shigella, and Campylobacter that are associated with food-borne diseases.

Irradiation is especially effective as a control measure for pathogenic microorganisms transmitted through solid food, especially foods of animal origin even when in the frozen state. Food processes such as heating, freezing, chemical treatment, and irradiation are not intended to serve as substitutes for good hygienic practice. Both at the national and international levels, good manufacturing practices (GMPs) govern the handling of specific foods and food products. They must be followed in the preparation of food, whether the food is intended for further processing by irradiation or any other means.

An additional step in the further processing of food, such as irradiation, requires a stricter adherence to GMP so that the products reach the final stages at the highest possible quality level.

Pasteurized milk was demonstrated to be safe, practical and fit for the needs of most urban consumers. It was very similar in taste and colour to fresh milk and required no change in consumption or cooking habits. However, the pasteurization of milk did not become a commercial reality for many years after its introduction in the early 1900s. A similar situation has arisen with irradiated food.

Although the safety and benefits of food irradiation have been thoroughly documented, the commercial application of the process has been hindered due to some misconception by the general public on its safety and the conservative position of the food industry. Other processes such as chemical and heat treatments can also kill insects, moulds and microorganisms, including pathogens in food. However, chemicals can leave residues, and heating food, such as canning, changes its texture, colour and flavour and converts it into a cooked product. Irradiation, on the other hand, achieves its effects without significantly raising the temperature of the food, leaving it closer to the unprocessed state.

Unlike the fumigants used for disinfestation and quarantine purposes, for example ethylene oxide and methyl bromide, irradiation does not leave residues in the food and is safer to use. Irradiation is unique, however, in its ability to inactivate pathogenic microorganisms, such as Salmonella, E. coli O157:H7 and Campylobacter, in food in the frozen state, particularly in food of animal origin.

Food irradiation has an important role to play in the production of safe, wholesome food just as heatpasteurization has. At a time when the number of food poisoning outbreaks is on the increase, when fumigants are being phased out, and the consumer is looking for safer, higher quality foods, the overwhelming benefits of food irradiation cannot be overlooked. Irradiation helps to ensure a safer and more plentiful food supply by extending shelf-life and controlling pests and pathogens in food. Most importantly, it is a safe process.

Facilities of Food Irradiation

Industrial food irradiation facilities must be licensed, regulated and inspected by national radiological safety and health authorities, many of whom base their rules upon irradiation standards and codes of practice jointly established by the IAEA, FAO and WHO. The common features of all commercial irradiation facilities are the irradiation room and a system to transport the food into and out of the room.

The major structural difference between this type of plant and any other industrial building is the concrete shielding surrounding the irradiation room, which ensures that ionising radiation does not escape to the outside of the room. In the case of a gamma irradiator, the radionuclide source continuously emits radiation and when not being used to treat food must be stored in a water pool (usually 6 metres in depth). Known as one of the best shields against radiation energy, water absorbs the radiation energy and protects workers from exposure if they must enter the room.

In contrast to gamma irradiators, machines producing high-energy electrons operate on electricity and can be switched off. The transport system employed in a large food irradiation facility is similar to that used for sterilization of medical products and can be either a conveyor or a rail system. In a gamma irradiator, the size of the containers in which the food is moved through the irradiation chamber can vary and pallets up to 1 m^3 may be used. On the other hand, with machines, the bulk or thickness of a product which can be treated is much less and hence there is a fundamental design difference between the two types of irradiator.

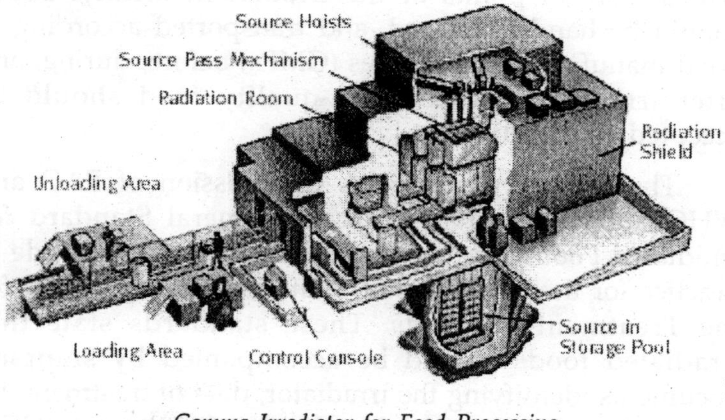

Gamma Irradiator for Food Processing

Over the past 30 years, laws and regulations have been promulgated to govern operations at industrial irradiators used to process non-food products, such as medical supplies. About 170 such irradiators are operating around the world. The plants, which must be approved by governmental authorities before construction, are subject to regular inspections, audits, and other reviews to ensure that they are safely and properly operated. These types of governmental controls would also be valid for irradiation facilities processing food.

At the international level, provisional guidelines for good manufacturing practices (GMPs) and good irradiation practices for a number of foods have been issued by the International Consultative Group on Food Irradiation (ICGFI). They cover all aspects of treatment, handling, and distribution. These guidelines provide a good basis for preparing the detailed protocols needed to implement irradiation on a commercial scale. Some of the guidelines have converted to standards of the American Society for Testing and Materials (ASTM).

As with all food technologies, effective quality control systems need to be installed and adequately monitored at critical control points at the irradiation facility. Foods should be handled, stored, and transported according to good manufacturing practices (GMPs) before, during, and after irradiation. Only high-quality food should be accepted for irradiation.

The Codex Alimentarius Commission of FAO and WHO adopted in 1983 a Codex General Standard for Irradiated Foods, and an associated International Code of Practice for the Operation of Radiation Facilities Used for the Treatment of Foods. These standards state that irradiated foods should be accompanied by shipping documents identifying the irradiator, date of treatment, lot identification, dose, and other details of treatment. ICGFI additionally has established an international registry of irradiators that meet standards for good operations.

It also organizes training courses for irradiator operators, plant managers, and supervisors on proper processing, with emphasis on GMPs, dosimetry, record-keeping, and lot identification, and for food control officials on proper inspection procedures required for food irradiation processing and trade in irradiated foods.

Any industrial activity includes certain risks to human beings and the environment. One of the risks at irradiation facilities is associated with the potential hazard of accidental exposure to ionizing radiation. Irradiators are designed with several levels of redundant protection to detect equipment malfunction and to protect personnel from accidental radiation exposure. Under normal operating conditions, all exposures of workers to radiation are prevented because the radiation source is shielded.

Potentially hazardous areas are monitored and a system of interlocks prevents unauthorized entry into the radiation room while products are being irradiated. Worker safety further rests upon strict operating procedures and proper training. All radiation plants must be licensed. In most countries, regulations require periodic inspection of facilities to ensure compliance with the terms of operating licenses. The plants are constructed with very heavy radiation shielding and thus the process presents no risk to the general public.

Over the past 30 years, there have been a few major accidents at industrial irradiation facilities that caused injury or death to workers because of accidental exposure to a lethal dose of radiation. All of the accidents happened because safety systems had been deliberately bypassed and proper control procedures had not been followed. None of these accidents endangered public health and environmental safety.

In most cases, reports of "accidents" have actually turned out to be operational incidents. Such incidents have caused the irradiator to be shut down but they did not harm anyone or pose a risk to the environment. The distinction between accidents and incidents is used by authorities responsible for safety in all industries. This is the case for many other food technologies, such as canning, fumigation and the agro-chemical industry, which are also potentially hazardous to workers.

At irradiation facilities, controls and formal protocols are strictly required to prevent accidents. The radiation processing industry is considered to have a very good safety record. Today there are about 170 industrial gamma irradiation facilities operating worldwide, a number of which process food in addition to other types of products. Most irradiation facilities are used for sterilizing disposable medical and pharmaceutical supplies, and for processing other non-food items. Facilities are constructed to standard designs with multiple safeguards to protect worker health and safeguard the community should a natural disaster such as an earthquake or tornado occur.

Radioactive materials required for irradiators is transported in lead-shielded steel casks. These casks meet national and international standards modelled upon the Regulations for Safe Transport of Radioactive Materials of the International Atomic Energy Agency (IAEA) and are designed to withstand the most severe accidents, including collisions, punctures, and exposure to fire and water depths. Large quantities of radioactive material are safely shipped all over the world to supply some 170 irradiators processing a variety of goods, mainly medical products such as syringes, physician gloves, sutures, and hospital gowns.

From 1955 to date, Canada has shipped approximately 480 million curies of cobalt-60 without any radiation hazard to the environment or release of radioactive materials. Over the same period, approximately one million shipments of radioisotopes for industrial, hospital, and research use were made in North America without radiation accidents. This excellent safety record far exceeds that of other industries shipping hazardous materials such as toxic chemicals, crude oil, or gasoline.

The same procedures used so successfully and safely to transport radioactive materials to existing irradiators will of course be used for transporting radioactive materials to any additional irradiators constructed for food processing.

It is impossible for a "meltdown" to occur in a gamma irradiator or for the radiation source to explode. The source of radiation energy used at irradiators cannot produce neutrons which can make materials radioactive, so no nuclear "chain reaction" can occur at an irradiator. The walls of the irradiation cell through which the food passes, the machinery inside the cell, and the product being processed cannot become radioactive. No radioactivity is released into the environment.

It is a misconception that the existence of gamma irradiation facilities will lead to a growing accumulation of radioactive waste material. At gamma irradiators, radionuclide sources, typically cobalt-60 or cesium-137, are used as the sources of radiation energy. These elements decay over time to nonradioactive nickel and non-radioactive barium, respectively. The sources are removed from the irradiator when the radioactivity falls to a low level, usually between 6% and 12% of the initial level (this takes 16 to 21 years for cobalt-60). The elements are then returned in a shipping container to the supplier who has the option of reactivating them in a nuclear reactor or storing them.

Safety of Irradiated Food

Irradiation does not make food radioactive. Everything in our environment, including food, contains trace amounts of radioactivity. This means that this trace amount (about 150 to 200 becquerels/kg) of natural radioactivity from elements such as potassium is unavoidable in our daily diets. In countries where food irradiation is permitted, both the sources of radiation and their energy levels are regulated and controlled.

The irradiation process involves passing the food through a radiation field at a set speed to control the amount of energy or dose absorbed by the food. The food itself never comes into direct contact with the radiation source. The maximum allowable energies for electrons and Xrays from the two machine-generated sources of radiation that can be used, are 10 million electron volts (MeV) and 5 MeV, respectively.

Even when foods are exposed to very high doses of radiation from these sources, the maximum level of radioactivity would be just one-thousandth of a becquerel per kilogram of food. This is 200,000 times smaller than the level of radioactivity naturally present in food. Food undergoing irradiation does not become radioactive any more than luggage passing through an airport X-ray scanner or teeth that have been X-rayed.

Irradiated Food and Radioactive Food: Irradiated foods are those that have been deliberately processed with certain types of radiation energy to bring about some desirable properties (for example, to inhibit sprouting or to destroy food-poisoning bacteria). Apart from foodstuffs, many other materials are commercially irradiated during manufacturing. These include cosmetics, wine bottle corks, hospital supplies and medical products, and some types of food packaging.

On the other hand, Radioactive foods are those that have become accidentally contaminated by radioactive substances from weapons testing or nuclear reactor accidents. This type of contamination is totally unrelated to irradiated food which has been processed for preservation and other purposes.

Irradiated Food never become Toxic. Since the late 1940s irradiated foods were considered to require careful toxicological investigation before this process could be applied to food manufacturing. In actual fact it was firmly concluded by a study conducted in Germany as far back as 1926 that irradiation did not produce any toxic factors in animal diets. The standard procedure for this purpose was to feed the foodstuff to be tested to laboratory animals and look for possible effects of longevity, reproductive capacity, tumour incidence, and other indicators of the animals' health status. Several hundred toxicological studies have been conducted on experimental animals over the past four decades. Many animal feeding tests including genetic studies of different types of irradiated food were carried out in many countries.

Among the many extensive animal feeding studies of irradiated food, those conducted at the Raltech Laboratory, USA, are generally acknowledged to be among the best and most statistically powerful of all. The studies involved using chicken irradiated either by a cobalt-60 source or electron machine up to a dose of 58 kGy. Some 134 tonnes of chicken meat, or nearly a quarter of a million birds, were used in the study to compare high-dose irradiation with heat-sterilization of chicken. The study involved chronic feeding studies in mice and dogs, teratology studies and mutagenicity tests.

The comprehensive results were reviewed by scientists of the United States Food and Drug Administration (FDA) at the time a petition for low dose irradiation of chicken was submitted in the mid-1980s. No adverse effects from consuming chicken processed with high doses of radiation were reported. The lack of treatment-related effects in the many well-conducted studies provides additional assurance that the consumption of irradiated food does not pose a hazard. Other types of extensive feeding tests also have been done. Over the last 20 years millions of mice, rats, and other laboratory animals have been bred and reared exclusively on an irradiated diet.

The diet, treated at doses between 25 and 50 kGy, has been fed to laboratory animals at many institutions involved in food, drug, and pharmaceutical research in Austria, Australia, Canada, France, Germany, Japan,

Switzerland, the United Kingdom, and the USA. No transmittable genetic defects - teratogenic or oncogenic - have been observed which could be attributed to the consumption of irradiated diets.

Issue of abnormal chromosomes as a result of eating irradiated food has been more sensationalised than any other. The claims focus on the incidence of "polyploidy", which is alleged to result from consumption of products made from wheat immediately after irradiation. Polyploidy means the occurrence of cells containing twice or more the number of chromosomes.

Human cells normally have 46 chromosomes. If they are polyploid they could have 92 or even 138 chromosomes. The incidence of polyploid cells is naturally occurring and varies among individuals, and even in one individual from day to day. It can also vary from organ to organ within one individual. The biological significance of polyploidy is unknown.

When undertaking studies on polyploidy, it is important that many thousands of cells are counted in order to see the effect of a treatment. As polyploid cells are rare, it is essential that enough cells are observed before any valid conclusions can be reached. It can also be extremely difficult to recognise polyploid cells; if normal (diploid) cells happen to be superimposed on the microscope slide they look very much like one polyploid cell.

Media reports have frequently cited results published in the mid-1970s by a group of scientists from the National Institute of Nutrition (NIN) in Hyderabad, India. This group of scientists reported increases in the frequency of polyploid cells in malnourished children, rats, mice and monkeys that they attributed to consumption of products made from wheat immediately after irradiation at 0.75 kGy.

When the report is examined more closely, among other shortcomings, it is found that only 100 cells from each of the five children in each group were counted - an incredibly small sample upon which to base any conclusion. In addition, although the results in each group were averaged, there is no indication of the actual incidence in each child. No polyploidy at all was seen when wheat was irradiated and stored for 12 weeks before consumption.

A number of institutions in India and elsewhere have tried to reproduce the results found at NIN based on information made available to them. Some used absorbed radiation doses as high as 45 kGy. For example, a rat feeding study carried out at the Bhabha Atomic Research Centre (BARC) in Mumbai, with freshly irradiated wheat, in which the incidence of polyploidy was determined by counting 3,000 cells from each animal, showed no effect from consuming the irradiated wheat.

Besides feeding tests using laboratory animals, there have been human feeding studies of irradiated foods. In the early 1980s, eight feeding studies using several irradiated food items, including irradiated wheat, were conducted in China using human volunteers. More than 400 individuals consumed irradiated food under controlled conditions for 7 to 15 weeks. One focus of the research was the possibility of chromosomal changes. Seven of the eight experiments involved investigation of chromosomal aberrations in 382 individuals.

No significant difference between the number of chromosomal aberrations in the control and test groups were discovered in any of the experiments. Incidence of polyploidy in those who consumed non-irradiated food and those who consumed irradiated samples were within normal range of the overall value of polyploid cells in participants. Although not aimed at testing the safety of irradiated foods it is worth noting at this point that radiation-sterilized foods are used in the diet of severely ill patients.

The so-called "radiolytic" products produced in irradiated food have proven to be familiar ones, such as glucose, formic acid, acetaldehyde, and carbon dioxide, that are naturally present in foods or are formed by thermal processing (thermolytic products). The safety of these radiolytic products has been examined very critically, and no evidence of their harmfulness has been found.

Irradiation causes the formation of free radicals - which in scientific terms are atoms or molecules with an unpaired electron - and that these are quite stable in dry foods has often been mentioned as a reason for special caution with irradiated dry foods. However, free radicals are also formed by other food treatments, such as toasting of bread, frying, and freeze drying, and during normal oxidation processes in food. They are generally very reactive, unstable structures, that continuously react with substances to form stable products.

Free radicals disappear by reacting with each other in the presence of liquids, such as saliva in the mouth. Consequently, their ingestion does not create any toxicological or other harmful effects. This has been confirmed by a long-term feeding study carried out a the Federal Research Centre for Nutrition in Karlsruhe, Gerınany. This study was especially designed to look for possible effects of a diet containing a high free radical concentration. Animals were fed a very dry milk powder irradiated with electrons at 45 kGy. No mutagenic effects were noted and no tumours were formed.

Nine generations of rats were continually fed this diet without any indication of toxic effects. Similarly, a slice of toasted bread (non-irradiated), which actually contains more free radicals than very dry foods that have been irradiated, can be expected to be harmless.

Under Good Manufacturing Practices (GMPs), irradiating food of animal origin to ensure its hygienic quality does not increase the risk from botulism any more than other "substerilizing" food processes, such as pasteurization. It is true that bacterial spores such as those of Clostridium botulinum are resistant to most preservation treatments, including low doses of irradiation. However, these spores are usually present in relatively low numbers and, although they survive sub-sterilizing doses of irradiation, other microorganisms also survive irradiation can grow, cause spoilage and inhibit the growth of Clostridium botulinum.

The survival of spores is therefore not considered to introduce any additional hazard in irradiated foods than in food subjected to other sub-sterilizing heat-treatments, for example, in pasteurized or cooked foods. Food treated by irradiation or traditional pasteurization must be handled, packaged, and stored following good manufacturing practices (GMPs). Doing so prevents the growth and toxin production of Clostridium botulinum.

Alternatively, highdose irradiation (30-60 kGy) can be used to destroy any Clostridium botulinum spores present in the food. Some types of clostridia cause more concern than others. Clostridium botulinum Type E, for example, is found at low levels in fish and seafood caught in some areas. It can grow and produce toxin even when the food is refrigerated at temperatures as low as 4° C.

Thus, fish and seafood, including their products, treated by any of the sub-sterilizing processes, including irradiation, must be kept at 3° C or below at all times during marketing. Most other types of Clostridium botulinum cannot grow and produce toxin at temperatures below 10° C. Good manufacturing practices (GMPs) require that raw foods such as fish, meat, and chicken are stored at a specific temperature, whether irradiated or not, to prevent the growth of Clostridium botulinum. It has been concluded by various workers in this field of research that low-dose irradiation does not increase the risk from sporogenous bacteria. On the contrary, it has been emphasised that lowdose irradiation can increase the safety of foods.

In this respect that is, only foods of good hygienic quality should be irradiated, irradiation does not differ from heat pasteurization, freezing, or other food processes. While these processes can destroy bacteria, they may not destroy preformed toxins and viruses already in the food. It is very important that foods intended for processing—by whatever method - are of good quality and handled and prepared according to GMPs established by national or international authorities. In some cases, strict regulations prohibit distribution of some foods.

Irradiated Foods and Nutritional Quality

As irradiation is a 'cold process', that is, it does not substantially raise the temperature of the food being processed, nutrient losses are small and often significantly less than losses associated with other methods of preservation such as canning, drying and heat pasteurization. Much of the early work on irradiation examined foods treated at sterilizing doses, but since recent applications often use doses well below 10 kGy, a realistic evaluation of the nutritional adequacy of irradiated food should be based on results of experiments carried out using doses likely to be used in commercial practice.

The change in nutritional value caused by irradiation depends on a number of factors. These include the irradiation dose to which the food has been exposed, the type of food, packaging, and processing conditions, such as temperature during irradiation and storage time. Carbohydrates, proteins and fats are the main components of foods. These macronutrients provide energy and serve as building blocks for the growth and maintenance of the body.

Extensive research has shown that carbohydrates, proteins, and fats, undergo little change during irradiation even at doses over 10 kGy. Similarly, the essential amino acids, minerals, trace elements and most vitamins do not suffer significant losses. Different types of vitamins have varied sensitivity to irradiation and to some other food processing methods. The sensitivity of the vitamins to irradiation depends on the complexity of the food system and the solubility of the vitamins in water or fat.

Irradiation of vitamins in pure solution results in considerable destruction of these compounds thus some reports in literature have overestimated the losses. For example, vitamin B_1 (thiamin) in aqueous solution showed 50% loss after irradiation at 0.5 kGy, while irradiation of dried whole egg at that dose caused less than 5% destruction of the same vitamin. This is due to the mutually protective action of various food constituents on each other. Vitamin losses can be minimized by irradiating the food in frozen form or by packaging it in an inert atmosphere such as under nitrogen.

Four vitamins are recognised as being highly sensitive to irradiation: B1, C (ascorbic acid), A (retinol) and E (?-tocopherol). However, B_1 is even more sensitive to heat than to irradiation. It has been demonstrated that pork and beef sterilized by irradiation retain much more vitamin B1 than canned meat sterilized thermally. Seemingly conflicting results of low versus high losses of vitamin C for some irradiated foods may be attributed to differences in analytical approaches used by researchers.

Some have measured only ascorbic acid, while others have measured total ascorbic acid, a mixture of ascorbic acid and dehydroascorbic acid. Both acids have vitamin C biological activity and are easily transformed from one to the other. If only ascorbic acid were measured, any apparent reduction in vitamin C level would be exaggerated. Research has shown that the natural differences in total vitamin C content of four varieties of strawberry are much greater than the reduction which occurs on irradiation.

The significance of any losses of vitamins E and A due to irradiation are marginal because the main sources of these vitamins in the human diet are butter and milk and these are unsuitable for irradiation treatment. Irradiation has practically no effect on the levels of beta carotene and other carotenoids, the precursors of vitamin A, formed in fruits during ripening. On the whole, the effects of irradiation on the nutritional value of foods are minimal and these observations are substantiated by the results of many feeding studies which have been undertaken to establish the wholesomeness of irradiated food. It should also be remembered that irradiated food will be consumed as part of a mixed diet, and therefore the process will have little impact on the total intake of specific nutrients.

The Joint Expert Committee of the Food and Agriculture Organization (FAO), World Health Organization (WHO), and International Atomic Energy Agency (IAEA), which examined these and other issues, stated in its conclusions in 1980 that irradiation does not introduce special nutritional problems in food. This was also the finding of the group of experts who convened at a meeting organised by the FAO, IAEA and WHO in Geneva, Switzerland in 1997 to discuss the effects of high dose irradiation. It was concluded at this meeting that doses greater than 10 kGy "will not lead to nutrient losses to an extent that would have an adverse effect on the nutritional status of individuals or populations".

Irradiated Foods Packaging

With the exception of such applications as sprout

inhibition in potatoes or onions, insect disinfestation in bulk grains, or delay of post-harvest ripening of fruits, irradiation of foodstuffs is usually carried out on packaged food items. There may be different reasons for this: prevention of microbial reinfection or insect exposure, prevention of water loss, exclusion of oxygen, prevention of mechanical damage during transport, or simply improved handling and marketing. The packaging material used must not release radiation-induced reaction products or additives onto the food, nor should it lose functional qualities such as mechanical strength, seal stability, or impermeability to water upon irradiation.

There is risk in irradiating foods in contact with plastic or other packaging materials. Results of extensive research have shown that almost all commonly used food packaging materials tested are suitable for use at any dose likely to be applied to food including sterilization treatment. Only packaging materials which have been specifically authorized for such use may be subjected to irradiation of prepackaged foods. Various types of packaging materials have been approved for use when food is irradiated. Their suitability for food intended for irradiation has been studied in Canada, the United Kingdom, the USA, and a few other countries.

A number of food packaging materials were approved for use in food irradiation by the United States Food and Drug Administration (FDA) more than 20 years ago. More recently, Canada, India and Poland have approved additional materials, including a multi-layered polyethylene film, as safe for packaging foods to be irradiated. Sophisticated tests have been used to evaluate the effect of radiation on plastic and other types of packaging materials. Researchers looked at the post-irradiation stability, mechanical strength, and permeability to water and gases of the packaging materials, and at the extractability of the plastics, additives, and adhesives.

Irradiated materials are used to package foods. Plastic films laminated with aluminium foil are routinely sterilized by radiation as part of the manufacturing process. They are used for hermetically sealed "bag-in-a-box" products, such as tomato paste, fruit juices, and wines. Other aseptic packaging materials, dairy product packaging, single-serving containers (for example, for cream), and wine bottle corks are also routinely sterilized by irradiation prior to filling and sealing to prevent product contamination. Other types of materials used to wrap food or other products also are routinely processed by radiation in many countries. The radiation process is used to "cross-link" the material's polymer chains for greater strength and heat resistance, and for producing plastics with special properties.

Costs of Food Irradiation

Any food process will add cost. In most cases, however, food prices do not necessarily rise just because a product has been treated. Many variables affect food costs, and one of them is the cost of processing. Canning, freezing, pasteurization, refrigeration, fumigation, and irradiation add cost to the product. These treatments will also bring benefits to consumers in terms of availability and quantity, storage life, convenience, and improved hygiene of the food. Reduced losses will bring revenue to producers and traders, thus in turn, compensating treatment costs.

The major factors influencing the economics of food irradiation using cobalt-60 include: irradiation design parameters such as applied dose, packing density of the products, handling conditions (dry versus perishable products), dose uniformity and throughput; capital costs consisting of the irradiator, radiation source, spare parts for linear accelerators, warehouse capacity; and operating costs such as salaries, utilities, replenishments of cobalt-60, maintenance, etc.

Irradiation costs range from US $10 to $15 per tonne for a low-dose application (for example, to inhibit the growth of sprouts in potatoes and onions) to US $100 to $250 per tonne for a high-dose application (for example, to ensure hygienic quality of spices). These costs are competitive with alternative treatments. In some cases, irradiation can be considerably less expensive. For disinfestation of fruit to satisfy the quarantine requirements of an importing country, for example, it has been estimated that the cost of irradiation would be only 10% to 20% of the cost of vapour-heat treatment.

Electron beam irradiators may have economic advantages over gamma irradiators where product throughput is large, the particle size or thickness of the product being treated is small, and where continuous treatment is possible by integrating the irradiator into the production line. As a result, they may be more efficient than gamma irradiators for treating large volumes of domestic or imported grains. In addition, these machine-type irradiators, based on electron acceleration rather than radionuclides, may not require as extensive regulatory approvals.

Typical Food Irradiation Facility Cost

The cost to build a commercial cobalt-60 food irradiation plant is in the range of US $3 million to $5 million, depending on its size, processing capacity, and other factors. This is within the range of plant costs for other technologies. For example, a moderately-sized, ultra-high temperature plant for sterilizing milk, fruit juices, and other liquids costs about US $2 million.

A small vapour-heat treatment plant for disinfestation of fruits costs about US $1 million. Often the capital costs of irradiation equipment are seen as prohibitive, even though low operating costs for most commodities make per unit costs very competitive with other treatments. Commercial contract multipurposeirradiators operate in many countries offering irradiation services at reasonable cost. Most of these facilities successfully combine irradiation of various food products and treatment of other non-food items such as cosmetics, pharmaceutical and disposable medical products. Since irradiation gives the added economic benefit of prolonged fresh market life for many foods, decreased waste and increased market potential of the food should be considered in a cost-benefit analysis.

Trade in Irradiated Foods

Food imports and exports are important to the health and economy of nations and people, yet trade barriers caused by pests, diseases and food safety issues continually threaten or inhibit trade. Several technologies work to remove trade barriers. Irradiation is one such technology that could assist in the improvement of trade.

Some irradiated foods such as spices and dried vegetable seasonings, as well as food ingredients such as mechanically deboned poultry meat, have entered international commerce for use mainly by the food industry in various types of processed food. The nature of the spice trade requires that spices, for example pepper from various sources, be mixed to achieve certain grades to satisfy market demand. Thus, it is possible that only a portion of the spices within one single shipment has been irradiated.

The production of, and trade in, irradiated spices have increased significantly in recent years from about 5,000 tonnes in 1990 to over 30,000 tonnes in 1994 to over 60,000 tonnes in 1997. Approximately 30,000 tonnes of irradiated spices and dried vegetable seasonings were produced in the USA alone in 1997. Fresh fruits and vegetables could be irradiated to overcome quarantine barriers against fruit flies in the near future. The United States Department of Agriculture (USDA) has accepted irradiation as a quarantine treatment against major fruit fly species regardless of host.

Labelled Irradiated Foods

Some national regulations require that irradiated food be labelled with a statement indicating the treatment and, often, with an international logo known as the radura symbol. Experience with market trials and commercial sale of irradiated food has proven that informed consumers are not against irradiated food but prefer it to be labelled as such. The label provides consumers with the opportunity to choose.

Label statements can also be used to state why products are irradiated. It has been demonstrated that people are more likely to buy irradiated food labelled with a statement conveying the positive benefits of the technology, for example, 'Irradiated to control microbes' or 'Irradiated to retard spoilage'. For irradiated foods that are not packaged, such as bulk containers of fruit and vegetables, retailers in some countries are required to display the logo and phrase.

Labelling regulations do, however, differ between countries. For example, in the USA, labelling requirements apply only to whole foods that have been irradiated but not to irradiated ingredients in a food. In the European Union it is proposed that food containing irradiated ingredients such as spices, but which are not themselves irradiated, must be labelled regardless of the percentage of irradiated product which has been incorporated. Many governments have introduced regulations requiring labelling of irradiated food but not to those treated by competitive treatments such as fumigation.

However, in August 1998 the United States Food and Drug Administration (FDA) amended the labelling requirements for irradiated food - a statement disclosing irradiation treatment is not required to be any more prominent than the declaration of ingredients.

A government can deny entry of any product into its territory. However, under the provision of the Agreement on the Application of Sanitary and Phytosanitary Measures (SPS), being enforced by the World Trade Organization (WTO), such a government, if a member of WTO, may be requested to furnish scientifically-based justification for regulations that are stricter than the only recognized international standards for food, which are the guidelines, and recommendations of the Codex Alimentarius Commission (food safety), the International Plant Protection Convention (IPPC) (plant protection and quarantine), and the International Office of Epizootics (animal health and quarantine).

With the existence of the Codex General Standard for Irradiated Foods, which recognizes the safety and effectiveness of food irradiation, and the endorsement of irradiation as a quarantine treatment of fresh agricultural produce by regional plant protection organizations operating within IPPC, irradiated food treated according to the principle of the Codex Standard can no longer be denied entry into countries on scientific grounds.

Detection Methods

The need for reliable and routine tests to determine whether or not food has been irradiated arose as a result of the progress made in commercialisation of the food irradiation process, greater international trade in irradiated foods, differing regulations relating to the use of the technology in many countries, and consumer demand for clear labelling of the treated food.

Although not essential for management of the process, it was envisaged that the availability of such tests would help strengthen national regulations on irradiation of specific foods, and enhance consumer confidence in such regulations. The availability of reliable identification methods would be of assistance in establishing a system of legislative control, and help to achieve acceptance of irradiated foods by consumers. In fact, an International Conference on Acceptance, Control of, and Trade in Irradiated Food held in Geneva in 1988 recommended that "governments should encourage research into methods of detection of irradiated foods so that administrative control of irradiated food once it leaves the facility can be supplemented by an additional means of enforcement, thus facilitating international trade and reinforcing consumer confidence in the overall process".

Since the mid 1980s extensive research has resulted in the development of a range of tests which can be used to reliably determine the irradiation status of a wide variety of food. The methods which have been studied most extensively and which have the greatest scope of application include electron spin resonance (ESR) spectroscopy, thermoluminescence (TL), and monitoring the formation of long-chain hydrocarbons and 2-alkylcyclobutanones. These methods have been successfully evaluated in a number of interlaboratory blind trials with the result that, in 1996, five tests were adopted as standard reference methods for the detection of irradiated food by the European Committee for Normalisation (CEN). These in turn are being adopted by some national authorities, such as Germany and the United Kingdom. More tests are being considered by CEN for implementation as reference methods.

IRRADIATED FOODS AND THE CONSUMER

The ultimate test for any product or process is the market

place, as it is the consumer who determines whether or not a product is better than previous or competitive products. Such is the case for irradiated food which, at the end of the day, will not be a technical or marketing success unless it is accepted by the consumer. Progress in the commercial use of irradiation has been slow, mainly because of misunderstanding.

Many people mistakenly fear, for instance, that the process may induce radioactivity in the food product and that irradiation will result in the formation of toxic byproducts in food. Given these fears, consumers often find it difficult to evaluate the benefits of this processing technique objectively.

Many market tests of irradiated foods have been carried out in several countries during the 1980s and 1990s, and to date, all have been successful. Market tests and the ongoing sales of irradiated foods provide the best source of information on whether irradiated foods meet consumer needs and wants. They provide excellent information about consumer acceptance and facilitate the commercialization of irradiation.

Several irradiated foods are used directly by the food industry. For example irradiated spices and mechanicallydeboned poultry meat are used for manufacturing various types of processed food. Many irradiated foods are also being marketed at the retail level.

A variety of processed food (for example, sauces, salad dressings, sandwich spread) also incorporate irradiated spices and vegetable seasonings. All irradiated products have to be labelled with an irradiation logo plus the word 'Radurised'. Since 1995, irradiated spices and dried vegetable seasonings have been marketed at retail levels in Belgium. Irradiated spices, condiments and seasonings are also available in China.

Successful market trials of other irradiated foods such as rice, mungbeans, potatoes and onions in several countries in recent years will likely lead to further commercialization of irradiated food in the near future. The actual sale of irradiated food in the market in several countries has clearly demonstrated that consumers will accept irradiated food if they have the choice.

10

Food and Energy

Food is the second most important way in which energy is taken into the body. It's the energy in food that sustains us, and the effect of food energy on our body is the basis for the dietary practice known as macrobiotics. Energy exists on a continuum, from yin, among whose attributes are cold, darkness, and contraction, to yang, characterized by heat, light, and expansion. Foods exist on this continuum and can be characterized as predominantly yin or yang, according to the effect they have on the body.

Yin foods-primarily sweeteners, oil, liquids, and most dairy products-have a cooling and lethargizing effect on us. Overconsumption of these foods disperses internal energy and is a primary cause of the weakness and degenerative diseases now prevalent. Caffeine, alcohol, and many drugs are also in this category. Although some of the latter substances (and many sweeteners) produce an initial burst of energy, their effect quickly abates and is followed by a letdown. Because their overall effect is lethargizing and cooling, they're classified as yin.

Yang foods-primarily meat, salt, eggs, and hard cheeses-have a heating and animating effect on the body; overconsumption results in tension and rigidity. Regular consumption of either category-now considered normal in the West-leads to imbalances in the body's energy that ultimately become manifest as physical problems. There are yin diseases and yang diseases, characterized by an excess of one or the other, and diseases resulting from both. It's therefore advisable to subsist more toward the center of the food-energy spectrum.

A diet based on this principle-the principle of balance-is grain-centered rather than meat-centered and includes vegetables, beans and bean products, soups and condiments, and in some cases fish and desserts. Foods that are packaged, processed, or chemically treated are avoided, as are most animal products. Methods of preparation affect the energy in foods and are also important-ingredients and preparation are suited to the season and locale, with an emphasis on variety, and the use of electricity in cooking is avoided. The five elements are also taken into consideration, as manifested in the five tastes: sweet, salty, sour, bitter, and pungent.

The point about macrobiotics as it relates to chi kung, however, is that despite its excellence, it can at best only remove self-imposed obstacles to health-halting the dissipation of our energy by wrong food choices, allowing our own healing processes to function optimally and unencumbered.

The importance of this achievement should not be underestimated. But if our energy is low to begin with and has been further depleted by disease or injury, merely halting its dissipation may not be enough. We must actively consolidate and rebuild and expand it for healing of deep or chronic problems to take place, and chi kung can do this. Macrobiotics is, in a sense, the yin or passive aspect of energy practice, while chi kung is the yang or active aspect. We can do either separately, but for the most rapid progress, both are essential.

CALORIE

A calorie refers to a non-SI unit of energy. There are two

common but different meanings: one is used in food and nutrition, the other was formerly widely used in chemistry, and a food calorie represents 1000 chemistry calories. The food calorie is sometimes capitalized as Calorie to distinguish it from the chemistry calorie; however, this capitalization is rarely observed in practice. Nutritionists measure the energy content of food in "calories" (sometimes capitalized and abbreviated as Cal or sometimes C, or abbreviated kcal as if small calories were being used), where each food calorie represents 4,184 joules. This is equivalent to 1000 of the calories used in chemistry, and thus the food Calorie would be called a kilocalorie if small calories were being used.

However, in chemistry calories have been deprecated as a scientific unit of measure in favour of joules, and therefore in common modern usage the word "calorie" usually refers to a food calorie. This situation provides two ways of talking about the amount of calories in food which look quite different but that express the exact same amount of energy. One may say that dietary fat has nine kilocalories (kcal) per gram, while proteins and carbohydrates have four kcal per gram, or, one may say that fat has nine Calories per gram while carbohydrates and proteins have four Calories per gram.

The amount of food energy in a particular food is measured by completely burning the food in a bomb calorimeter, a method known as direct calorimetry. Dieticians recommend counting calories to avoid obesity. The government of the United Kingdom recommends consumption of no more than 2000 Calories (2000 kcal) by women each day and 2500 Calories (2500 kcal) by men each day. In physics or chemistry, a calorie (abbreviated cal) is a unit of energy that equals the amount of heat necessary to raise the temperature of one gram of water by 1 degree Celsius, at a pressure of 1 atm. This amount of heat depends somewhat on the initial temperature of the water, which results in various different units sharing the name of "calorie" but having slightly different energy values:

— the 15 °C calorie,

— the 4 °C calorie,

— the mean 0 °C to 100 °C calorie,

— the International Steam Table calorie,

— the thermochemical calorie,

The slight variations in these units can be seen if you convert them to joules. For example, one 15 °C calorie is the amount of heat necessary to raise the temperature of 1 g of water from 14.5 °C to 15.5 °C. This is approximately equal to 4.1855 J or 3.968×10^{-3} Btu. The International Steam Table calorie is approximately equal to 4.1868 J and the thermochemical calorie 4.184 J. Of these various units, what is most commonly meant by calorie in contemporary English text is the 15 °C calorie. The nutritional Calorie represents 1000 of these 15 °C calories.

Since this could be a source of confusion and error, these units are now deprecated. The International System of Units (SI) unit for heat (and for all other forms of energy) is the joule (J), while the (obsolete) cgs system uses the erg.

Estimates of requirements relate to the maintenance of health in already healthy individuals. Health is understood to include patterns of activity that are judged to be consistent with satisfactory physiological and social function. The requirements for energy and protein of an individual are defined in the following terms:

Energy: The energy requirement of an individual is the level of energy intake from food that will balance energy expenditure when the individual has a body size and composition, and level of physical activity, consistent with long-term good health; and that will allow for the maintenance of economically necessary and socially desirable physical activity. In children and pregnant or lactating women the energy requirement includes the energy needs associated with the deposition of tissues or the secretion of milk at rates consistent with good health.

Protein: The protein requirement of an individual is defined as the lowest level of dietary protein intake that will balance the losses of nitrogen from the body in persons maintaining energy balance at modest levels of physical activity. In children and pregnant or lactating women, the protein requirement is taken to include the needs associated with the deposition of tissues or the secretion of milk at rates consistent with good health.

All requirement estimates refer to needs persisting over moderate periods of time. The corresponding intakes may be referred to as "habitual" or "usual", to distinguish them from intakes on a particular day. However, as a matter of convention and convenience they are expressed as daily rates (of intake). However, there is no implication that these amounts must be consumed each day.

There are important physiological differences between the requirements for energy and protein, as defined above. For energy, it is usually considered that once the level of body weight and physical activity has been fixed and the appropriate growth rate defined, there is only one level of intake at which energy balance can be achieved; in consequence, this becomes that individual's requirement for energy. Even if some degree of adaptation is possible, it is likely that this range is fairly narrow. If the intake is either above or below the requirement, defined in this way, a change in body energy stores is to be expected unless energy expenditure is correspondingly altered.

If such changes in expenditure do not occur, the energy store, mainly in the form of adipose tissue, will increase when the intake exceeds requirement and decrease when it is below requirement. It is clearly contrary to experience to suppose that for each individual there is one fixed setpoint for body weight and adipose tissue mass compatible with health. In fact, we recognize that for any individual there is probably a range of acceptable body weights, and this also applies to the individuals in a group. However, if the imbalance is too great, or continues over long periods, the resulting changes in body weight and composition can be detrimental to function and health. Consequently, there may be risks associated with intakes either above or below actual requirements.

For protein, the requirements of individuals are also expressed in terms of the amount of dietary protein needed to prevent losses of body protein and to allow, where appropriate, for desirable rates of deposition of protein during growth and pregnancy. In this respect, the requirements of the individual for both protein and energy are analogous. However, in contrast to energy, if more protein is ingested than is needed for metabolic purposes, essentially all the excess is metabolized and the end-products are excreted, since protein is not stored in the body in the way that energy is stored in adipose tissue.

Furthermore, again in contrast to energy, no detrimental effect has been identified with intakes of protein moderately above the actual requirement. For an individual, the range between the intake that is just sufficient to compensate for losses (or permit growth) and intakes that are associated with harmful effects is therefore wide. The individual's requirement is thus defined as the lower end of this range. This fundamental biological difference between energy and protein has important consequences for describing the distribution of requirements among the individuals of a group.

Estimates of requirements are derived from measurements on individuals. Actual measurements on people of the same sex and of similar age, body size, and physical activity are in practice grouped together to give the average energy or protein requirement of that set of people, together with a measure of their variability. These results are then used to predict the requirements of other individuals or collections of individuals who have the same characteristics, but on whom measurements have not been made. Such a collection of similar individuals may be referred to as a class.

The characteristics of the class are that obvious factors that may affect requirements-age, sex, weight, etc.-have been matched. However, in spite of the matching there remain many unknown factors producing variation between individuals, so that there is a distribution of requirements within the class. Changes in the variables that characterize the class will involve a change in the average requirement and therefore a change in the position of the distribution.

These concepts apply to both energy and protein requirements. For a class of similar individuals, the descriptor of energy requirements is the average of the individual requirements, without specific provision for the known individual variation in requirement.

The descriptor of the protein requirement of a class of similar individuals is the safe level of intake, an amount that will meet or exceed the requirements of practically all the individuals in the group, explicitly taking into account individual variation in requirement.

The contrast between the two descriptors is illustrated in Fig. 1, in which it is assumed that the statistical distributions are Gaussian, although the principles hold for other types of distribution. Fig. 2 shows the proportion of randomly selected individuals whose requirement would not be met when a particular level of intake is provided. The curve describes the probability that the intake would or would not meet an individual's requirement.

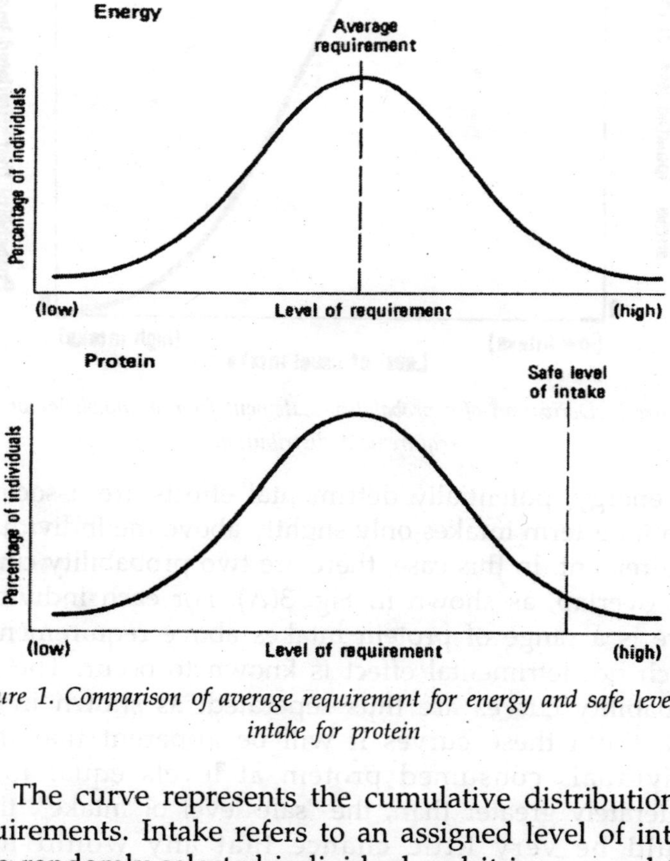

Figure 1. Comparison of average requirement for energy and safe level of intake for protein

The curve represents the cumulative distribution of requirements. Intake refers to an assigned level of intake for a randomly selected individual and it is assumed that there is no correlation between intake and requirement among similar individuals. In a similar way, one can consider the probability that a high intake will be associated with detrimental effects for a randomly selected individual. As noted above, there is a major biological difference between energy and protein in this respect.

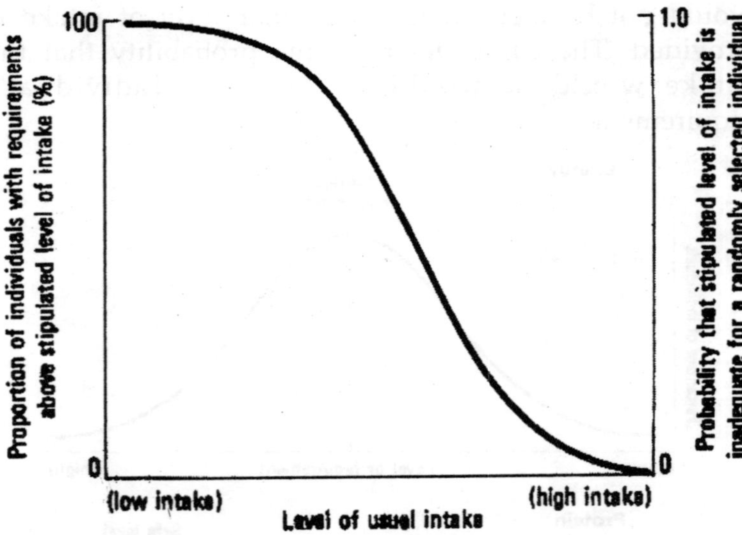

Figure 2. Derivation of a probability statement from a knowledge of the requirement distribution

For energy, potentially detrimental effects are associated with long-term intakes only slightly above the individual's requirement. In this case, there are two probability curves that overlap, as shown in Fig. 3(A). For each individual there is a range of protein intakes above requirement at which no detrimental effect is known to occur. The two probability curves are thus separated, as shown in Fig. 3(B). From these curves it will be apparent that if all individuals consumed protein at levels equal to, or moderately greater than, the "safe level of intake", there would be very little chance that any would have inadequate intakes.

Most people have the ability to select their food intake in accordance with their energy requirement over the long-term, since it is believed that regulatory mechanisms operate to maintain a balance between energy intake and energy requirement over long periods of time. This implies that one would expect there to be a correlation between energy intake and energy requirement among individuals if sufficient food is available in the absence of interfering factors. In the examples cited above (Fig. 3), food intake was taken as fixed at each level, and the probabilities of inadequacy or excess at that level for a random individual were considered.

If self-selection is allowed to operate, it is to be expected that individuals will make selections according to energy need and the probability of inadequacy or excess will below across the whole range shown in Fig. 3. If the average energy intake of a class were equal to the average requirement of the class, almost all individuals would be at low risk because of processes regulating energy balance and the resultant correlation between intake and requirement. Thus, when one is considering the requirements of classes, the estimate of average requirement is an appropriate descriptor for the distribution of requirement.

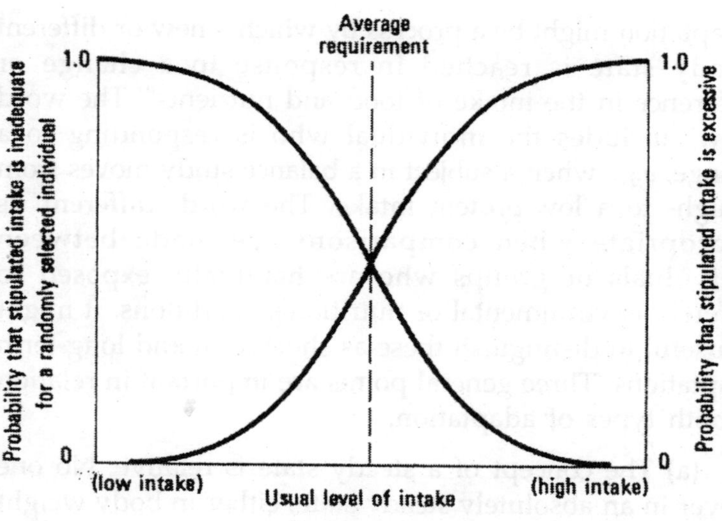

Figure 3. Probability that a particular intake is inadequate or excessive for a randomly selected individual with regard to energy intake (A) and protein intake (B)

In the case of energy, the two probability curves overlap. In the case of protein the curves are separated by a "safe range of intake" that will be associated with low probabilities of either inadequacy or excess for almost all individuals. For protein, there is very little evidence of a correlation between intake and requirement among individuals consuming self-selected diets. Thus, the probability descriptions presented in Fig. 3 apply whether the random individual consumes a self-selected diet or is given an arbitrarily selected amount of protein. Consequently, if the average protein intake of a group is equal to the average protein requirement of that group, it cannot be assumed that the probability of inadequacy will be low for most individuals. On the contrary, this would be an "unsafe" situation.

Requirements of Energy and Protien

Adaptation

Adaptation might be a process by which a new or different steady state is reached in response to a change or difference in the intake of food and nutrients". The word "new" includes the individual who is responding to a change, e.g., when a subject in a balance study moves from a high- to a low-protein intake. The word "different" is appropriate when comparisons are made between individuals or groups who are habitually exposed to different environmental or nutritional conditions. It might be useful to distinguish these as short-term and long-term adaptations. Three general points are important in relation to both types of adaptation.

(a) The concept of a steady state is relative. No one is ever in an absolutely steady state, either in body weight or in nitrogen balance. During the day, when food is being eaten, nitrogen balance is positive; during the night, in the absence of food, it becomes negative. Over 24 hours these fluctuations even out. The situation is precisely analogous to the oxygen debt incurred during strenuous exercise, which is made up during rest. The time-scale over which a state may be considered steady will vary for different functions. It is also clear that in biological systems no so-called steady state is completely stable. This is illustrated by the slow changes in body composition and function that occur as adults age.

(b) Adaptations may be of fundamentally different kindsmetabolic, biological/genetic, and social/behavioural. The response to a change in protein intake is one of the best worked out examples of a metabolic adaptation, but even in this case we do not know the limits of human adaptability. Reduction in physical activity as a consequence of a reduced energy intake could be regarded as a behavioural adaptation, with both good and bad effects. For example, the energy intakes of children may be adequate to support satisfactory growth rates, but only at the expense of a reduction in total energy expenditure, notably through less physical activity. The result is to impair the child's capacity for exploration and play, and hence his mental, functional, and social development. It has often been suggested that a decrease in body size might be an advantageous adaptation to shortage in food supply.

The determinants of body size are complex and depend upon both environmental and genetic factors. In developing countries large numbers of children are small for their age compared with the NCHS standards. This reduction in linear growth ("stunting") is the result of environmental factors because it is reversible under favourable conditions. Whether it represents a handicap is hotly debated. It has also been suggested that selection might occur in favour of those who are genetically smaller and hence have lower needs. A full analysis of the significance of differences in body size would have to take account also of the secular changes that have occurred in a number of countries and of the established relationship between the heights of parents and their children.

(c) It follows from these considerations that adaptation implies a range of steady states and it is impossible to define a single point within the range that represents the "normal". Different adapted states will carry different advantages and penalties. A decision about which is optimal or preferable can only be made in the light of a particular set of values. If the criteria are life expectancy and freedom from disease in the early years of life, then perhaps the nutritional state in industrialized societies might be preferred to that of developing countries, but there may be other criteria of optimal functional capacity.

Reference Standards for Children, Adolescents, and Adults

Although the energy and protein requirements for the process of growth are relatively small compared with those for maintenance, except in the young infant, satisfactory growth is nevertheless a sensitive criterion of whether needs are being met. Therefore, the definition of satisfactory growth is the first step in estimating the requirements of infants and children. An example of the dilemma mentioned above is whether reference standards for the growth of children in industrialized countries should be accepted as universally relevant or whether local standards should be used.

Children in many developing countries are smaller at birth than those in industrialized countries and grow at a slower rate during infancy and early childhood. The evidence suggests that in young children these differences are due primarily to environmental factors, including inadequate nutrition, and that genetic and ethnic factors are of lesser importance, sò that young children of different ethnic groups should be considered as having the same or similar growth potential. Even in a healthy privileged population there is a wide range of variation in the size of children. In such a population there is no indication that differences in size per se are related to health, wellbeing, or physiological function.

However, in communities where children's growth is limited by environmental factors, there is evidence of an association between functional impairment and deficit in linear growth. In such situations, it is extremely difficult to separate the effects of undernutrition from those of other aspects of social deprivation. Therefore, it remains a matter for further research how far small size in children represents a handicap or an adaptation, whether minor limitations of genetic growth potential are harmful, and whether maximum growth is necessarily an indicator of optimal nutrition.

Nevertheless, the Consultation feels it desirable that the growth potential of children should be fully expressed, and estimates of energy and protein requirements should allow for this. Estimates of the requirements of children up to 10 years are therefore based on the reference growth standards published for international use by WHO, which are derived from the United States National Center for Health Statistics (NCHS). The use of this particular reference population is recommended on the basis of a number of criteria. Surprisingly, in contrast to adults, there appear to be no recommendations for children concerning the ranges within which weight or height at any given age may be regarded as satisfactory.

This is partly because information about the risk attached to given degrees of deficit is only just becoming available, and partly because children start with different birth-weights, and therefore their attained weights will continue for some time to be above or below the median. In epidemiological studies of childhood undernutrition it is conventional to accept -2 SD from the median as the cut-off point between "normal" and "malnourished", corresponding approximately to the 3rd centile or to 80% of the median for weight and 90% for height. Similarly, +2 SD in weight for height may be taken as a cut-off point for obesity.

In relation to growth, two further points must be taken into account. Previous committees have based their estimates of the daily requirements for growth on increments in body weight of the reference population over intervals of 3 months for infants below 1 year and intervals of 1 year for older children. This procedure assumes that growth occurs at the same rate from day to day. It must be recognized that this is not so, and that even in normal children free from infection growth occurs in spurts. As a result, the variability in weight gain over short periods such as one month is extremely high. For example, in two longitudinal studies from birth to 3-6 months, the coefficient of variation of weight gain over 4-week periods was approximately 37%.

The reasons for this variability in the rate of weight gain are not clear. The data of Fomon show that it is greater than the variability in energy intake. One factor, therefore, may be day-to-day fluctuations in physical activity. From the point of view of protein requirements, the phenomenon could be regarded as analogous, on a longer time-scale, to the metabolic differences that have been observed between the day, when food is consumed, and the night, when it is not. Studies on adults have shown that during the night there is a negative nitrogen balance that is cancelled out by a positive balance during the day. In children it has been suggested that growth occurs in spurts in relation to food intake.

The variability in growth would not affect requirements averaged over a period of time if it were a consequence simply of fluctuations in food intake, so that intake and rate of growth each day were exactly matched.

It seems unlikely, however, that this is the full explanation. Since this exact matching does not happen, the effect of the variability in growth may be to increase the growth component of the requirement, as a reduction in growth over one period will have to be compensated by an increased growth rate later on. A second question that should be raised, although it cannot at present be answered, results from the fact that all allowances for growth are based on increments of body weight. It is conceivable that growth might be limited by special requirements of particular tissues; for example, the relative amounts of energy and protein needed to achieve a given gain in body weight might not be the same as the amounts needed to secure an appropriate increase in height. This is a subject on which further research is needed.

The desirable heights and weights of children over 10 years of age present special problems, because there is considerable variation between individuals and groups in the timing of the adolescent growth spurt, which starts at different calendar ages in boys and girls. Furthermore, if children have been growing slowly from infancy, as happens in many developing countries, by 10 years of age the gap between their actual weight and their expected weight, based on that of adolescents in industrialized countries, will be very large. It is not known whether extra food at this stage can increase the extent and duration of the pubertal growth spurt.

For these reasons it is considered more realistic, after the age of 10 years, to relate requirements to the appropriate weight for height rather than weight for age. In order to maintain uniformity with the reference values for the earlier years of childhood, the standards published by WHO for height up to 18 years have again been chosen, but they do not include values of weight for height beyond 10 years. To provide these values the Consultation used data from a large sample of children measured in the

United States of America earlier in this century. By using actual height and median weight for height, it is possible to allow for the fact that puberty begins at different ages in different groups of adolescents. Again, as with younger children, there are no clear recommendations about the "acceptable" range of weight for height.

Adult groups in various parts of the world show substantial differences in height, and height variations are also common within countries and races. In general, there is no reason to suppose that adults of either short or tall stature have a health risk attributable to their stature, except perhaps in relation to pregnancy and childbirth. However, body weight, when expressed in relation to height, does influence health, and a range of desirable or acceptable weights for height has been proposed. The upper limit of the acceptable range, at which there is an increased risk to health, has been reasonably well defined.

Long-term prospective studies on large numbers of adults in developing countries are not available. At present the average weight of adults in many countries is below the mid-point of that range, and sometimes even below the lower limit. There is no direct evidence that this in itself is either beneficial or harmful. More information relating body weight and composition to health risk in these communities would be valuable. A useful simplification is to express the weight for height as the body mass index (BMI), since this function gives a measure of weight for height that is largely independent of actual height.

Body Composition

Estimates of requirements based on body weight are an approximation, since they do not take account of differences in body composition, which will determine true requirements. In recent decades the emergence of methods for estimating some body components in living subjects has resulted in observations on several thousand people ranging from newborn infants to the very old. At birth the neonate averages 14% body fat, which rises to about 23% at 12 months and declines to 18% at 6 years of age. During this period girls have slightly more body fat than boys, and this difference becomes more pronounced after 6 years.

During adolescence the difference in the body fat content between the sexes becomes strikingly accentuated and persists throughout adult life as shown by differences in the thickness of the subcutaneous fat layers. There is evidence that body composition is also influenced by genetic factors, since obesity tends to be familial and monozygous twins are more concordant in fatness than dizygous twins. Adolescence is also characterized by a major sex difference in the rate of acquisition of lean weight. Boys show a rapid and sustained spurt in lean weight, whereas there is a modest acquisition of body fat in the early phase of puberty, followed by a decline. In contrast, girls have a smaller spurt in lean weight, but they acquire more body fat.

In adolescent boys the time of the spurt in lean weight has been found to coincide with the most rapid growth in height, and to continue until 20-25 years of age, whereas in girls the pubertal increase in lean weight ceases by about 18 years, in keeping with the marked decrease in the rate of gain in stature after menarche. During the second decade of life boys thus double their lean weight, while the increase in girls is only 1.5-fold. The end result at maturity is a fat-free weight of about 60 kg in males averaging 70 kg total body weight, and 42 kg in females averaging 63 kg. The variability in lean weight is less than that of total body weight.

The adult years are characterized by a decline in lean body mass in both sexes, which becomes obvious by the age of 40; by 85 years the lean body mass has reached a value about three-quarters of that characteristic of the young adult. Simultaneous measurements of body nitrogen by neutron activation and body potassium as 40K show that, with advancing age, more potassium than nitrogen is lost, implying that the potassium-rich muscle mass is especially reduced. The relative loss of potassium is about 10% between the sixth and eighth decades. Autopsy data confirm that subjects over 70 years of age have 40% less muscle than young adults, with a smaller reduction in the mass of visceral organs.

Preferential loss of muscle with aging is also demonstrated by the decline in creatinine output and the fall in 3-methyl histidine output. This age-related loss of lean body mass is commonly accompanied by an increase in body fat. Consequently, in relation to body weight, the lean tissue content of the body declines with age, and this accounts in part for a progressive fall in basal metabolic rate in relation to body size. In the elderly there is a decrease in the proportion of skeletal mass, as well as muscle. Within the lean body mass there are also differences in the proportion of various tissues at different ages. From birth to maturity the brain increases its mass 5-fold, the liver, heart, and kidneys, which are even more metabolically active, increase 10- to 12-fold, while muscle multiplies its mass by about 40-fold.

Physical Fitness

Estimates of requirements for energy and protein are based primarily on metabolic and balance studies of limited duration. However, the estimated requirements should be enough to maintain health and sustain optimal bodily function, including physical and mental fitness. During growth, in addition to the increases in weight and height, there are marked functional changes. In boys, aerobic capacity and heart volume in relation to lean body mass increase up to the age of 14-15 years. The natural peak in functional capacity coincides with high levels of spontaneous physical activity, and estimates of requirements must allow for this. Conversely, in the fourth to the fifth decade of life aerobic capacity starts to decline, with decreasing physical activity and energy requirements.

Intakes of energy or protein above as well as below those needed for optimal function may be detrimental if they exceed the adaptive capacity of the organism. Excessive energy intakes lead to obesity, with reductions in cardiorespiratory efficiency, physical performance, and endurance. It has already been suggested that stunting in linear growth may represent an adaptation that does not necessarily present any health hazard beyond early life. For example, cardiorespiratory function, physical performance, and muscular strength were found to be significantly better in stunted Tunisian children from a poor socioeconomic group than in children from affluent families, whose growth was closer to that of the standard in developed countries.

Similarly, Italian children from poor families performed better in physical fitness tests than their counterparts from more prosperous families, in spite of their smaller size and lower habitual energy intakes. These findings suggest that habitual physical activity is a more important determinant of fitness than is body size per se. Nor do the effects of small stature necessarily carry penalties in adult life except for tasks requiring a particular body build and strength. Thus high aerobic capacity related to body weight was found in Indian miners with very low weights and heights compared with their counterparts in other countries. On the other hand, in another study in India low weight and height were significant handicaps for obtaining employment in agriculture. Therefore, while stunting in height is a rather sensitive marker of socioeconomically disadvantaged populations, the consequences need to be carefully evaluated for evidence of any functional handicap.

Relation Between Weight and Age

Protein: Within a given age range, the requirement for protein per kg of body weight is considered to be constant. Therefore, the primary expression of protein requirement is in grams of protein per kilogram. This principle applies to all ages, although absolute additions, in units of grams of protein per day, are made for pregnancy and lactation.

Energy: For energy the position is more complicated, because at a given age the main component of the energy requirement, the basal metabolic rate (BMR) varies not only with absolute body weight but also per kg. The total energy requirement per kg, therefore, cannot be taken as constant. Hence the primary expression of energy requirement is the total requirement per person, derived from that person's body weight.

With adults less than 60 years old the effect of age is relatively unimportant, since at a given weight the BMR decreases by only about 1% per decade. With children the change of BMR per kg with age is much greater-about 5% per year between 3 and 10 years. At present, we do not know to what extent this reflects an age-related change per se, or age-related changes in body weight.

The energy requirements of adolescents are treated in the same way as those of adults. If at each age weight is the main determinant of requirements, the question then arises, what weight should be used? Within the acceptable range, many people will have weights that differ by 10% or more from the median. If the actual weight is used, it will tend to maintain the status quo. If the median of the reference range is used, the result will have a normative effect. The existing needs of those who are at the lower end of the weight range for age or height will be overestimated and the needs of those at the upper end will be underestimated.

If the requirements so calculated are fulfilled, there will be a tendency for weight to move towards the median. This is what is meant by the term "normative". It will be for the user to choose the most appropriate body weight for calculating requirements, depending on the circumstances and his aims. For the purposes of tabulation it is necessary to group together individuals, according to age, weight for height, etc. The wider the ranges chosen, the less homogeneous such groups will be. The problem then is to decide on operationally useful ranges. No hard-and-fast guideline can be laid down. A large number of narrow ranges is more precise than a small number of wide ones, but also more complex.

The variability of requirements within a group defined by any chosen range will clearly be greater than in a completely homogeneous class. This has implications for calculating the requirements of the group as a whole which are of great importance for the application of requirement estimates. The requirements specified for each range in the tables represent those of the individual or homogeneous class whose weight for age or weight for height is at the mid-point of the range. Such estimates do not necessarily correspond with the average requirement of the group as a whole, since this will depend on the distribution of individuals within the group.

11

Digestion, Absorption and Metabolism

Digestion is the process whereby the body breaks down food into absorbable nutrients. The digestive tract is a long tube surrounded by muscles. These muscles alternate contracting and relaxing (peristaltic motion) pushing food along the digestion tract. Digestion begins shortly after food is in the mouth. The teeth grind solid foods to reduce the size of the food pieces. Saliva is released which helps moisten the food. The tongue pushes the moisten chewed food to the back of the mouth, starting the swallowing reflex.

The moist food passes through the esophagus and enters the stomach. The stomach is a distended pouch of the digestive tube. Strong circular muscles at each end of the stomach control food entering and leaving the stomach. The stomach mixes food by muscular contractions, causing food particles to break up further. The stomach secretes hydrochloric acid and other digestive enzymes, mostly for protein digestion, and also kills many microorganisms in food. The stomach does not absorb nutrients, except for some water and alcohol. Most nutrients are absorbed later in the small intestine. When food reaches a liquid consistency, the stomach releases some of the food mixture into the small intestine.

Most digestion and nutrient absorption occurs in the small intestine. The gall bladder releases bile into the small intestine, which contains bile salts for fat digestion. Bile salts help break up fat into smaller particles so fat digestive enzymes are able to work. The pancreas, connected to the small intestine, releases many of the digestive enzymes. Some enzymes digest protein, other enzymes digest carbohydrates, and others fats. The pancreas also produces hormones, such as insulin. These hormones are released into the blood, not the intestines. Enzymes needed for the final steps in digestion of proteins, carbohydrates and fats are found in the cells lining the small intestine. Digestive enzymes break down food particles into final breakdown products.

The final breakdown products of protein digestion are single amino acids or small chains of two or three amino acids. The final products of carbohydrate digestion are monosaccharides. The final digestive products of triglyceride digestion are free fatty acids and glycerol and monoglycerides. Vitamins, minerals, water, and some larger fat-like compounds such as cholesterol are not broken down before they are absorbed.

The cells lining the small intestine absorb the digestion breakdown products from carbohydrates, proteins and fats, vitamins, minerals and most water. Once inside the intestinal wall the breakdown products of digestion are released into the body through one of two transport systems; the bloodstream or the lymphatic system. The water-soluble nutrients and short fatty acids are released directly into the bloodstream. Longer fatty acids, fat-soluble vitamins, and fat-like compounds such as cholesterol are not water-soluble and the blood is mostly water.

In the intestinal wall the longer fatty acids and glycerol reform triglycerides, and they are packed with the fat-soluble vitamins and fat-like compounds into chylomicrons. The chylomicrons are released into the lymphatic system which flows into the bloodstream near the heart. After digestion and absorption of nutrients is completed, indigestible matter, such as fiber moves into the large intestine. In the large intestine the indigestible matter is compacted by removing water. Little nutrient absorption occurs in the large intestine.

All the chemical reactions that occur in the body is called *metabolism*. For metabolism to occur the body needs water, energy, oxygen, and nutrients. The body uses nutrients released into the blood stream to:

— build and maintain body tissues, hormones, etc.;

— regulate body functions performed by the heart, blood, liver, kidneys, brain, etc.;

— supply energy for body functions and for physical activity.

The gastrointestinal (GI) system includes the gastrointestinal tract (mouth, pharynx, esophagus, stomach, small intestine, large intestine) and accessory organs (salivary gland, liver, gallbladder, pancreas) that secrete substances into the tract via connecting ducts. GI system breaks down particles of ingested food into molecular forms by enzymes (digestion) that are then transferred to the internal environment (absorption).

Functions of GI organs The GI tract begins at the mouth, where digestion begins with chewing. Saliva containing mucus and the enzyme amylase is secreted from 3 pairs of salivary glands, located in the head. Mucus moistens the food and amylase partially digests polysaccharides (starches). Food then reaches the stomach through the pharynx and esophagus. The stomach is the sac that stores and digests food macromolecules into a solution called chyme. Glands lining the stomach secrete hydrochloric acid that dissolves food particles and protein-digesting enzymes, called pepsin.

Final stages of digestion and most of the nutrient absorption occurs in next portion of the tract: the small intestine. The small intestine is divided into 3 segments - duodenum, jejunum, and ileum. The pancreas is a gland located behind the stomach. From its exocrine portion it secretes (1) digestive enzymes and (2) a fluid rich in HCO_3- ions to neutralize the acid from stomach. The liver secretes bile. Bile contains HCO_3- ions and bile salts to solubilize fats.

Bile reaches the gall bladder through hepatic ducts and is stored in the gall bladder between meals. During a meal, bile is secreted from the gland by smooth muscle contraction and reaches the duodenum portion of the small intestine by the common bile duct. Monosaccharides, amino acids and mineral salts are absorbed by transporter-mediated processes while fatty acid water diffuse passively. Undigested material is passed to large intestine, where it is temporarily stored and concentrated by reabsorption of salts and water. Finally, contractions of rectum, the last part of large intestine, expel the feces through the anus. Structure of GI Tract Wall The luminar surface is covered by a single layer of epithelium containing exocrine and endocrine cells.

The exocrine cells disintegrate and discharge into the lumen, releasing their enzymes. The epithelia with an underlying layer of connective tissue (lamnia propia) and muscle (muscularis mucosa) are called mucosa. Below the mucosa is a layer of inner circular and outer longitudinal smooth muscle called muscularis externa, which provides the forces for moving and mixing the GI contents. The outermost layer of the tube is made up of connective tissue called serosa. The luminar surface of the tube is highly convoluted into projections called villi and microvilli; both of which increase total surface area for absorption. The center of each villus has a single blunt-ended lymphatic vessel called lacteal. Venous drainage from the intestine transports absorbed materials to the liver for processing via the hepatic portal vein.

Carbohydrate

Digestion begins in the mouth by salivary amylase and completed in the small intestine by pancreatic amylase. Monosaccharides, such as glucose, galactose and fructose, are produced by the breakdown of polysaccharides and are transported to the intestinal epithelium by facilitated diffusion or active transport. Facilitated diffusion moves the sugars to the bloodstream.

Protein

Proteins are broken down to peptide fragments by pepsin in the stomach, and by pancreatic trypsin and chemotrypsin in the small intestine. The fragments are then digested to free amino acids by carboxypeptidase from the pancreas and aminopeptidase from the intestinal epithelium. Free amino acids enter the epithelium by secondary active transport and leave it by facilitated diffusion. Small amounts of intact proteins can enter interstitial fluid by endo- and exocytosis.

Fat

Fat digestion occurs by pancreatic lipase in small intestine. A monoglyceride and two fatty acids are produced in the digestive process. Large lipid droplets are first broken down into smaller droplets, by a process called emulsification. Emulsification is driven by mechanical disruption (by contractile activity of GI tract) and emulsifying agents (amphipathic bile salts). Pancreatic colipase binds the water-soluble lipase to the lipid substrate.

Digested products and bile salts form amphipathic micelles. These micelles keep the insoluble products in soluble aggregates from which small amounts are released and absorbed by epithelial cells via diffusion. Free fatty acids and monoglycerides then recombine into triacylglycerols at the smooth ER, are processed further in the Golgi and enter the interstitial fluid as droplets called chylomicrons, which are then taken up by the lacteals in the intestine.

Vitamins

Fat-soluble vitamins are absorbed and stored along with fats. Most water-soluble vitamins are absorbed by diffusion or mediated transport. Vitamin B_{12}, because of its large size and charged nature, first binds to a protein, called intrinsic factor, which is secreted by the stomach epithelium, and is then absorbed by endocytosis. Water The stomach absorbs some water but most is absorbed at small intestine by diffusion.

Regulation of GI Processes

Control mechanisms of the GI system regulate conditions in the lumen of the tract. Reflexes are initiated by:

— Distension of wall by volume of luminal contents

— Chyme osmolarity

— Chyme pH

— Chyme concentrations of specific products.

Neural Regulation of the GI tract: Impulses to the GI muscles and exocrine glands are supplied by enteric nervous system, the local nervous system of GI tract, which allows local, short reflexes, independent of CNS. Long reflexes through the CNS are possible via sympathetic and parasympathetic nerves, which also innervate the GI tract.

Hormonal Regulation: Endocrine cells are scattered throughout GI epithelia and surface of these cells is exposed to the lumen. Chemical substances in the chyme stimulate them to release hormones into blood.

Phases of GI control: Each phase is named according to where the receptor for a reflex is located. These phases do not occur in temporal sequence.

— The cephalic phase is initiated when sight, smell, taste, chewing, and emotional states stimulate receptors in the head. Reflexes mediated by sympathetic and parasympathetic fibers activate secretory and contractile activity.

— The gastric phase is initiated by distension, acidity, and the presence of amino acids and peptides in the stomach. This phase is mediated by short and long reflexes and activates the secretion of gastrin.

— The intestinal phase is initiated by distension, acidity, osmolarity of digestive products in intestine and is mediated by GI hormones and short and long neural reflexes.

Mouth, Pharynx, and Esophagus

Chewing is controlled by somatic nerves to the skeletal muscles and the reflex activation of mechanoreceptors on the palate, gums and tongue. Autonomic nerves in response to chemoreceptors and pressure receptors in mouth stimulate saliva secretion. Swallowing is mediated by pressure receptors on walls of pharynx, which send impulses to the swallowing center in the medulla oblongata.

The center activates muscles in the pharynx and esophagus. Multiple responses occur in a temporal sequence. The palate is elevated to prevent food from entering the nasal cavity, respiration is inhibited and the epiglottis covers the glottis to prevent food from entering trachea (windpipe). The upper esophageal sphincter opens and food enters the esophagus and moves toward the stomach by muscle contractions called peristaltic waves. Food then moves to the stomach when the lower esophageal sphincter opens.

A less efficient, or faulty, lower esophageal sphincter results in the reflux of gastric contents into the esophagus (gastro-esophageal reflux), this reversal results in heartburn and over time contributes to ulceration of esophagus. Epithelium lining the stomach invaginates into the mucosa, forming tubular glands. Parietal (oxyntic) cells secrete acid and intrinsic factor and chief cells secrete pepsinogen. Also scattered throughout are enterochromaffin-like (ECL) cells, which secrete histamine, and other cells that secrete somatostatin. The antrum, a lower portion of the stomach, secretes gastrin.

Increased protein content in a meal stimulates release of gastrin and histamine, which in turn stimulates HCl secretion. Somatostatin inhibits acid secretion by inhibiting the release of gastrin and histamine. Enterogastones in the duodenum also inhibit gastric acid secretion. The precursor pepsinogen, which is produced by chief cells, is converted to pepsin by the acid in the stomach. The stomach produces peristaltic waves in response to the arrival of food.

The pyloric sphincter between the stomach and duodenum opens to release small amounts of chyme into the duodenum with each wave. These waves are generated by pacemaker cells in the longitudinal smooth muscle layer and are spread out by gap junctions. Gastrin, distension of stomach etc. stimulate gastric motility while distension of duodenum inhibits it.

Pancreatic Secretions

Inactive trypsinogen is secreted by pancreas and is later

converted by the intestinal enzyme enterokinase to active trypsin, which digests proteins. Pancreatic amylase and lipase are secreted in active forms. The pancreas also secretes bicarbonate ions. Secretion of pancreatic enzymes is stimulated by cholecystokinin (CCK), the secretion of which is triggered by the detected presence of fatty acids and amino acids in the small intestine. The secretion of bicarbonate ions is stimulated by secretin, which is triggered by acidity in small intestine.

Bile Secretion

Bile contains bile salts, which solubilize fats, and bicarbonate ions, which in turn are used to neutralize stomach acids. Bile salts, secreted by hepatocytes (liver cells) enter the GI tract and are reabsorbed by transporters in the intestine and are returned to the liver via the portal vein. This recycling pathway is called the entero-hepatic circulation. The sphincter of Oddi controls the entry of the bile duct into the duodenum. When the sphincter is closed, secreted bile is shunted into the gallbladder. The presence of fat in the intestine releases CCK, which relaxes the sphincter to discharge bile salts into the duodenum.

Small Intestine

The most common motion of the small intestine is stationary contraction and relaxation, called segmentation. Segmentation results in little net movement. The chyme is mixed and brought into contact with the intestine wall and then moved slowly toward the large intestine. The movements are initiated by pacemaker cells in the smooth muscle layer. After most of the materials are absorbed, segmentation is replaced by peristaltic activity called migrating motility complex, which moves any undigested material to the large intestine. The candidate intestinal hormone, motilin, initiates migrating motility.

Large Intestine

The large intestine consists of 3 parts: the cecum, colon and rectum. The primary function is to store and concentrate fecal material for elimination. Chyme enters the cecum through the ileocecal sphincter, which relaxes and opens as a result of the gastroileal reflex. Na+ is absorbed along with water. K+ and HCO_3- ions are secreted into the lumen. Undigested polysaccharides (fiber) are metabolized to short-chain fatty acids by the residing bacteria and these are then absorbed by diffusion. A small amount of vitamin K is also produced and absorbed. Bacterial metabolism produces a mixture of gases, called flatus.

Motility and Defecation

Regular contractions of the circular smooth muscle produce a slow rhythmic segmentation movement. The undigested material moves slowly in order to provide resident bacteria time to grow and multiply. Following a meal, there is a wave of intense contraction, called mass movement. The internal anal sphincter is made of smooth muscle and closes the anus, while the external anal sphincter is made of skeletal muscle and is under voluntary control. Both sphincters regulate the anal opening and closing.

Mass movement of fecal material into the anus initiates the defecation reflex, which is mediated by mechanoreceptors. The two sphincters open to expel the feces. If defecation is delayed, rectal contents are driven back into colon by reverse peristalsis until the next mass movement.

Pathophysiology of the GI Tract Ulcers: Ulcers are eroded areas of gastric surface and breaks in the mucosal barrier, which expose the underlying tissue to corrosive action of acid and pepsin. Damage to underlying blood vessels may cause bleeding.

Vomiting

The vomit reflex results in the forceful expulsion of toxic gastric contents. This reflex is coordinated by the vomiting center in the medulla oblongata. Various mechano- and chemo- receptors in the stomach and elsewhere can trigger this reflex.

Increased salivation, sweating, heart rate, pallor etc. accompany the reflex. Abdominal muscles contract to raise abdominal pressure while the lower esophageal sphincter opens and gastric contents are forced into the esophagus (retching). If the upper esophageal sphincter opens, contents are then expelled from the mouth (vomiting). Excessive vomiting can lead to loss of water and salts, which will ultimately result in dehydration.

Gallstones

Excessive secretion of water insoluble cholesterol in bile results in formation of crystals, called gallstones, which can close the opening of gallbladder or the bile duct. If a stone prevents bile from entering the intestine fat digestion and absorption decreases. If a stone blocks the entry of the pancreatic duct, it prevents pancreatic enzymes from entering the intestine, thus preventing the digestion of other nutrients. A blocked bile duct inhibits further secretion of bile, resulting in accumulation of bilirubin in tissues, producing a yellowish coloration called jaundice. Jaundice is common in newborns and is rectified by sunlight exposure.

Lactose Intolerance: Lactose intolerance results from a lack of the enzyme lactase which digests lactose, the sugar in milk. The lack of lactase results in the incomplete digestion of lactose to glucose and galactose.

Constipation and Diarrhea

Constipation is the absence of defecation due to decreased

motility of the large intestine. This results in excess absorption of water from feces, making it hard to expel. Dietary fiber, which is not digested in small intestine, can produce distension and increase motility. Diarrhea results from decreased fluid absorption, or increased fluid secretion resulting in increased luminal fluid, which in turn, causes distension and increased motility. Diarrhea results in decreased blood volume, loss of water and other nutrients.

Regulation of Organic Metabolism

Absorptive state is the period during which ingested nutrients enter blood and some of these nutrients supply the energy need of the body while the remainder is stored. Post-absorptive state is the period during which the GI tract is empty of nutrients and body stores must supply required energy.

Absorptive State

Carbohydrates and proteins are absorbed primarily as monosaccharides and amino acids, respectively, into the blood while fat is absorbed as triacylglycerols into the lymph.

- *Absorbed Carbohydrates*:During the absorptive state, glucose is the major energy source and some of it is converted to glycogen and stored in skeletal muscle and liver. In adipose tissue, glucose is transformed and stored as fat.
- *Absorbed Triacylglycerols*: Fatty acids of plasma chylomicrons are released within adipose tissue capillaries and form triacylglycerols.
- *Absorbed Amino Acids*: Most amino acids enter cells and are used to synthesize proteins and any excess amino acids are converted to carbohydrate or fat.

Post Absorptive State

In this state, the net synthesis of glycogen, fat, and protein ceases, and net catabolism of these substances begins. Plasma glucose level is maintained by:

— Glycogenolysis, which is the hydrolysis of glycogen stores in liver and skeletal muscles.

— Lipolysis, catabolism of triacylglycerols into glycerol and fatty acids in adipose tissues. Any glycerol reaching the liver is converted to glucose.

— Protein is catabolized to glucose. Such new synthesis of glucose is called gluconeogenesis.

Glucose Sparing (Fat Utilization): Glucose sparing means the reduction of glucose catabolism and increase in fat utilization by most tissues. This spares glucose for the brain and thus protein breakdown is minimized.

Endocrine and Neural Control

Insulin

A peptide hormone secreted by beta (B) cells of islets of Langerhans, in the pancreas. Its secretion is increased during the absorptive state and decreased during the post-absorptive state. Insulin targets are muscular, adipose and liver-tissues. The main roles of insulin are to stimulate the movement of glucose from extracellular fluid into cells by facilitated diffusion, stimulate glycogen synthesis and inhibit glycogen catabolism.

Control of Insulin Secretion: Insulin is controlled by an increase in plasma glucose or amino acid concentration, and the hormone glucose dependent insulinotropic peptide (GIP), which is secreted in the GI tract to stimulate insulin secretion. Parasympathetic fibers stimulate insulin secretion.

Glucagon

Glucagon is a peptide hormone secreted by alpha (A) cells of the pancreas. Its target is the liver tissue and its actions are opposed to that of insulin. Glucagon increases glycogen breakdown and gluconeogenesis to increase the plasma concentration of glucose during the post-absorptive state or when plasma glucose is low (hypoglycemia). Sympathetic nerves stimulate glucagon secretion. On a side note, cortisol and growth hormone also have effects similar to that of glucagon.

Diabetes Mellitus

Diabetes mellitus results from a deficiency of insulin or hyporesponsiveness (slowed response) to insulin. In insulin dependent diabetes mellitus (IDDM) or type 1 diabetes, insulin is very low or absent as a result of destruction of beta cells. Large amounts of glucose are excreted as the plasma glucose level is very high and the filtered load of glucose exceeds the maximum tubular reabsorptive capacity. Treatment must involve administration of insulin.

In noninsulin-dependent diabetes mellitus (NIDDM) or type 2 diabetes, plasma insulin level is normal but there is target-cell hyporesponsiveness to insulin, termed insulin resistance, which is also related to obesity.

Hypoglycemia: A low plasma glucose level will result from an excess of insulin (beta cells) or deficiency of glucagon (alpha cells).

Regulation of Plasma Cholesterol: The two sources of cholesterol are diet and synthesis by the liver. The liver also excretes cholesterol by adding it to bile. The homeostatic control that keeps the plasma cholesterol constant mainly involves hepatic synthesis.

The ingestion of saturated fatty acids (animal fats) raises plasma cholesterol while unsaturated fatty acids (vegetable fats) lowers it. Low-density lipoproteins (LDL) deliver cholesterol to cells throughout body while high-density lipoproteins (HDL) removes excess cholesterol from blood and tissue and delivers it to the liver for excretion. The ratio of LDL to HDL is important and the lower the ratio, the lower the deposition of extra cholesterol in the blood vessels.

Control of Growth

1. *Environmental factors*: Adequacy of nutrient supply is a vital factor in growth.

2. *Hormone Influences*:

— Growth Hormone (GH) secreted by anterior pituitary, is the single most important hormone for postnatal growth. An excess of GH produces gigantism, whereas a deficiency produces dwarfism. When excess GH produces bone thickening without lengthening and overgrowth of other organs, it is called acromegaly. GH exerts its effect on growth by promoting secretion of IGF-I from liver and other tissues. IGF-I promotes cell division, and stimulates protein synthesis by promoting the uptake of amino acids by cells.

— *Thyroid Hormone*: TH is important for controlling metabolism and plays a permissive role in the normal development and maintenance of the nervous system. A decrease in TH during infancy leads to mental retardation, called endemic cretinism.

— *Insulin*: Insulin is an anabolic (building) hormone and inhibits protein degradation. It also promotes cell division and differentiation because it is required for production of IGF-I.

— *Sex Hormones*: Sex hormones stimulate the secretion of GH and IGF-I. Testosterone exerts an anabolic effect by stimulating protein synthesis.

— *Cortisol*: Cortisol exerts antigrowth effects by stimulating protein catabolism (breakdown).

Concepts of Energy Expenditure: The breakdown of organic molecules liberates the energy stored in their bonds. The energy produced is used by cells to perform biological work - muscle contraction (external work) and active transport, molecular synthesis. Energy that is liberated (ΔE) during breakdown of an organic molecule can either appear as heat (H) or be used to perform work (W).

$$\Delta E = H + W$$

Energy for work must first be incorporated into ATP. Heat cannot be converted to work but is used to maintain body temperature and thus homeostasis.

Metabolic Rate

Metabolic rate is the total energy expenditure per unit time. Basal metabolic rate (BMR) is the metabolic rate under certain standardized conditions. Most of the activity contributing to basal metabolic rate is from the activity of the heart, liver, kidney and brain.

— *Thyroid Hormones*: Thyroid hormones are the most important determinant of BMR. They can increase BMR by increasing oxygen consumption and heat-production in most body tissues, which is termed a calorigenic effect, by reducing ATP production.

— *Epinephrine*: Epinephrine increases metabolic rate by calorigenic effect. Epinephrine stimulates the catabolism of glycogen and triacylglycerols.

— *Food-Induced Thermogenesis*: Ingestion of food raises body temperature and protein has the greatest effect in producing temperature changes.

— *Muscle Activity*: Muscle activity increases muscle contraction, e.g., during exercise or shivering, which in turn increases the metabolic rate.

— *Regulation of Total-Body Energy Stores*: Energy stored = Energy from food intake - (Internal heat produced + External work). The body weight of adults is regulated around a set point by reflexively adjusting caloric intake and/or energy expenditure.

Control of food intake: A hormone, leptin, synthesized by adipose tissue, is released in proportion to the amount of fat in adipose tissue. The hormone acts on the hypothalamus to cause a reduction in food intake by inhibiting the release of a neuropeptide that stimulates eating. It also stimulates metabolic rate and therefore controls changes in energy expenditure. Leptin is important in long-term control. In short-term, various satiety signals such as insulin, body temperature, presence of food in GI tract act on the hypothalamus to regulate the duration and frequency of meals..

Overweight and obesity: Overweight is a term to describe an increased amount of fat in the body and obesity is the state of being excessively overweight. The body mass index (BMI) is an index of weight and is calculated by dividing a person's weight by the square of their height. Low calorie diets have limited effectiveness to control weight since it results in a drop in metabolic rate, preventing further weight loss. Exercise, however, lowers the set point around which total body stores of fat are regulated. Exercise is an effective method, over time, in managing weight and body fat stores.

Eating disorders: Anorexia nervosa is the pathological fear of gaining weight and consequent reduction of food intake. This disorder leads to low blood pressure, low body temperature and altered secretion of many hormones and a severe case may lead to death. Bulimia is recurrent episodes of binge eating associated with self-induced vomiting, laxatives, diuretics, dieting or exercise in order to rid the body of ingested food.

Regulation of body temperature: The ability to maintain body temperatures within narrow limits is called homeothermy. The total heat content of the body is net difference between heat production and heat loss. In steady state, heat production equals heat loss.

Mechanisms of heat loss or gain: The body surface can lose heat by radiation, conduction, convection and by the evaporation of water.

Temperature-regulating reflexes: Changes in body temperature are detected by two types of thermoreceptors, ones in the skin (peripheral thermoreceptors) and ones in hypothalamus, spinal cord etc. (central thermoreceptors). Central thermoreceptors provide the essential negative feedback for maintenance of core body temperature while peripheral thermoreceptors provide feedforward information. The hypothalamus serves as the overall integrator of reflexes and sends outputs via sympathetic nerves to sweat glands, skin arterioles, and adrenal medulla and via motor neurons to skeletal muscles.

Control of heat production: Changes in muscle activity constitute the major control of heat production and a decrease in core body temperature leads to an increase in skeletal muscle contraction, which then leads to shivering (rhythmical muscle contractions). No external work is performed by shivering and all liberated energy appears as internal heat, called shivering thermogenesis. Voluntary muscle contractions are also used to produce heat.

Control of heat loss by radiation and conduction: The skin's effectiveness as an insulator is subject to physiological control by a change in blood flow to the skin cells. As more blood reaches the skin from the core the closer the two temperatures become. Blood vessels reduce the insulating capacity of skin by carrying heat to the surface to be lost to the external environment.

Vasoconstrictor sympathetic nerves, firing of which is increased in response to cold and decreased in response to heat, control these vessels. Behavioral mechanisms, such as curling up into a ball when cold, reduce the surface area exposed to the environment, thus decreasing heat loss by radiation and conduction.

Control of heat loss by evaporation: Water loss through skin, sweat and respiratory tract can also contribute to heat loss.

Integration of effector mechanisms: The range of environmental temperatures over which body temperature can be maintained by vasoconstriction or vasodilation alone is called the thermoneutral zone. Below and above this zone, the body must increase its heat production and increase heat loss respectively.

Temperature acclimatization: Changes in sweating onset, volume and composition determine adaptation to high temperatures. Sodium loss through sweat is reduced by its increased reabsorption due to aldosterone secretion.

Fever and hyperthermia: Fever is the elevation of body temperature due to a resetting of the thermostat in the hypothalamus. Body temperature is always maintained during a fever. Fevers are caused by infection or stress. The raising of the body thermostat results in the overall sensation of feeling cold. Vasoconstriction and shivering occur to drive up body temperature. When the thermostat is reset and the fever breaks, it leads to person feeling hot, vasodilation and sweating occurs. Sometimes this process is referred to as fever and chills.

The thermostat is reset by chemical messengers, called endogenous pyrogen (EP), which consists of interleukin 1 (IL-1) and IL6. Both of which are released from macrophages, acting upon hypothalamus. Excessive and potentially damaging fever is prevented and temperature is brought back to normal. Increased body temperature stimulates defensive responses to infection. An elevation in body temperature not due to infection is called hyperthermia. Exercise and retention of heat is a common cause.

Heat exhaustion and heat stroke: Heat exhaustion is a state of collapse due to hypotension from: (1) depletion of plasma volume secondary to sweating, resulting in decreased cardiac output and (2) extreme dilation of skin blood vessels resulting in decreased peripheral resistance. It is a safety device to force cessation of work in a hot environment when heat loss mechanisms are overtaxed, preventing a large rise in body temperature.

Heat Stroke is a complete breakdown of heat-regulating systems so that the body temperature keeps going up. It is characterized by collapse, delirium, seizures, and unconsciousness. Heat stroke occurs due to overexertion in hot environments. It works in a positive feedback manner, raising body temperature, increasing metabolism and producing still further heat.

Bibliography

ACC/SCN, "4th Report on the World Nutrition Situation: Nutrition throughout the life cycle". *ACC/SCN in collaboration with IFPRI*, 2000.

Bender, Arnold E. *Dictionary of Nutrition and Food Technology*. 7th ed. London, England and Boston, MA: Butterworths, 1999..

Burkhalter, B.R., Abel, E., Aguayo, V., Diene, S.M., Parlato, M.B. & Ross, J.S., *Nutrition advocacy and national development: the PROFILES programme and its application*. Bulletin of the World Health Organization. 77(5): 407-415, 1999.

Ensminger, Audrey H, et al. *The Concise Encyclopedia of Foods and Nutrition*. Boca Raton, FL: CRC Press, 1995.

Grantham-McGregor, S.M., Walker, S.P. & Chang, S., "Nutritional deficiencies and later behavioural development". *Proceedings of the Nutrition Society*. 59: 47-54, 2000.

Haddad, L. and H. Bouis, The Impact of Nutritional Status on Agricultural Productivity: Wage Evidence from the Philippines. Oxford Bulletin of Economics and Statistics 53:45-68, 1991.

Jamison, D. T., "Child Malnutrition and School Performance in China". *Journal of Development Economics, 20*(2), 299-309, 1986.

Latham, M.C. et al., "Parasitic infections, anaemia and nutritional status: a study of their interrelationships and the effect of prophylaxis and treatment on workers in Kwale District, Kenya". *Transactions of the Royal Society of Tropical Medicine and Hygiene* 77 (1): 41-8, 1983.

Laqua, Rosalinda T. *Nutrition and Diet Therapy Reference Dictionary*. 4th ed. New York, NY: Van Nostrand Reinhold, 1996.

Leslie, J. & Jamison, D.T., "Health and nutrition considerations in education planning". 1. Educational consequences of health problems among school-age children. *Food and Nutrition Bulletin*. 12: 191-203, 1990.

Roberts, Arthur J., Mary E. O'Brien, and Genell Subak-Sharpe (eds.). *Nutraceuticals : The Complete Encyclopedia of Supplements, Herbs, Vitamins, and Healing Foods*. New York, NY: Perigee Book, 2001.

World Health Organization, "Energy and Protein Requirements". *WHO Technical Report Series* No. 724. Geneva, 1985.

______________, "Measuring change in nutritional status: guidelines for assessing the impact of supplementary feeding programmes for nulnerable groups". *WHO*. Geneva, 1983.

Index